THE MAMMOTH BOOK OF
TASTELESS JOKES

★　★　★　★　★

Also available

THE MAMMOTH BOOK OF TASTELESS JOKES

★ ★ ★ ★ ★

E. Henry Thripshaw

RUNNING PRESS
PHILADELPHIA · LONDON

ROBINSON

Constable & Robinson Ltd
3 The Lanchesters
162 Fulham Palace Road
London W6 9ER
www.constablerobinson.com

First published in the UK by Robinson,
an imprint of Constable & Robinson, 2010

A copy of the British Library Cataloguing in Publication
Data is available from the British Library

UK ISBN 978-1-84901-055-9

3 5 7 9 10 8 6 4

First published in the United States in 2010 by Running Press Book Publishers

US Library of Congress number: 2009943393
US ISBN 978-0-7624-4000-9

Running Press Book Publishers
2300 Chestnut Street
Philadelphia, PA 19103-4371

Visit us on the web!

www.runningpress.com

Printed and bound in the EU

AUTHOR'S NOTE

Congratulations on buying the special "bad taste" edition of this book. You have chosen wisely. No depth has been left unplumbed, no barrel unscraped, no bar unlowered to bring you this epic collection of xxx-rated jokes.

There is little or no inoffensive material in this book, apart from a few bland acknowledgments and as they only appear in this opening introduction you are almost past them now. The book itself is printed on non-recycled paper from non-renewable sources, hand bound and printed using very cheap third world labour, the pages glued into place using gelatin from rendered donkey hides and flown thousands of miles to a bookshop near you, thus achieving a carbon footprint at least fifteen times larger than normal for a book even of this size. By the simple act of buying this unnecessarily fat volume, thus increasing the risk of a reprint, you can congratulate yourself upon joining the ranks of some of the worst carbon polluters on the planet.

Finally, I would like to thank the Royal Family for giving me access to the Windsor joke archive, especially their large collection of gratuitously offensive racist material. A special personal thanks also of course to HRH the Duke of Edinburgh for his fine Diana jokes. It was also a great honour to have been one of the first non-royals ever to have set eyes upon the Saxe Coburg Gotha dirty joke archive, which I spent many happy hours poring over, although, alas, the legendary Queen Mary "fisting joke" proved elusive.

In short, something to offend everyone, I hope.

E. Henry Thripshaw (Colonel)

★   ★   ★   ★   ★

CONTENTS

★   ★   ★   ★   ★

AARDVARKS

* An aardvark walks into a bar, orders a pint of beer, sits down and starts to read his newspaper. The barman pulls a pint and takes it over to the aardvark, who proffers a £10 note. The barman goes back to the till, returns with a pound coin and duly gives it the aardvark, who doesn't say a word.

   The aardvark eventually downs his beer and calls for another one. The barman says to him, "You know, we don't get many aardvarks in here."

   The aardvark replies, "At £9 a pint, I'm not fucking surprised."

* What do you call an aardvark that keeps getting his head kicked in?
   A vark.

*   *   *   *   *

ABORTIONS

* Have you heard about the Irish abortion clinic?
   There's a twelve-month waiting list.

* What two purchased items are most likely to freak out a cashier?
   A pregnancy test and a coat hanger.

* Why is the Catholic Church so opposed to abortion?
   Because it would mean fewer children to molest.

★ What do you call a man at an abortion clinic?
    Relieved.

★ What's the difference between a television and a pregnant girlfriend?
    If you put a coat hanger inside your pregnant girlfriend you don't get a very good reception.

★ Hear about the back-street abortionist whose business folded?
    His ferret died.

What do you call an abortion in Prague?
A cancelled Czech.

★ Why can't you fool an aborted foetus?
    Because it wasn't born yesterday.

★ My girlfriend recently had an abortion.
    Looking on the bright side, she also won Slimmer of the Week.

★ Two women were sitting in the waiting room of an abortion clinic. One noticed that the other was knitting what appeared to be a little blue romper suit.
    The first lady said to the knitter, "Excuse me, but don't you think it is just a little bit tasteless to be knitting a romper suit when you are about to have an abortion?"
    "Not even remotely," the second lady replied. "It's a body bag."

★   ★   ★   ★   ★

ACCIDENTS

❖ Two lumberjacks, Mark and his mate Jim, were cutting wood when Jim accidentally sawed his arm off. Mark carefully wrapped the severed arm in a plastic bag and rushed it and Jim to the nearest hospital. "Your friend is in luck!" the surgeon told Mark. "I'm an expert at reattaching limbs. Come back in four hours."

When Mark returned four hours later the surgeon said, "I got through the operation much faster than expected. Your friend said to tell you that he has gone to the pub." Mark found this news quite hard to believe but he went to the pub, and, amazingly, his friend Jim was enjoying a pint and a game of darts.

A few months later, Mark and Jim were sawing wood again when the accident-prone Jim cut his leg off. Mark placed the leg in a plastic bag and took it and Jim back to the surgeon. The surgeon said, "Legs are a little more complicated – come back in six hours." Mark returned in six hours and the surgeon said, "I finished early – your mate said to tell you he has gone to the park to play football." Mark went to the local playing fields and, sure enough, there was Jim, kicking a ball about.

A few months later the hapless Jim had yet another freak sawing accident and was decapitated. Mark put the head in a plastic bag and took it and the rest of Jim to the surgeon. The surgeon said, "Heads are extremely difficult. Come back in twelve hours." So Mark returned in twelve hours, but was shocked when the surgeon told him, "I'm sorry, your friend died."

"I don't understand, you said heads were just difficult."

The surgeon replied, "No, the surgery went well. I'm afraid your friend suffocated in that plastic bag."

❖ Tom was in a terrible accident at work. He fell through the floor and ripped off both of his ears. As he was permanently disfigured, he settled for a very large sum of money and left the company. At first he was highly self-conscious about his disability and he stayed at home, keeping himself to himself. A few months later, however, Tom decided to invest his money in a small, but lucrative, franchise business. After weeks of negotiations he bought the company outright. But, after signing on the dotted line, he realized that he knew little about running a business. He decided he had to hire someone who could help him out. After advertising in the local press he received several interesting CVs and eventually set up three interviews.

The first candidate was very promising. He was intelligent, friendly and seemed to know everything he needed to. As the interview drew to a conclusion, the applicant commented, "I couldn't help but notice, but you don't appear to have any ears." Tom was very disappointed by his lack of tact and decided there and then that he was not right for the job.

The second interviewee was a woman and she was even better than the first. At the end of the interview he asked her directly: "Do you notice anything different about me?"

She replied: "Well, you have no ears."

Tom again felt slightly offended and decided not to employ her.

The third and final interviewee was the best of all three, a young graduate fresh out of business school. He was very smart, he was very easy to get along with and he seemed to have more about him than the first two put together.

Tom was apprehensive, but went ahead and asked the young man the same question: "Do you notice anything different about me?"

To his surprise, the young man answered: "Yes. You wear contact lenses."

Tom was shocked, and said, "What an incredibly observant young man. How in the world did you know that?"

The young man replied, "Well, it's obvious really. You can't wear glasses if you haven't got any fucking ears!"

A man calls his wife from Accident and Emergency. He tells her that he lost his finger in a building site accident. "Oh my God!" cries the wife, "The whole finger?"

"No," replies her husband. "The one next to it."

* One evening a man was at home watching TV and eating a bowl of peanuts. Every now and then he would toss a peanut in the air and catch it in his mouth. Just as he was in mid-toss his wife asked him a question and as he turned to answer her, a peanut fell in his ear. He tried to dig it out but in his desperation succeeded in only pushing it in deeper. He asked his wife to help him dislodge it but after hours of trying they decided to go to the hospital.

As they were heading out of the door, their daughter came home with her date. After being informed of the problem, their daughter's' young male companion suggested he might be able to get the peanut out. He told the father to sit down and relax, then proceeded to shove two fingers up the father's nose and told him to blow hard. The father blew as he was told, and to everyone's huge relief the peanut flew out of his ear. The mother and father thanked him profusely for helping them out. "It was nothing," the young man insisted modestly. Once he was gone, the mother turned to the father and said, "That's wonderful! Isn't he a smart young man? What do you think he's going to be when he grows older?"

The father replied, "Judging from the smell of his fingers, our son-in-law."

A man rushes into a bar and orders a double brandy. While the barman is pouring, the man extends his hand at knee height and asks: "Do penguins grow this big?"

"I should think so," the barman replies.

The man raises his hand. "How about this big?"

"Well, perhaps a king penguin, but I'm not sure . . ."

The man holds his hand at shoulder level: "This big?"

"Not a cat in hell's chance."

The man knocks back his drink in one. "Bollocks. I just ran over a nun."

★　　★　　★　　★　　★

ACNE

✳ When did the teenager realize he had bad acne?
  When his dog called him Spot.

✳ How do you know if you have bad acne?
  a. When the blind can read your face.
  b. When your pores have stretch marks.

★　　★　　★　　★　　★

ADAM AND EVE

* Adam is talking to God and asks him: "God, why did you make women so beautiful?"
    God replies: "So that you would find them attractive."
    Then Adam asks: "Okay. God, but why did you have to make them so stupid?"
    God replies: "So that they would find you attractive."

* God found Adam in the Garden of Eden.
    "Where's Eve?" asked God.
    "She started bleeding, God, so she went down by the stream to wash," replied Adam.
    "Oh no!" said God, "We have to stop her!"
    "Why?" said Adam.
    "Because I'll never get the smell out of the fish!"

* Adam and Eve were walking through the Garden of Eden one day when God spoke to them. "All right, kids," said God, "I have a couple of items left here in my goody bag. Who wants the ability to urinate standing up?"
    Eve immediately replied, "Please, God, Me! Me! Me!"
    So God in his infinite wisdom granted her the ability to pee while standing. But Eve saw that Adam's face was a picture of utter despair because he too badly wanted the ability to pee while standing. So Eve was generous and said to God, "He may have it if he wants it so much."
    So, God gave the ability to Adam instead, and he was so happy that he immediately ran behind a bush and urinated standing up.
    When he came back, Eve looked at God and said, "Well, do you have anything left for me?" God looked back in the bag. Looking back at Eve he said, "Sorry love, all I have left is multiple orgasms."

* ## Why did God create Eve?
    ## To iron Adam's leaf.

★ God says to Adam, "I have some good news and some bad news, what do you want to hear first?"

Adam says, "Tell me the good news first."

God says, "I'm going to give you a penis and a brain. From these two gifts you will derive great pleasure and great intellect."

"Wow, God," Adam replies, "that's great. But what's the bad news?"

God says, "I'm only going to give you enough of a blood supply to work one at a time."

★ Why did God create Adam first?

Because he didn't want anyone telling him how to make Adam.

★ One day God decided to make a companion for Adam. He summoned St Peter and told him of his decision. He explained to St Peter that he was going to make a human being who was similar to man, yet was different and could offer him comfort, companionship and pleasure. God said he would call this new creation "woman". So God went about creating this being which was similar to man yet was different in ways that would be appealing and could provide physical pleasure to man. When he had finished creating this being that would now be called woman he summoned St Peter.

"Oh Lord, once again you have done a cracking job," said St Peter when he saw the woman.

"Thank you, you are very kind," replied God, looking pleased with himself. "I am now ready to provide the brain, nerve endings and senses to this being, this woman. I require your assistance on this matter, St Peter. I am thinking of making her brain slightly smaller, yet more intuitive, more feeling, more compassionate and more adaptable than man's."

"Good idea again, Lord," said St Peter.

"What about nerve endings? How many should I put in her hands?"

"How many did you put in Adam?" asked St Peter.

"Two hundred," replied God.

"Then do the same for this woman," said St Peter.

"And how many nerve endings shall we put in her feet?"

"How many did we put in Adam?"

"Seventy-five," replied God. "These beings are constantly on their feet so they benefit from having fewer nerve endings there, so I think I will do the same for woman."

"Nice one," said St Peter.

"How many nerve endings should we put in woman's genitals?"

How many did you put in Adam?" asked St Peter.

"Four hundred and twenty," replied God. "Of course, I wanted Adam to have a means of receiving extra pleasure in his life, didn't I? Do you think I should do the same for woman?"

"Again, good idea, Oh Lord," said St Peter.

"No, wait." said God. "Fuck it. Let's give her ten thousand. I want her to scream out my name."

How do you know Adam and Eve weren't black?

Have you ever tried to take a rib from a black man?

ADVERTISEMENTS

❖ A woman places an ad in the local newspaper: "Looking for man with three qualifications: won't beat me up, won't run away from me and is great in bed."

Two days later her doorbell rings.

"Hi," her visitor announces. "I'm Tim. I have no arms so I won't beat you up and no legs so I won't run away."

"What makes you think you are great in bed?"

"I rang the door bell, didn't I?"

❖ A man is browsing the small ads in his local paper looking for a pet when he comes across an advert: "Intelligent, adorable golden Labrador – free to a good home." He calls the number and arranges to see the dog. When he arrives at the house a man lets him in. The man asks the owner "Does the dog have a pedigree?"

The owner replies: "Why don't you ask him yourself. He's in the kitchen."

The man goes into the kitchen and sure enough there is the dog, a very handsome golden Labrador. Feeling a bit silly, he goes along with it and says to the dog: "Do have a pedigree?"

To his amazement, the dog replies. "Yes I have a pedigree. I'm Kennel Club registered and both my mother and father have won best of breed at Crufts." The dog continues, "I used to work for Customs and Excise at Heathrow Airport and I've been in several films and TV ads."

His mouth agape, the man turns to the owner. "What an incredible dog. He talks and he's been a top sniffer dog. I just don't understand it. Why do you want to give him away?"

"Because", the owner replies, "I'm sick of his fucking lies."

❖ An Australian woman takes out a personal advert to find herself a man who has never slept with a woman before. She finally gets a reply from a man who has spent his entire life in the outback. They meet and hit it off immediately and, after a brief engagement, they get married. On the wedding night, she walks into their bedroom to find her new husband standing in the middle of the room, totally naked and all the furniture from the room piled into one corner.

"What happened?" she asks.

"I have never been with a woman," he says, "but if it's anything like a kangaroo, I'm going to need all the room I can get."

What Women's Personal Ads Really Mean

Adventurous: has slept with all your mates

Athletic: flat chested

Average looking: has a face like an arse

Beautiful: pathological liar

Contagious smile: does a lot of prescription drugs

Educated: had the arse shagged off her by everybody at university

Emotionally secure: on medication

Feminist: obese

40-ish: 49

Free spirit: heroin addict

Friendship first: former slut

Fun: irritating

Gentle: boring

Good listener: autistic

Large lady: morbidly obese

Looking for soul mate: stalker

New Age: excessive body hair

Old-fashioned: no blow jobs or anal

Open-minded: desperate

Outgoing: loud and embarrassing

Passionate: sloppy drunk

Poetic: depressive

Professional: bitch

Romantic: frigid

Sociable: fanny like a yawning donkey

Voluptuous: super-morbidly obese

Widow: murderer

❖ An old man whose wife had recently passed away decided to place an obituary in the local paper. He went to see the editor and was told it would cost £1 a word. After turning out the contents of his pocket, the old man found £3 in loose change. He wrote: "Doris Smith Dead".

Seeing this, the editor felt so sorry for him he said; "For £3 you can have seven words."

The old man thanked him and thought for a while. Then he wrote: "Doris Smith Dead. Ford Focus for Sale".

★   ★   ★   ★   ★

ADVICE

My dad always told me that you should live each day as if it is your last. That's why he spent the last fifteen years in an intensive care unit with an oxygen mask and a tube up his arse.

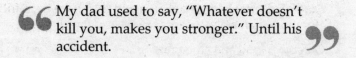 My dad used to say, "Whatever doesn't kill you, makes you stronger." Until his accident.

★   ★   ★   ★   ★

AFTERLIFE

✳ A couple made a pact that whoever died first would come back and tell their partner if there was an afterlife. The husband was the first to go and, true to his word, he made contact with his wife one night when she was lying in bed.

"Sarah, Sarah . . ."

"Is that you, Ted?"

"Yes, I've come back just as we agreed."

"What's it like?"

"Well, I get up in the morning, I have sex, I have breakfast, go off to the golf course, I have sex, I bathe in the sun, and then I have sex twice. I have lunch, another romp around the golf course, then sex pretty much all afternoon. After that it's supper and the golf course again. Then have sex until late at night. The next day it starts again."

"Oh, Ted! You surely must be in Heaven."

"Not exactly, I'm a rabbit in Essex."

✳ Two old Yorkshiremen, Ted and Frank, have been mates for as long as either can remember. They are now both in their nineties and throughout their friendship they have shared a love of cricket, both as players in their youth and now as devoted spectators. One day while they are sitting at Headingley watching a county game, Ted turns to Frank and says, "You know Frank, me and thee have been friends for more than eighty years and we've enjoyed our cricket all that time."

"Aye," replies Frank.

"Well," Ted continues, "we've both had a decent innings and are now getting towards the point where we've got to carry our bat for the last dignified walk back to the pavilion."

"Aye," replies Frank.

"Do you think they have cricket in Heaven?" asks Ted.

Frank says: "I don't know, lad. But if one of us takes the walk to the pavilion before the other, let's promise that if it's at all possible, we will come back and let the other know."

"Sounds good to me," says Frank.

A couple of months later Ted gets ill and unfortunately a few days later takes the long walk back to the pavilion. About a week after Ted dies, Frank is asleep in bed and is woken by a voice he recognizes as his old deceased mate.

Franks says: "Ted, is it thee?"

"Aye," says Ted. "We agreed that the first one would come back and let the other know if there was cricket in Heaven."

Frank answers, "Aye."

"Well," says Ted, "there is some good news and some bad news, which would you like first?"

Frank considers his options for a moment. "I'll have the good news first, please."

So Ted starts with the good news. "There is test match cricket in Heaven and the weather is always a warm summer afternoon. All of our old friends are here and you have the strength and vitality of your youth so that you can bat and bowl all day without getting tried. And Frank, the afternoon teas are to die for."

"That's great," says Frank, "but, what's the bad news then?"

Ted replies: "You're opening the batting for us next Monday."

* Charlie came home drunk one night, collapsed into bed beside his sleeping wife and fell into a deep slumber. When he awoke he was standing in front of the Pearly Gates where St Peter said, "You died in your sleep, Charlie."

Charlie was shocked. "I'm dead? No, I can't be! I've got too much to live for. Send me back!"

St Peter said, "I'm sorry, but there's only one way you can go back, and that is as a chicken."

Charlie was devastated but begged St Peter to send him to a farm somewhere near his home. The next thing he knew he was in a farmyard, covered with feathers, clucking, and pecking the ground.

A cock strolled past. "So, you're the new hen, eh? How's it going?"

"Not bad," replied Charlie, "but I have this odd feeling inside. Like I'm going to explode!"

"You're ovulating," explained the cock. "Don't tell me you've never laid an egg before."

"Never," said Charlie.

"Well, just relax and let it happen," says the cock. "It's no big deal."

Charlie did as the cock said and a few very uncomfortable seconds later, out popped an egg.

Charlie was overwhelmed as he experienced motherhood for the first time. He soon laid another egg, and then another. His joy was overwhelming.

Just he was about to lay his fourth egg, he felt a smack on the back of his head, and heard his wife shout, "For fuck's sake, Charlie! Wake up you drunken bastard. You've shat the bed!"

★　　★　　★　　★　　★

AGONY AUNTS

Dear Marge,

I'm writing to tell you my problem. For the past twenty years I have been married to a sex maniac. My husband won't leave me alone. He fucks me regardless of what I am doing: cooking, ironing, washing dishes, sweeping, even doing anything that askjsh l;sasp wth nd f unothel gothsl ehj fpslth fjsl;s;;o{*&^ ^ .lp sld mpskdli dlks; "+**

If Men Were Agony Aunts . . .

Q: My husband continually asks me to perform oral sex on him.

A: Do as he says. Semen can help you lose weight and makes your skin glow. Most men know this and his offer to allow you to perform oral sex on him is totally selfless and shows he loves you. Even better, thank him by performing it twice a day; then cook him a nice meal.

Q: My husband doesn't know where my clitoris is.

A: Your clitoris is of no concern to your husband. If you must play with it do it in your own time or ask your best friend to help. You may wish to film yourself while doing this and present it to your husband as a birthday gift. To ease your guilt, perform oral sex on him and cook him a delicious meal.

Q: My husband stays out late most evenings with his friends.

A: This is perfectly natural behaviour and it should be encouraged. The male is a hunter and he needs to prove his prowess with other men. A night out chasing young single girls is a great stress relief and can foster a more peaceful and relaxing home. Nothing will rekindle your relationship better than the man being away for a day or two (it's a great time to clean the house, too)! See how emotional and happy he is when he returns to his stable home. The best thing to do when he gets home is for you and your best friend to perform oral sex on him. Then cook him a nice meal.

Q: My husband always has an orgasm then rolls over and goes to sleep without giving me one.

A: I'm not sure I understand the problem. Perhaps you forgot to cook him a nice meal?

Q: My husband wants a threesome with my best friend and me.

A: Clearly, your husband can't get enough of you! Knowing that there is only one of you he can only settle for the next best thing – your best friend. Far from being an issue, this can bring you closer together. Why not get some of your old college friends involved as well? If you are still not sure about this maybe you should let him be with your friends without you. If you're still not quite sure, then just perform oral sex on him and cook him a nice meal while you think about it.

Q: My husband is uninterested in foreplay.

A: You are a bad person for bringing it up and should seek sensitivity training. Foreplay to a man is very stressful and time consuming. Sex should be available to your husband on demand with no strings attached. Requests for foreplay only indicate that you do not care for your man as much as you should. Stop being so selfish! Perhaps you can make it up to him by performing oral sex on him and cooking him a nice meal.

❖ Dear Marge,

I am a sailor in the Australian Navy. My parents live in the suburbs of Melbourne, and one of my sisters, who lives in Dandenong, is married to a guy from Salford, England. My mum and dad are awaiting trial for the sale of Class A drugs and are currently dependent on my two sisters, who are prostitutes in Canberra. I also have two brothers: one who is currently serving a non-parole life sentence for the rape and murder of a teenage boy in 2004, the other is currently being held on remand on charges of incest with his three children. I have recently become engaged to marry a former Thai prostitute who is currently a part-time working girl in a Melbourne brothel. Unfortunately her time there is limited, as she has recently been infected with HIV AIDS. We intend to marry as soon as possible and are currently looking into the possibility of opening our own brothel with my fiancée using her knowledge of the industry working as the brothel madam. We are hoping my two sisters will be interested in joining our team. Although I would prefer them not to prostitute themselves at least it would get them off the streets and hopefully the heroin. My problem is this: I love my fiancée and look forward to bringing her into the family and of course I want to be totally honest with her. Should I tell her about my brother-in-law being a Manchester United fan?

* * * * *

AGORAPHOBIA

* There's always light at the end of the tunnel.
  Unless you're agoraphobic.

* My friend is an agoraphobic homosexual. He's been trying to come out of the closet for thirty years.

* * * * *

AIDS

* What's the difference between AIDS and cancer?
  When you have cancer you still get visitors.

★ I read once that you can get AIDS from a mosquito. If you ask me, anyone sick enough to have sex with a mosquito deserves to get AIDS.

★ "Doctor, can I get AIDS from a toilet seat?"
  "Yes, but only by sitting down before the last guy gets up."

> 66 They say a problem shared is a problem halved. Not if it's AIDS. 99

★ A man went to his doctor after a brief but debilitating illness. The doctor, after a lengthy examination, looked him in the eye and said, "I've some bad news for you . . . you have a cancer and it can't be cured. I give you two weeks to a month." The man was shocked and saddened by the news, but being a man of solid character, managed to compose himself and walk from the doctor's office to meet his son, who was waiting for him outside.

  "Son," he said, "as Rudyard Kipling once said, if you can meet with triumph and disaster, and treat those two impostors just the same – you'll be a man. It turns out that I have cancer and I've been given a short time to live. But we're going to celebrate my life. Let's head for the pub and have a few pints."

  His son was shocked at first, but after three or four pints the two were feeling a little less sombre. They had a laugh, shed a few tears and drank some more beers. After a while, they were eventually approached by some of the man's old friends, who asked what the two were celebrating. He told his friends, "I've only got a few weeks to live as I have been diagnosed with AIDS."The friends gave him their condolences and they all had a few more beers.

  After his friends left, the man's son leaned over and whispered in confusion, "Dad, you are dying of cancer. Why did you tell your friends that you are dying of AIDS?"

  "Well, son," the father replied, "I don't want them fucking your mother when I'm gone."

★ A man goes to the doctor's to get his test results. The doctor tells him: "I'm not going to beat around the bush. You have AIDS."

The man is devastated. "Doctor, what can I do?"

"Eat one curried sausage, one head of cabbage, twenty unpeeled carrots drenched in hot sauce, ten chilli peppers, fifty walnuts, a box of grape nuts cereal, then top it off with a gallon of prune juice."

The man asks, bewildered, "Will that cure me?"

"Sadly, no," replies the doctor. "But it should leave you with a better understanding of what your arse is for."

★ What do you call a homosexual who doesn't have AIDS?

A lucky cocksucker.

★　　★　　★　　★　　★

AIR TRAVEL

❖ A man is sitting in the airport departure lounge when a gorgeous young girl in a stewardess uniform parks herself next to him. She's so stunning that he tries to overcome his natural shyness and seize the moment with a witty and original chat-up line. He's struggling for something to say, then it occurs to him that she might work for British Airways. He taps her on the shoulder and, quoting the BA slogan, says to her: "We take good care of you." The girl just gives him a strange sideways look.

"Shit, I've blown it," he thinks to himself. "Hang on, maybe she is with Air France." So he says to her: "So, we get you there faster." This time she glares at him.

"Bugger, wrong again. Maybe she works for American Airlines." He turns to her again and says, "So, luxury is our middle name in the skies?"

The girl turns to him and says, "Listen, mate, why don't you just fuck off."

"Ah, now I get it," says the man. "You're with Ryannair."

❖   Bob is sitting in the VIP lounge of Virgin Airways when he sees Richard Branson walk past. Bob walks up to him and says: "I don't believe it! Richard Branson . . . I'm your biggest fan!" Flattered, the billionaire businessman shakes his hand warmly.

"Would you mind if I asked a small favour? I'm meeting an important client in a few minutes," says Bob. "Could you just pass by and say hello? It would really impress my client if he thought I knew you."

Being a friendly and approachable sort of guy, Mr Branson agrees to this harmless request and a few minutes later he spots Bob deep in conversation with his client. He walks over, taps Bob on the shoulder, and says, "Hi, Bob. How are you doing?"

Bob turns round and says, "Fuck off, Branson, you cunt, can't you see I'm busy?"

❖   One day at a busy airport terminal the passengers on a commercial airliner are sitting on the plane waiting for the crew to arrive so that they can get on their way. Finally the pilot and the co-pilot make their way out of the terminal and begin walking across the tarmac towards the plane. Everyone notices that both pilot and co-pilot are clutching white sticks and wearing dark glasses. Both of them only narrowly avoid being hit by a shuttle bus on the runway. The passengers laugh uneasily at the joke as the "blind" crew pair climb the stairway and feel their way to the cockpit.

After a few minutes, the engines power up and the aircraft begins to move down the runway. Suddenly the plane accelerates rapidly and panic sets in. Some passengers start praying while others get down on the floor. As the plane speeds closer and closer to the end of the runway, the voices become more and more hysterical until finally, when the plane has less than twenty feet of runway left to go everyone screams at once and at the very last moment the nose begins to lift and the plane takes off into the sky.

In the cockpit the co-pilot breathes a huge sigh of relief and turns to the pilot: "You know," he says, "one of these days those fuckers back there aren't going to scream and we're all going to get killed."

❖ A rock star is on a flight to London, drinking too much and being generally loud and obnoxious. He gets up to use the toilet but finds them all engaged. He grabs hold of a stewardess and says: "If I don't get to use the toilet in the next two minutes I'm going to sue your ass and the whole of your motherfucking airline!"

The hostess replies "Okay, please calm down, sir. You can use the staff toilet at the front of the plane. But please don't press any of the three buttons."

So the rock star agrees, staggers off down the aisle into the staff toilet at the front of the plane and sits down to do his business. He sees three buttons in front of him, marked WW, WA and ATR. Curiosity gets the better of him so he decides to press WW. Suddenly warm water sprays up his bum.

"Mmmm," he says to himself. "That was good". So he presses WA and a jet of warm air dries his bum. "Mmmm. Nice!" So finally he can't resist pressing the ATR button. The next thing he knows he is waking up in a hospital ward just as the nurse is entering the room.

"Nurse! Nurse! Where am I? What happened?"

The nurse replies: "Well, apparently you were on a plane and a stewardess told you not to press any of the buttons, but you pressed the ATR button."

"What does ATR mean exactly?"

"Automatic Tampon Remover. Your testicles are under your pillow."

A pilot addresses his passengers but forgets to turn off the intercom. They hear him say to his co-pilot: "I'm going to have a shit, then shag the arse off that new air hostess."

At this, the air hostess runs up the aisle to warn the pilot that the intercom is still on, but she trips and falls over.

"No need to hurry, love," says an old lady. "He's having a shit first."

❖ A Muslim was sitting next to an Aussie on a flight from Singapore bound for Sydney, Australia. When the plane was airborne, the stewardesses took orders for drinks. The Aussie said: "I'll have a Scotch on the rocks, please." The drink was brought and placed before him. The stewardess asked the Muslim if he would like a drink.

He replied: "I would rather be raped by a dozen infidel whores and have my head stuffed up a sheep's arsehole than let alcohol touch my lips."

The Aussie handed his drink back to the stewardess and said, "Sorry, darling, I didn't realize there was a choice."

❖ What do you call a black man flying a plane?
A pilot, you racist.

❖ A man gets to his plane seat and is surprised to find a parrot strapped into the seat next to him. Once in the air, the stewardess comes round and the man asks her for a coffee. The parrot meanwhile squawks: "And get me a fucking whisky, you bitch."

The stewardess, somewhat taken aback, remains composed and brings a whisky for the parrot, but forgets the coffee. When the man points this out to her, the parrot immediately drains its glass and yells, "And get me another fucking whisky while you're at it, bitch!" Visibly upset, the shaking stewardess returns shortly with a whisky for the parrot, but still no coffee.

Unaccustomed to such slackness, the man loses his temper and decides to try the parrot's approach: "I've asked you twice for a coffee, bitch, now go and get it or I'll give you a slap!"

In a couple of seconds, two burly stewards grab both him and the parrot, take them to the emergency exits and throw them out. As they are ejected from the plane, the parrot turns to the man and says:

"You know, for someone who can't fly, you're a right lippy fucker."

❖ As an airplane was about to crash, a female passenger jumped up and frantically announced, "If I'm going to die, I want to die feeling like a woman."

She removed all her clothing and shouted: "Is there someone on this plane who is man enough to make me feel like a woman?"

A male passenger stood up, removed his shirt and says, "Here, iron this."

★   ★   ★   ★   ★

ALIENS

✳ Two aliens land in the mid-west of America near an abandoned gas station.

They approach one of the gas pumps and one of the aliens says, "Greetings, Earthling. We come in peace. Take us to your leader."

The alien repeats the greeting, to no avail. Annoyed by what he perceives to be the gas pump's bad manners, he produces his ray gun and says, "Greetings, Earthling. We come in peace. Take us to your leader, or I'll fire!"

The other alien interrupts and urges his comrade, "No, don't shoot, you don't want to make him mad!" But before he can finish his warning, the first alien fires. There is a huge explosion and both aliens are blasted 200 metres into the air.

When they finally regain consciousness, the first alien says, "The Earthling is truly a formidable creature – he nearly killed us both! How did you know he was so dangerous?"

The other alien replies, "My friend, if there's one thing I've learned during my travels through the galaxy, it is that anyone who can wrap his penis around himself twice and then stick it in his own ear is someone you shouldn't fuck with."

★   ★   ★   ★   ★

AL-QAEDA

✳ Al-Qaeda has hidden some bombs in tins of Alphabetti Spaghetti. Police have warned that if they go off it could spell disaster.

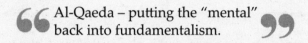 Al-Qaeda – putting the "mental" back into fundamentalism.

❖ Al-Qaeda accidentally recruited a dyslexic into their ranks. They now have the world's first suicide bummer.

★   ★   ★   ★   ★

ALZHEIMER'S

✳ A man takes his sick wife to the doctor. The doctor examines her and says, "Well, it's either Alzheimer's disease or AIDS."

"What do you mean?" the man says. "You can't tell the difference?"

"Unfortunately not," replies the doc. "The two conditions look very similar in the early stages."

"So, what am I supposed to do about it?" asks the man anxiously.

"Tell you what," says the doctor. "Drive her way out into the country, kick her out of the car, and if she finds her way back, don't fuck her."

✳ Knock knock . . .
Who's there?
Alzheimer's.
Alzheimer's who?
Knock knock . . .

The Benefits of Alzheimer's

1   You make new friends every day.
2   You can laugh at all the old jokes.
3   You make new friends every day.
4   You can hide your own Easter eggs.

❋   A stand-up comedian got a gig at the local Alzheimer's Association annual party. He was very nervous because he hadn't worked for a while but he need not have worried. They liked his first joke so much that he told it again and again and again. In fact he told it eighty-six times. After the show, an old man went up to him and shook his hand: "You were brilliant," he said. "I don't know how you remember them all!"

❋   I was in the shopping centre this morning when a man approached me, collecting for Alzheimer's. I told him, "Piss off, I've already given, don't you remember?"

❋   "It's bad news, I'm afraid," the doctor tells his patient. "You have cancer and Alzheimer's."
    "Thank you, doctor. Oh well, it could be worse. At least I don't have cancer."

❋   Did you hear about the Alzheimer's protest march?
    "What do we want?"
    "We don't know!"
    "When do we want it?"
    "Want what?"

❋   The Alzheimer's Society is doing its bit for Comic Relief. It will be known as Fuck Nose Day.

❋   My side of the family has a history of Alzheimer's. Or was it my wife's side?

✳ An elderly man walks into a bar and sees a gorgeous much younger woman sitting on her own. He walks over, sits next to her and says: "Do I come here often?"

✳ The old man suffering from Alzheimer's who lives just down the road groped my wife this morning. I'm going to go down there later and give him a hiding he will never remember.

✳ How does every Alzheimer's joke end?
   No, sorry, it's gone.

*   *   *   *   *

AMERICA AND AMERICANS

✳ Apparently about 60 per cent of Americans don't own a passport. It's not that they don't want to leave their country, they're just too fat to fit into a photo booth.

✳ Recent studies have shown that 60 per cent of Americans suffer from obesity.
   The other 40 per cent couldn't care less.

✳ What do you say to a thin American?
   "How's the chemotherapy going?"

I was driving along when I saw a big fat American standing in the middle of the road. I ran straight over him: I could have gone around him but I wasn't sure if I had enough petrol.

★ Why is American beer always served very cold?
   So you can tell it from piss.

★ An American couple are on holiday travelling through Wales. On their way they see a sign for a place called Llanfair-pwllgwyngyllgogerychwyrndrob-wllllantysiliogogogoch and decide to head there for something to eat. As they make their way there they debate the pronunciation of the town's name.

They stop for lunch and one tourist asks the girl serving them "Before we order, could you please settle an argument for us?" The waitress nods.

"Would you please pronounce where we are for us – very slowly?"

The waitress leans over the counter and says, "Buurrrrgerrrrr Kinnnnggg."

★ Americans – chasing the American dream does not count as exercise.

★ A man is showing an American tourist around London. When they come to a Pelican crossing, he presses the button and the pedestrian signal goes "bleep-bleep-bleep-bleep . . ."

"What's that for?" asks the American.

"Oh, that's just to let the blind know that the lights have changed," explained the guide.

"My God," replied the visitor. "In the States we don't even let them drive."

★ Americans. They say tomato; we say, "Please don't shoot me, I'm on your side."

★　　★　　★　　★　　★

AMISH

❖ What goes clip-clop clip-clop bang!?
An Amish drive-by shooting.

❖ What do you call an Amish guy with his hand up a horse's arse?
A mechanic.

❖ Two Amish women are peeling spuds. One says: "These potatoes remind me of my husband's balls."
"Why?" asks the other. "Are they very big?"
"No, because they're dirty."

❖ Did you see the first Amish porn film?
Ninety minutes of bare ankles.

Ten Signs that
Your Amish Teenage Son is Going
Through a "Difficult" Phase

1 He stays in bed till after 5 a.m.
2 In his sock drawer you find pictures of women without bonnets.
3 He drinks molasses until he throws up.
4 He gets a tattoo that says: "Born to Raise Barns".
5 His name is Jeremiah, but he goes by "J Daddy".
6 He defiantly says, "If I had a radio, I'd listen to rap!"
7 You come upon his secret stash of colourful Y-fronts.
8 He uses slang expressions like: "Talk to the hand, 'cause the beard ain't listening."
9 He was recently pulled over for "driving under the influence of cottage cheese".
10 He's wearing his big black hat backwards.

❖ An Amish woman is trotting down the road in her horse and buggy when she is pulled over by a traffic cop. "Ma'am, I'm not going to give you a ticket right now, but I do have to issue you a warning. You have a broken reflector on your buggy."

"Oh, I'm sorry," she replies. "I'll get my husband, Jacob, to take a look at it as soon as I get home."

"That's fine. Another thing, ma'am. I don't like the way that one rein loops across the horse's back and around one of his testicles. I consider that animal abuse. Please ask your husband to take care of that right away. Have a nice day now, ma'am."

Later at home the Amish lady explains to her husband about her encounter with the cop.

"Well, what exactly did he say?"

"He said the reflector is broken."

"I can fix that in a couple of minutes. Anything else?"

"Er . . . I'm not really sure to be honest. Something about the emergency brake?"

❖ What is every Amish woman's fantasy?
Two Mennonite.

*　　*　　*　　*　　*

AMPUTEES

✳ A little girl wakes up from surgery in hospital, having survived stepping on a land mine. She screams: "Doctor, something is wrong . . . I can't feel my legs!"

"That's quite normal," said the doctor, "we've had to amputate both your arms."

✳ A bus hit my brother and he had both of his legs amputated. Now he's my half-brother.

* A gang of amputees robbed a bank. The police say they are stumped.

Police have arrested a one-legged man for extortion. They said he was leaning on people.

* If you ever saw an amputee being hanged, could you suppress the urge to shout out letters?

★ ★ ★ ★ ★

ANAL SEX

* I joined a fisting club last month. It has really widened the circle of my friends.

* I shagged some bird up the arse last night. The poor thing hasn't flown since.

* I used to go out with an English-language teacher but she dumped me.
   She didn't like my improper use of the colon.

* A man complains to his doctor: "I've been banging the wife for so long and so often that she's rather big and loose. Is there anything you can suggest?"
   "Well," says the doctor, a little awkwardly, "it's a bit of a taboo subject frankly, but have you thought about taking her up the other hole?"
   "What?" the man replies. "And risk getting her pregnant?"

★ Ulrika Jonsson has been rushed to hospital after accidentally sitting on her mobile phone. Doctors are not too worried. Apparently it isn't the first time she's had an Ericsson up her arse.

★ My girlfriend likes it doggy style. It's great because she fetches my paper and slippers afterwards.

★ What do a nine-volt battery and a woman's arsehole have in common?
You know it's wrong but nevertheless you will end up touching it with your tongue.

★   ★   ★   ★   ★

ANIMALS

❖ A lion, a tiger and a chicken were sitting around discussing who was the toughest. The tiger said, "I'm the toughest sonofabitch in the animal kingdom. When I roar, all of the animals run and hide."

The lion said, "No, I'm the hardest motherfucker in the animal kingdom. When I roar, all the animals quake with fear."

The chicken said quietly, "Sorry guys, but I'm the toughest. When I sneeze, the whole world shits itself."

❖ A female tortoise was walking down an alley when she was ambushed and viciously raped by a gang of snails. When the police arrived they asked her if she got a good look at his attackers. The tortoise, with a confused look on her face, replied: "I don't know, it all happened so fast."

❖ A camel and his son are grazing. The younger camel looks up to his father and says: "Dad, why have we got these great big humps on our backs?"

The father camel looks down on the son and says: "Well, son, it is so that we can travel for miles in the desert without stopping for water."

The young camel listens intently and says, "Wow, I never knew that!"

A few minutes later, the younger camel says: "Dad, why do we have really thick eyelids?"

The father answers, "To protect our eyes so that our pupils are not scratched by sand storms."

"Wow!" the young camel says.

A couple of minutes later the younger camel says: "Dad, why have we got such huge feet?"

"Well, son," the father camel replies, "we have to walk over sand dunes and because our feet are big we can travel much more easily."

"Wow," says the son. "Dad, what the fuck are we doing in a zoo, then?"

❖ **What's yellow and smells of bananas?**
  Monkey sick.

❖ What's blue and comes in pints?
  A whale.

❖ **What's pink and hard?**
  A pig with a flick knife.

❖ What's the worst smell in the world?
  A kipper's cunt.

❖ Why do cows always look so miserable when they are being milked?
  Well, if someone woke you up early, rubbed your tits for two hours and didn't shag you, wouldn't you be depressed?

❖ What did the slug say to the snail?
   "*Big Issue*, mate?"

❖ What do Tupperware and a walrus have in common?
   They both like a tight seal.

❖ Little Red Riding Hood was skipping through the forest to visit her grandma, when all of a sudden, she bumped into a big bad wolf sitting under a tree with his ears erect and his mouth stretched in a big toothy grin.
   "My, Mr Wolf, what big sticky out ears you have."
   "Yes, my dear," replied the wolf. "All the better to hear with."
   "My, Mr Wolf, what big flared nostrils you have."
   "Yes, my dear, all the better to smell with," replied the wolf.
   "My, Mr Wolf, what big bulging eyes you have."
   "Yes, my dear, all the better to see with," replied the wolf.
   "My, Mr Wolf, what big teeth you have," said Little Red Riding Hood.
   "Yes, my dear, all the better to eat with. Now, do you mind? I'm trying to have a shit."

Why do black widow spiders kill their males after mating?
   To stop the snoring before it starts.

❖ Two sheep in a field. One says to the other: "BA AAA BA AAAA BA AAA."
   The other says: "Fuck, I was going to say that."

❖ How can you tell if a crab is an insomniac?
   It only sleeps in snatches.

❖ A baby seal walks into a club . . .

❖ Why do hippos make love underwater?
Have you ever tried keeping a nine-pound clitoris damp?

❖ A married couple are driving along the road one night when they see a wounded skunk on the side of the road. They stop and the wife gets out, picks it up, and takes it into the car. She says, "Look, it's shivering, it must be freezing to death. What should I do?"

Her husband replies, "Put it between your legs to keep it warm."

She asks, "What about the smell?"

He replies: "Hold its nose."

❖ What's the difference between a hamster and a cow?
Cows survive the branding.

❖ A male whale and his partner were swimming off the coast of Japan when they spotted a whaling ship. The male whale recognized it immediately as the whaling ship that had harpooned and killed his father many years earlier. He said to the female whale, "I've got an idea. Let's both swim under the ship and blow out of our air holes at the same time. It should make the ship turn over and sink."

They tried it and sure enough, the ship turned over and quickly sank. Soon, however, the whales realized that the ship's crew had escaped by jumping overboard and were swimming to the safety of shore. The male whale was furious that they were going to get away and said to his female companion: "Let's swim after them and gobble them up before they reach the shore."

At this point, he realized that the female was reluctant to follow him. "Is there a problem?" he asked her.

"Look," she replied. "I went along with the blow job, but there's no way I'm going to swallow the seamen."

❖ Which animal has a cunt in the middle of its back?
A police horse.

ANNE FRANK

* Did you hear about the Anne Frank Museum closing down because of a lack of visitors?
  No one could find it.

Excerpt from a Week of the Diary of Anne Frank

15 June 1944: Hid.
16 June 1944: Hid.
17 June 1944: Hid.
18 June 1944: Hid.
19 June 1944: Hid.
20 June 1944: Hid.
21 June 1944: Bugger.

---

* You have to feel sorry for Anne Frank. First she gets her diary published, which is every girl's worst nightmare, on top of that she doesn't get to make any money from it, which is every Jew's worst nightmare.

* What's brown and hides in the attic?
  The diarrhoea of Anne Frank.

★   ★   ★   ★   ★

ANNIVERSARIES

★ A man and his wife went to their honeymoon hotel to celebrate their twenty-fifth wedding anniversary. As the couple reflected upon on that magical evening twenty-five years ago, the wife asked her husband: "When you first saw my naked body in front of you, what was going through your mind?"

The husband replied: "All I wanted to do was to fuck your brains out, and suck your tits dry."

The wife slipped off her clothes and stood in front of him wearing only a negligee. She asked: "What are you thinking now?"

He replied, "I'm thinking it looks like I did a pretty good job."

★ Alf and Mabel had been married for fifty years. On the night of their wedding anniversary after the celebrations were over they retired to bed in a romantic mood. Mabel said to Alf: "I remember when you used to kiss me every chance you had." Alf leaned over and gave her a loving peck on the cheek.

Then Mabel said, "I also remember when you used to hold my hand all the time." Alf gently took her hand in his.

Mabel went on: "I also remember how you used to nibble my ear and it sent chills up and down my spine."

Alf got out of bed and walked toward the door. As he exited the room, she called after him, "Do you need a pee?"

"No, I'm just going to get my teeth."

★ An elderly couple are having dinner to celebrate their golden wedding anniversary. The old man leans forward and says to his wife, "There is something I need to say. It has always slightly bothered me that our ninth child never quite looked anything like the rest of our children. These past fifty years have been the most wonderful experience I could have ever hoped for and your answer will never take all that away. But I must know, did he have a different father?"

The wife stares at her plate, unable to look her husband in the eye. Eventually, she swallows hard then says. "Yes, he did."

The old man is stunned into silence. After a few moments he summons up the courage to ask: "Who was he?"

The old woman gulps down her wine and says: "You."

★   My wife said to me in bed one night, "Since it is our wedding anniversary, why don't I let you act out one of your fantasies?"

"Okay," I replied. "You sit at the end of the bed and I'll sit behind you."

A little surprised, she did as I asked, then she said, "What is this supposed to be?"

"You driving me down to the pub."

★   ★   ★   ★   ★

ARABS

❖ What do you call a first-time offender in Saudi Arabia?
   Lefty.

❖ What does Tehran have in common with Hiroshima?
   Nothing, yet.

❖ When is it okay to spit in an Arab woman's face?
   When her moustache is on fire.

❖ What do you call an Arab standing between two buildings?
   Ali.

❖ How do you tell a Sunni from a Shi'ite?
   The Sunnis are the ones with the Shi'ite blown out of them.

❖ Arab scientists have invented a time-travel device that can transport an entire country back to the middle ages. They're calling it "Islam".

❖ A Bangladeshi called Abdul was bragging that in his country there were seventy-nine different ways to make mad passionate love. An Englishman listened intently, then said: "Why, that's amazing. Where I come from there's only one way."

"Just one?" Abdul asked. "And which way is that?"

"Well there's a man and there's a woman . . ."

"Praise Allah!!" shouted Abdul. "Number eighty!"

❖ Why are camels known as ships of the desert?

Because they are full of Arab semen.

❖ Two Arabs board a flight out of London. One takes a window seat and the other sits next to him in the middle seat. Just before takeoff, a rabbi sits down in the aisle seat. After takeoff, the rabbi kicks his shoes off and is settling in when the Arab in the window seat says, "I need to get up and get a Coke."

"Don't get up," says the rabbi, "I'm in the aisle seat, I'll get it for you." As soon as he leaves, one of the Arabs picks up the rabbi's shoe and spits in it.

When the rabbi returns with the Coke, the other Arab says, "That looks good, I'd like one as well." Again, the rabbi offers to go to fetch it. While he is gone the other Arab picks up the rabbi's other shoe and spits in it.

When the rabbi returns they all sit back and enjoy the rest of the flight. As the plane is landing, the rabbi slips his feet into his shoes and realizes immediately that they are full of phlegm. He leans over and says to his Arab neighbours, "Gentlemen, why does it have to be this way? How long must this go on? This fighting between our nations! This hatred! This animosity! This spitting in shoes and pissing in Cokes?"

★   ★   ★   ★   ★

AUSTRALIANS

✳ An Australian bloke is walking though the bush when he comes across an isolated homestead with a girl standing by the gate. "G'day," says the Aussie. "Fancy a fuck?"
"Not really," replies the girl. "But you've talked me into it, you silver-tongued bastard."

✳ How many Aborigines does it take to eat a dead kangaroo?
Five. One to do the eating and four to stop the traffic.

✳ Why do Australians call their beer XXXX?
Because they can't spell PISS.

✳ An Englishman walks into an Aussie bar in the outback and orders a white wine. Suddenly a deathly silence descends as everyone turns to look at the stranger. The barman says: "You ain't from around here, are ya . . . where ya from, mate?"
The man says, "I'm from Sussex, England."
The barman asks, "What the hell you do in Sussex, mate?"
The man responds, "I'm a taxidermist."
The barman asks, "A taxidermist . . . now just what the hell is a taxidermist?"
He says, "I mount animals."
The barman grins and shouts out to the whole bar, "It's okay, boys, he's one of us!"

✳ What's the definition of Australian aristocracy?
An Aussie who can trace his lineage back to his father.

✳ What's an Australians idea of foreplay?
"You awake?"

✳ What's a Tasmanian's idea of foreplay?
"You awake, mum?"

✳ An Aussie bloke meets a young New Zealander and they fall in love and get married. On their wedding night, she turns to him and says, "Can you please be gentle with me? I'm still a virgin."

The groom quickly gets out of bed and phones his father. "Strewth, dad, she's a virgin. What the hell do I do?"

His dad replies, "Tell her to sling her hook, son! If she's not good enough for her own family, then she ain't good enough for ours!"

What is the definition of an Australian gentleman?
Someone who will always offer to light his girlfriend's farts before lighting his own.

✳ An Aussie was driving along through the outback in his four-wheel-drive, when he saw an Aborigine carrying two sheets of corrugated iron and a crate of beer. He stopped to give him a lift and the Aborigine chucked the two sheets of corrugated iron and beer in the back and hopped in beside the driver. "What the hell are you doing, mate, wandering around the outback with two sheets of corrugated iron and a crate of beer?" the driver asked.

"The wife kicked me out," the Aborigine explained. "We had a court case. She got the kids, I got the house and contents."

✳ A British tourist arrived in Australia, hired a car and set off for the outback. On his way he saw a man having sex with a sheep. Horrified, he pulled up at the nearest pub and ordered a straight double whisky. Just as he was about to knock it back, he saw a bloke with one leg masturbating furiously at the bar.

"For pity's sake!" the Brit cried. "What the hell is wrong with this country? I've been here one hour and I've seen a bloke shagging a sheep and now some bloke's wanking himself off in the bar!"

"Fair dinkum, mate," replied the barman. "You can't expect a man with one leg to catch a sheep, can you?"

✳ Once upon a time in the Kingdom of Heaven God went missing for six days. On the seventh, Michael the Archangel found him resting. He enquired, "Where have you been, God?"

God sighed a deep sigh of satisfaction and proudly pointed downwards through the clouds, "Look, Michael, look what I've made."

Archangel Michael looked puzzled and said, "What is it?"

"It's a planet," replied God, "and I've put life on it. I'm going to call it Earth and it's going to be a great place of balance."

"Balance?" enquired the Archangel, a trifle confused.

God pointed to different parts of Earth. "Look over there, for example. That is Northern Europe. It will be cold but it will be a place of great opportunity and wealth. Southern Europe, however, will have good weather but it is going to be relatively poor."

"I think I get it," said Michael the Archangel.

God continued: "Over there I've placed a continent of white people and over there is a continent of black people. And over there, I call this place America. North Americans will be rich and powerful and cold and everyone will hate them, while South Americans will be poor and hot and happy and friendly. Can you see the balance?"

"Yes," said Michael the Archangel, impressed by God's work. Then he pointed to a smallish land mass and asked, "What's that one, God?"

"Ah," said God. "That's New Zealand, the most glorious place on Earth. There are beautiful mountains, rainforests, rivers, streams and a fabulous coastline. The people are good looking, intelligent, extremely sociable, hard working and high achieving, and they will be known throughout the world as diplomats and carriers of peace. They will also be strong in character and will admired and respected by all who come across them."

Michael gasped in wonder and admiration. "But, God, you said there will be balance."

"Yes," God replied. "Just wait until you see the twats I'm putting next door to them."

Ten Reasons
Why it's Great to Be Australian

1 You know that your great-great-grandfather was a murdering bastard that no civilized nation on earth wanted.
2 Fosters Lager.
3 You get to dispossess Aborigines who have lived in your country for 40,000 years because you think it belongs to you.
4 Your cricket captain is not afraid to cry live on TV.
5 Tact and sensitivity.
6 Bondi Beach.
7 Other beaches.
8 Liberated attitudes to homosexuals.
9 Drinking cold lager on the beach.
10 Having a bit of a swim and then drinking some cold lager on the beach.

＊ How do you tell the difference between an Australian and a New Zealander?

Ask them both "Have you ever fucked a nine-year-old?" – the Kiwi will answer, "Christ, no way, mate! That's gross." The Aussie will have a puzzled look on his face and reply, "A nine-year-old what?"

＊ A New Zealander and an Aussie were chewing the fat one afternoon over a cold tinny. After a while the Aussie said to the Kiwi, "If I was to sneak over to your house and shag your wife while you were off fishing, and she got pregnant and had a baby, would that make us related, mate?"

The Kiwi thought about it for a couple of minutes, scratched his head, and squinted his eyes, thinking real hard about the question. Finally, he said, "Well, I'm not sure about related, mate, but it would make us even."

✳ An Australian walks into a bar in London. The barmaid takes his order and notices his Australian accent. They get chatting and at the end of her shift he asks her if she fancies a quick shag. Although she is really attracted to him she sensibly declines. He then offers to pay her £200 for sex. As the barmaid is on a gap year and travelling the world and because she is short of funds she agrees.

The next night the Aussie guy turns up at the bar again and after showing her plenty of attention throughout the evening he asks if she fancies a shag again for £200. She thinks to herself, "What the hell – I had a great night last night and I could do with the money" – so she agrees. This goes on for five nights.

On the sixth night the Aussie walks into the bar again and orders a beer, but this time he takes his drink and just sits in the corner. The barmaid is disappointed and goes over and sits next to him.

She asks him where he is from.

"Near Melbourne."

"Really? So am I," she says. "Whereabouts near Melbourne?"

"Box Hill," he says.

"That's amazing," she says, "so am I – what street?"

"North Albert Road," he says.

"This is unbelievable," she says, "what number?"

He says "Number 20."

She is astonished: "You are not going to believe this," she says, "I'm from number 22 – my parents still live there!"

"I know," he says, "your dad gave me £1,000 to give you."

✳ Why do so many Australian men suffer from premature ejaculation?

Because they always have to rush back to the pub to tell their mates about it.

❋ An Aussie tour guide was driving a group of foreign tourists through the desert to Ayer's Rock. Along the way he was describing the legendary abilities of the Australian Aborigine to track man or beast over land, through the air, under the sea. The tourists were amazed.

Along the road, the tour rounded a bend on the highway and discovered, lying in the middle of the road, an Aborigine. He had one ear pressed to the white line whilst his left leg was held high in the air. The tour stopped and the guide and the tourists gathered around the prostrate Aborigine.

"Jacky," said the tour guide, "what are you tracking and what are you listening for?"

The aborigine replied, "Down the road about twenty-five miles is a 1974 Valiant Ute. It's red and the left front tyre is bald. The front end is out of whack and it has dents in every panel. There are nine blokes in the back, all drinking warm sherry. There are three dead kangaroos on the roof rack and six dogs on the front seat."

The tourists were astounded by the precision and detail of the information.

"That is amazing – how do you know all that?" asked one.

The Aborigine replied, "I fell out of the fucker about twenty minutes ago."

ASSASSINS

★ The CIA had an opening for an assassin. As this was a highly classified position to fill, it involved a lot of testing and background checks before the applicants could even be considered for the position. After sending some would-be assassins through the various background checks and training and testing, they finally narrowed the possible choices down to three male applicants.

The day came for the final test to see which man would get the job. The CIA men in charge of the test took the first of the men to a large metal door and handed him a gun.

"We need to know that you will follow your orders, no matter what," he was told. "Inside this room you will find your wife sitting in a chair. Take this gun and kill her."

The man was visibly shocked. "You can't be serious! I could never shoot my own wife."

"In that case," said the CIA man, "you are undoubtedly the wrong man for the job. Take your wife and go home."

The second man is taken to the same door and handed a gun.

"We must know that you will follow instructions, no matter what," they explained to the second man. "Inside you will find your wife sitting in a chair. Take this gun and kill her."

The second man looked a little shocked, but he took the gun and went into the room. All was quiet for about five minutes and then the door opened and the man came out with tears in his eyes.

"I tried but I just couldn't pull the trigger and shoot my own wife. I guess I'm not the right man for the job."

"Correct," the CIA man replied. "You do not have what it takes. Take your wife and go home."

The third and final applicant was led to the same door of the same room and given the same gun. "We must be sure that you will follow instructions, no matter what the circumstances. This is your final test. Inside you will find your wife sitting in a chair, take this gun and shoot her."

The third man took the gun, opened the door and went into the room. Outside, the CIA man heard the gun start firing, one shot after another, six times. Then all hell broke loose in the room. They heard screaming, crashing, banging on walls. This commotion went on for several minutes then all went quiet. The door opened and there stood the third man. He wiped the sweat from his brow and said: "You never told me the gun was loaded with fucking blanks. I had to beat the bitch to death with the chair."

★ What's the difference between Bill Clinton and John F. Kennedy?

One had his head blown off, the other was assassinated.

★ ★ ★ ★ ★

AUTISM

❖ Did you know that if you counted up all the pies bought at football matches every weekend in the UK, the chances are, you're autistic.

> A friend of mine was a sadistic autistic. Just by the sound of your screams, he could tell the exact temperature of the boiling hot water he threw in your face.

❖ I used to share a flat with a guy who was autistic. It was great. I used to put rice in his slippers before I went out. He went absolutely nuts – but not before he had counted them all.

❖ What's the last thing you should ever say to an autistic person?

You do the maths.

❖ How do you know if your child might be autistic?

When you can't save their drawings because they're drawn in faeces all over your nice white carpet.

AUTOPSIES

* Three corpses arrive at the mortuary on the same day, all with very big smiles on their faces. A police inspector, thinking that this strange coincidence requires an explanation, arrives to ask the coroner how they died.

The coroner shows him the first body. "Englishman, sixty years old, died of heart failure whilst making love to his mistress. Hence the enormous smile, Inspector," says the coroner.

He shows the inspector the second corpse. "Scotsman, about twenty-five years old, won £1,000 on the lottery, spent it all on whisky. Died of alcohol poisoning, hence the smile."

"Nothing unusual here," says the inspector and asks to be shown the last body.

"Ah," says the coroner, "Irishman, about thirty years old, struck by lightning."

"Why is he smiling then?" enquires the Inspector.

The coroner replies: "Thought he was having his picture taken."

* A professor is giving the first-year medical students their first lecture on autopsies and decides to give them a few basics before starting.

"You must be capable of two things for a successful autopsy. The most important factor is that you must have no fear." At this point, the lecturer sticks his finger into the dead man's arsehole and then licks it. He then asks all the students to do the same thing with the corpses in front of them. After a few seconds of uncomfortable silence, they all reluctantly follow suit. Two students throw up, a third faints to the floor.

"The second thing", continues the lecturer, "is that you must have an acute sense of observation. For example, you may or may not have noticed that just now I stuck my middle finger into the corpse's anus, but I licked my index finger."

BANKERS

★ What's the difference between a cattle grid and a banker?

Nobody slows down to drive over a banker.

★ A city financier parks his brand-new Porsche in front of the wine bar to show it off to his colleagues. As he is getting out of the car a van comes flying along and takes the door clean off before speeding away. Distraught, the financier grabs his mobile and calls the police. Five minutes later the police arrive. Before the copper has a chance to ask any questions the financier starts screaming, "My Porsche, my beautiful red Porsche is ruined! It'll never be the same again."

After the anguished financier finally finishes his ranting and raving, the copper shakes his head in disbelief. "I can't believe how materialistic you city twats are," he says. "You don't care about anything but money. You're so busy thinking about your precious possessions that you don't know what's going in your own lives."

"How dare you!?" snaps the financier.

The copper replies, "Well, you're so concerned about your car that you didn't even notice that your arm was torn off when the van hit you."

The financier looks down in horror at his bleeding shoulder socket. "FUCKING HELL!" he screams, "WHERE'S MY ROLEX??!!"

What's the difference between a Lehman Brothers employee and a pigeon?

A pigeon can still leave a deposit on a brand-new Porsche.

★ A little old woman walked into the Bank of Scotland carrying a large bag full of money. She insisted on speaking with the bank manager to open a savings account because, "It's a lot of money." After a great deal of negotiating, the bank staff decided to humour her and finally ushered her into the manager's office. The bank manager asked her how much she would like to deposit. To his astonishment she replied, "£150,000!" and dumped the cash out of her bag on to his desk.

The manager was curious as to how she came by all this cash, so he asked her, "Madam, it is a little unusual for someone to be carrying so much cash around. Where did you get this money?"

The old lady replied, "Gambling."

The manager then asked, "Gambling? What kind of gambling?"

The old woman said, "Well, for example, I'll bet you £25,000 that your testicles are square."

"Ahem!" coughed the bank manager, "If you don't mind me saying so, that's a rather silly bet. You can never win that kind of bet."

The old lady challenged him, "So, would you like to take my bet?"

"If you insist," said the bank manager. "I'll be very happy to bet £25,000 that my testicles are not square!"

The little old woman said, "Okay, but since there is a lot of money involved, may I bring my lawyer with me tomorrow morning at 10 a.m. as a witness?"

"Certainly," replied the bank manager.

That evening after work the bank manager started to have second thoughts about the bet and spent ages in front of a mirror checking his balls, turning from side to side until he was sure there was absolutely no way his balls were square and that he would win the bet.

The next morning, at precisely 10 a.m., the little old woman appeared with her lawyer at the bank manager's office. She introduced the lawyer to the head of the bank and repeated the bet: "£25,000 says the bank manager's balls are square!" The banker agreed with the bet again and the old lady asked him to drop his pants so they could all see.

The little old lady peered closely at his balls and then asked if she could feel them. "Well, if you must," said the bank manager, "£25,000 is a lot of money so you are entitled to be absolutely certain."

Just then, he noticed that the lawyer was quietly banging his head against the wall. The bank manager said to the old lady, "What's wrong with him?"

She replied, "Nothing, except I bet him £100,000 that at 10 a.m. today I would have the Bank of Scotland's manager's balls in my hand."

★ Two tigers were stalking through the jungle. Suddenly, the one at the rear reached out with his tongue and licked the arse of the tiger in front of him. The startled front tiger turned and said, "Pack it in!" The rear tiger apologized, and they continued onward.

About five minutes later, it happened again. The front tiger turned, growling, "I said pack it in." The rear tiger again apologized, and they continued.

Another five minutes passed, and again the front tiger felt the unwanted tongue. The front tiger turned, giving the rear tiger a ferocious glare, angrily hissing, "What the fuck is it with you?"

The rear tiger replied, "Sorry. I really didn't mean to offend. But I just ate a merchant banker on safari and I'm trying to get the taste out of my mouth."

BAR JOKES

❖ A Roman centurion walks into a bar.
   "What can I get you?" asks the barman.
   "I'll have a Martinum please."
   "Don't you mean a Martini?"
   "If I want a fucking double I'll ask for one."

❖ A man walks into a bar with a crocodile under his arm. He says to the barman, "I'll have a pint of bitter, please, and a nigger for the crocodile."

The barman pours the pint and goes out the back. When he returns he says to the customer: "Sorry, pal, we only have pygmies left."

"No thanks," replies the customer, "I'm not starting him on shorts this early in the day."

❖ A man walks into a bar with his pet monkey. He orders a drink and, while he's drinking, the monkey jumps all over the place. It steals some olives from behind the bar and eats them, then takes some pickled eggs from a jar and eats them, then jumps up on the pool table, grabs the cue ball, sticks it in his mouth and swallows it whole. The barman shouts at the monkey's owner: "Oi, did you see what your monkey just did?"

"No, what?"

"The little bastard just ate the cue ball off my pool table!" says the barman.

"That doesn't surprise me," replies the customer "He eats everything in sight. I'll pay for the cue ball and everything." He finishes his drink, pays his bill and leaves.

Two weeks later he's back in the bar and he has his monkey with him again. He orders a drink and the monkey starts running amok around the bar again. While the man is enjoying his drink, the monkey finds a cherry in a customer's glass. He grabs it, sticks it up his arse, pulls it out, and eats it.

The barman is appalled. "Oi, did you see what your monkey did now?" he asks.

"Now what?" responds the customer.

"Well, the little bastard pinched a cherry from that guy's drink, stuck the cherry up his arse, then pulled it out and ate it!" says the barman.

"Well, that doesn't surprise me," replied the customer. "He still eats everything in sight but ever since he ate that cue ball he measures everything first."

❖   I went to the pub last night and the barman asked me what I wanted. I said, "Surprise me!" So he showed me a naked picture of my daughter.

❖   **A man walks into a bar and asks the barmaid for a double entendre, so she gives him one.**

❖   A couple are sitting in a bar when a man comes up to them. "Excuse me," he says to the couple, "VD?" The boyfriend jumps up and punches him in the face, knocking him to the floor with a bloody nose. The man picks himself up and goes to the toilet to clean himself up.

   A couple of minutes later he's back in the bar approaching another couple. "Excuse me," he says to them, "VD?" The same thing happens. Three couples and three more beatings later he sees a bloke in the corner with a scabby face. He goes over and says, "VD, mate?"

   "Yeah," replies the bloke.

   "Oh good. You're next on the dartboard."

> An Englishman, a Welshman and a Scot are sitting in a beer garden drinking a beer. A fly falls into each one's mug. The Englishman pours away his beer with the fly and orders a new beer. The Welshman picks the fly out of his mug with his fingers and continues drinking. The Scot picks out the fly and then forces it to spit out the beer it has swallowed.

❖   A horse walks into a bar and the bartender asks, "Why the long face?"

   The horse replies, "I've got Down's Syndrome."

❖   A man walks into a bar. The barmaid asks what he wants.

"I want to put my head between your tits and lick the sweat off," he replies.

"You bloody pervert!" shrieks the barmaid. "Get out before I get my husband."

The bloke apologizes and says he will never do it again. The barmaid accepts his apology and again asks what he wants.

"I want to pull down your knickers, spread chocolate all over your cunt and lick it off," he replies.

"That's it!" shrieks the barmaid. "You're barred, you dirty bastard. Leave now!"

Once again the man apologizes profusely and swears that he will never, ever, do it again. "Right. I'll give you one last chance," says the barmaid. "Now, what do you want?"

"I want to turn you upside down, fill your cunt with scrumpy cider and suck it all out of you."

The barmaid runs sobbing upstairs to her husband, who is watching the telly.

"What's up, love?" says the husband.

"There's this disgusting pervert downstairs! When I asked him what he wanted, he said that he wanted to put his head between my tits and lick the sweat off," she said in a flood of tears.

"He did what? He's a dead man!" shouts the husband, getting out of his chair.

"Then he said he wanted to pull down my knickers and spread chocolate all over my pussy and lick it clean!" screams the wife.

"I don't believe it! The bastard!" shouts the husband, rolling up his sleeves and picking up a baseball bat.

"Then he said he wanted to turn me upside down, fill my pussy with scrumpy cider and drink it out of me," she concludes.

The husband puts the baseball bat down and sits back down in his chair.

"Aren't you going to do something?" shouts the wife, in hysterics.

"Sorry, love, I'm not messing with someone who can drink fourteen pints of scrumpy cider."

❖ A man walks into a bar. The barman asks: "Why the long face?"

   The man says: "My mother was raped by a horse."

❖ How do you know when a barmaid is mad at you?
   There's a string hanging out of your Bloody Mary.

A strip of tarmac goes into a bar and orders a pint. After serving him, the barman asks if he wants to join his friend in the corner. He looks around and sees sitting in the corner a strip of green tarmac. The strip of tarmac shakes his head violently: "I'm not going near him, he's a fucking cycle path!"

❖ A man was drinking alone at the bar. "How come I never see you in here with Phil any more?" the barman asks him.

   "Well, would you drink with a bloke who's a liar, always late, borrows money he never pays back, never offers to buy a round, is jealous of everything you have and as soon as your back is turned he tries to fuck your wife and daughter?"

   "Bloody hell, no!" says the barman.

   "Well, neither would Phil."

★ A man walks into a bar. He's massive, heavily tattooed and menacing. He knocks back a beer and snarls, "All the men on this side of the bar are cocksuckers! Anyone got a problem with that?" You could hear a pin drop.

   He then knocks back another beer and snarls, "All the men on the other side of the bar are motherfuckers! Anyone got a problem with that?" Everyone is silent again.

   Then one man gets up from his stool and starts to walk towards the man.

   "You got a problem, pal?"

   "No, I'm just on the wrong side of the bar."

❖ A man walks into a bar with an ostrich and a cat. The barman walks over to them and says, "What can I get for you?"

The man replies, "I'll have pint of bitter."

The ostrich says, "I'll have pint of bitter."

The cat says, "I'll have half a pint and I'm not paying."

So the barman says, "Okay, that will be £5.50."

The man reaches into his pocket and places the exact amount on the bar. About an hour later the barman goes back over to them and says, "What'll you gentlemen have?"

The man says, "I'll have another pint of bitter."

The ostrich says, "I'll have a another pint of bitter."

The cat says, "I'll have another half but I'm not paying."

The barman serves them and says, "That'll be £5.50."

The man reaches into his pocket and brings out the exact change and pays him. A couple of days later they come back into the bar and the barman walks over and asks, "What do you guys want today?"

The man says, "I'll have a whisky."

The ostrich says, "I'll have a whisky."

The cat says, "I'll have half of bitter but I'm not paying."

So the barman says "Okay, that will be £8.53." The man reaches into his pocket and brings out the exact change and pays him.

So, the barman can't help but ask: "Why is it that every time I tell you the amount you owe you always have the exact change in your pocket?"

The man said, "I found a bottle with a genie in it and she granted me three wishes. My first wish was that I always have the exact change in my pocket for anything I buy."

The barman says, "That's a really clever wish. That's better than asking for a lottery win. A lottery win will run out eventually but that never will. What were your other two wishes?"

The man says, "That, unfortunately, is where I fucked up. I asked for a bird with long legs and a tight pussy."

❖ Three women walk into a bar. "Congratulations," says the barman. "You've subverted a male-dominated joke format."

Two fat blokes in a bar. One says to the other: "Your round."

His mate replies: "You can talk, you fat fuck."

❖ James Bond walks into a bar and takes a seat next to a very attractive woman. He gives her a quick glance, then casually glances at his watch.

The woman asks, "Is your date running late?"

"No," 007 replies, "I am here alone. Q has just given me this state-of-the-art watch and I was just testing it."

The woman says, "A state-of-the-art watch? What's so special about it?"

"It uses alpha waves to telepathically talk to me," he explains.

"What's it telling you now?"

"Well, it says you're not wearing any knickers."

The woman laughs and replies, "Well, your state-of-the-art gadget must be faulty because I am most certainly wearing panties!"

007 taps his watch, and says, "Blast, the damn thing must be an hour fast."

❖ An man walks into a bar and sees a sign:
CHEESEBURGER: £1.50
CHICKEN SANDWICH: £2.50
HAND JOB: £10.00
He walks up to one of the three attractive barmaids:

"Yes?" she enquires with a smile. "Can I help you?"

"I was wondering," whispers the man, "are you the one who gives the hand jobs?"

"Yes," she purrs, "I am."

"Well," he replies, "go wash your hands and get me a cheeseburger."

❖ A young guy was sitting in the pub enjoying a quiet pint when in walked the most stunning woman he had ever laid eyes on. She was tall with brown eyes, silky blonde hair and an incredible figure barely covered by a tiny mini skirt and a flimsy T-shirt. He could see that she was bra-less and her incredibly pert breasts were on show. After watching her walk in, he turned back to his beer and shrugged – she was way out of his league. No sooner had he taken a sip of his beer, however, when she pulled up another bar stool and sat right next to him.

"Hi," she said, then took his hand and placed it on her perfect inner thigh, rubbing it up and down. "So, does that make you feel good?" she asked. "I'll bet you feel good," she continued. "In fact, I'll bet you've never felt this good before."

"Actually, I have," the young guy corrected her. "You see, when I was eighteen, I was picked to play for the school football team to play in the regional cup final in front of a crowd of about 500 people and I felt fantastic."

No sooner had the words left his mouth that he realized his mistake. Instead of getting up to leave, as might be expected, the woman took his hand off her thigh and put it up the front of her top. Her nipple pushed into his palm as she massaged his hand into her perfect breast.

"So, how do you feel now," she purred.

"Not bad," the man replied.

"I'll bet you do," said the woman. "In fact, I'll bet you've never felt this good before!"

Unbelievably, the young guy replied, "Well, actually I have. In that game I was telling you about we were 1–1 with only about one minute left on the clock. The opposition knocked the ball deep into our half, where I picked it up, ran half the length of the pitch, dribbled past four defenders, nutmegged a fifth, than just as I was about to score I was scythed down by their keeper. He was shown the red card and I had a simple penalty kick to win the match."

"Christ," he muttered under his breath to himself, not believing what he had just said. He was amazed therefore when she pulled his hand from under her top and thrust it down the front of her skirt. His fingers immediately met her moist fanny.

"Okay, smartarse," she said. "But I bet you never felt a cunt like this before?"

"Certainly have," he answered, "I put it over the bar".

❖ A beautiful woman approaches the bar in a quiet rural pub. She beckons alluringly to the barman, who immediately goes to serve her. She asks him to come closer, then leans over and seductively caresses his beard.

"Are you the manager?" she asks, softly stroking his face with both hands.

"Actually, no," the man replies.

"Then can you get him for me? I need to speak to him," she says, running her hands through his beard.

"I'm afraid I can't," says the barman breathlessly. "Is there anything I can do?"

"Yes there is. I need you to give him a message," she continues, running her finger through his hair.

"What should I tell him?" the bartender just manages to say.

"Tell him", she whispers, now sliding two fingers inside his mouth, "that there is no toilet paper or hand soap in the ladies' room."

❖ A man walks into a bar and orders a beer. After a few minutes he goes to the cigarette-vending machine to buy a pack of smokes. As he approaches the machine he hears a voice coming from it: "You're a fucking prick," says the voice. "You're a cunt and a waste of space. Piss off, you tosser, before I insult you some more."

He runs to the bar and complains to the barman. The barman apologizes profusely: "I'm sorry, sir, the cigarette machine is out of order."

An Englishman, an Irishman, a Scotsman, an Australian, an Arab, a homosexual, a horse, a Jew and a crocodile walk into a bar. The barman says, "Is this some kind of joke?"

BEARS

* What's the most manic and psychotic animal in the world?
  The bi-polar bear.

* A bear wakes up in the forest and goes behind a bush to take a shit. While he's taking a dump he sees a little rabbit nearby doing the same. "Hey there, little fella, what you doin'?" the bear says, trying to strike up a friendly conversation.

  "Hi there, Mr Bear," replies the rabbit. "I'm taking a dump."

  "You ever have problems with shit sticking to your fur?" enquires the bear.

  "Nope," replies the rabbit.

  So the bear picks up the rabbit and wipes his arse with it.

* A bear walks into a bar in Boise, Idaho. He sits down and says to the barman "I'll have a beer, please."

  The barman replies, "Sorry, we don't serve beer to bears in bars in Boise."

  The bear persists, "Give me a break, I'm really thirsty."

  The barman says, "Sorry we don't serve beer to bears in bars in Boise."

  So the bear says, "Look, I'm spitting feathers here. I'll pay you double."

  But again the barman says, "Sorry, we don't serve beer to bears in bars in Boise."

  The bear is really angry by now so he grabs the woman sitting in the stool next to him, rips her head off and eats her whole. Then he says to the barman, "Give me a fucking beer or you're next!"

  The barman replies, "Look, I already told you we don't serve beer to bears in bars in Boise, and we certainly don't serve it to bears on drugs!"

  "Drugs, I'm not on drugs!" roars the bear.

  "Why of course you are," says the bartender. "That was a bar bitch you ate."

✳ A koala bear from Australia took a holiday in London to experience a different culture. After arriving at Heathrow and getting settled in at his hotel, the koala bear decided to take a walk. After touring Soho for a few hours he noticed several women on the side of the street strutting their stuff.

The koala bear approached one of them and asked, "What are you doing?"

The woman replied, "I'm a prostitute. Are you looking for a good time?"

The koala bear immediately replied that he was.

"Do you want sex?" the prostitute asked.

"Well, I think so, I did come here to live the true London experience," said the bear, with a grin on his face.

The prostitute grabbed the bear's hand and directed him to her dingy flat, where they had sex. Soon after, the koala bear got out of bed and headed for the door.

The prostitute shouted, "Where do you think you're going?"

The bear told her that he was done and it was time for him to go. "I'm a prostitute. You have to pay me!" she protested.

The bear said with disgust, "Since when do I have to pay for sex?"

The prostitute replied, "Everyone I have sex with has to pay. It's in the dictionary, look it up." The koala bear agreed to pull out a dictionary from one of her shelves to look up the word "prostitute". It said: "A woman who has sex in exchange for money."

The koala bear then remarked, "Okay, to make it even, why don't you look up the word koala bear?"

The prostitute grabbed the dictionary and looked up "koala bear". The bear said, "Go ahead, read it aloud!"

The prostitute read the definition out loud: "An Australian animal that eats bush and leaves."

✳ How do you make a bear cross?
Nail a couple of them together.

* What you call a bear with no paw?
   Rupert the bastard.

* * * * *

THE BEATLES

* What caused audiences to scream so loud at Beatles concerts?
   The shock of seeing four Scousers working.

* What's yellow and lives off dead beetles?
   Yoko Ono.

* The Beatles have reformed and have brought out a new album. It's mostly drum and bass.

* What would it take to re-unite The Beatles?
   Two bullets.

What was John Lennon's last hit?
   The pavement.

* Why did Mark Chapman shoot John Lennon?
   Yoko ducked.

* What was tall and thin and came in a yellow bag?
   John Lennon.

* * * * *

BEREAVEMENT

❖ A man called the undertaker one afternoon and sobbed: "Please come and bury my wife."

"But I buried your wife ten years ago," replied the undertaker.

"I got married again," the man sobbed.

"I didn't know," said the undertaker. "Congratulations."

> My uncle died the other day after drinking a bottle of varnish. The doctors said it was a terrible end, but a lovely finish.

❖ Sid won a ticket in a raffle to go to the FA Cup Final at Wembley. When he gets inside the stadium he realizes that the seat is quite low down at pitch level, right behind a bank of photographers restricting his view. About five minutes into the game, however, he spots an empty seat about ten rows up right on the half-way line. He decides to take a chance and makes his way through the stadium and around the security guards to the empty seat. As he sits down he asks the gentleman sitting next to him, "Excuse me, is anyone sitting here?"

"No. help yourself," he replied.

"This is incredible!" said Sid. "I wonder, who in their right mind would have a seat like this at the FA Cup Final and not use it?"

The man replies, "Well, actually, the seat belongs to me, I was supposed to come with my wife, but she passed away. This is the first FA Cup Final we haven't been to together since we got married in 1967."

"Well, I'm really sorry to hear that," says Sid, "but all the same, couldn't you find someone to take the seat? A relative or a close friend?"

"No," the man replies, "they're all at the funeral."

❖   A well-dressed young man is sitting alone in a bar, staring grimly into his drink. "Is there anything wrong?" asks the barman.

"Well, three months ago my grandfather died and left me £100,000," replies the young man.

"That doesn't sound like anything to be upset about," says the barman.

"Yeah," said the young man, "but then two months ago an uncle on my mother's side died. He left me £95,000. And only last month an aunt passed away, leaving me her house."

"So why are you sitting here looking so unhappy?" asks the barman.

The young guy takes a swig of his drink and replies, "This month, so far, fuck all."

❖   I've noticed that whenever someone dies of cancer, people always say, "They died after a long battle with cancer." My wife passed away last week. She died after a short battle with a number 22 bus.

*   *   *   *   *

BESTIALITY

*   My wife and I decided to try a threesome with my best friend last night.

It was some of the best sex we've ever had. And I know he enjoyed it as well. His tail hasn't stopped wagging since.

*   A man goes to the doctor's and says, "I've got a mole on my dick, can you remove it please?"

"Okay. Let's have look." So the chap pulls his trousers and pants down and the doctor examines him. "Yes, sir, I can remove that mole. But I'm afraid I'm going to have to report you to the RSPCA."

* What's the worst thing about washing your cat?

  Getting the fur off your tongue afterwards.

* A man goes to the doctor and says, "I've got a huge hole in my arse."

  The doctor says, "Drop your pants, bend over and let me have a look."

  The man does as he's told. "My God!!" exclaims the doctor. "What could have made a hole as big as that?"

  He replies, "I've been fucked by an elephant."

  The doctor says, "An elephant's penis is long and thin . . . this hole is enormous!"

  "I know. He fingered me first."

* I had sex with a chicken last night. It turns out the chicken came first, after all.

* I put my dick inside my daughter's pet rabbit. He is not a happy bunny.

* I was forcing the dog to give me a blow job this morning when he suddenly turned on me. Fortunately his arse was just as good.

* A miserable-looking man walks into a bar, sits down and orders a treble whisky. "Wow, that's some strong poison you're ordering, you must be miserable," says the barman.

  The man replies, "Well, I just found my wife in bed with my best friend, so yes, I'm feeling pretty bad."

  The barman is deeply saddened by the man's plight so he gives him the drink on the house and encourages him to tell him the fully story.

  "Well, I came home and walked into our bedroom, then I saw them together. I told her that we were through and to pack her things."

  "And what did you do with your friend?" the barman enquires.

  He replies, "Well, I looked him right in the eye and I said, 'bad dog!'"

> " I love a nice tight pussy. That's why
> I'm in big trouble with the RSPCA. "

* A man walks into his bedroom with a sheep under his arm. His wife is lying in bed reading. The man says, "This is the pig I have been fucking."
   His wife replies, "I think you'll find that is a sheep."
   The man replies, "I think you'll find I was talking to the sheep."

* Why did the pervert cross the road?
   Because his dick was stuck inside the chicken.

* What's the worst thing about giving anal to a horse?
   The horse's turn.

* ## Why did the zoophile cross the road?
   ## Because he saw the zebra crossing.

* I went home and caught the plumber with his dick up the dog's arse! I can't believe the police won't do anything! It turns out the cunt is Corgi registered.

* If the dog's tail is still wagging, can you really call it rape?

★   ★   ★   ★   ★

BIRDS

★ Why don't cockerels have hands?
   Because chickens don't have tits.

A pheasant waddles up close alongside a grouse, looks around and asks in a hushed tone, "If I stick my beak up your arse, would you be interested in returning the favour?"
   "Okay," says the grouse. "I'm game if you are."

★ What do you call a female peacock?
   A peacunt.

★ What do you get if you cross a hedgehog with an owl?
   A prick that stays up all night.

★ Animal rights activists claim that cutting a chicken's head off is cruel because it still runs around in pain. Not if you cut its legs off first.

★ What should you do if a bird craps on your car?
   Don't take her out again.

★ The mating call of a robin: "Tweet tweet chirrup."
   The mating call of an owl: "A twit to woo. A twit to woo."
   The mating call of a blackbird: "Stick it up my ass Winston."

★ ★ ★ ★ ★

BLINDNESS

❖ A coach driver is transporting a group of blind children back from a school trip. It is a hot summer's day and he decides to stop for a break at a country inn. As the blind children get out of the coach he notices them carrying a football.

"How are you going to play football?" he enquires.

"We've got a special football with a bell in it," says one of the boys. "Go and have a drink, we'll be fine!"

So the driver goes into the pub, gets himself a drink, and sits down to read the newspaper. About half an hour later a police officer enters the inn.

"Who's in charge of those blind kids outside?" asks the officer.

"I am, officer. Is there a problem?"

"I should say so, sir. They have just kicked a Morris dancer to death."

❖ Two neighbours are out walking their dogs. One, a German shepherd owner, says, "Fancy a pint?"

The other, a Chihuahua owner, says: "They'll never let us in with the dogs."

The first replies: "Just follow my lead," as he puts on a pair of sunglasses. He goes up to the bar and asks for a drink.

The bartender says, "You can't bring that dog in here!"

The man says, "This is my guide dog."

The bartender apologizes, "I'm sorry, sir, here . . . the first one's on me." The man takes his drink and goes to a table near the door.

The second man walks into the bar with a Chihuahua. He asks for a drink. The bartender says, "Hey, you can't bring that dog in here!"

"This is my guide dog," the man says.

The bartender says, "No, I don't think so. They don't have Chihuahuas as guide dogs."

The man replies, "What? The bastards gave me a Chihuahua?"

❖ A blind man was walking down the street with his guide dog when it led him to walk smack into a post, breaking his nose. When he recovered, the blind man reached into his pocket and fetched out a treat to feed the dog.

A passer-by remarked: "That's very kind of you. Even after he's made a mistake like that, you're giving him a treat."

"Not exactly," says the blind man. "I'm just trying to find which end is which so I can kick him in the bollocks."

❖ **How do you drive a blind girl crazy?**
Make her read a stucco wall.

❖ A blind millionaire businessman went on a trip in his private jet. At 20,000 feet the pilot called him into the cockpit to tell him he was feeling ill and had chest pains. Suddenly the pilot keeled over with a fatal heart attack. The blind man panicked as he felt the plane nose-diving and rocking violently, so he dragged the pilot out of his seat and strapped himself in. After a lot of frantic fumbling around he located the radio and called into it: "Mayday! Mayday!"

Ground control heard the call for help and enquired what the problem was.

"I am blind and alone in a plane, the pilot is dead and I'm flying upside down. Mayday! Mayday!"

Ground control said: "Calm down, sir. Just to clarify, you are blind, is that correct? If so how do you know you are flying upside down"

The blind man replied: "Because I can feel the shit running up my back."

❖ **A blind man says to his mate, "What's 'F' in Braille?"**

He replies, "It's so we can fucking read, you soft cunt."

❖ A blind man was in a bar bragging about how his disability had given him a heightened sense of smell. His claimed that his olfactory senses were now so highly developed that he could identify any type of wood purely by smell alone. He challenged fellow drinkers that for every piece of wood they brought him that he was unable to name, he would buy them a drink.

The customers took up his challenge and started to bring in bits of wood and twigs for him to sniff. The first man came up to him with a leg from an old desk for him to sniff. "That's easy, it's oak, I would say approximately thirty years old."

Next, a lady came up to him holding a piece of branch. "Another easy one, that's a branch from an elm tree."

So this went on for ages and the customers were starting to get a bit bored with the whole sniffing thing, until a man came in with a black piano key.

The blind man sniffed and furrowed his brow. "Slightly trickier, that one. It's definitely ebony, but I was thrown somewhat by the smell of stale sweat from the pianist's fingers and the fact that it's been placed between the ivory keys for so long."

By this time the onlookers were pretty pissed off by the whole business and the barman decides he's had enough. So he gets his wife to take off her knickers and stand in front of the blind man in an effort to confuse him. He sniffs and sniffs again.

"This one's a little harder, can you turn it over please!"

The women turns around and presents her arse quite close to his face.

"Yep, I've got it now. That's the shit house door off a Newquay sardine trawler."

Is it just me, or is it obvious there would be less litter if blind people were given pointed sticks?

❖ Did you hear about the blind circumcisionist who got the sack?

❖ A blind man goes to visit an Irish optician with his guide dog. Both the blind man and the dog are facing the eye-test chart on the wall. The optician takes the guide dog away and replaces it with another guide dog, and asks, "Is that better or worse?"

❖ Did you hear about the blind horny skunk?
   It attempted to rape a fart.

❖ How do blind people know when to stop wiping their backsides?
   When the toilet paper doesn't smell of shit.

★　　★　　★　　★　　★

BLONDES

✳ A young brunette walks into the doctor's. "Doctor, my body hurts wherever I touch it."

"Hmmm. Highly unusual, not to mention unlikely," says the doctor. "Show me."

So the girl takes her finger and pokes her elbow and screams in agony. She pokes her knee and screams, pokes her ankle and screams. Everywhere she touches makes her scream.

"You're not really a brunette, are you?" says the doctor.

She says, "No, I'm really a blonde."

"I thought so," he replies. "You have a broken finger."

* A blind man goes into a lesbian bar by mistake. He finds his way to a barstool and orders a drink. After sitting there for a while, he shouts in a loud voice, "Oi, barman, you want to hear the best thick blonde joke ever?"

  The bar immediately falls deathly quiet. In a deep, husky voice, the woman next to him says, "Before you tell that joke, sir, I think it is fair, given that you are blind, that I should enlighten you on a few points. Number one, the 'barman' is in fact a blonde lady. Number two, the bouncer on the door is also a blonde lady. Number three, the lady sitting next to me is also blonde and is a professional boxer. Number four, the lady to your right is a blonde and is also a professional wrestler. Number five, I'm a 6-foot, 200-pound blonde woman with a black belt in karate and a very short fuse. Now, I want you to think about this carefully. Do you still want to tell that joke?"

  The blind man thinks for a second, shakes his head and says: "Nah, forget it, not if I'm going to have to explain it five times."

* ## What's the difference between a blonde and a shopping trolley?

  ## A shopping trolley has a mind of its own.

* A blonde is at the hairdressers, having her roots done, chatting to the stylist.

  "My boyfriend has very bad dandruff," she says.

  "Why don't you give him head and shoulders?" suggests the stylist.

  "Okay," says the blonde. "How do I give him shoulders?"

* A blonde takes her car to be repaired. The mechanic fixes it in less than five minutes.

  "Nothing serious, love," he tells her, "just shit in the air filter."

  "Oh," she replies. "How often?"

﹡ How can you tell when a blonde is having a bad day?

When there is tampon behind her ear and she can't find her pencil.

﹡ What do a blonde and a turtle have in common?

Every time they are on their backs, they are fucked.

﹡ A young lad starts a new job in a sex shop. His boss has to go on an errand, so he leaves the lad in charge of the shop. After a while a black lady enters the shop and starts browsing the dildoes.

"May I be of assistance, madam?" enquires the lad.

"How much are your dildoes?" she replies.

"They're all £40."

"In that case I'll have a white one. I've never had a white one before."

Next, in comes a white woman, who asks the same question and gets the same answer. "I'll buy a black one," she says, "I've never had a black one before."

In comes a blonde. "How much are your dildoes?"

"They're all the same, £40 for the white, £40 for the black."

"Okay. But how much is that tartan one on the shelf?"

"That's a very special dildo, madam. It's £165."

"I'll have it," says the blonde, and she leaves with her purchase.

The boss returns and asks the lad how he got on. "Pretty good, actually," came the reply, "I sold one white dildo, one black dildo, and I sold your Thermos flask for £165."

﹡ How can you tell if a blonde has been in your fridge?

By the lipstick on the cucumber.

* One evening a blonde looked outside and to her surprise she saw the house next door was on fire. Being a good neighbour she called the emergency services. The operator asked what her emergency was.

  The blonde replied, "The house next door is on fire."

  "Okay, but how do we get there."

  The blonde replied, "Don't you still have those big red trucks?"

* What do you call a blonde with half a brain?
  Gifted.

> ❝ What do you call a blonde with a whole brain?
> A golden retriever. ❞

* A blonde phones her boyfriend and says, "Please come over and help me. I've got this killer jigsaw puzzle and I can't figure out how to get started."

  Her boyfriend asks, "What is it supposed to be when it's finished?"

  The girlfriend says, "According to the picture it's a giant hen."

  The boyfriend decides to go over and help with the puzzle. When he arrives the girlfriend has the puzzle spread all over the table. He studies the pieces for a moment, then looks at the box, then turns to her and says, "First of all, no matter what we do, we're not going to be able to assemble these pieces into anything resembling a giant hen. So let's forget about the jigsaw and have a nice cup of tea."

  "And then," he says with a deep sigh, "we're going to put all the Corn Flakes back in the box."

* A brunette, a blonde and a redhead are all in fifth grade. Who has the biggest tits?
  The blonde, because she's eighteen.

* What do you get when a naked blonde does a handstand?
  A brunette with very bad breath.

* A white guy is walking along a beach when he comes across a lamp partially buried in the sand. He picks up the lamp and gives it a rub. Two blonde genies appear and grant him three wishes. He makes his three wishes and the blonde genies vanish. Suddenly he finds himself in a bedroom in a fabulous mansion, surrounded by a bevy of stunningly beautiful women. He makes love to all of them.

  The following morning he starts to explore the house. Suddenly he feels something rustling under his feet. He looks down and notices the floor is covered in £50 notes. Next, there is a knock at the door, so he answers it! Standing outside are two people dressed in Ku Klux Klan outfits. They drag him outside to the nearest tree, throw a rope over a sturdy limb and hang him by the neck until dead.

  As the Klansmen are walking away they remove their hoods, revealing their true identities as the two blonde genies of the lamp. One blonde genie says to the other, "I can understand his first wish . . . banging all those beautiful women in a big mansion, etc. I also get the bit about him wanting to be a millionaire. But why he wanted to be hung like a black man is beyond me."

* * * * *

BREASTS

* Women don't care how big your penis is. They would, except they're too busy worrying about the size of their tits.

* Why is the part of a woman between her hips and her breasts called a waist?

  Because they could have easily fitted in another pair of tits there.

★ What are the small bumps around a woman's' nipples for?
  They are Braille for "suck here".

★ An old man was lying on the beach next to a voluptuous young girl in a bikini. "Excuse me," the old man said to her. "Would you mind if I feel your tits?"

"Clear off, you old pervert!" she replied.

"I will give you ten quid if you let me feel your tits," he said.

"£10, are you mad!? Get away from me!"

"Okay I'll give you £100 if you let me feel your tits," he persisted.

"NO! Get away from me!"

"£200," he offered.

She paused to think about it for a couple of seconds, but then came to her senses and said, "I said NO!"

"£500 if you let me feel your tits," he continued. At this point she thought, well he is old, and he seems harmless enough, and £500 IS a lot of money, and it might be the only way to get rid of him.

"Well, okay," she said, "but only for a minute."

She loosened her bikini top and while both of them are standing there on the beach, he slid his hands underneath and began to cop a feel. Then the old man started to moan, "OH MY GOD . . . OH MY GOD . . . OH MY GOD," all the time he was caressing her tits.

She asked him, "Er . . . if you don't mind me asking, why do you keep saying, 'Oh my God, oh my God'?"

He went on feeling her tits and said, "OH MY GOD . . . OH MY GOD . . . OH MY GOD . . . OH MY GOD, where am I going to get £500?"

★ A magazine article listing the top ten of the most painful things women endure says that the worst is having your nipples clamped. Surely having them towed away is worse?

Ten Signs that Your Son has Outgrown Breastfeeding

1 He opens your blouse by himself.
2 While suckling at one breast, he caresses the other.
3 He has developed a bad habit of flicking his tongue.
4 He keeps slipping fivers in your belt.
5 He uses your milk as creamer for his coffee.
6 Your birth control pills interfere with his acne medicine.
7 After each feeding he lights up a cigarette.
8 He frequently invites his friends over for dinner.
9 You feel an uncontrollable urge to listen to country music.
10 Beard abrasions on your areola.

★ How do you make five pounds of fat look good?
    Put a nipple on it.

★ A woman comes home after visiting the hospital. Her husband looks her up and down and says, "You seem very pleased with yourself. What's up?"

His wife replies, "Actually I have good reason to look pleased. I just came back from having a mammogram and the doctor said not only am I healthy, but I have the breasts of an eighteen-year-old."

The husband asks, "What did he say about your fifty-two-year-old arse?"

"No," she replies, "he never mentioned you".

★　　★　　★　　★　　★

BROTHELS

❖ A man is walking through Soho when it suddenly starts raining so he takes shelter in a clip joint, paying £50 to get in. Once inside he finds himself confronted by three doors. They read "Blonde", "Brunette" and "Black".

He chooses "Blonde", only to be confronted by three more doors, this time reading "Small Tits", "Medium Tits" and "Big Tits".

This time he chooses "Big Tits", only to be again confronted by three more doors reading "Large Cunt", "Tight Cunt" and "Wet Cunt".

Somewhat excited now, he chooses "Wet Cunt", pushes his way through the door, and finds himself back outside in the rain.

Why does a single-storey brothel usually make more money than a two-storey brothel?
Because there's no fucking overhead.

❖ A young man was in town looking for some action with the ladies. A taxi driver gave him an address. "Take this. You'll find everything you want there."

When the young man arrived at the address he saw a door with a small panel on it. He knocked and the panel slid open. A female voice asked what he wanted. "I want to get screwed," said the young man.

"Okay, but this is a private club. Slide twenty quid in the slot as an initiation fee," answered the voice.

The young man slid a £20 note in the slot, the panel closed. Ten minutes passed and nothing happened. He began to pound on the door. Eventually the panel slid open.

"Excuse me," said the young man, "I want to get screwed!"

"What?" said the voice, "Again?"

❖ A man walks into a brothel and tells one of the girls he wants a blow job. The girl takes him to a room and proceeds to suck him off without a condom. While she does so, he sees a half-full bucket of sperm beside the bed.

He disregards this unsettling sight as he enjoys the best blow job of his life and shoots his load into her mouth. Instead of swallowing, she promptly spits the semen into the bucket.

"I get it," says the punter. "You don't like swallowing, eh?"

She wipes her mouth and replies, "Actually, I have a bet with one of the other girls. Whoever fills up a bucket first gets to drink both buckets."

❖ This guy is feeling really horny, so he walks into a brothel to get himself a good seeing-to. Once inside he remembers that he's a bit short of cash so he says to the mistress: "I only have £5, can you help me out?"

The lady says: "Okay, go down the corridor and take the door on the right." The guy goes in through the door and sees a chicken sitting on a table. He is very disappointed but has a raging hard-on so he figures, "What the hell – you get what you pay for!" and he fucks that chicken senseless. There are feathers flying everywhere.

A week later he returns to the brothel and says to the madam: "Listen, lady, I've only got £2 today. Is there anything at all you can do for me?"

The madam replies, "Go down the corridor and take the door on the left."

So the guy goes in through the door on the left and finds a bunch of guys staring through a two-way mirror at two lesbians having sex.

"This has got to be the bargain of the century," he says to the other guys. "Only two quid for this!"

One of the men turns to him and says, "Yes, but you should have been here last week – there was guy in there fucking a chicken."

★   A teenager gets £50 for his eighteenth birthday from his dad, who tells him to go and get himself sorted with a prostitute from the local brothel.

"But remember," says his dad, "get any slut except Sandpaper Sally."

The teenager thanks his dad and heads for the brothel. When he gets there he discovers that all of the girls are busy except for Sandpaper Sally, so he decides to come back later. After about an hour, he returns, but yet again the only girl available is Sandpaper Sally. "Okay," he says to himself, "screw it, I am not waiting any longer, I'll take my chances with her."

A couple of minutes after penetration he discovers that his dick is as sore as hell. "Owww!" he complains. "That really hurts!"

She replies, "Hang on a minute." So she goes to the bathroom for about ten minutes then comes out. They start having sex again. "Wow," says the teenager, "that feels much better. How do you do it?"

"Oh," she replies, "I just picked my scabs."

❖   A lorry driver from Birmingham who has been driving around Europe for two weeks stops at a brothel outside Amsterdam. He walks straight up to the madam, drops £300 and says, "I want your ugliest woman and a grilled cheese sandwich."

The madam is astonished. "For that kind of money you could have one of my best girls and a three-course meal."

The driver replies, "I'm not horny, I'm just homesick."

❖ What do you call children born in whorehouses?
   Brothel sprouts.

❖   One day at the brothel, the girls are surprised to see a young boy enter, aged about nine. In his hand is a length of string, which is fastened around the neck of what appears to be a lifeless frog. The boy picks the frog up and places the deceased amphibian on to the counter, and says, "I want a bitch with herpes."

The madam is flabbergasted. "I beg your pardon?"

"I said 'I want a bitch with herpes'," replies the child.

"Well, I'm afraid we don't have any ladies that fit that description," says the madam.

"I want a bitch with herpes and I am not leaving until I get a bitch with herpes," says the boy, placing £1,000 on the counter, next to the dead frog.

The madam considers her options for a while and sends for one of her many venereally challenged sluts. The boy follows the girl to her room, his dead frog trailing behind him. After an hour or so of Lord knows what, the boy returns to the counter, frog in tow, to thank the madam. She takes this opportunity to ask the question that had been puzzling her for the previous hour, "Why did you want a whore with herpes?"

"Well," explains the boy, "my parents are going out tonight. In the evening I'm going to shag my babysitter. When my dad drives her back home, he's going to shag her. Then he's going home to shag mum. In the morning she's going to shag the milkman. He's going to shag his wife, she's going to shag her boss, he's going to fuck his wife, my English teacher, and she's going to fuck my headmaster. And he's the cunt who killed my frog!"

*　　*　　*　　*　　*

BUILDERS

* What was the difference between Joseph Fritzl and Fred West?

One supported his victims in the cellar, the other supported the cellar with his victims.

* Two builders went into the bar after a hard day's work. They had been sitting drinking for a while when a very smartly dressed man walked in and ordered a beer. The two began to speculate about what the man did for a living.

"I'll bet he's a banker," said the first builder.

"Looks more like a hedge fund manager to me," argued the second. They continued to debate the subject for a while until eventually the first builder went to use the toilet, where he saw the smartly dressed man standing at the urinal.

"Excuse me, but me and my mate have been arguing over what a smartly dressed bloke like you might do for a living?" the builder said to the man.

The man replied, smiling, "I'm a logician."

"A what?" asked the builder.

"Let me explain," the man continued, "Do you have a goldfish at home?"

A bit puzzled, the builder replied, "Yes, I do, as it happens."

"Well, then it's logical to assume that you either keep it in a bowl or a pond. Which is it?"

"A pond," the builder replied.

"Well, then it's logical to assume that you have a big garden." The builder nodded his agreement. The man continued, "Which means that it is quite logical to assume you have a large house."

"Yep, I have a six-bedroom house I built myself," the builder said proudly.

"Okay, given that you have such a large house, it is also logical to assume that you have a wife."

The builder nodded again, "Yes, I'm married and we have four kids."

"Then it's logical to assume that you have a healthy sex life."

"Five nights a week!" the builder boasted.

The man smiled, "Therefore it's logical to assume you don't masturbate often."

"Never!" the builder exclaimed.

"Well, there you have it," the man explained. "That's logical science at work. From finding out that you have a goldfish, I've discovered the size of your garden, all about your house, your family and your sex life!"

The builder left, hugely impressed. When he returned to the bar the other builder asked, "Did you find out what he does?"

"Yeah," replied the first, "he's a logician."

"A what?" the puzzled second builder asked.

"Let me explain," the first builder continued. "Do you have a goldfish at home?"

"No," replied his mate.

"Well, you're a wanker, then!"

* A young family moved into a house on a new housing estate next door to a vacant building plot. A couple of weeks later a gang of construction workers turned up to start building a house on the empty plot. The young family's five-year-old daughter took an interest in all the activity going on next door and sat on her garden swing, watching the workers. They got to know her name and by the end of the summer they more or less adopted the little girl as a sort of project mascot. They chatted with her, let her sit with them while they had tea and lunch breaks and gave her little jobs to do here and there to make her feel important. They even gave her her very own little hard hat and visibility vest.

One Friday they gave her a little wages envelope containing £2 in 10p coins. The little girl took her pay home to her mum, who suggested that they take the money she had earned to the bank the next day to start a savings account.

When they got to the bank the cashier was tickled pink by the story of the little girl and her job on the building site and her little pay packet. "You must have worked very hard to earn all this," said the bank cashier.

The little girl replied, "I worked all last week with the men building a big house."

"Goodness me," said the cashier. "And will you be working on the house again this week as well?"

The little girl thought for a moment and said. "I think so. Provided those cunts at Jewson deliver the fucking bricks."

✳ A builder goes to the doctor and says, "Doctor, I'm constipated."

The doctor examines him for a minute and then says, "Lean over the table." The construction worker leans over the table, the doctor whacks him on the arse with a cricket bat and then sends him into the bathroom.

He comes out a few minutes later and says, "Doc, I feel great. What should I do?"

The doctor replies, "Stop wiping your arse with cement bags."

Fred West's daughter was trying on a new dress. She said: "Dad, does this look good on me?'"

"Yes, it's lovely!" Fred replied. "But then again, you'd look good in a bin bag."

★   ★   ★   ★   ★

BURNS VICTIMS

★ How do burns victims pick their noses?
   From a catalogue.

★ What's black and peeps through a letterbox?
   An agoraphobic in a house fire.

★ What's charred and stands between two sticks?
   A burnt cripple.

★ I saw the most horrific film ever last night. It was about a little boy who accidentally knocked over a kettle and scalded himself with hot tea and suffered terrible third degree burns. It should have had a PG rating.

★ Build a man a fire and he's warm for a night. Set a man on fire and he's warm for the rest of his life.

★ The Australian entertainer Rolf Harris was asked to leave the scene of the Australian bushfire as he was causing some distress to mourners at the scene. According to press reports, he was seen pulling the charred remains from the smouldering ashes and asking onlookers, "Can you guess what it is yet?"

★ Say what you like about burns victims, but they always stick together.

★ Do burns victims get a discount if they're cremated?

★   ★   ★   ★   ★

CANADIANS

Ten Reasons Why it's Great to Be Canadian

1 It beats being American.
2 You belong to the only country to successfully invade the US and burn its capital to the ground.
3 You can play hockey twelve months a year, outdoors.
4 You belong to the only country to successfully invade the US and burn its capital to the ground.
5 Where else can you travel 1,000 miles over fresh water in a canoe?

6   A political leader can admit to smoking pot and his/
    her popularity ratings will rise.
7   You belong to the only country to successfully invade
    the US and burn its capital to the ground.
8   You get to kill grizzly bears with huge shotguns and
    cover your house in their skins.
9   Own-an-Eskimo scheme.
10 You belong to the only country that has successfully
    invaded the US and burnt its capital to the ground.

★   ★   ★   ★   ★

CANCER

❖   A woman who discovers that she has terminal cancer turns
    to God and becomes a born-again Christian. Early in her
    sickness, a surgeon proposes radical surgery. "No," she tells
    him, "I don't want to be mutilated and suffer unnecessary
    pain. God will help me."

    A few weeks later, she sees a radiologist who proposes
    radiation to treat her rapidly growing tumour. "No," she
    says, "I don't want radiation burns inside and out. It's not
    necessary. God will help me."

    A few weeks later she is referred to an oncologist;
    chemotherapy is advised. "No," she says, "I don't want to
    be sick all the time and lose my hair. God will help me."

    Soon after, she dies. She goes to Heaven and demands
    an audience with God. "Why didn't you help me?" she
    whines.

    "What? I sent you help three times: a surgeon, a radiologist
    and an oncologist. What more did you fucking want?"

❖   I got thrown out of the cancer ward in the local hospital
    yesterday. Apparently laughter isn't the best medicine.

❖ A woman goes to her doctor with a swollen abdomen. The doctor examines her and says: "How's your appetite?"

"I'm eating well, thanks doctor."

"Well, that's only natural . . . now that you are eating for two," replied the doctor.

The woman was overjoyed. "Me and my baby?"

"No – you and your fast-growing tumour."

❖ My wife is forever saying I don't pay her any attention. So yesterday I was expecting brownie points when I said, "Have you had your hair done, dear? You look different." She went ballistic. I won't forget she's having chemotherapy again in a hurry.

❖ What's the best thing about having cancer?

Quicker showers.

❖ A young man went to his doctor for a routine check-up. When he came back in for the results, the doctor said gravely, "I think you'd better sit down. I've got some good news and some bad news."

"Okay, doctor," said the young man. "Give me the bad news first."

"Well," said the doctor, "you have cancer. It's spreading at an unbelievably rapid rate, it's totally inoperable and you've about three weeks to live."

"Jesus," said the young patient, wiping a bead of sweat off his brow. "What's the good news?"

"You know that receptionist out in the front office? The one with the big tits and the long blonde hair? Well," said the doctor, leaning forward with a grin, "I'm shagging her."

What's the best thing about dating a girl who is having chemotherapy?

You don't have to hold her hair back when she throws up.

❖ A woman visits her doctor complaining of a swelling in her lower abdomen.

The doctor examines her and says, "Well, I can tell you that you'll need to be buying lots of nappies in about nine months' time."

"This is wonderful news – am I pregnant?"

"No, you have bowel cancer."

❖ A cancer victim walks into a bar. The barman says, "So, what'll you be having?"

He replies, "A malignant tumour eating away my decrepit body."

❖ They say time is a great healer. Unless you have terminal cancer.

❖ Doctor: "I'm afraid the tests show that your cancer is advanced. You have six months to live."

Patient: "But, doctor, I can't pay off my private medical bills in six months."

Doctor: "In that case, you have another six months."

❖ An apple a day keeps the doctor away. Not if you have leukaemia.

❖ Why did the cancer victim cross the road?

He was hoping to get hit by a truck.

❖ A sixteen-year-old girl goes to see her doctor for a check-up. She complains, "Doctor, every other girl my age has large breasts but I never seemed to develop. Are they ever going to get bigger?"

"Actually," the doctor replies, "I've got some good news and some bad news for you. The good news is that your breasts should start growing in the next few weeks."

"Oh, that's great!" the girl replies. "What's the bad news?"

"The tumour is malignant."

❖ Say what you like about cancer. It's still the best way for bald kids to meet sports stars.

❖ I have just received the devastating news that my girlfriend has terminal cancer and the doctor has given her less than nine months to live. On the bright side, at least I don't have to worry now about getting her pregnant.

❖ Why is a beetroot like prostate cancer? It turns your piss red.

❖ My mother told me she was dying from cancer. I told her not to worry: those horoscopes usually get it wrong.

❖ A man goes to the doctor's for his test results. The doctor says, "I'm afraid you have cancer. You only have six months left to live."

"God, no!" says the man, "What can I do?"

The doctor says, "I recommend you move to Stoke-on-Trent, marry a fat lass and start supporting Port Vale."

"Will that cure me?" says the man.

"No," says the doctor, "but it will make the six months seem a lot longer."

❖ A doctor calls a patient to report on a bone scan and biopsy. The patient is out so the doctor leaves a message to call. As usual, no medical details are left.

After a day of missing each other on the phone the doctor and the patient finally get together. Says the doctor in a matter of fact voice, "I have good news and bad news. Which will you have first?"

"The good news."

"Okay. The reports say that your cancer has spread and that you have forty-eight hours to live."

"You call that good news? It must be the bad news. What could possibly be worse?"

"Well, the bad news is that I've been trying to call you since yesterday."

❖ I'll never forget the day my wife was diagnosed with cancer. She never bloody well shuts up about it.

* * * * *

CANNIBALS

* What did the cannibal do after dumping his girlfriend?
He wiped his arse.

* Did you hear about the cannibal who turned up late for lunch?
They gave him the cold shoulder.

* Two cannibals are eating a clown. One says to the other: "Does this taste funny to you?"

* A Frenchman, an Englishman and an Irishman are captured by cannibals. The cannibal chief says, "The bad news is that now that we've caught you, we're going to kill and eat you. We will put you in a pot and cook you and then after we have eaten you we'll use your skins to build a canoe. The good news is that you get to choose how you die."
The Frenchman says, "I choose to die by the sword." The chief gives him a sword, the Frenchman cries, "Vive la France!" and runs himself through.
The Englishman says, "A pistol for me, please." The chief hands him a gun, the Englishman points it at his head, saying, "God save the Queen!" and blows his brains out.
The Irishman says, "Give me a fork." The chief is baffled, but shrugs and hands him a fork. The Irishman takes the fork and starts jabbing himself all over, shouting: "So much for your fucking canoe, suckers!"

* What is the definition of trust?
  Two cannibals giving each other a blow job.

> 66 Did you hear about the cannibal who passed his uncle in the woods? 99

* Two cannibals, a father and son, were sent by their tribe to go out and get something to eat. They walked deep into the jungle and waited behind a tree. After a while along came a little old man. The son said, "Dad, there's one."

  "No," said the father. "There's not enough meat on that one even to feed the dogs. We'll wait."

  A little while later, along came this really fat guy. The son said, "Dad, let's eat the bastard."

  "No," the father said. "We'd all die of a heart attack from the cholesterol in that one. We'll wait."

  About an hour later, along comes this absolutely gorgeous woman. The son said, "Now, there's nothing wrong with that one, dad. Let's eat her."

  "No," said the father. "We'll not eat her either."

  "Why not?" asked the son.

  "We're going to take her back alive and eat your mother."

* What did Hannibal Lecter say about Britney Spears and Christina Aguilera?
  "Mmmm . . . pop-tarts!"

★　　★　　★　　★　　★

CARS

★ A Mini Cooper with dark tinted windows pulls up next to a Rolls Royce at a red light. The Mini driver rolls down his window and asks the Rolls Royce driver, "You got a telephone in that Roller?"

"As a matter of fact I do, right here on the seat beside me," says the Roller driver.

"Me too," says the Mini driver. "You got a TV in that Roller?"

The Roller driver replies: "Yes I do, right here on the dash."

"Me too," says the Mini driver. "You got a twin bed in the back seat?"

The Roller driver replies: "Er . . . no."

"I do," says the Mini driver, just as the light turns green and he shoots off. The Rolls Royce driver makes a note of the registration number then heads straight to the nearest Rolls Royce dealer. "Yes," the dealership assistant tells him, "we do carry and can install a twin bed in the rear seat of your car." So, after about a week the Roller driver picks up his car with the newly installed twin bed.

A couple of days later he spots the Mini Cooper in a car park. He gets out of his car, walks over to the Mini and starts rapping on the back window.

No response. He raps on the window again. No response, so he raps some more. The window lowers a couple of inches and the Mini driver says, "Yes?"

"Remember me?" says the Roller driver. "I just wanted you to know that I have a twin bed in the back seat of my Roller now."

The Mini driver frowns and says: "You get me out of the fucking shower just to tell me that?"

★ Why do men pay more for car insurance?
Because women don't get blow jobs while they're driving.

It was our wedding anniversary and my wife demanded I take her somewhere expensive. So I took her to a gas station.

★ A little boy is walking down the street after school when a car slows down and pulls up alongside him. The window goes down and a man from inside says, "Hey, do you want to get in the car with me?"

The little boy looks at him then quickens his step. A couple of minutes later, further down the road, the car pulls up again. The window goes down: "I'll give you a bag of sweets if you get in the car with me."

The little boy ignores him again and hurries on. A couple of hundred yards down the road, the car pulls up and the window goes down again. The man says, "I'll give you £10 and two bags of sweets if you get in the car with me."

The little boy stops. He looks at the man and says, "Dad, you bought the Rover, live with it!"

★ What's the difference between a Jehovah's Witness and a Rover?

You can shut the door on a Jehovah's Witness.

★ Two old women were driving through town. They came to a set of traffic lights on red, but they just sailed through without stopping. The woman in the passenger seat thought to herself: "I could have sworn we just went through a red light!"

After a couple more minutes they came to another set of traffic lights on red and sailed through. Again, the old woman in the passenger seat was almost sure that the light had been red and was getting nervous but said nothing.

At the next set of lights, sure enough, the light was red and they sailed through. So, she turned to the other woman and said, "Ethel, do you know that we just ran through three red lights in a row? You could have killed us both!"

Ethel turned to her and said, "Shit . . . am I driving?"

★ Petrol is so expensive these days, I can't afford to use my car. In fact, the last time I went dogging, I had to ask my mum to give me a lift.

★ An elderly man is driving down the M1 when his mobile rings. Answering it, he hears his wife on the other end. "Derek," she says, "please be careful when you're driving back. I just heard on the radio that there's a maniac on the M1 near Luton. He's driving the wrong way!"

"It's not just one," Derek replies. "There's fucking hundreds of them!"

★   ★   ★   ★   ★

CATS

❖ A sadist, a masochist, a psychopath, a necrophiliac, a zoophile and a pyromaniac are all sitting on a bench in a mental institution.

"How about having sex with a cat?" says the zoophile.

"Let's have sex with the cat and then torture it," says the sadist.

"Let's have sex with the cat, torture it and then kill it," shouts the psychopath.

"Let's have sex with the cat, torture it, kill it and then have sex with it again," says the necrophiliac.

"Let's have sex with the cat, torture it, kill it, have sex with it again and then burn it," says the pyromaniac.

Everyone turns to the masochist and asked: "So, what's it going to be?"

The masochist replies, "Miaow."

❖ When I was a small child my kitten died, so my mum went out and bought an identical replacement, hoping that I wouldn't realize. But I did. And I killed that one as well.

❖ Curiosity killed the cat, but I was curious to see what it would look like if I hit it with a hammer.

> Cats have nine lives, which of course makes them perfect for animal experimentation. But I was wondering, does a radioactive cat have eighteen half-lives?

❖ A man hates his wife's cat so much that the next time she is out shopping he secretly drives to the next town and dumps it. He can't believe his eyes when he gets home and finds the cat sitting outside the front door. A couple of days later his wife goes out shopping again, so he drives fifty miles and dumps the cat on the motorway. When he gets home, to his amazement, the cat is sitting outside the front door. This goes on for a couple of weeks, then one day he drives 200 miles and dumps the cat on the other side of the country. A couple of hours later he rings his wife and asks, "Is the cat home?"

"Yes, why?" asks his wife.

"Put the little bastard on the phone," he says, "I'm lost."

❖ What do you do if a kitten spits at you?
Turn the grill down.

❖ How do you make a cat flap?
Throw it off a cliff.

❖ Two female cats are sitting on the fence when a really good-looking tom walks by and winks at them. "Did you see that?" one of the cats says. "I wouldn't mind sharing a dead mouse with him!"

"Oh, forget about him," her friend tells her. "I went out with him once, and all he did was go on and on about his fucking operation."

❖ A little boy was at the supermarket checkout with a huge box of detergent. The checkout girl, trying to be friendly, asked him he had a lot of laundry to do.

"Not laundry," the boy said. "I'm going to wash my kitten."

"You shouldn't use this to wash your kitten. It is very powerful and if you wash your cat in this, you'll make him very ill. You might even kill him."

Nevertheless the little boy paid for his box of detergent and went on his way. A couple of weeks later the little boy was back in the supermarket buying some chocolate. The checkout girl asked the boy how his kitten was doing.

"Oh, he died," the boy said.

"I tried to tell you not to use that detergent on your kitten."

The little boy replied, "I don't think it was the detergent that killed him."

"Oh, I'm sorry. How did he die?"

"Dunno," says the boy, "but I think it might have been the spin cycle."

❖ **I bought a "Bag For Life" from Tesco. They are so much better for drowning kittens than normal bin bags.**

❖ Little Jimmy was in the garden filling in a hole when his neighbour peered over the fence. Interested in what the youngster was up to, he politely asked, "What goes on there, Jimmy?"

"My goldfish died," replied Jimmy tearfully, "and I've just buried him."

The neighbour was perplexed. "That's an awfully big hole for a goldfish, isn't it?"

Jimmy patted down the last heap of earth. "Yes it is," he replied. "That's because he's inside your cat."

★   ★   ★   ★   ★

CHAVS

* What do you say to a chav when he's at work?
   "Big Mac and fries, please."

* ## What do you call a chav in a suit?
   ## The accused.

* What do you call a chav in a white shell suit?
   The bride.

* Two chavs in a car without any music – who's driving?
   The police.

* What do you call a thirty-year-old female chav?
   Granny.

* How do you know if you're definitely a chav?
   You let your fifteen-year-old daughter smoke at the dinner table in front of her children.

* ## Why should you never run over a chav on a bike?
   ## It's probably your bike.

* What's the most confusing day of the year for a chav?
   Father's Day.

* Two chavs race their Vauxhall Novas off a cliff to see who hits the bottom first – who wins?
   Society.

*   *   *   *   *

CHILDBIRTH

❖ A white guy is awaiting his newborn baby in the delivery room. The midwife comes in and hands him a black baby. "Is this yours?" asks the nurse.

"Quite probably," he replies, "she burns everything."

❖ A young girl in the maternity ward is just about to go into labour when the midwife asks her if she would like her husband to be present at the birth. "I'm afraid I don't have a husband," she replies.

"Okay. Do you have a boyfriend?" asks the midwife.

"No, no boyfriend either."

"Do you have a partner, then?"

"No, I'm single, I'll be having my baby on my own."

After the birth the midwife again speaks to the young woman. "You have a healthy bouncing baby girl, but I must warn you before you see her that the baby is black."

"Well," replies the girl, "I was very down on my luck, with no money and nowhere to live and so I accepted a job in a porno film. The lead man was black."

"Oh, I see," says the midwife. "That's really none of my business and I'm sorry I have to ask you these awkward questions but I must also tell you that the baby has blonde hair."

"I'm not surprised," the girl again replies. "You see, the co-star in the movie was this Swedish guy."

"Oh, I'm sorry," the midwife repeats, "that's really none of my business either and I hate to pry further but your baby also has slanted eyes."

"Okay," continues the girl, "there was also a little Chinese man in the movie, and I really had no choice."

At this, the midwife again apologizes, collects the baby and gives it a slap on the backside, whereupon the baby starts crying.

The mother says, "Thank Christ for that!"

"What do you mean?" asks the midwife.

"Well," says the girl, extremely relieved, "I had this horrible feeling that she was going to bark."

❖ A woman goes to her doctor, who confirms that she is pregnant. As this is her first pregnancy, the doctor asks her if she has any questions. "Well, I'm a little bit worried about the pain. How much will childbirth hurt?"

"Well, it varies from woman to woman and pregnancy to pregnancy and it is hard to describe pain."

"Can't you give me some idea, doctor?" she asks.

He thinks for a while and says, "Okay, try this. Hold your upper lip between your forefinger and thumb and pull it out a little.

"Like this?"

"Yes. Does that hurt?"

"Yes, but only a little."

"Now pull out a bit more. Does that hurt?

"Yes!"

"Okay. Now stretch it over the top of your head."

A woman is in labour, screaming in pain and ranting and raving at everyone in the maternity ward. She turns to her boyfriend and says, "You did this to me, you bastard!"

He replies casually, "If you recall, my sweet, I wanted to stick it up your arse. But you said, 'Fuck off, it'll be too painful.'"

❖ An Englishman, a Welshman and a Jamaican are in hospital, waiting for their wives to give birth. After much pacing up and down, the nurse emerges from the maternity ward and announces that each is the father of a bouncing baby boy.

"Unfortunately there's just one small problem," she adds. "Because they were all born at the same time we got the tags mixed up and we don't know which baby belongs to which parent. Would you mind identifying them?" The three men agree and walk into the delivery room and look at the babies.

Immediately the Englishman stoops down and picks up the black baby. "Yes, this is definitely my baby," he says confidently.

"Er, excuse me," says the Jamaican, "but I think it's obvious that this is my son."

The Englishman pulls him aside and says, "I see where you're coming from, mate, but one of these babies is Welsh and I'm not prepared to gamble."

❖ A man was pacing nervously up and down the waiting room at a maternity ward when he looked up and saw a doctor approaching. The doctor took a deep breath and announced: "You have a baby daughter. There's nothing wrong, exactly, but your child is a little bit different. Your baby is a hermaphrodite."

The man looked back blankly. "A hermaphrodite? What's that?" he asked the doctor.

"It means your baby has the features of a male and a female," the doctor replied.

The man turned pale. "Oh my God! You mean it has a vagina and a brain?"

★   ★   ★   ★   ★

CHINA AND THE CHINESE

✳ A Chinese man calls into work and says, "Solly boss, I no come work today, I really sick. Got headache, stomach ache and legs hurt, I no come work."

"You know something," his employer replies, "I really need you in here today. Tell you what, when I feel sick like you do, I go to my wife and ask her to give me sex. That makes everything better and I go to work. You try that."

A couple of hours later he calls in again. "I do what you say boss and I feel great. I be at work soon."

"Didn't I tell you?" says his employer, feeling quite pleased with himself. "I look forward to seeing you later."

"Okay, boss. By the way, you got velly nice house."

✳ **What does a Chinaman do when he has an erection?**
He votes.

✳ Why can't Chinese couples have Caucasian babies?
Because two Wongs don't make a white.

✳ Three Chinese labourers are working on a building site when the foreman calls them over. If they can carry an extra pallet of bricks, he tells them that there will be an extra £50 in their wages.

The first man adds an extra pallet of bricks and the foreman is well pleased.

The second man also lifts an extra pallet and the foreman is even more pleased.

The third one tries with all his might but he just can't lift an extra pallet. The foreman tells him: "You are the weakest chink. Goodbye."

✳ A young man was lost in the woods when he came across a small house. He knocked on the door and was greeted by an ancient Chinese man with a long grey beard.

"I'm lost," said the man. "Can you put me up for the night?"

"Certainly," the Chinese man said, "but on one condition. If you lay a finger on my daughter, I will inflict upon you the three worst Chinese tortures known to man."

"Okay," said the man, thinking that the daughter must be pretty old as well, and entered the house. Before dinner, the daughter came down the stairs. She was young and attractive with an amazing figure. She was also obviously very sex-starved because she couldn't keep her eyes off the young man during the meal. Remembering the old man's warning, he politely ignored her and went up to bed alone. But during the night, he could bear it no longer and sneaked into her room for a night of passion. He was careful to keep everything quiet so the old man wouldn't hear.

He crept back to his room, exhausted but happy. The next morning he awoke to a feeling of pressure on his chest. Opening his eyes he saw a large rock on his chest with a note on it that read, "Chinese Torture 1: Large rock on chest."

"Well," he smiled to himself, "if that's the best the old man can do then I don't have too much to worry about." He picked the boulder up, walked over to the window and threw it out of the window. As he did so he noticed another note on it that read: "Chinese Torture 2: Rock tied to left testicle." In a panic he looked down and saw the rope that was already getting close to the end. Thinking quickly on his feet, and figuring that a couple of broken legs were better than castration, he jumped out of the window after the boulder. As he plummeted downward he spotted a large sign on the ground looming towards him that read, "Chinese Torture 3: Right testicle tied to bedpost."

✳ What's the definition of a clunt?

Someone who runs away from a Chinese chip shop without paying.

✳ A deaf mute man works his way up in the Chinese Triads and gets the job of collecting protection money on a small patch in Chinatown. After a couple of months in the job, however, he gets greedy and starts to cream off some of the money and stashes it in a safe place. His Triad bosses soon realize that they are short by about £50,000. They send their best enforcer to sort it out. He finds the deaf mute money collector to ask him where the money is, but they can't communicate so the enforcer drags him off to a poor Chinese restaurant owner who knows sign language.

"Ask him where the money is," demands the enforcer.

The restaurant owner signs to the man, who he knew had been terrorizing the neighbourhood for weeks: "He wants to know where the money is."

The deaf mute signs back, "I have no idea what you're talking about. Go fuck yourself."

The interpreter relays this to the enforcer, who promptly pulls out a gun and points in the money collector's mouth.

"Now, ask him again where the money is."

The terrified deaf mute signs back, "The £50,000 is in a deposit box at Euston Station. The key to the box is in the glove compartment of my car, box number 432."

"What did he say?" demands the Triad enforcer.

The restaurant owner replies: "He says he still doesn't know what you're talking about. He thinks you're a slitty-eyed cunt who doesn't have the balls to pull the trigger and your mother sucks cock for money."

Why are there so many Chinese people in Harrow?

Because they get off the plane at Heathrow, climb into the taxi and say "Harrow".

* A Chinese couple get married and the bride is a virgin. On the wedding night, she cowers naked under the bed sheets as her husband undresses.

  He climbs in bed and tries to gently reassure her.

  "Darring," he says, "I know dis you firt time and you velly flightened but I plomise you, I give you anyting you want, I do anyting you want. What you want?"

  "I would rike number 69," she replies.

  He says, "You want beef with bloccolli?"

* A refuse collector is doing his rounds and notices one house in the street that doesn't have a wheelie bin outside, so he goes to the door and knocks. After a few minutes an old Chinese man comes to the door.

  "Where's your bin?" the refuse collector asks.

  "I bin upstairs," the Chinese man replies.

  "No," the refuse collector continues, "where's your WHEELIE bin?"

  The old man thinks for a minute then says: "Okay, you got me. I was upstairs having a clafty wank."

⋆　⋆　⋆　⋆　⋆

CHRISTMAS

⋆ Have you heard about the new doll out this Christmas?

  It comes without shoes, clothes, or any possessions at all. It's called a Zimbarbie doll.

⋆ Have you heard about the new line of tampons with bells and tinsel?

  They're for the Christmas period.

⋆ The wife gave me a nice long blow job for Christmas. I didn't have the heart to tell her that our daughter got me the same.

> My family believes in enjoying a very traditional Christmas. Our grandad hanged himself on Christmas Eve. They didn't take his body down until 6 January.

★ It was Boxing Day and little Robbie and Timmy are comparing their presents.

"So what did what did you get?" asks little Robbie.

"I got a football, a rugby ball, a tennis set, some DVDs, a Wii and loads of games, a 32-inch plasma screen TV, and some books, and a remote control car, and a remote control plane, and a little motorbike. I also got shed loads of sweets and chocolate, and I got to go to Lapland to meet Santa!"

"Wow!" says Robbie.

"Yeah, I know! So what did you get?"

"I got a football and a selection box," says Robbie.

"That's a bit shit, isn't it?" says Timmy.

"Yeah, I suppose it is. But then I'm not the one with leukaemia."

★ Three men died on Christmas Eve and were met by St Peter at the pearly gates. "You've all led sinful lives," said St Peter, "but as this is the season of goodwill to all men, I'll give you a sporting chance. If you can show me something that symbolizes Christmas I will allow you to enter."

The first man fumbled through his pockets and pulled out a lighter. He flicked it on. "It represents a candle," he said.

"You may pass through the pearly gates," St Peter said.

The second man reached into his pocket and pulled out a set of keys. He shook them and said, "They're bells."

St Peter said: "Okay, you may pass through the pearly gates."

The third man started searching desperately through his pockets and finally pulled out a pair of women's knickers.

St Peter looked at the man with a raised eyebrow and asked, "And just what do those symbolize?"

The man replied, "They're Carol's."

★   Remember, a doggy is not just for Christmas.
It's a great position all the year round.

★ I bought a Liverpool FC advent calendar for Christmas. Fucking typical; all the windows are boarded up and some bastard had stolen the chocolate.

★   ★   ★   ★   ★

CHURCH

❖ A church service was just about to commence and the congregation were sitting in their pews. Suddenly, Satan himself appeared at the front of the church. Pandemonium ensued as the church was filled with screams, and everyone was fighting to get out, trampling each other in a frantic effort to get away. Very soon the church was empty except for one man, who sat calmly in his pew without moving, apparently oblivious that evil incarnate was just a few yards away. Satan walked up to the man and said, "Do you know who I am?"

"Yes," the man replied.

"Do you not fear me?" Satan asked.

"No, mate," said the man.

"Don't you realize that I can make you fry by lifting one finger?" said Satan.

"It wouldn't surprise me," replied the man, calmly.

"Do you know that I can cause you horrifying agony for all eternity?" persisted Satan.

"That wouldn't surprise me either," replied the man.

"And yet you are not afraid?" said the evil one.

"Not really," said the man.

Satan asked, "Why do you not fear me?"

The man calmly replied, "Because I have been married to your sister for thirty years."

❖ One day Mr Smith went to see the minister at the local church. "Reverend," he said, "I have a problem. Mrs Smith keeps falling asleep during your sermons and it's very embarrassing. Is there anything I can do?"

"I have an idea," said the minister. "Take this hatpin with you. I will be able to see your wife from the pulpit and when she falls asleep I will give you a signal. When I give the signal, you stick the hatpin in her leg."

The following Sunday, Mrs Smith dozed off once again in church. Seeing this, the preacher put his plan to work.

"And who, pray, made the ultimate sacrifice for you?" he said, nodding to Mr Smith.

"Jesus!" Mrs Smith cried out as her husband jabbed her in the leg with the hatpin.

"Yes, that's correct, Mrs Smith," said the minister.

Before long, Mrs Smith nodded off again. Once again the minister put his plan to work. "Who is your redeemer?" he asked the congregation, motioning towards Mr Smith.

"God!" Mrs Smith shouted out, as she was harpooned again in the leg.

"Correct again," said the minister, smiling.

Before long, Mrs Smith again dozed off. This time, however, the preacher failed to notice and as he picked up the tempo of his sermon, he made a few hand motions that Mr Smith incorrectly interpreted as signals to stick his wife with the hatpin again. The minister asked, "And what did Eve say to Adam after she bore him his 99th son?"

Mr Smith poked his slumbering wife, who cried out, "You stick that motherfucker in me one more time and I'll break it off and shove it up your ass!"

❖ Three couples, an elderly couple, a middle-aged couple and a young newlywed couple visit a parish church for the first time. The vicar says, "We have special requirements for new parishioners. You must abstain from sex for two weeks."

A couple of weeks later the vicar goes to the elderly couple and asks, "Were you able to abstain from sex for the two weeks?"

The old man replies, "No problem at all, vicar."

"Well done," says the vicar. "Welcome to the church."

He goes to the middle-aged couple and asks, "Were you able to abstain from sex for the two weeks?"

The man replies, "The first week wasn't a problem. I confess the second week was a struggle but, yes, we made it."

"Well done. Welcome to the church," says the vicar.

The pastor then addresses the newlywed couple. "Well, were you able to abstain from sex for two weeks?"

"Well, vicar, unfortunately we failed."

"Oh dear," says the pastor. "That is disappointing."

"Well we tried our best. We went twelve days without sex but then one day my wife was reaching for a can of beans on the top shelf and dropped it. When she bent over to pick it up, I was overcome with lust and I had to fuck her up the arse."

"Oh dear," says the vicar, "we don't much like that sort of thing in here."

"We understand, vicar," says the young man. "They're not too happy about it in Morrisons either."

CINEMA

* A man and his wife are enjoying a nice afternoon in the cinema. After half an hour or so she leans over to her husband and whispers: "The man next to me is having a wank."

"Just ignore him," he says, engrossed in the film.

"I can't," she replies, "he's using my hand."

* A man took his dog to the cinema. At the end of the film the dog applauded.

"That's amazing," said the usherette.

"Yes, it is," said the man. "He thought the book was crap."

A boy and a girl are sitting at the back of the cinema, kissing passionately.

When they come up for air, the boy says, "I love kissing you, but do you mind not passing me your chewing gum."

"It's not chewing gum," the girl replies. "I've got bronchitis."

*　　*　　*　　*　　*

CLIFF RICHARD

★ Sir Cliff Richard went to an old people's home to perform a concert but was disconcerted to find that none of the residents recognized him. Puzzled, he took an old lady aside and enquired, "Excuse me, but do you have any idea who I am?"

"Sorry, dear," said the old lady, "but if you ask one of the nurses, they'll tell you."

★ Sir Cliff is performing live in Japan on the last leg of his world tour. The audience go wild as Cliff asks them if there is anything he can sing especially for them.

"Tits and fanny!" scream the audience. "Tits and fanny!"

Cliff is shocked. "I can't sing that," he says. "I'm a devout Christian."

"Tits and fanny!" scream the audience. "Tits and fanny!"

"Oh, come on . . . please!" Cliff pleads. "What about 'Devil Woman' or 'Livin' Doll', at least something I know!"

"Tits and fanny!" scream the crowd.

"Okay, okay," says Cliff. "But I don't know how it goes."

"Tits and fanny," . . . sing the crowd in unison . . . "how we don't talk any more."

COMAS

❖ A man had been slipping in and out of a coma for several months and all the while his wife kept vigil at his bedside, every single hour of every single day. One day, while conscious, he motioned for her to come nearer.

As she sat by him, he whispered, eyes filling with tears. "You know what? You have been with me all through the bad times. When I lost my job, you were there for me. When my business failed, you supported us both. When I got shot, you nursed me back to health. When we lost the house, you endured living in a shabby rented flat.

"Now my health has started failing and you are still right by my side. You know what?"

"What dear?" She softly asked, choking back the tears as she gently rubbed his forehead.

"I'm beginning to think you're a jinx, so why don't you just fuck off."

❖ My father is in a coma. He's just living the dream.

❖ A young woman in a coma is moved to a new room in the hospital. After a few days her nurse notices that every time she sponge bathes the patient around her bits, the nearby monitor indicates that the patient's vital signs increase significantly. She has a bright idea: perhaps oral sex might just provide the stimulus to bring the woman out of her coma. She calls the woman's husband, and tells him that there is a just a chance oral sex can revive his wife, and he agrees.

When he arrives at the hospital, the nurse ushers him into the room, closes the curtain around the bed and closes the door. Five minutes later, the husband rushes out of the room, clearly distressed. All of his wife's vital signs have plummeted to zero and she needs a doctor immediately. The nurse is very upset that her idea not only didn't work, but had threatened the life of the woman she had sought to save.

She asks the husband: "What happened?"

"I'm not sure," he replied. "But I think she choked."

* * * * *

CONTRACEPTION

* I bought myself my first black condom today. My wife died last night and her sister is visiting later, so I thought I had better show a bit of respect.

* A couple have just had sex. The woman says, "If I got pregnant, what would we call the baby?"

The man takes off his condom, ties a knot in it and flushes it down the toilet. He says, "If he can get out of that, we'll call him Houdini."

There's nothing worse than having sex, then when you've finished, looking down and seeing a limp used condom hanging off the end of your cock. Especially when you weren't wearing one when you started.

* How do Australians practise safe sex?

They brand the sheep that kick.

* I bought some of these flavoured condoms last week. I said to my wife, "Let's play a game. I put one of these flavoured condoms on and you try to guess what flavour it is."

So she closed her eyes and went under the duvet and said: "Mmmm. Cheese and onion flavour."

I replied: "Hang on, give me chance to put one on!"

✳ Did you hear about the new "morning after" pill for men?
It works by changing your blood type.

✳ What's a diaphragm?
A trampoline for dick heads.

✳ The Russian President Vladimir Putin called Barack Obama with an emergency request. "Mr President, we need help. Our largest condom factory has exploded," the Russian President explained. "My people now have no method of birth control! This is a true disaster!"

"Vladimir," said Obama, "the American people would be happy to do anything within their power to help you."

"We do need your help," said Putin. "Could you possibly send one million condoms to tide us over?"

"No problem, I'm on it," said Obama.

"Oh, and one more small favour, please?" said Putin.

"Yes?" said Obama.

"Can you supply the condoms red in colour and at least ten inches long and four inches in diameter?"

"No problem," replied Obama, and with that, he hung up and called the CEO of Durex. "I need a favour, you've got to make one million condoms right away and send them to Russia."

"Consider it done," said the CEO of Durex.

"Great! Now listen, they have to be red in colour, ten inches long and four inches wide."

"Easily done. Anything else?"

"Yes," says Obama. "Print 'MADE IN USA, SIZE MEDIUM' on each one."

✳ What's the best form of birth control for people over fifty?
Nudity.

✳ A man walks into a pharmacist's with his eight-year-old son. As they walk past the condom display, the little boy asks, "What are these, dad?"

"Those are called condoms, son. Men use them to have safe sex."

"Oh, I see," replies the boy, thoughtfully. "I think I've heard about that at school." He looks over the display and picks up a package of three and asks, "Why are there three in this pack?"

"Those are for students, son. One for Friday, one for Saturday and one for Sunday."

"Cool!" says the boy. He notices a six-pack and asks, "Then who are these for, dad?"

"Those are for single men. Two for Friday, two for Saturday and two for Sunday."

"WOW!" says the boy. "Then who uses THESE?" he asks, picking up a twelve-pack.

With a sigh, his dad replies, "Those are for married men. One for January, one for February, one for . . ."

✳ A young guy goes into a pharmacist's to buy some condoms. The pharmacist tells him that the condoms come in packs of three, nine or twelve and asks which pack size he wants.

"Well," he says, "I've been seeing this bird for a while and she's really hot and I'm pretty sure tonight's the night. She's invited me to have dinner with her folks – a bit of a bummer! – but after that we're going out and I'm pretty sure I'm going to get lucky. Once she's seen my dick she isn't going to want anyone else, so you'd better give me the twelve-pack."

The young man makes his purchase and leaves. Later that evening, he sits down to dinner with his girlfriend and her parents. He asks if he might give the blessing and they agree. He begins the prayer: "Lord, for what we are about to receive . . ." then continues praying for several minutes.

The girl leans over to him and says, "You never told me that you were such a religious person."

He leans over to her and whispers, "You never told me your dad was a pharmacist."

COSMETIC SURGERY

A man approaching his fiftieth birthday decides to have a facelift. He spends £5,000 on the operation and is very happy with the results. On his way home from surgery, he stops at a kiosk and buys some cigarettes. Before leaving, he says to the vendor, "I hope you don't mind me asking, but how old do you think I am?"

"About thirty-five," is the reply.

"I'm actually forty-nine," the man replies smugly, feeling really good about himself.

After that he goes into a Starbucks for a coffee and asks the young girl behind the counter the same question, to which the reply is, "Oh you look about twenty-nine."

"I am actually forty-nine." By now he's feeling fantastic.

While standing at the bus stop, he asks a really old woman the same question. She replies, "I am ninety years old and my eyesight is going. But when I was young there was a sure way of telling a man's age. If I put my hand down your pants and play with your balls for ten minutes, I will be able to tell your exact age."

As there is no one around, the man lets her slip her hand down his pants.

The old lady rummages around for ten minutes and says: "Okay, it's done. You are forty-nine."

The man is stunned. "That was brilliant! How did you do that?"

The old lady replies, "I was standing behind you in Starbucks."

★　　★　　★　　★　　★

COURTS

❖ A defendant was on trial for murder at the Old Bailey. There was strong circumstantial evidence indicating guilt, but no corpse. In his closing statement the counsel for the defence, realizing that in all likelihood his client would probably be convicted, resorted to a trick. "Ladies and gentlemen of the jury, I have a surprise for you all," the lawyer said as he looked at his watch. "Within one minute, the person presumed dead in this case will walk into this courtroom." He looked towards the courtroom door. The jurors, somewhat stunned, all did likewise. A minute passed and nothing happened. Finally the lawyer said, "Actually, I made up the previous statement. But you all looked at the door to see if someone walked in. I put it to you, therefore, that there is reasonable doubt in this case as to whether anyone was actually killed and insist that you return a verdict of not guilty."

The jury retired in confusion to deliberate. A few minutes later, the foreman of the jury returned and told the judge that they had arrived at a unanimous verdict. "We find the defendant guilty."

The lawyer's jaw dropped in disbelief. "But how?" he enquired. "You must have had some doubt: I saw all of you stare at the door."

The jury foreman replied: "Yes, we did. But your client didn't."

A judge asks a defendant if he has anything to say for himself. The defendant mutters under his breath, "Fuck all."

"What did you say?" asks the judge.

The court clerk turns to the judge and says, "The defendant said 'fuck all', your honour."

"Really?" says the judge, "I could have sworn I saw his lips move."

✳ Did you hear about the two gay judges?
   They tried each other.

❖ The judge says to a double-murder defendant, "You're
charged with beating your wife to death with a hammer."
   A voice at the back of the courtroom yells out, "You
bastard!"
   The judge adds, "You're also charged with beating your
mother-in-law to death with a hammer."
   The voice in the back of the courtroom yells out, "You
bastard!"
   The judge stops and says to the man in the back of the
courtroom, "Sir, I can understand your anger and frustration
at this crime. But no more outbursts from you, or I'll charge
you with contempt. Is that understood?"
   The man in the back of the court stands up and says, "I'm
sorry, your honour. But for fifteen years I've lived next door
to that bastard and every time I asked to borrow a hammer
he said he didn't fucking have one."

★   ★   ★   ★   ★

COWBOYS

✳ A cowboy and his brand-new bride check into a hotel for
their honeymoon. The husband goes to the front desk and
asks for a room.
   "This here is a very special occasion," he informs the
receptionist. "We done got married today and we need a
good room with a strong bed."
   The receptionist winks and asks, "Do you want the
Bridal?"
   The cowboy thinks about it a while and then replies,
"Nope, I guess not. I'll just hold on to her ears until she gets
used to it."

✳ A young cowboy wanted more than anything to be the greatest gunfighter in the American West. He practised every minute of his spare time but knew that he wasn't yet first rate and that there was room for improvement. He was sitting in a saloon one night when he saw an old gunslinger at the bar who had once been recognized as the fastest gun of his day. The young cowboy sat himself down next to the old-timer, bought him a drink and told him the story of his great ambition. "Do you think you could give me some tips?" he asked.

The old man looked him up and down and said, "Well, for one thing, son, you're wearing your gun way too high. Tie the holster lower down on your leg." The young man did as he was told, stood up, whipped out his .44 and shot the bow tie off the piano player.

"That's fantastic!" said the young buck. "Got any more tips for me?"

"Yep," said the old man, "cut a notch out of your holster where the hammer hits it. That'll give you a smoother draw."

The young man took out his knife, cut the notch, stood up, drew his gun in a blur, and shot a cufflink off the piano player.

"Wow!" said the cowboy. "Even better! Got any more tips?"

The old man pointed to a large can in a corner of the saloon. "See that tin of grease over there? Coat your gun with it."

The young man went over to the can and smeared some of the grease on the barrel of his gun.

"No," said the old-timer. "You've gotta smear it all over the gun, handle and all."

"Will that make me a better gunfighter?" asked the young man.

"No," said the old-timer, "but when Wyatt Earp over there is done playing the piano, he's going to shove that gun up your arse and it won't hurt as much."

✳   Three cowboys are sitting around a campfire out on the lonesome prairie. They are chewing tobacco and swapping tales of bravado for which cowboys are famous. The first cowboy says, "I reckon I must be the meanest, toughest cowboy on the prairie."

"You reckon, dude? How come?" asks the second.

"Why, just the other day, a bull got loose in the corral and gored six men before I wrestled it to the ground by the horns, with my bare hands."

The second cowboy says: "Why that's nothing. I was walking down the trail yesterday and a twenty-foot rattlesnake slid out from under a rock and came straight at me. I grabbed that snake with my bare hands, bit its head off and sucked the poison down in one gulp."

The third cowboy said nothing. He just sat there, chewing his tobacco, slowly stirring the coals with his cock.

✳   One day the Lone Ranger and his trusty sidekick Tonto were out riding through the prairie when the Lone Ranger had to stop to take a piss. So he dismounted his horse Silver and went over to a bush and pulled down his pants. Just then, Tonto heard a scream. The Lone Ranger staggered out from behind the bush and said, "Tonto, I've been bitten by a rattlesnake on my dick! Go to town and ask the doctor what to do!"

So Tonto rode to town and went to the doctor. "Doctor, Lone Ranger has been bit by a rattlesnake. What do I do?"

The doctor replied, "You take a knife and make a small incision on the spot where he was bit, then you suck out the venom."

Tonto thanked the doctor and rode back to Lone Ranger.

"Tonto!" said the Lone Ranger, mightily relieved to see his friend. "Well, what did the doctor say?"

Tonto looks at the Lone Ranger and replied: "Doctor say you going to die!"

✳   An old cowboy went to a bar and ordered a drink. As he sat sipping his whisky a young lady sat down next to him. She turned to the cowboy and asked, "Are you a real cowboy?"

"Well," he replied, "I've spent my whole life on the ranch, herding and branding cattle, mending fences and so forth, so I guess I am. How about you?"

"I'm a lesbian," the woman replied. "I spend my whole day thinking about women. As soon as I get up in the morning I think about women. When I take a shower I think about women. While I watch TV or even eat I think about women. Everything seems to make me think about women."

The two sat sipping in silence. A short time later a man sat down on the other side of the old cowboy and asked, "Are you a real cowboy?"

"Well, I always thought I was," he replied, "but it turns out I'm a lesbian."

Two cowboys in a saloon. One says to the other, "I bet you fifty bucks you can't take a sip of that spittoon over there." With that, the other cowboy puts the spittoon to his mouth and knocks back the entire contents in one go.

"Well, I'll be darned!" says the first cowboy. "I only told you to take a sip!"

"I couldn't," replies the other. "It was all in one lump."

* Two cowboys walk into a saloon to wash the dust from their throats. As they stand by the bar drinking their beers and chewing the fat, a woman at a table near to them starts to choke. After a minute or so it becomes apparent that she is in distress. One of the cowboys asks her, "Ma'am, can ya swaller?"

No, signals the woman, desperately shaking her head.

"Can ya breathe?" asks the other.

The woman shakes her head again, by now beginning to turn blue.

The first cowboy walks over to her, lifts up the back of her skirt, yanks down her knickers and slowly runs his tongue up and down her arse. This shocks the woman into a violent spasm, the obstruction flies out of her mouth, and she begins to breathe again. The cowboy slowly walks back over to the bar and takes a swig of his beer. His partner says in admiration, "You know, I'd heard about that there Hind Lick Manoeuvre, but I ain't never seen nobody do it."

★   ★   ★   ★   ★

CREMATION

★ A woman who had recently lost her husband had him cremated and brought his ashes home. She picked up his urn and poured him out on to the kitchen table. Then, tracing her fingers in the ashes, she started talking to her deceased spouse. "Colin, you know that dishwasher you promised me? I bought it with the insurance money!"

She paused for a minute, tracing her fingers in the ashes then said, "Colin, remember that car you promised me? Well, I also bought it with the insurance money."

Again, she paused for a few minutes and, while tracing her fingers in the ashes, said, "Colin, that diamond ring you promised me? Yep. Bought it with the insurance money."

Finally, still tracing her fingers in the ashes, she said, "Colin, remember that blow job I promised you? Here it comes."

★ Shortly before the cremation, the undertaker quietly sat down next to the grieving widow. "How old was your husband? " he asked.

"He was ninety-eight," she sobbed. "Two years older than I am."

"Really?" the undertaker said. "Hardly worth going home, is it?"

* My grandfather swore by adding a spoonful of gunpowder to his tea every morning. He said it was a very old remedy to help him live longer, and it worked: he lived to the ripe old age of ninety-seven. He left a widow, two children, fourteen grandchildren and a fifty-foot crater where the crematorium used to be.

* ## My dad recently died of asbestos poisoning. It took three weeks to cremate him.

* Three gay men died and were going to be cremated. Their lovers were waiting in line at the crematorium at the same time and were discussing what they planned to do with the ashes.

   The first said, "My partner loved to fly, so I'm going up in a plane to scatter his ashes in the sky."

   The second said, "My partner was a good fisherman, so I'm going to scatter his ashes in his favourite lake."

   The third man said, "My partner was sex mad. I'm going to dump his ashes in a chicken vindaloo so he can tear my arse up just one more time."

* My grandmother used to have terrible arthritis, which left her completely crippled. She used to drink a litre of olive oil a day. It didn't help combat the arthritis but it made her cremation a lot quicker.

*   *   *   *   *

CRICKET

* A man goes to the doctor and says: "I've got a cricket ball stuck up my arse."

   The doctor says, "How's that?"

   The man replies, "Don't you fucking start!"

❖ The English cricket team went to Australia to try to win the Ashes. As they were going through customs their captain was stopped by immigration control and asked if he had a criminal record. "Nah," he replied. "To be honest, I didn't think you needed one any more."

❖ A woman walks into a police station and goes up to the reception desk.

"I've just been raped," she tells the desk sergeant.

He takes down her personal details and then asks her, "Did you get a look at your assailant, miss?"

"Yes. He was a New Zealand cricketer," she replies.

"How do you know he was a cricketer?"

"Well, he was dressed all in white. White shirt, white jumper, white trousers and shoes," replied the woman.

"I see. Could he possibly have been a crown green bowler, miss? They also wear white clothing," points out the sergeant.

"No, he was definitely a cricketer. He still had his pads on."

"Fair enough, so he's a cricketer. But how do you know he's a New Zealand cricketer?" asks the sergeant.

The woman replies, "Well, he wasn't in for long."

★   ★   ★   ★   ★

CRIME

✳ Tomorrow, I'm going to dress up as Hitler but without any trousers or underwear. I'm going to carry a pig under one arm and a can of spray-paint under the other. Then I'm going to rob my local bank, spray offensive messages on all the walls, fuck the pig seven ways, then leave a big turd out on every desk, before walking out with the money. Let's see *Crimewatch* re-create that.

> **❝** Apparently someone in London gets stabbed every two minutes. Of course the poor bastard must be used to it by now. **❞**

✳ According to government statistics, hippopotamuses kill more people every year than knives. A knife, however, is much easier to conceal.

✳ A man walks into a police station and says to the duty sergeant, "I live just down the road. You arrested a burglar breaking into my house last night. I'd like to speak to him, please."

"Sorry, sir, but you'll get your chance in court," says the duty officer.

"No," says the man. "I want to know how he got in the fucking house without waking the wife. I've been trying to do that for years."

✳ A hoodie goes into a Manchester library. The librarian tells him, "In order to borrow a book, you need to prove that you are a resident of Moss Side." So he stabs her four times.

✳ The credit crunch has seen elderly women get hit the hardest. The old slags should learn to just let go of their handbags.

✳ Another indiscriminate shooting spree in America has left fifteen dead, this time in a nursing home for the elderly. During the shooting the gunman was offered a cup of tea twenty-eight times.

DEAD CELEBRITIES

❖ What did Robert Maxwell and Freddie Mercury have in common?
  They were both bumped off by dodgy seamen.

❖ **What did Rod Hull and Emu have in common?**
  Neither could fly.

❖ What sits in the corner of the lounge and crackles?
  Rod Hull's television.

❖ What's the difference between Vanessa Feltz and Rod Hull's roof?
  One is big, hard to get on top of and covered in green slime, and the other is Rod Hull's roof.

❖ Why didn't Jill Dando drink much alcohol?
  One shot went straight to her head.

  What's pink and fluffy and hasn't moved in years?
  Freddie Mercury's slippers.

❖ What's the difference between Jill Dando and a white shirt?
  The white shirt survived the doorstep challenge.

❖ What did the war in Kosovo and a bullet have in common?
  Jill Dando couldn't stop either of them.

❖ Jill Dando's fiancé wanted to paint the front door red. She was dead against it.

❖ What was the last thing to go through Kurt Cobain's mind as he pulled the trigger?
A bullet.

❖ ## What's the difference between Kurt Cobain and a pint of cider?
A pint of cider always looks better without a head.

❖ What's the difference between Grace Kelly and Kenny Dalglish?
Kenny Dalglish could take corners.

❖ Why did Bob Geldof take up karate?
Because he heard he could kill Michael Hutchence with a black belt.

❖ What did Kermit the frog say when Jim Henson died?
Nothing.

❖ What's the difference between Michael Hutchence and Princess Di?
Hutchence wore his belt.

❖ Why was Paula Yates attracted to Michael Hutchence?
Because he was well hung.

❖ Paula Yates was being considered for the position of England cricket coach at the time of her death. The English Cricket Board thought that her experience of fucking Australians and bringing home the ashes would be invaluable.

❖ ## What did Elton John sing at Mother Theresa's funeral?
"Sandals in the Bin".

❖ What's red and gathers dust?
   Natasha Richardson's passport.

❖ What's black and white and goes to bed hungry?
   Heath Ledger's cat.

❖ What was Marc Bolan's last hit?
   Tie a yellow mini round the old oak tree.

❖ What's black and very pissed off?
The reincarnation of Bernard Manning.

❖ What's black and shoots across a room?
   Marvin Gaye's dad.

❖ "Knock knock"
   "Who's there?"
   "Diana, Princess of Wales."
   "Sorry, but I don't open the door for dead people."
   "Knock knock."
   "Who's there?"
   "Mother Theresa."
   "I said I don't answer the door for dead people!"
   "Knock knock."
   "Who's there?"
   "Elvis Presley."
   "Hurry up, Burger King shuts in half an hour . . ."

❖ Roy Castle finally made it into the *Guinness Book of Records*.
   They gave him six months to live and he did it in two.

❖ Did you hear they had to pull Steve Irwin's line of sun care
   products?
   Apparently they don't protect you from harmful rays.

❖ What's blue, hangs from the ceiling and doesn't fit any
   more?
   Ian Curtis.

❖ Gene Pitney's undertakers have said that it will take ten weeks to make him a coffin from oak . . . or twenty-four hours from balsa.

❖ How does Bob Marley like his doughnuts?
    He doesn't, he's dead.

John Lennon, John F. Kennedy and Martin Luther King went out for a beer.
    Who got the first round in?
    The sniper behind the grassy knoll.

✦   ✦   ✦   ✦   ✦

DEAFNESS

✳ I met a girl the other day and took her home to meet my parents. My dad whispered to me, "Where the hell did you get her from, son? She's cross-eyed, bow-legged and all her teeth are black!"
    I told him, "Dad, there's no need to whisper, she's also deaf."

✳ Why did the deaf boy's girlfriend wear tight jeans?
    So he could read her lips.

✳ Why do deaf women masturbate with one hand?
    So they can moan with the other.

✳ How do deaf people have phone sex?
    By fax.

❋ A deaf mute walks into a chemist's to buy some condoms. He has difficulty making himself understood and can't see any condoms on the shelf to point to. Out of sheer frustration he unzips his trousers and flops his cock on the counter then puts down a £5 note next to it.

The chemist looks at the customer's penis and the fiver, then unzips his trousers and does the same as the deaf mute. Then he picks up both fivers and stuffs them in his pocket. Baffled and angry, the deaf mute curses the chemist wildly in sign language and storms out of the shop.

Meanwhile another customer has been looking on, completely bemused. "That was a bit harsh, wasn't it?" he says to the chemist.

"Look," the chemist replies, "if he couldn't afford to lose, he shouldn't have been betting."

> 66 When the police arrest a deaf and dumb person, do they tell him he has the right to remain silent? 99

❋ A man was sitting in a pub and noticed a group of people using sign language. He was also intrigued to note that the barman was using sign language to speak to them. When the barman served him next, the man asked how he had learned to sign. The barman explained that these were regular customers and he picked it up from them.

The man thought that this was highly commendable. A few minutes later, however, the man noticed that the people in the group were waving their hands around very wildly.

The barman looked over and signed to them, then shouted, "I warned you about that. Now fuck off out!" and threw the group out of the bar.

The customer was taken aback and asked what had just taken place.

"If I told them once I told them 100 times," replied the barman. "NO SINGING IN THE BAR!"

❋ Why didn't the deaf girl scream when she fell off the cliff?
Because she was wearing mittens.

* A mute was walking down the street one day when he came across a mute friend. He used sign language to greet his friend and ask how he had been doing. "Oh, enough of that hand-waving shit," replied his friend. "I can talk now."

Amazed, the mute pressed him for details. It seems that his friend had been to see a specialist, who, upon finding no physical damage to his vocal cords, had put him on a treatment programme that had restored the use of his voice. Gesturing enthusiastically, the mute asked if he might meet this specialist and they got an appointment that very afternoon.

After a thorough physical examination, the specialist told him that, indeed, he could find no permanent damage, that the mute was essentially in the same condition as his friend, and there was no reason why he couldn't be helped as well.

"Yes, yes," signed the mute. "Let's have the first treatment right now!"

"Very well," replied the specialist. "Please go into the next room, drop your trousers and pants and lean over the examining table. I'll be right in."

The mute did as instructed and the doctor sneaked in with a broomstick, a mallet and jar of Vaseline. Greasing the broom handle, he rammed it home with a couple of deft swipes of the mallet. The mute jumped from the table, screaming, "AAAaaaaaaaaaa aaaaaaaaaa aaaaaaaaaaa!!!"

"Very good," smiled the doctor. "Next week, we move on to 'B'."

* My ex-wife was deaf. She left me for a deaf friend of hers. To be honest, I should have seen the signs.

* You can say what you like about deaf people . . .

★   ★   ★   ★   ★

DENTISTS

★ An old lady went to visit her dentist. When it was her turn she sat in the chair, lowered her knickers and raised her legs. The dentist said, "Excuse me, but I'm not a gynaecologist."

"I know," said the old lady. "I want you to take my husband's teeth out."

★ **What's worse than having your doctor tell you that you have gonorrhoea?**
Getting the news from your dentist.

★ A Scotsman phoned a dentist to enquire about the cost for a tooth extraction.

"£85 for an extraction, sir," the dentist replied.

"£85? You're joking, mon. Have ye nae got anything cheaper?"

"That's the normal tariff, sir," replied the dentist.

"I know; what aboot if ye did'nae use any anaesthetic?" enquired the Scot.

"That would be highly unusual, sir, but I could do it and would knock £15 off."

"What aboot if yon dental nurse did the extraction instead of you and still wi' nae anaesthetic?"

"Well, I can't guarantee the standard of professionalism and it would be very painful. But yes, the price could drop by £20."

"Och, now you're talking laddie! It's a deal," said the Scot. "Can ye confirm an appointment for the wife next Tuesday, then?"

★ **What's red and very bad for your teeth?**
A house brick.

★ I went to the dentist and he said, "Say Aaah."
   I said, "Why?'"
   He said, "My dog's died."

> 66 My dentist has been voted Dental
> Surgeon of the Year. Sadly, all he got
> for it was a little plaque. 99

★ A man goes to the dentist's for an examination. The dentist tells him: "This tooth on the lower right has to come out. I'm going to give you a local anaesthetic and I'll be back in a few minutes."

The man grabs the dentist's arm, "Please. I hate needles. I'm not having any injection."

"Okay," says the dentist. "We'll have to go with the gas."

The man replies, "Please. No gas. It makes me really sick for a couple of days. I'm not having gas."

So the dentist steps out and comes back with a glass of water, "Here," he says. "Take this pill."

The man asks, "What is it?"

The dentist replies, "Viagra."

The man looks surprised, "Will that kill the pain?" he asks.

"No," replies the dentist, "but it will give you something to hang on to while I pull your tooth."

★ What do you get when you have thirty-two Glaswegians in a room?
   A full set of teeth.

★ A man goes to his dentist for a regular check-up. After the dentist has had a look at the man's mouth he says, "Hmm. Been licking your wife's fanny recently?"

The man looks up in horror and replies: "Oh, God, how embarrassing. Yes, I have. Er, why? Have I got pubes between my teeth?"

"Not at all," the dentist replies. "But you have got shit in your nostrils."

★ Why did the Buddhist monk refuse Novocain?

Because he wanted to transcend dental medication.

★   ★   ★   ★   ★

DESERT ISLANDS

❖ A plane carrying some Christian missionaries crash lands in the middle of the south Atlantic ocean. Miraculously, two priests and a nun survive and make it to a remote, barren island. Stranded alone with no expectation of rescue, the three are unable to resist sexual temptation.

Three months later, however, the nun is overcome by guilt at the sins she has committed and she kills herself.

Six months later, the two priests also have a crisis of conscience and realize they also cannot cope with the guilt of what they are doing. So they bury the nun.

❖ A black guy is marooned on a desert island. He finds a lamp on the beach one day, thinking it might be worth a bit if it was cleaned up. He gives it a rub. Poof – out pops a genie! "For freeing me from the lamp I will grant you three wishes," says the genie.

The guy panics, and says the first thing to pop into his head.

"Give me an ice cream!"

Poof – an ice-cream stand appears with his name on it. A bit stunned, he sits there for a while eating his ice cream, thinking long and hard before making his final two wishes. Finally he turns to the genie and says . . .

"I want to be white and surrounded by women!"

Poof – he turns into a tampon.

❖ A plane travelling from London to Sydney is suddenly hit by a severe engine problem and plummets into the Indian Ocean. The impact is such that the plane is ripped apart, leaving only one male survivor. After hours of swimming he spies an island and drags himself on to the shore. Although he is half drowned he can't help but admire the beauty of the island he finds himself on. Looking down the beach he sees a figure lying on the sand, another survivor from the crash! He runs over and sees that she is not breathing, so quickly he gives her the kiss of life. After several attempts she coughs and splutters into life. To his amazement he see that it is Kylie Minogue!

Deeply grateful to him for saving her life, Kylie and the stranger form an immediate bond and over the following weeks, while stranded on the island, they fall madly in love. One day Kylie is walking down the beach and notices her new-found love sitting on the rocks by the beach, staring out to sea, with a melancholy look on his face. She wanders over to him.

"What's wrong, love?" says Kylie.

"Kylie," he says, "the last few weeks have been the greatest of my life. We've found this island paradise. We have all the food and water we need and I have you, but still I can't help feeling there's something missing."

"What, my darling?" says Kylie. "What do you need? I'll do anything."

"Well there is one thing. Would you mind putting on my shirt and my trousers?"

"Okay, if that's what you want," says Kylie.

"Okay. Now, would you mind walking around the island, and I'll set off in the other direction and meet you on the beach half-way?"

"Okay, my love, whatever will make you happy," says Kylie.

So they set off in opposite directions. After an hour walking he eventually sees her heading towards him along the beach. He breaks into a run, goes up to her and grabs her by the shoulders and says: "Fucking hell mate, you'll never guess who I'm shagging!"

❖   A man is shipwrecked on a desert island. One day he is amazed to see a stunningly curvaceous female scuba diver walking out of the water, looking as though she had been poured into her wetsuit. He runs to greet her and tells her she is the first human contact he has had in three years.

"Sounds like you could use a drink, honey," she says, as she unzips one of her pockets and offers the man a flask of single malt whisky.

"That's the best drink I've ever had!" he tells her.

"No problem. Would you like a smoke?" she asks, as she unzips another pocket on her suit and offers the man a Cuban cigar.

"This must be the best cigar in the world!" he shouts, as he blows smoke rings in the air. As she begins to unzip the front of her wetsuit, she asks with an alluring wink, "Would you like to play around?"

"No shit!" he shouts. "You got golf clubs in there as well?"

★   ★   ★   ★   ★

DIARRHOEA

✳   An elderly man died and his wife put a death notice in the local paper, noting that he died of gonorrhoea. No sooner were the papers delivered when a relative phoned and complained bitterly: "You know very well that he died of diarrhoea."

The widow replied:, "I know. I nursed him night and day."

"So why did you claim he died of gonorrhoea?"

"I thought it would be better for posterity to remember him as a great lover rather than the big shit he always was."

✳   If one out of ten people suffer from diarrhoea, does that mean that the other nine enjoy it?

✳ "Doctor, I need some help. I keep shitting myself. I think I suffer from hereditary diarrhoea."

"I'm afraid that's impossible," replies the doctor. "Diarrhoea is not hereditary."

"Are you sure? It's in my jeans."

★　★　★　★　★

DINING OUT

★ We took dad to Australia for his eightieth birthday. We were in this really nice restaurant in Sydney when suddenly he shouted out: "I fucking hate aborigines!"

We said: "Dad, you can't say that here." But he just wouldn't shut up.

Again he shouted: "I fucking hate aborigines!"

"Dad, you just can't say that in a restaurant. And in any case, it's pronounced aubergines."

An Englishman was in a Paris restaurant and had just had the soup he ordered put in front of him. As the waiter departed, he called him back. "Garçon, il y à un mouche dans ma soupe."

The waiter, seeing that there was indeed a fly in the soup, corrected him: "UNE mouche, monsieur."

"Fuck me," said the Englishman, peering even closer at the fly, "you've got good eyesight!"

★ I was out with the wife having a meal at the local pub when I decided to sneak into the kitchen to see how hygienic it was. To my shock, I saw the chef using his false teeth to put the edgings on the pastry for the pies.

I said, "You dirty bastard, haven't you got a tool?"

He replied, "Yes, but I use that for putting the rings in the doughnuts."

★ One cold winter's evening, a little elderly couple walked slowly into a McDonalds. They looked completely out of place among all the young families and young couples eating there. Lots of customers looked at them admiringly. "Look," they were all thinking, "there is an old couple who has been through a lot together, probably for sixty years or more."

Eventually the little old man shuffled up to the cash register and placed his order, then paid for their meal. The couple took a table and started taking food off the tray. There was just one cheeseburger, one order of French fries and one Coke. The little old man unwrapped the cheeseburger and carefully cut it in half, then placed one half in front of his wife. Then he carefully counted out the French fries, divided them in two small piles and neatly placed one pile in front of his wife. Then he took a sip of the Coke, and then his wife took a sip as the man began to eat his meal. "Ah, that poor old couple," everyone was thinking.

As the old man began eating his French fries, a young man walked over to them and politely offered to buy another meal. "No thanks," replied the old man, "we're just fine. We are used to sharing everything."

The young man returned to his table and sat down. He couldn't help noticing, however, that the little old lady still hadn't eaten a thing. She just sat there watching her husband eat and occasionally sipping some Coke. Again, the young man went over and begged them to let him buy them another meal. This time, the lady explained that no, they were happy sharing.

As the little old man finished eating, the young man could stand it no longer and asked again. After being politely knocked back again, he finally asked the little old lady, "Madam, why aren't you eating. You said that you share everything."

"We do," she replied. "I'm waiting for my turn to use the teeth."

★ An American tourist goes into a restaurant in Spain and orders the speciality of the house. When his meal arrives, he asks the waiter what it is. "These, senor," replies the waiter, "are the cojones, how you say, the testicles, of the bull killed in the ring today." The American swallows hard but tries the dish anyway and to his surprise finds it delicious. He enjoys it so much that he returns the next evening and orders the same item. When he has finished, the waiter asks him if everything was okay.

"Superb, thank you," says the American. "But these cojones, or whatever you call them, they were much smaller than the ones I had last night."

"Yes, senor," replies the waiter. "You see, the bull, he does not always lose."

★ A couple go into a restaurant and order a meal. When the waiter brings out their soup course they notice he has his thumbs stuck in both bowls. Being English, they are reluctant to complain, so they shrug and laugh it off.

"Would you like anything else?" the waiter enquires. "We have some excellent lamb shank today." They both order lamb shank, so the waiter goes off and comes back with two plates of lamb shank. Once again they notice that the waiter's thumbs are in the gravy. Again, they let it go.

"Would sir and madam like any desert? Our special today is apple pie," says the waiter.

"Fine," they reply. The waiter returns with his thumbs stuck in the custard. By now they have just about lost their appetites but are still reluctant to force a confrontation.

"Would you like some coffee?" asks the waiter. They nod, and he returns with his thumbs stuck in the cups of coffee.

By now the man can no longer restrain himself: "I say, what the hell's going on here? Every time you have come to this table you've had your thumbs stuck in our food!"

"I'm terribly sorry, sir," mumbles the waiter. "I've got an infection and my doctor told me to keep my thumb in a hot, moist place."

"Why don't you just stick it up your arse?"

"That's where I put it when I'm in the kitchen."

DISABILITY

❖ Little Jimmy's next-door neighbour had a baby, which unfortunately was born without ears. When mother and new baby arrive home from the hospital, Jimmy's family are invited round to see the baby. Before they leave their house, Jimmy's father explains to his son that the newborn baby next door hasn't any ears. His dad warns him severely not to mention anything about the baby's predicament. To even mention the word "ears", Jimmy's dad tells him sternly, would invite the hiding of his life when they got back home. Little Jimmy tells his dad that he understands completely.

When Jimmy looks in the cot, he says, "What a beautiful baby."

The mother says, "Why, thank you, Jimmy."

Jimmy continues, "He has lovely little feet and lovely little hands, a lovely little nose and really lovely eyes. Can he see?"

"Yes," the mother replies, "we are so thankful; the doctor says he will have 20/20 vision."

"That's great," says Jimmy, "because he'd be fucked if he needed glasses."

❖ What is the best way to fuck a woman in a wheelchair?
   Slash her tyres.

❖ One-armed waiters. They can take it, but they can't dish it out.

❖ Last night I had sex with a girl who was suffering from brittle-bone disease. What a little cracker she was.

❖ What's the definition of perfect balance?
   A pregnant hunchback.

❖ What's the best thing about being a hunchback?
   Being able to rock yourself to sleep at night.

❖ What's the difference between shagging a girl with arms and shagging a girl without arms?
   When you are shagging a girl with no arms and your dick slips out you have to put it back in yourself.

> " I had a parcel delivered today and it was covered in crayon. That's the last time I pay for a special delivery. "

❖ A man was walking along the beach one day when he passed by a young woman who did not have any arms or legs. He couldn't help noticing that she was gently sobbing to herself. "Why the tears?" he asked.
   She said: "I'm eighteen years old and I've never been kissed."
   The man paused for a moment, then smiled and gave her a soft kiss on the forehead. She brightened up a little and smiled, so he gave her a big kiss on the lips. They pause for an unsure moment, and then she said, "You know, I'm eighteen years old and . . . I've never been fucked."
   The man stood up, started smiling and grabbed the young woman by the hair and tossed her into the sea. As she started screaming and bobbing up and down, the man shouted, "Consider yourself fucked, love!"

❖ Did you hear about the strawberry picker who hadn't any legs?
   She was a right jammy cunt.

❖ ## What do you call a man without any shins?
   Neil.

❖ What do you call a retard on a trampoline?
   Spring cabbage.

❖ I was very upset when my doctor told me I was in the advanced stages of Motor Neurone Disease. I could hardly control myself.

❖ One day a little boy runs up to his mother, and says "Mummy, mummy! Why am I called Leaf?"

His Mother replies: "Because when you were a baby, a leaf fell on your head."

The next day, his little sister runs in, saying "Mummy, mummy! Why am I called Petal?"

Mother replies: "Because when you were a baby, a petal fell on your head."

The following day, their little brother says: "kslsiehsjk mrblkshju mmrbbl drubksjl ls gggg".

Mother says: "Be quiet, Fridge."

❖ **I live near a remedial school. There's a road sign outside that says, "SLOW CHILDREN". It can't be good for their self-esteem.**

❖ How did the quadriplegic fall off the cliff?

He was pushed.

❖ I went to see this quadriplegic juggler. He wasn't very good, he kept dropping the quadriplegics.

❖ I've got nothing against disabled people. I've even got one of their stickers on my car.

❖ When is the best time to add insult to injury?

When you're signing somebody's plaster cast.

❖ What's the opposite of Christopher Reeve?

Christopher Walken.

❖ Isn't it quite ironic that people with "club feet" are generally crap at dancing?

❖ A man is in hospital waiting for his wife to give birth when a doctor walks over. "You have a baby son, however there were complications," the doctor informs him gravely. "Your baby is alive, however it has no body, legs or arms, it is just a head."

The new father lets the news sink in, then immediately resolves to raise the head like any normal child. He takes it to football games, takes it to the park, then on his son's eighteenth birthday he takes the head to the pub for a pint. He walks up to the bar and asks for two pints of Carling.

He pours the beer into the head's mouth when, suddenly, a body sprouts from nowhere. The father is amazed and orders his lad two pints of Fosters, which the boy knocks back. Suddenly two arms sprout. The lad then has two pints of Stella Artois and grows two legs. He is now like any normal eighteen-year-old.

Father and son drink all night to celebrate, and at the end of the night they walk out of the pub. The son, unused to alcohol, staggers into the road and a lorry knocks him twenty feet through the air, killing him outright.

The moral of the story? Quit while you're a head.

Following the confirmation of London as the venue for the Paraplegic Olympics, the organizers have published a leaflet containing cockney rhyming slang for the disabled:

Mutton Jeff: deaf
Bacon rind: blind
Canary Wharf: dwarf
Cardinal Wolsey: cerebral palsy
Raspberry ripple: cripple
Wasps and bees: amputees
Rubber and plastic: spastic
Tulips and roses: multiple sclerosis
Diet Pepsi: epilepsy
Benny and the Jets: Tourette's

❖ What goes PLOP PLOP FIZZ FIZZ?
   Two paraplegics in an acid bath.

❖ Three pregnant women are sitting outside a doctor's surgery. They are all knitting in expectation of their new kids' imminent arrivals.
   The first one takes out a tablet, and pops it in her mouth. "It's a calcium supplement so my baby's bones grow nice and strong," she explains to the other two, and carries on knitting.
   The second woman also pops a pill. "It's vitamin C to ward off colds and boost its immune system," she tells her companions, and carries on knitting.
   The third woman takes a tablet. "Its Thalidomide," she says. "I can't do sleeves."

❖ What do you say to a girl with no arms and no legs?
   Nice tits.

❖ A boy was born with just a head, no body. His parents were at a cocktail party one evening when, quite by chance, they bumped into a fellow guest who introduced himself as a research biochemist. "My colleagues and I are working on a method to regenerate missing limbs," he told them.
   Then the dad said: "Actually, our son has several missing limbs. In fact, he's just a head. Will you be able to possibly generate a body for him?"
   "Sure," the biochemist said. "If the formulae work out, we'll be able to generate a whole new body for your son."
   The parents dashed home to tell their son the wonderful news. They went into the house, went to the little head's bedroom, turned on the light, walked over and tapped him on the head, saying "Son, son, wake up. We have a big surprise for you."
   The boy opened his eyes, looked up at them, and said: "Let me guess, another fucking hat?"

❖ I was refused entry to remedial school the other day. Apparently, a blow job a day is not a "special need".

DIVORCE

* A divorcee spots his ex-wife's new husband in a bar. After knocking back a few drinks, he walks over to the guy and says: "So, how do you like using second-hand goods?"

    "No problem," the new husband replies. "Once you get past the first three inches, it's all brand new."

* When I got divorced my wife said she would fight for custody of the kids, which she then did. Fortunately I was able to take her out with a single punch.

* ## Why don't cannibals eat divorced women? Because they're very bitter.

* A man and his wife were driving along the motorway doing 55 mph. The wife looked over at the husband and said, "We've been married for twelve years and I want a divorce." The husband said nothing but slowly increased the speed to 60 mph.

    She went on: "There's no point you trying to talk me out of it, I've been having an affair with your best friend and he's much better in bed than you are." The husband said nothing, he just slowly increased his speed.

    She went on, "I want the house." By now he's doing 70 mph. She continued, "I want the children as well." He put his foot down, up to 80 mph.

    She continued, "I want the car, the bank account and all the credit cards as well." He increased his speed to 90 mph and pointed the car towards a concrete support under a motorway bridge.

    "Well?" she said. "Aren't you going to say something?"

    He replied, "No thanks, I've got everything I need."

    She asks, "Like what?"

    Just before they hit the bridge at 95 mph, he replied, "I've got the only airbag."

DIY

★ I got myself arrested in B&Q yesterday for punching a black woman in the tits. I blame my father. He told me to go to a DIY shop and find a Black & Decker.

> A woman goes into a DIY store and buys a wall mirror. The assistant asks: "Do you want a screw for that?"
> She replies: "No, but I will suck your cock for a lawnmower."

★ A husband and wife had just finished having sex, when she says to her man: "I've never told you this before, but you make love like you decorate."
He replies: "You mean slowly, with smooth strokes and a professional finish?"
"No, more like the council. You just bang it up, leave a fucking mess and I have to finish the job myself."

★　　★　　★　　★　　★

DOCTORS

❖ A man goes to the doctor's complaining about a pain in his backside. The doctor instructs him to remove his clothes and hop on the bed.
"My God!" says the doctor, pulling a lettuce leaf from the man's arse.
"Tell me the worse doc, how serious is this?"
The doctor looks up with a worried expression on his face and says grimly: "I'm afraid this is just the tip of the iceberg."

❖ A women walks into a doctor's with badly grazed knees. The doctor says: "How did you do this?"

The women replies, "Oh, you know, just having the usual sex, doggie style".

"Do you know any other positions apart from doggie style?" asks the doctor.

"Yes," the women replies. "But my dog doesn't."

❖ A man goes into the doctor's office feeling really ill. After a thorough examination the doctor calls him into his office and says, "I have some bad news. You have HAGS."

"What the hell is HAGS?" the patient asks.

"It's herpes, AIDS, gonorrhoea and swine flu," replies the doctor.

"Christ!" says the man. "What happens next?"

"We are going to put you in an isolated room and feed you pancakes, flapjacks and pizza."

"Is that going to cure me?"

"No, you're going to die," says the doctor. "But it's the only food we know of that we can slide under the door".

❖ I went to see the doctor today with severe headaches. He asked me if I'd suffered any memory loss. I replied, "How the fuck would I know?"

❖ A man goes into see his doctor and says, "Every time I see a lorry, I get a hard-on."

The doctor laughs. "I don't believe you. Show me."

So the man walks over to the window and after a lorry passes by, he pulls his trousers down to reveal a huge erection. The doctor says, "I still don't believe it. Do it again." So the man goes over to the window, another lorry goes by and sure enough he gets another erection.

"This isn't possible," says the doctor, scratching his head. "Give me a blood sample and come back in a couple of weeks time."

Two weeks later the man returns to the doctor. "Sit down, I have some bad news for you. It appears that you are HGV positive."

❖ A man goes to the doctor for a check-up. The doctor finishes his examination and tells the man, "I have some bad news. Your situation is very bleak. I estimate you only have about two weeks left to live."

The man is deeply shocked. He asks the doctor, "Is there is anything I can do?"

The doctor thinks for a while. "Tell you what, there is one thing that you could try."

"Just name it, doctor, I'll do whatever it takes."

The doctor replies: "Take a lot of mud baths, at least two or three a day."

"Will that help my condition?"

The doctor says, "No. But it will get you used to the idea of being covered in dirt."

❖ An attractive young woman with a baby was shown into the examining room. The doctor examined the baby and asked her, "Is he breast fed or bottle fed?"

"Breast fed," replied the woman.

"Strip down to your waist," the doctor ordered.

The woman did as she was told and the doctor examined her breasts.

He squeezed and pulled each one for a while and then he sucked hard on each nipple. Finally he remarked, "No wonder this child is suffering from malnutrition. You don't have any milk!"

"That's correct," said the woman. "This is my sister's child."

"I'm sorry, I had no idea," the doctor blurted. "You really shouldn't have come."

"I didn't," replied the woman, "until you started sucking my right nipple."

A doctor walked into a bank to sign a cheque. Searching inside his pocket, he pulled out a rectal thermometer. "Bollocks!" said the doctor. "Some arsehole's got my pen!"

❖ "Doctor, I have a strawberry stuck up my arse."
"Don't worry. I've got some cream for that."

❖ I went to see my doctor to get my prostate checked. He gave me the thumbs up.

❖ A young couple were sunning themselves on a nudist beach when a wasp buzzed into the woman's vagina. The girl started screaming "Oh my God, help me, there's a wasp inside me!"

The boyfriend quickly covered her with his jacket, carried her to the car and raced to the hospital where he explained the situation. After examining her, the doctor realized that the wasp was in too deep to be reached. The doctor thought for a moment and said "Hmm, tricky situation. But I have a solution to the problem if the young sir would permit."

The boyfriend agreed that he willing to do whatever it took to get the wasp out. The doctor said, "Okay, what I suggest you do is rub some jam over the top of your penis and insert it into your young lady. When you feel the wasp getting closer to the tip, withdraw it and the wasp should hopefully follow it out."

The boyfriend agreed, but was so upset and nervous that he was unable to rise to the occasion.

"If neither of you object, I could give it a try," suggested the doctor.

The boyfriend nodded and gave his approval. The young lady said "Yes, yes, whatever, please just get on with it!"

The doctor quickly undressed, dipped his penis in jam and mounted the woman. Her boyfriend watched with alarm as the doctor began thrusting forcefully and showed no signs of pulling out.

The boyfriend, at this point, suddenly became very annoyed and shouted: "Now, wait a minute, what the hell do you think you're doing?"

"Change of plan," gasped the doctor. "The wasp is in too deep. I'm going to try to drown the little fucker."

❖ "I have to inform you," a doctor tells his patient, "that your condition is terminal."

"Give it to me straight, doctor. How long have I got?"

The doctor replies, "Ten . . ."

"Ten what? Months? Weeks?"

The doctor continues: "Nine, eight, seven . . ."

A beautiful woman asks her doctor: "Will you kiss me, doc?"

"No, it would be against my code of ethics," replies the doctor, firmly.

"Please just one kiss," begs the woman.

"Sorry," says the doctor, "it's completely out of the question. Strictly speaking I shouldn't even really be shagging you."

❖ One night a man and a woman are both at a bar, knocking back a few drinks. They start talking and it turns that they're both doctors. After about an hour or so the man says to the woman, "How about a quick shag, no strings attached? It'll just be one night of fun." The woman doctor agrees to it.

So they go back to her place and he goes in the bedroom. She goes in the bathroom and starts scrubbing up, as if she's about to go into the operating room. After scrubbing for what seems like an eternity, she finally goes in the bedroom and they have sex.

Afterwards, the man says to the woman, "You're a surgeon, aren't you?"

"Yes, I am, how did you know?"

The man says, "I could tell by the way you scrubbed up before we started."

"Oh, that makes sense," says the woman. "You're an anaesthesiologist, aren't you?"

"Yeah," says the man, a bit surprised. "How did you know?"

The woman answers, "Because I never felt a thing."

❖ "Doctor, I have an embarrassing sexual problem. I can't get it up for my wife any more."

"Okay, Mr Smith, bring her back with you tomorrow and let me see what I can do."

The following day, the worried husband returns with his spouse.

"Take off your clothes please, Mrs Smith," the doctor orders. "Now turn all the way around. Lie down, please. I see. Fine, you may put your clothes back on."

The doctor takes the husband aside. "There's nothing wrong with you, Mr Smith," he says. "Your wife didn't give me an erection either."

❖ A man goes to his doctor, complaining of multiple illnesses. After a thorough examination the doctor informs him, "You have hypochondria."

"Bugger," says the patient, "not that as well."

❖ A woman goes to her doctor for some tests. The doctor says to her, "I'm sorry to tell you, you only have a few weeks to live."

She says, "I want a second opinion."

The doctor replies, "Okay, you're a fat ugly bint."

❖ A woman walks into the doctor's office with a huge boil on her arse. The doctor squeezes it, pushes it and prods it. He says, "This is too big a job for me, I'm sending for Pete the pus-sucker."

Pete the pus-sucker comes in, takes one look at the huge, inflamed boil festering with pus and says, "Bloody hell. It's a big one all right, but I'm going to give it a go. Stand back everyone."

Pete puts on a lab coat, gets on his knees, presses his lips to her arse and begins to suck the pus from the massive white core of the boil.

About half-way through, the woman slips out a fart. Pete stops what he's doing and throws up all over the floor. When he's finished retching, he looks up and says, "You know, lady, it's people like you that make this job so gross!"

❖ "Doctor, doctor, I think I've got problems with my hearing."

"What are the symptoms?"

"Aren't they those yellow people on TV?"

❖ A man went to the doctor's, sporting an ominous-looking green ring around his cock. He was sitting in the waiting room and got into casual conversation with the bloke next to him, who whipped his own prick out to reveal a similar blemish, only this one was deep red. The bloke next to him was called in for his appointment. A minute later, he walked out whistling. On the way out he cheerfully assured the other man that there was nothing to worry about and waved goodbye.

Hugely relieved, he was in two minds whether or not to leave right there and then when the doctor called him in. Deciding he didn't want to have wasted his doctor's time, he walked into the office. "What can I do for you today?" enquired the doctor.

"This is a bit embarrassing, but I wonder if you could take a look at my penis. It's just a little bit discoloured, but I'm sure I may have overreacted."

The doctor instructed the man to pull down his trousers. After studying the knob for several minutes, the doctor tucked his patient's cock and testicles back into his underpants and broke the news.

"I'm very sorry to have to inform you that your penis will have to be amputated immediately."

"What?" gasped the patient. "The other bloke was just in here just now with the same problem and he said his prick was fine afterwards!"

"That's true," said the doctor. "Unfortunately there is a world of difference between lipstick and gangrene."

❖ A man goes in to his doctor's surgery and asks, "Doctor, do you think I will live until I'm 100?"

The doctor asks, "Do you drink, smoke or do drugs?"

The man replies, "No."

The doctor then asks, "Do you like to sleep around with women, and go out partying?"

The man replies, "No, I don't."

The doctor then asks, "Well, why the fuck do you want to live until you're 100?"

❖ A man has been feeling ill and off his food for several days when finally he decides to see his doctor. After hearing the man's symptoms and examining him with a stethoscope, the doctor tells him that he had a tapeworm.

"Is that bad? How can I get rid of it?" asks the man.

"Come back tomorrow and bring a hard-boiled egg and a Mars Bar," replies the doctor. A puzzled look crosses the man's face. "Trust me," says the doctor. "I'm the doctor."

So, the following day the man brings in the hard-boiled egg and the Mars Bar. "Please remove everything below the waist and bend over," says the doctor.

"Excuse me?" says the man.

"Trust me. I'm the doctor," says the doctor. So, the man removes his trousers and underwear and bends over. WHAM! – the doctor shoves the egg up the man's arse.

"Whoa! Hold on a minute," shouts the man.

"Trust me. I'm the doctor," says the doctor. About a minute later, WHAM! – up goes the Mars Bar. "Now pull up your pants and come back tomorrow. And bring with you a hard-boiled egg and a Mars Bar," says the doctor. As the man starts to protest the doctor says, "Trust me. I'm the doctor."

The man returns the next day and he brings the hard-boiled egg and the Mars Bar. "Drop your trousers and underwear and bend over," says the doctor.

"This again?" says the man.

"Trust me. I'm the doctor," says the doctor.

So, the man drops his pants and bends over. WHAM! – the doctor shoves the egg up his rear. "Oh! I can't believe I'm doing this!" says the man.

"Hold still now and trust me. I'm the doctor," says the doctor. About a minute later, WHAM! – up goes the Mars Bar. "Now pull up your pants and come back tomorrow with another hard-boiled egg and another Mars Bar," says the doctor. As the man starts to protest again, the doctor says, "Trust me. I'm the doctor."

This routine goes on for several days, until one day, after the man pulls up his trousers, the doctor says, "Now I want to see you tomorrow with a hard-boiled egg and a cricket bat." As the man turns pale the doctor says, "Trust me. I'm the doctor."

The man spends a sleepless night imagining what could happen on his next visit. He almost bottles it and stays home, but he still feels ill. So the man arrives the next day as instructed, with the hard-boiled egg and the cricket bat.

"Drop your trousers and bend over," says the doctor.

"But why do we need a cricket bat?" asks the man nervously.

"Trust me. I'm the doctor," says the doctor.

The man drops his pants and bends over. WHAM! – the doctor shoves the egg up his anus. "Oh God!" says the man, terrified of what is to come next.

"Hold still and trust me. I'm the doctor," says the doctor. About a minute later, the man is just about on the verge of passing out from sheer terror and can't help clenching his buttocks as tight as he can. Nothing happens. A couple more minutes pass and he starts to relax.

Suddenly the tapeworm sticks its head out of his rear and says, "Where's my fucking Mars Bar?" WHAM! – down comes the cricket bat.

★   ★   ★   ★   ★

DOGS

❋ Three large German Shepherd dogs were sitting in the waiting room at the vet's surgery when they struck up a conversation. The first dog turned to the second and said, "So, why are you here?"

The second dog replied, "I'm a pisser. I piss on everything – the settee, the drapes, the table, the cat and the kids. But the final straw was last night, when I pissed in the middle of my owner's bed."

The first dog said, "So, what is the vet going to do?"

"Going to give me Prozac, apparently," came the reply from the second. "All the vets are prescribing it. It works for everything."

The first dog then turned to the third dog and asked, "Why are you here?"

The third dog replied: "I'm a digger. I dig under fences, dig up flowers and trees, and I dig just for the hell of it. When I'm in the house, I dig up the carpets. Unfortunately I went over the line last night when I dug a great big hole in my owner's brand new leather settee."

"So, what are they going to do to you?" the first dog asks.

"Looks like Prozac for me too," the dejected dog replies.

The third dog then turned to the first dog and asked, "So, what's your story?"

"I'm a shagger," the first dog said. "I'll shag anything. I shag the cat, a pillow, the table, the kids, whatever. I want to shag everything I see. Yesterday, my owner had just got out of the shower and was bending down to dry her toes, and I just couldn't help myself. I hopped on her back and started humping away."

The first and second dogs exchanged a glance and enquired: "So, Prozac for you too, pal, eh?"

"Actually, no," said the first dog. "I'm here to have my nails clipped."

* What do you get when you cross a Rottweiler and a St Bernard?

    A dog that rips your face off then goes to fetch help.

* ## What do you call a dog with metal balls and no back legs?
    ### Sparky.

* A dog is truly a man's best friend. If you don't believe it, just try this simple experiment. Lock your dog and your wife in the boot of the car for an hour.

    When you open the boot, which one is happiest to see you?

* What is the most popular name for a dog in Korea?

    Starters.

* Where do you find a dog with no legs?

    Where you left him.

* ## What do you do if a pit bull mounts your leg?
    ### Fake an orgasm.

* How do you make a dog drink?

    Stick it in a blender.

* How do you know you're really ugly?

    Your dog closes his eyes when he humps your leg.

* What is the best thing about play fighting with your pet dog?

    The make up sex.

* What has four legs and one arm?

    A Doberman in a playground.

✳ I was in a bar in the Black Country standing next to a guy with the most docile-looking dog imaginable. When the Walsall score was read out on Sky Sports, however, the dog went completely berserk. It was growling and barking and baring its teeth at the customers.

"Bloody hell, mate, what's going on there?" I said.

He replied, "Oh yeah. He does that every time Walsall lose."

I said, "Well, what does he do when they win?"

He replied, "Don't know mate. I've only had him six months."

✳ Why does a dog lick his arsehole?

Because he knows that in a couple of minutes he'll be licking your face.

> ❝ They say that a dog is man's best friend. Personally speaking, I can't see how that can be true. I mean, how many of your friends have you neutered? ❞

✳ A man buys a dog from a pet shop and teaches it to recite the Lord's Prayer, word-for-word, until the dog has it down perfect. He takes the dog to the pub and announces: "I bet anyone here a fiver that this dog can recite the Lord's Prayer!" Unsurprisingly, several people take up the bet, upon which the dog is placed upon on the bar. "Okay," says the man to the dog. "Let's do it."

"Wuff! Wuff! Wuff!" says the dog, and starts licking its balls.

The man loses all of his money and is despondent. On the way home, he says to the dog, "What the fuck was that all about? I trained you to recite it perfectly!"

"Dead right," says the dog, "but consider what the odds will be tomorrow night."

✳ What's the best way to give your dog a bone?

Tickle his balls.

* How do you stop a dog from humping your leg?
  Pick him up and suck his dick.

* A dog walks into a butcher's shop with a £10 note in his mouth and a note reading "10 lamb chops, please". Amazed, the butcher takes the money, puts a bag of chops in the dog's mouth. He decides to follow the dog and watches him wait for a green light, look both ways and trot across the road to a bus stop. The dog checks the bus timetable and sits patiently in the bus shelter. When a bus arrives, he walks around to the front and looks at the number, then boards the bus. The butcher follows, unable to believe his eyes.

  As the bus travels out of town, the dog looks though the window, casually taking in the scenery. After awhile he stands on his back paws to push the "stop" button, then the butcher follows him off.

  The dog runs up to a house and drops his bag on the porch. He then starts to scratch furiously at the front door. He does this again and again, but there is no answer. So he jumps on a wall, walks around the garden, beats his head against a window, jumps off, and waits at the front door.

  Eventually a huge man opens it and starts cursing and kicking the dog. Oblivious to the dog's pitiful yelps and whines, he pummels the mutt into a bloodied pulp.

  The butcher runs up and screams at the dog owner: "What the hell are you doing? This dog's a genius!"

  The owner says, "Genius my arse, this is the second time this week he's forgotten his key!"

* Why do dogs lick their balls?
  Because they can't make a fist.

* What do you call a dog that hears voices?
  A shitzu-phrenic.

* What did you say to a mongol dog?
  "Down, Syndrome!"

✳ What do you get if you cross a pit bull with a prostitute?
   Your last blow job.

✳ Four men were bragging about how clever their dogs were. One was a building engineer, the second man was an accountant, the third man was a chemist and the fourth was an IT engineer.

   The building engineer called to his dog. "T-square, do your stuff!"

   T-square trotted over to a desk, took out some paper and a pen and drew a circle, a square and a triangle. Everyone agreed that that was pretty clever, just like his clever owner.

   The accountant, however, was not to be outdone. He called to his dog and said, "Spreadsheet, do your stuff!" Spreadsheet went out into the kitchen and returned with a packet of biscuits. He divided them into four equal piles of three biscuits each. Everyone agreed that that was very clever, just like his owner.

   But the chemist said his dog could do better. He called to his dog and said, "Measure, do your stuff!" Measure got up, walked over to the fridge, took out a pint of milk, took a 10-ounce glass from the cupboard and poured exactly ten ounces without spilling a drop. Everyone agreed that that was pretty impressive, just like his owner.

   Then the three men turned to the IT engineer and said, "What can your dog do?" The IT engineer called to his dog and said, "Keyboard, do your stuff!"

   Keyboard jumped to his feet, ate the biscuits, drank the milk, dumped on the floor, shagged the other three dogs and wrote out an invoice for £750.

✳ **My dog jumped in the washing machine yesterday. Don't worry; at least he died in Comfort.**

✳ What's got four legs and goes "Miaow"?
   A frozen dog on a bench saw.

* What has two legs and bleeds?
  Half a dog.

* A vicar was walking though the park, when he saw a little blonde-haired blue-eyed little girl playing with her dog. "Hello, little girl," he said. "What's your name?"
  "My name is Cherry."
  "That's a beautiful name," said the vicar.
  "Yes," said the little girl. "My mummy was sitting under a cherry blossom tree just before I was born, and some cherry blossom fell on her tummy. She said that it she had a girl, she would name her Cherry."
  "That's a really sweet story," the vicar replied. "What's your dog's name?"
  "Porky."
  "That's an unusual name for a dog. Why is he called that? Is it because he has a curly little tail?"
  "No," said the little girl. "He fucks pigs."

A poodle walks into a telegram office, takes out a blank form and writes: "Woof. Woof. Woof. Woof. Woof. Woof. Woof. Woof. Woof."

The clerk examines the paper and tells the poodle: "There are only nine words here. You could send another 'Woof' for the same price."

"Fuck off," the poodle replies, "that wouldn't make any sense at all."

* My dog kept getting up in the middle of the night and setting the house alarm off. My wife told me to disable it, so I broke its legs with a golf club.

★　★　★　★　★

DROWNING

❖ How do you stop a politician from drowning?
  Shoot him before he hits the water.

❖ What is the most dangerous stretch of water in the world?
  The shallow end of Michael Barrymore's pool.

❖ Mick worked at the brewery for twenty years, but one day he tripped on the walkway and fell over into the beer vat and drowned. The foreman volunteered to inform Mick's widow of her husband's death. He went to her house and when she answered the door, he said: "I'm sorry but I have bad news. I'm afraid your husband passed away at work today when he fell into a vat and drowned."

  Mick's wife was inconsolable and she wept for several minutes. Eventually she pulled herself together and wiped the tears from her eyes with her apron. She asked the foreman, "Tell me, did he suffer?"

  "We don't think so," the foreman replied. "He got out three times to take a piss."

❖ A married woman died in a scuba-diving accident while on holiday with her girlfriends. A day later her husband was paid a visit by two grim-faced policemen. "We're sorry to disturb you, sir, but we have some information concerning your wife. Actually, we have some bad news, some fairly good news and some really great news. Which would you like to hear first?"

  Fearing the worst, the husband took a deep breath and asked for the bad news first.

  "We're sorry to inform you, sir," the policeman said, "the authorities found your wife's body in the sea yesterday."

"Oh, my God!" said the distraught husband. Remembering what the policeman had said, he asked, "What's the good news?"

"When we pulled her up," said the policeman, "she had two seven-pound lobsters and a dozen crabs attached to her body."

"Good God! So, what's the great news?"

The officer replied, "They're going to pull her up again tomorrow."

*   *   *   *   *

DRUGS

* My younger brother is an example of what can happen to people who get involved with drugs. He has a Porsche and his own house by the age of nineteen.

* How do you plant dope?
Bury a blonde.

* A tabloid newspaper published a picture of the Olympic swimmer Michael Phelps at a party taking a huge hit from a huge reefer.

I think there's an important lesson to be learned here, children – never share your bong with someone who has the lung capacity of a dolphin.

Did you hear about the two Asian heroin addicts who accidentally injected themselves with curry powder by mistake?

Both men are in intensive care. One has a dodgy tikka and the other is in a korma.

* Jesus sits down one day and considers the high rate of drug abuse that will follow long after his time on earth. He thinks it is a bit hypocritical of him to condemn them without first trying them himself, so he sends his apostles out to see what drugs they can find. A couple of days later Jesus hears a knock at the door. "Who is it?"

  "Paul."

  Jesus opens the door. "What did you bring, Paul?"

  "Hashish from Morocco."

  A few minutes later there is a second knock. "Who is it?"

  "It's Mark."

  Jesus opens the door. "What did you bring, Mark?"

  "Cocaine from Colombia."

  Another knock. "Who is it?"

  "It's Matthew."

  Jesus opens the door. "What did you bring, Matthew?"

  "Heroin from Afghanistan."

  This continues for a while, until eventually there is a twelfth knock on the door

  "Who is it?"

  "It's Judas."

  Jesus opens the door. "What did you bring, Judas?"

  "The FBI, motherfuckers!"

* ## My doctor warned me to stay away from methamphetamine. So I bought a fifteen-foot straw.

* Naomi Campbell and Jeremy Clarkson met at a celebrity bash.

  "I'm a model," says Naomi. "What do you do?"

  Jeremy replies, "I do *Top Gear*."

  "Cool," says Naomi. "I'll have an eighth."

* What did the heroin addict get on his IQ test?

  Drool.

★   ★   ★   ★   ★

DRUNKS

★ A guy is out on the lash with the lads and gets wildly drunk. By the time he staggers home he is covered in vomit and, sure enough, his wife is waiting up for him. The following weekend he's out again with his mates, but avoiding the booze. When one of his friends asks why, he explains that he is still reeling from the almighty bollocking his wife gave him last time he got home drunk.

"No problem," says his mate. "When it happens again, make sure you have £20 in your shirt pocket so you can tell your wife that someone else puked on you and put the money in there for the dry cleaning!" Emboldened by this brilliant plan he proceeds to get completely pissed.

Much later that evening he falls through the front door, again covered in vomit. Predictably, his wife completely freaks.

"I can explain!" he protests. "A guy threw up over me and gave me £20 for dry cleaning! Check my pocket!"

His wife looks in his shirt pocket and says, "There's £40 here."

"Yeah," her husband replies. "He shat in my pants as well."

★ How do you know when you've had enough to drink?

When you see a mop and don't understand why you're getting an erection.

★ A man was stumbling down the street with one foot on the curb and one foot in the gutter. A policeman pulled up and said, "I've got to take you in, pal. You're obviously drunk."

"Officer, are you absolutely sure I'm drunk?"

"Yes, sir, I'm sure," said the copper. "Let's go."

Breathing a sigh of relief, the man said, "Thank God. I thought I was a cripple."

⋆ A man is at the bar, blind drunk. Some of the customers decide to be good Samaritans and get him home. They pick him up off the floor and drag him out of the door. On the way to the car, he falls down three times.

When they get to his house, they help him out of the car, and he falls down four more times. They ring the doorbell and a woman answers.

"Here's your husband!"

"Thanks," says the man's wife. "What did you do with his wheelchair?"

⋆ What do you call an Pakistani alcoholic? Mustafa pint.

⋆ A drunk comes staggering into the park blind drunk and sits himself down on a bench next to some other drunks. "Where have you been all night?" asks his friend.

"At this fantastic new bar," he says. "The Golden Saloon. Everything there is golden."

"Bollocks! There's no such place!" snorts his mate.

The drunk says, "Sure there is! The joint's got these huge golden doors and a golden floor. Fuck, even the toilets are gold!" His mate doesn't believe his story, so the next day checks the phone book, and, sure enough, there is a place across town called the Golden Saloon. He calls up the place to check his mate's story.

"Is this the Golden Saloon?" he asks.

"Yes, it is," a woman answers.

"Do you have huge golden doors?"

"We certainly do."

"Do you have golden floors?"

"Most certainly do."

"What about golden toilets?"

There's a long pause, then he hears the woman shouting, "Eric, I think I got a lead on the guy who shat in your saxophone!"

⋆ There is nothing uglier than a drunken woman. Apart from Andrew Lloyd Webber.

* A drunk gets on a bus one day, dishevelled and stinking of alcohol and stale urine. He sits down next to a priest, opens his newspaper and starts reading. A couple of minutes later, he asks the priest, "Father, what causes arthritis?"

   "My friend, it's caused by loose living, being with cheap, wicked women, too much alcohol and contempt for your fellow man," the priest replies.

   "Imagine that," the drunk mutters. He returned to reading his paper.

   The priest, thinking about what he had said, turns to the man and apologizes. "I'm sorry, I didn't mean to come on so strong. How long have you had arthritis?"

   "I don't have arthritis, Father. But I just read in the paper that the Pope does."

* I made that classic mistake last night that all guys make. I got really drunk and I ended up having sex with my best friend. Now I can't even bring myself to talk to him. To be honest, I can't even bring myself to play fetch with him.

* I really need to stop drinking. If my liver becomes any more black and bloated, it's going end up getting adopted by Madonna.

* A policeman is walking down the high street one night when he finds a totally inebriated man collapsed against a building with his car keys in his hands. The officer approaches and asks: "Excuse me sir, what are planning to do with those car keys?"

   The drunk looks at his keys and says: "Shit! My car, it was right on the end of my key. Some bastard stole my car!"

   "Okay," says the copper. "I also have to inform you that your penis is hanging out."

   The man looks down, sees his prick hanging there and screams, "Oh my God, they took my girlfriend as well!"

★ You should never use alcohol as a substitute for a woman. Last time I did that, I got my cock stuck in the neck of the bottle.

★ A car in central London was weaving all over the road one night. A patrol car spotted him and pulled him over. The officer approached the car and said, "Sir, get out of the car, I need you to blow into this breathalyser."

The driver reached into his pocket and produced a doctor's note. It read: "This man suffers from chronic asthma. Do not make him perform any action that may leave him short of breath."

The officer said, "Okay, I need you to come with me, sir, and give a blood sample." The man produced another letter. This one read: "This man is a haemophiliac. Please do not cause him to bleed in any way." So the officer said, "Right, a urine sample then."

The man produced a third letter from his pocket. It read, "This man is an American. Please don't take the piss."

★ A man walks into a bar and shouts at the barman rudely: "Give me a shot of twelve-year-old single malt." The barman thinks to himself, "This fool won't know the difference," so he pours a shot of cheap two-year-old whisky.

The customer takes one sip and spits it out. "I said twelve-year-old whisky, dickhead!"

Quietly fuming, the barman pours some six-year-old scotch. The customer takes a sip – same reaction.

But the barman still thinks he can put one over him, so he pours a shot of ten-year-old scotch. Again, same reaction from the customer.

Finally, the barman is cowed into submission and he pours the man a glass of twelve-year-old single malt whisky. The customer takes a sip and is completely satisfied.

Meanwhile a drunk at the end of the bar slides a glass down the bar to the whisky expert and says: "Mister, taste this!" He obliges . . . and quickly spits it out.

"It tastes like piss," he shoots back at the drunk.

The drunk replies: "So it should. How old am I then?"

There's nothing worse after a night on the lash than waking up next to someone and not being able to remember who they are, or how you met, or why they're dead.

★ A drunk walks into a bar full of bikers and orders a drink. He looks around and sees three big, hairy bikers sitting at a corner table. He gets up and staggers over to the table, looks the biggest, meanest biker square in the face and says: "I went past your grandmother's house today and I saw her in the window, stark naked. Fuck me, she is one fine-looking woman!"

The biker looks at him but doesn't say a word. His friends are both mad and confused because he is the baddest biker in the bar and afraid of no man. The drunk leans on the table again and says: "I shagged your grandmother. I fucked her six ways and she was the best I ever had!"

The biker's friends are starting to get really, really agitated but the biker still says nothing. The drunk leans on the table one more time and says, "I'll tell you something else, boy, your grandma liked it. She squealed like a bitch on heat!"

At this point the biker stands up, grabs the drunk by his lapels, looks him square in the eyes and says, "Grandad, go home, you're drunk."

★ Did you hear about the dyslexic alcoholic? He choked on his own Vimto.

★ The latest pub craze is filling a woman's vagina with vodka then sucking it out using a straw. Doctors, however, are warning about the dangers of minge drinking.

★   ★   ★   ★   ★

DUCKS

❖ A young hedgehog made his way down to the riverbank and gingerly dipped his toes into the water. He waded in and, as the water got deeper, he soldiered on, gasping for breath. Suddenly he disappeared under the water and was only just able to get back to the bank. After resting for a few minutes, the young hedgehog tried again – after going under twice more, he managed to get back to dry land before collapsing. This time it took him longer to recover, but once he felt fit enough he started back into the water. Meanwhile two ducks were watching from the other side of the bank. One said to the other: "Don't you think it's time we told him he was adopted?"

Three ducks walk into a bar.

"Hello, who are you?" the barman asks.

The first duck replies, "I'm Huey."

"I bet you are," says the barman. "And how's your day been, Huey?"

"Great, thanks. I've been in and out of puddles all day. What else could a duck want?" smiles Huey.

"That's nice," says the bartender, turning to the second duck. "Hi, and who are you?"

"Dewey," comes the reply.

"So how's your day been, Dewey?" asks the barman.

"Great. I've been in and out of puddles all day as well. What more could a duck want?"

The barman turns to the third duck and says, "So, I bet you must be Louie?"

"No," she says, with a coy smile. "I'm Puddles."

❖   A duck walks into a chemist's and says to the assistant, "Give me a chap stick."

The assistant says to the duck, "Are you paying cash?"

The duck replies, "Just put it on my bill."

The next day, the duck goes back to the chemist's and says to the assistant: "Give me a box of condoms."

The assistant says, "Do you want me to put them on your bill?"

The duck says, "Hell, no, I'm not that kind of duck."

❖ How do you turn a duck into a soul singer?

Put it in the microwave until it's Bill Withers.

❖   A duck walks into a bar and says; "Got any bread?"

The barman says: "No."

The duck says: "Got any bread?"

The barman says: "No."

The duck says: "Got any bread?"

The barman says: "No, we do not have any bread."

The duck says: "Got any bread?"

The barman says: "No, we haven't got any fucking bread."

The duck says: "Got any bread?"

The barman says: "No, are you deaf? We haven't got any fucking bread. Ask me again and I'll nail your fucking beak to the bar, you irritating little twat, NOW FUCK OFF!!"

The duck says: "Got any nails?"

The barman says: "No!"

The duck says: "Got any bread?"

★   ★   ★   ★   ★

DYSLEXIA

* My friend left the doctor's today looking really worried. "What's the matter?" I asked.
  "I've got the big C," he said.
  "What, cancer?"
  "No, dyslexia."

* Did you hear about the agnostic dyslexic insomniac?
  He stayed up all night wondering if there really is a dog.

* ## Two dyslexics walk into a bra.

* Did you hear about the dyslexic devil worshipper?
  He sacrificed his mum to Santa.

* There is one great advantage in being dyslexic. It doesn't cost a fortune to get a personal number plate for your car.

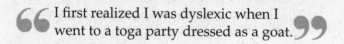 I first realized I was dyslexic when I went to a toga party dressed as a goat.

* Two dyslexics were working in a kitchen.
  The first says, "Can you smell gas?"
  The second replies: "Fuck off. I can't even smell my own name."

* ## Two dyslexics robbers ran into a bank. One shouts: "Air in the hands, mother stickers this is a fuck up!"

* Did you hear about the dyslexic student who entered a spelling bee?
  She came in salt.

✳ A dyslexic bloke goes on a skiing trip to Austria. When he arrives at the resort he asks a local where the ski slope is.

   "Don't know," replies the local, "I'm a tabogganist myself."

   "That's okay," says the dyslexic. "Give me twenty Benson and Hedges then."

✳ Dyslexia: it means you never have to say you're syror.

★   ★   ★   ★   ★

EATING DISORDERS

★ How do you know you're at a bulimic bachelor party?
   The cake jumps out of the girl.

★ My girlfriend suffers from depression brought on by her having anorexia. I told her she should lighten up.

★ What does a bulimic call two fingers?
   Dessert.

★ What do you call an anorexic with three teeth missing?
   A rake.

★ Why do bulimics love KFC?
   Because it comes with a bucket.

★ What do you call an anorexic with a yeast infection?
   A quarter pounder with cheese.

★ I dumped my bulimic girlfriend the other day. I've never had a problem with her illness, it was just that she was always bringing it up whenever we were eating.

★ I'm thinking of becoming an anorexic because, according to medical experts, one in ten people with anorexia die. A ninety per cent chance of immortality? That's good enough for me!

My mother suffers from both bulimia and Alzheimer's. She sits there all day long stuffing her face with cakes, chocolates, crisps and ice cream, and then forgets to be sick.

★ Top astrophysicists have announced this week that the universe actually weighs less than previously thought. Apparently the Hubble Telescope adds an extra 10–15 light-years to the universe's arse and thighs.

★ I'm dating an anorexic but it's not going too well. These days, I'm seeing less and less of her.

★ I was annoyed to be woken up last night by the bulimic in the flat above me. I banged on the ceiling and shouted, "For fuck's sake, love! Keep it down!"

★ I have just bought a puppy. When I Googled "BRINGING UP A DOG", I got thirty Korean bulimia websites.

★ What did the anorexic say to her boyfriend?
    Does this tampon make me look fat?"

★ Anorexia – ribbed for her pleasure.

★   ★   ★   ★   ★

ECONOMISTS

❖ Two economists are walking down the road when they come across a pile of dog shit lying on the pavement. The first economist says to the other, "If you eat it, I'll give you £10,000!" The second economist does some number-crunching and figures out he's better off eating the shit, so he does and collects the money.

Continuing along the same road they almost step into yet another pile of dog shit. The second economist says to his friend, "Now, if you eat this pile of shit, I'll give you £10,000." After evaluating the proposal, the first economist eats the dog shit and takes the money.

They continue on. The first economist starts thinking and finally says to his friend, "Listen, we both have the same amount of money we had before, but we both ate shit. I don't see us being better off."

The second economist replies, "True . . . however, there is one important fact you have overlooked".

"What's that?"

"We have both just been involved in £20,000 of trade."

★   ★   ★   ★   ★

ELEPHANTS

✳ How do you know when an elephant has been screwing in your garden?

The flower beds are crushed and you are missing a bin liner.

✳ What do you get when you cross an elephant with a poodle?

A dead poodle with an eighteen-inch diameter arsehole.

* One day a female elephant was walking through the woods and she got a thorn stuck in her foot. She saw an ant passing and asked him to help her get the thorn out.

  The ant asked, "Okay, but what do I get in return?"

  The elephant replied, "I'll do anything."

  "Anything?" said the ant. "Will you let me fuck you up the arse?"

  The elephant thought to herself, "What's this little guy going to do anyway?" So she replied, "Anything – just get this thorn out of my foot!"

  So the ant got busy taking the thorn out. When he finally got it out, he looked up at the elephant and said, "Okay it's out, are you ready?"

  The ant climbed up and started to work away. Just then a monkey overhead dropped a coconut on the elephant's head.

  "Ouch," said the elephant, "that hurt!"

  The ant responded, "Yeah, yeah! Take it all, bitch!"

* What's big, red and slimy?
  An inside-out elephant.

* How do you make a dead elephant float?
  You hire a large flatbed truck, put about half a dozen dead elephants on top, decorate it, add a sound system and some dancers.

* How can you tell that there are two elephants in your fridge?
  You have to put the partly eaten and dismembered body parts of your infant daughter in the freezer instead.

* What do elephants use as tampons?
  Sheep.

✳ Why do elephants have trunks?
Because sheep don't have string.

✳ An elephant is walking through the jungle when, all of a sudden, he falls into a deep pit. The elephant realizes that there is no chance of him being able to climb out and he is going to die there, so he starts to shout for help.

By chance a passing chicken hears the elephant's cries and decides to investigate. He sees the elephant stuck in the pit and shouts down to him: "Don't worry, elephant. I am going to save you."

The chicken then calls on the King of the Jungle. The King of the Jungle promptly arrives in his Red Porsche. He throws a rope from the Porsche into the pit, the elephant ties it around his waist and the King of the Jungle pulls him out of the pit.

The elephant is so grateful to the chicken that he promises him that he will one day do the same for him if the chicken should ever be in mortal danger.

As chance would have it, a couple of weeks later the elephant is walking through the jungle minding his own business when he hears the sound of a chicken in distress. He wanders over and sees that his friend the chicken is stuck in a pit. The elephant shouts "Don't worry chicken, I will save you."

The elephant throws his tail into the pit. Unfortunately, the tail is too short and the chicken can't reach it. Undeterred by this, the elephant throws in his trunk. Alas, the trunk is also too small. As a last desperate effort the elephant throws in his penis. Hurrah! The chicken grabs the elephant's enormous dong and climbs out to safety.

The moral of the story: if you have a big dick you don't need a red Porsche to pull a chick.

★   ★   ★   ★   ★

ENGLISHMEN

★ What's an Englishman's idea of foreplay?
   Half an hour of begging.

Ten Reasons
Why it's Great to Be English

1 Two world wars and one world cup, doo-dah
   doo-dah.
2 Proper beer.
3 You get to confuse everyone with the rules of cricket.
4 You get to accept defeat graciously in nearly all major
   sporting events.
5 Union Jack underpants.
6 Water shortages guaranteed every single summer.
7 You can live in the past and imagine you are still a
   world power.
8 Bathing once a week, whether you need it or not.
9 Ditto changing underwear.
10 It beats being Welsh.

★ Three Englishmen are in a bar. They see an Irishman
  drinking alone and they decide to wind him up. One of the
  Englishmen walks over to the Irishman and taps him on the
  shoulder. "Hey, I hear your St Patrick was an arse bandit."
      "Oh really, hmm, I didn't know that."
      Puzzled, the Englishman walks back to his mates.
      "I told him St Patrick was a turd-burglar and he didn't bat
  an eyelid."
      "You just don't know how to set him off," says one of his
  friends. "Watch and learn."
      The second Englishman walks over and taps the Irishman
  on the shoulder. "I hear your St Patrick was a transvestite!"

"Really?" shrugs the Irishman. "I didn't know that, thanks."

The Englishman goes back to his buddies. "You're right, he's unshakeable."

The third Englishman says: "No, let me try."

He walks over to the Irishman, taps him on the shoulder and says, "I hear your St Patrick was an Englishman!"

"I know," says the Irishman "that's what your mates were saying."

★ ★ ★ ★ ★

EPILEPSY

An Englishman is on holiday in the American mid-west when he wanders into a local bar and has a few beers. After a while he notices there's one of those mechanical bulls in the corner and he asks the barman if he can have a go.

The barman says "Be my guest."The Englishman climbs on and the bull starts moving. "No one's ever made it past five minutes on their first try, Limey!" the barman warns him. To everyone's amazement, however, the Englishman sails through the five-minute mark. He blasts past ten and fifteen, and even after twenty minutes is still holding on.

The locals are awestruck. He's fast approaching the world record. The barman cranks the bull up to eleven and it goes mad, but the plucky Englishman hangs on, unfazed. Eventually, after forty-five minutes, the bull breaks down and comes to a halt. The crowd are cheering and whooping as the barman grabs the hand of the Englishman and shoves a microphone in his face. "Holy shit, boy! You done broke the world record by a clear fifteen minutes! How you do that?"

"Easy," the Englishman replies, "I'm married to an epileptic. If you can fuck her for five minutes, you can ride anything."

❖ **What do you call a good-looking epileptic?
   Fit.**

❖ What's blue and doesn't fit?
   A dead epileptic.

❖ What does it say on a black epileptic's t-shirt?
   Help me, I'm not break dancing.

❖ What do you call an epileptic with a Hoover?
   Shake 'n' Vac.

❖ **What do you call an epileptic in a bush?
   Russell.**

❖ What do you get if an epileptic falls into a lettuce patch?
   Seizure salad.

ESSEX GIRLS

✳ How do you know when an Essex girl is on her period?
   She's only wearing one sock.

✳ What's the difference between a bowling ball and an Essex girl?
   You can only get three fingers in a bowling ball.

✳ What do Essex girls use as protection during sex?
   A bus shelter.

❋ An Essex girl goes to the DSS to register for child benefit.

"How many children do you have?" asks the assessor.

"Ten," replies the Essex girl."

"Ten? Are you sure? What are their names?"

"Duane, Duane, Duane, Duane, Duane, Duane, Duane, Duane, Duane, and then there's little Duane."

"Doesn't that get confusing?" asks the assessor.

"Nah," says the Essex girl. "Its great, because if they are out playing in the street I just have to shout, "DUANE, YA DINNER"S READY" or "DUANE, GO TO BED NOW" and it's sorted."

"Yes, but what if you want to speak to one individually?"

"That's easy," says the Essex girl, "I just use their surnames."

❋ How can you tell if an Essex girl really likes oral sex?
She hitches up her skirt when you yawn.

❋ What's the difference between an Essex girl and an Arab girl?
The Essex girl gets stoned before she commits adultery.

An Essex girl is walking down the road with her left tit hanging out. A police car pulls up beside her and the officer says, "Miss, put your breast back in your top or I will arrest you."

The Essex girl looks down and says, "OH MY GOD, I'VE LEFT THE BABY ON THE BUS AGAIN!"

❋ Why do Essex girls wear knickers?
To keep their ankles warm.

❋ Why do Essex girls like cars with sun roofs?
Extra leg room.

* What is the difference between an Essex girl and the *Titanic*?
    Only 1,500 people went down on the *Titanic*.

* Where does an Essex girl go to lose weight?
    The abortion clinic.

* ## What does an Essex girl put behind her ears to make her more attractive to men?
    ### Her feet.

* What is the difference between an Essex girl and a plate of spaghetti?
    Spaghetti moves when you eat it.

* An Essex girl was in bed with this fella. "Go on," she said, "put a finger inside me." The man obliged.
    "Go on, put two fingers inside me." The man obliged.
    "Go on, put your hand inside me." The man obliged.
    "Go on, put two hands inside me." The man obliged.
    "Okay, now clap your hands."
    The man replied: "That's impossible!"
    The girl said: "I know, tight aren't I?"

* What does an Essex girl do with her arsehole after sex?
    She takes him down the pub.

* ## How do you know an Essex girl is having an orgasm?
    ### She drops her chips.

* An Essex girl walks into the local dry cleaners. She places a garment on the counter. "I'll be back tomorrow afternoon to pick up me dress," she says.
    "Come again?" says the clerk, cupping his ear.
    "No," she replies. "This time it's mayonnaise."

＊ An ambulance arrives at the scene of a terrible air crash on the A127 just outside Basildon in Essex. The paramedic says to a girl passenger, "How many fingers have I got up?"
She screams: "FUCK! I'M PARALYSED!"

＊ What does an Essex girl say after her eleventh orgasm?
"So, do you all play for the same team?"

＊ An Essex girl goes to the police station to report a rape. They ask her: "Did you get a good look at your assailant?"
"Yes," she replies, "I'm fairly certain he worked for the council."
"How do you know that?" she is asked.
"I had to do all the work."

＊ How do you get an Essex girl into a lift?
Grease her hips and throw in a bag of crisps.

＊ What's the difference between an Essex girl and an empty crisp bag?
You only get one bang out of an empty crisp bag.

＊ An Essex girl was involved in a nasty car crash and lay in the wreckage, trapped and bleeding. A paramedic arrives and says to her: "It's okay, I'm a paramedic and I'm going to ask you some questions. What's your name?"
"Chantelle."
"Okay, Chantelle, is this your car?"
"Yes."
"Where are you bleeding from?"
"Epping."

＊ An Essex girl goes into labour and she phones for an ambulance. "My waters have broke, I'm having a baby!" she tells the operator.
The operator asks, "Where are you ringing from?"
The Essex girl replies, "From my fanny to my feet!"

FARMERS

❖   A farmhand is driving around the farm, checking the fences. After a few minutes, he calls his boss on his mobile.

"Boss, I've got a problem. I hit a pig on the road and he's stuck in the front grille of my truck. He's still wriggling – what should I do?"

"In the back of your truck there's a shotgun," his boss tells him. "Shoot the pig in the head, and when it stops wriggling you can pull it out and throw it in a bush."

"Okay," says the farm worker.

About ten minutes later he calls back.

"Boss. I did what you said, I shot the pig and dragged it out and threw it in a bush."

"So what's the problem?" his boss snapped.

"The blue light on his motorcycle is still flashing!"

❖   A student of criminal psychology is writing his thesis on people who sexually abuse animals. In particular, he is studying men who molest sheep. He takes a flight to Australia where he meets a sheep farmer. The farmer agrees to an interview about the mechanics of sex with sheep.

"Well it's quite simple, you Pommie bastard. You grab the sheep by the tail, hold tight and slip your cock in."

The student thanks him and travels to New Zealand where he asks a farmer there the same question.

"Ah, we're with the Aussies on that one. Grab the bastard by the tail, hold on and fuck it from behind."

Finally, the student goes to Wales and asks a farmer there how he does it.

"Well it's bloody awkward, see – first you find your sheep, then you finds a stone wall, then you grabs the sheep by the front paws, bend its back over the wall and fucks it like that."

The student enquires: "If you don't mind me asking, why don't you fuck it from behind like they do in Australia and New Zealand?"

The Welsh farmer looks bewildered. "Fuck it from behind? How are you supposed to kiss it?"

❖ A farmer has successfully grown a crop of dildoes. Unfortunately he's having trouble with squatters.

❖ A young journalism student at Swansea University was assigned to write a human-interest story, so he went up into the mountains, where he found a farmer sitting on his porch. He introduced himself, explained his mission, and asked, "Has anything ever happened here that made you really happy?"

The farmer thought for a moment, then said, "I remember one time my neighbour's daughter, a fine looking girl, got lost, see. So we formed a posse and went to look for her, and when we found her, we all took turns to screw her."

"I can't print that!" said the young student. "Can't you think of anything else that happened that made you happy?"

The farmer thought for a while longer, then smiled. "Oh! One time a neighbour's sheep got lost, see. We formed a posse to look for it, and when we found it, we all took turns to screw it."

Again, the young man said "I can't write about that either. Let's try another approach. Has anything ever happened around here that made you really sad?"

The old farmer dropped his head in shame. After a couple of seconds he looked up timidly at the young man and said, "This one time, I got lost . . ."

❖ Two farmers are in a bar. One says to the other, "I think my dog is gay."

"How do you work that out then?" the other one asks.

"Because his cock tastes like shit."

★   ★   ★   ★   ★

FEMINISTS

✳ At the World Women's Conference, a feminist speaker from Germany stood up: "At last year's conference we talked about being more assertive with our husbands. After the conference I went home and told my husband that I would no longer cook for him and that he would have to do it himself. After the first day I saw nothing. After the second day I saw nothing. But after the third day I saw that he had cooked a wonderful full roast with all the trimmings." The crowd clapped and cheered.

A second speaker from America stood up: "After last year's conference I went home and told my husband that I would no longer do his ironing and that he would have to do it himself. After the first day I saw nothing. After the second day I saw nothing. But after the third day I saw that he had done not only his own ironing but my ironing as well." The crowd clapped and cheered.

A third speaker from England stood up: "After last year's conference I went home and told my husband that I wasn't going to do his laundry any more and that he would have to do it himself. After the first day I saw nothing. After the second day I saw nothing. But after the third day I could see a little bit out of my left eye."

Why do Japanese Sumo wrestlers shave their legs?

So you can tell them apart from feminists.

✳ Feminists: if only they put all that passion into their cooking.

✶   ✶   ✶   ✶   ✶

FIRST DATES

★ A man and a woman meet in a bar. They click, have a couple of drinks and end up leaving together. They go back to his apartment and, as he shows her around, she notices that one wall of his bedroom is completely filled with soft, cuddly teddy bears. There are three shelves on the bedroom wall, containing what must be hundreds of cute, cuddly teddy bears, lovingly arranged in rows covering the entire wall. There were small bears all along the bottom shelf, medium-sized bears covering the length of the middle shelf and massive teddy bears all the way along the top shelf. She didn't think it was odd for a man to have such a large collection of teddy bears: on the contrary, she was quite impressed because it demonstrated his sensitive side.

Anyway, they share a bottle of wine, and then another, and after a while, she finds herself thinking, "Maybe this guy could be the one! Could this be the father of my children?" She leans over and kisses him on the lips. They embrace and the passion builds, then he takes her in his arms, gently sweeps her off her feet and carries her into his bedroom where they rip off each other's clothes and make passionate love.

After a steamy night of raw passion with this sensitive gentleman, they lie there together in the afterglow. The woman rolls over, gently strokes his chest and asks coyly, "Well, how was it?"

He smiles at her, strokes her cheek, looks deeply into her eyes, and says: "It was great. Help yourself to any prize from the middle shelf."

> I took this girl home last week, got her stripped and saw she had the biggest vagina I'd ever seen. She asked, "Have you taken any precautions?"
>
> "Yes," I told her. "I've tied my feet to the bed rail."

★ What should you do when your blind date starts smoking?
  Slow down and use a lubricant.

★ I went on a blind date last night with a stunning girl. We seemed to have a lot in common and had similar taste in films, music and hobbies. It was going really well until she asked me if I had any children. Unfortunately, "Yes, thousands on my hard drive" wasn't really the answer she was looking for.

★ I went out with a girl last week and she told me she wanted to be "treated like a princess". So I put her in the back of a Mercedes and drove it into a wall.

★ This bloke and his date were parked up in a country lane some distance from town when they started kissing and fondling each other. Just then the girl stops and sits up. "What's the matter?" asks the guy.
  She replies: "I really should have mentioned this earlier, but I'm actually a prostitute and I charge £20 for sex."
  The man thinks about this for a few seconds, but then reluctantly gets a £20 note out of his wallet, pays her and they have sex. After a cigarette, he just sits in the driver's seat looking out of the window.
  "Why aren't we going anywhere?" asks the girl.
  "Well, I should have mentioned this before," replies the man, "but I'm actually a taxi driver, and the fare back to town is £25."

★ I met this girl in the pub the other night. After several drinks, I said to her, "Would you like to sit on my face?"
  She replied, "Why? Is your nose bigger than your dick?"

★ How can you tell if your date is a macho woman?
  She rolls her own tampons.

★ A man and woman meet at a speed-dating service. The man sits down and says, "I have just three questions."

"Okay," replies the woman.

He asks, "Do you like to clean?"

She says, "I love cleaning."

He asks, "Do you like to cook?"

She says, "I love cooking."

"Fantastic. I have one last question. Do you like sex?"

She replies, "I like it infrequently."

He pauses and says, "Is that one word or two?"

★ I'll never forget the first ever time I had sex. That's because I kept the receipt.

★ A man was dining in a fancy restaurant, sitting opposite a stunning brunette who was alone at the next table. He has been checking her out ever since he sat down but didn't have the nerve to strike up a conversation with her. Suddenly, she sneezed, and her glass eye flew out of its socket in the man's direction. Instinctively, he reached out and grabbed it out of the air and handed it back to her.

"Oh my God, I am so sorry," the woman said as she popped her eye back in place. "Please, allow me to buy you dinner to make it up to you."

The man was delighted to accept her generous offer and they enjoyed a wonderful dinner together. Afterwards the woman invited him to the theatre, followed by drinks. They talked, they laughed, they flirted. Eventually she asked him if he would like to come to her place for a nightcap and perhaps stay for breakfast the next morning.

The following morning she cooked a beautiful breakfast and brought it to him in bed. The man couldn't believe it was happening to him. It was his dream date!

"You know," he said, "you are the perfect woman. Are you this nice to every man you meet?"

"No," she replied. "You just happened to catch my eye."

★ What do you call a man who expects sex on the second date?
  Slow.

★ I lost my virginity to a retard. I always wanted the first to be special.

★ How do you know when a date is going badly?
  When you spike your own drink with Rohypnol.

★   ★   ★   ★   ★

FISHING

❖ It's a beautiful sunny day so Tom decides to go fishing at his usual spot at a local river. When he gets there he is surprised to see an unfamiliar face fishing on the opposite side of the river. When Tom leaves that evening, the stranger is still sitting there. Tom comes back early the next morning, and the stranger is there again and is still fishing when Tom leaves that evening.

This routine continues for a few days until Tom can't contain his curiosity any more. He approaches the stranger and says, "Excuse me, I can't help noticing that every morning when I arrive you are sitting there, and you're still there when I leave every night. Don't you have a home to go to?"

"I'm on my honeymoon," replies the stranger. "My wife is in that log cabin up there on the hillside."

"Shouldn't you be up there with her then?" says Tom.

"I can't touch her. She's got gonorrhoea," says the stranger.

"What about doing it in her tradesman's entrance?" jokes Tom.

"I can't. She suffers from chronic diarrhoea."

"Well, it's still your honeymoon, couldn't you get her to give you a blow job?"

"Nope. She's got pyorrhoea."

"That's terrible," says Tom. "Why did you marry her then?"

"For the maggots."

❖ A youth walking along the pier notices an old man with his shoes off, trouser legs rolled up, legs dangling in the sea and fishing with an imaginary rod.

Puzzled, the youth asks, "What are you doing?"

The old man replies, "Fishing for cunts."

"Sounds good. Can I join you?" replied the youth.

"No problem, son."

The young man sits down and casts an imaginary rod out, and then says, "So, how many cunts have you caught today?"

The old man replies, "You're the third this morning."

Two fishermen, Tom and Sid, were out in a fishing boat on their favourite lake, catching very few fish but sinking a lot of beers. Suddenly Tom felt a little tug. Reeling it in, he found a bottle with a cork in it. He uncorked the bottle and a genie appeared. The genie said, "I will grant you one wish."

Tom thought for a while and said, "I wish this whole lake was beer." His wish came true. The lake was now filled with their favourite brew.

Sid said, "You stupid cunt. Now we have to piss in the boat."

❖ Two men are sitting by a pond, fishing and enjoying a warm summer's day.

A swimmer passes by and waves to the men. Suddenly, the swimmer sinks and fails to re-surface. After about ten minutes, the first angler casually asks the other if he saw what happened.

"Aye."

"Don't you think we ought to look for him?" says the first.

"Aye."

So they put down their fishing rods, go in with their waders and drag out a lifeless body.

"I suppose we'd better give him the kiss of life," says the second.

He gets down and opens the mouth of the victim.

"Fuck me, I'm not breathing into that, his breath smells fucking revolting."

"Don't be so fucking sensitive," says the other angler, "it's life or death, you cunt."

The other angler attempts to give him the kiss of life, but is also repelled by the bad breath.

A third man, who had been watching from nearby, says, "I think you might have got the wrong man!"

"Say again?" ask the anglers.

"Only that one's still got his ice skates on, see?"

★   ★   ★   ★   ★

FLATULENCE

✳ A couple had been happily married for years. The only friction in their otherwise idyllic marriage arose from the husband's habit of farting loudly every morning when he awoke. The noise would disturb his wife and the smell would make her eyes water and make her gasp for air. Every morning she would plead with him to stop farting because it was making her sick. He told her he couldn't stop it; after all, it was perfectly natural. She told him to see a doctor; she was concerned that one day he would blow his guts out. The years when by, however, and he continued to let rip.

One Christmas morning she had had enough. As she was preparing the turkey for dinner and her husband lay upstairs sound asleep, she looked at the bowl where she had put the turkey innards and neck, gizzard, liver and all the spare parts, and a malicious thought came to her. She took the bowl and went upstairs where her husband was sound asleep. Gently pulling back the bed covers, she pulled back the waistband of his Y-fronts and emptied the bowl of turkey guts into his underpants. A while later she heard her husband wake and let rip the usual blast, followed by a blood-curdling scream and the sound of frantic footsteps as he hurtled into the bathroom. The wife could hardly control herself as she rolled on the floor laughing, tears in her eyes! After years of torture she reckoned she had her revenge. About half an hour later, her husband came downstairs in his bloodstained underpants, with a look of horror on his face. She bit her lip and asked him what was the matter.

"You were right," he said. "All these years you have warned me and I didn't listen to you."

"What do you mean?" asked the wife.

"Well, you always told me that one day I would end up farting my guts out and today it finally happened. But, by the grace of God, some Vaseline and these two fingers, I think I got most of them back in."

✳ I went to the doctor and asked if he could give me something for persistent wind. He gave me a kite.

✳ An elderly Welshman and his wife are lying in bed. After a few minutes the old man lets loose a huge fart and says, "Four points."

His wife rolls over and asks, "What the hell was that?"

The old man says, "A try. I'm ahead four-nil."

A few minutes later the wife lets one go and says, "Try, converted."

After about ten minutes, the old man farts again and says, "Try, conversion. I'm ahead fourteen to seven."

Now starting to get into this, the wife quickly farts again and says, "Try, conversion – fourteen all."

The old man strains really hard, but to no avail: he can't fart. So as not to be outdone by his wife, he gives it everything he has and strains real hard to get out just one more fart. Straining too hard, he shits in the bed.

His wife asks, "Now what was that?"

The old man replies, "Half-time, switch sides."

✳ An old woman is riding the lift in Harrods when a young, beautiful woman gets into the lift, smelling of very expensive perfume. She sees that she has the old lady's attention and turns to her and says arrogantly, "'Romance' by Ralph Lauren, £100 an ounce."

Then another young and equally beautiful woman gets into the lift, also smelling strongly of expensive perfume. She turns to the old woman and says, "'Chanel No. 5', £120 an ounce."

A couple of floors later the old woman has reached her destination and is about to get out of the lift. Before she leaves, she looks both beautiful women in the eye, then bends over and farts in their direction and says, "Broccoli – 70 pence a pound."

* Why do men fart louder than woman?

  Woman can't keep their mouths shut long enough to build up pressure.

* What's the definition of a fart?

  A turd honking for the right-of-way.

A little old lady goes to the doctor's. "I can't stop dropping these silent little farts," she says to him.

"I can help you," replies the doctor. "Take these pills and come back next week."

The following week, the lady returns. "Doctor," she says, "I don't know what you gave me, but now my farts stink!"

The doctor says, "Good, we fixed your sinuses. Now let's work on your hearing aid."

* Two medical students were sitting on a park bench and they decided to play a game. They try to spot physical abnormalities in passers-by and attempt to make a correct diagnosis. After a while, an old man walked slowly past with his legs wide apart. "He has a bad case of haemorrhoids," asserted the first student.

  "No, he has a hernia," said the second.

  They went over to talk to the old man and told him that they couldn't agree with each other's diagnosis of his problem.

  One said: "My friend thinks you have a bad case of haemorrhoids, and I think you have a hernia. Which of us is correct?"

  The old man replied, "Well, I thought it was just a fart, but it looks like we were all wrong."

                    *   *   *   *   *

FOOD

★ How do you make German chocolate cake?
First, you occupy the kitchen . . .

★ What do you call a cheese factory in the Middle East?
Cheeses of Nazareth.

★ The other day I phoned my local pizza delivery firm and asked for a thin and crusty supreme. They sent me Diana Ross.

★ How many potatoes does it take to kill an Irishman?
None.

★ What do you call someone who covers his genitals in chickpeas and garlic?
A hummusexual.

★ What tastes good on pizza but not on pussy?
Crust.

★ Have you tried the new German–Chinese fusion cuisine?
The food is okay, but an hour later you're hungry for power.

★ ★ ★ ★ ★

FORTUNE TELLERS

❖ A small frog goes to see a fortune teller. The medium tells the frog: "You are soon going to meet a beautiful young girl who will want to know everything about you."

The frog replies, "That's brilliant. When will I meet her and where? In a bar? At a party?"

"No," the fortune teller replies. "Next term, in her biology class."

> I read my horoscope today. It said I should invest in something fun on four wheels. I don't know if that meant I should get a new car or a prostitute on one roller skate.

★　★　★　★　★

FROGS

✳ A princess is skipping alongside a pond in the royal gardens when she spied a really ugly frog. Being a very simple princess, she picked the frog up anyway and immediately recoils at the unfortunate creature's totally hideous appearance.

"My!" said the princess. "You really are a very ugly frog!"

"I know, I know," replied the frog. "I got a really bad spell cast on me."

"Well, I've seen frogs with spells, but never one as ugly as you," said the princess.

"Yeah, yeah, well, it's like I said," explained the frog, "this was a really, really bad spell."

"Nevertheless," replied the princess, "I will kiss you, and you will turn into a prince."

"As you wish," replied the frog. "However, I'm afraid it is not going to be quite as simple as that. I'm afraid a spell this bad will almost certainly require a blow job."

✳ A man walks into a bar. "Hey, barman, I'm a bit strapped for cash. If I show you something truly amazing, will you give me a free beer?"

"Everybody tries that one on and I've seen it all," says the barman. "But you're certainly welcome to try me."

The man reaches in his pocket and takes out a frog and a tiny piano and sets them on the bar. The frog begins to play the piano so beautifully that it brings a tear to the barman's eye.

"I have to admit, that was pretty amazing," says the barman, wiping his eye. "Here's your free beer."

A few minutes pass, and the man finishes the beer while the frog continues to play.

"Barman, I could use another beer. If I show you something even more amazing, can I drink for free all night?"

"You're pushing your luck," says the barman. "This had better be good."

The man takes a hamster from his pocket, sets it next to the piano, and it begins to sing while the frog plays the piano!

"Well, bugger me, that's a hell of a show," says the barman. "You can drink all night for free."

Meanwhile, another customer sidles up and sits next to him.

"Say, pal," he says. "I'll give you fifty quid for that there hamster."

"Sure, it's a deal," he replies.

The money changes hands and the customer leaves with the hamster.

The barman says: "Are you mad? You just sold a singing hamster for fifty quid. You could have a lifetime of free beer with that thing!"

"Nah, don't worry about it," says the man. "The frog is a ventriloquist."

✳ **What did one lesbian frog say to the other lesbian frog?**
   "Christ, we really do taste like chicken."

✳ **What's green and red and goes round and round and round?**
A frog in a blender.

✳ A buxom brunette goes to her local pet shop in search of an exotic pet. As she looks about the shop, she notices a box full of frogs. The sign says: "Sex Frogs – complete with instruction manual, only £20 each. Money Back Guarantee!"

The girl looks around to see if anybody's watching her and whispers to the man behind the counter, "I'll take one." The man packages the frog and says quietly, "Just follow the instructions carefully."

The girl nods, grabs the box and is quickly on her way home. As soon as she closes the door to her apartment, she takes out the instructions and reads them thoroughly, doing exactly what it says to do:

1. Take a shower.
2. Splash on some nice smelling perfume.
3. Crawl into bed and position the frog.

She then quickly gets into bed with the frog and, to her annoyance, absolutely nothing happens. The girl is totally frustrated and quite upset. She re-reads the instructions and notices at the bottom of the paper it says, "If you have any problems or questions, please call the pet shop."

So, the girl calls the pet shop. The owner is sympathetic: "Sorry. In fact I had some complaints about this earlier today. I'll be right over." Within twenty minutes, the man is ringing her doorbell. The girl welcomes him in and says, "I've done everything according to the instructions and the damn thing just sits there."

The man, looking very concerned, picks up the frog, stares directly into its eyes and says sternly: "Listen to me! I'm only going to show you how to do this one more time!"

✳ A huge bloke walks into a bar and orders a beer. The barman starts to pull him a pint, but can't take his eyes off the guy, because on top of this huge, muscle-bound body the man has a tiny head, about the size of a peach.

So the barman gives the customer his beer and says, "You must work out, you have an amazing physique."

"Thanks," says the customer.

"It really is phenomenal. But if you don't mind me asking, home come your head is so small?"

The big guy nods slowly. He's obviously fielded this question many times. "One day," he begins, "I was hunting and got lost in the woods. I heard someone shouting for help. I followed the cries and they led me to a frog sitting next to a stream."

"No shit?" says the barman.

"Yeah, so I picks up the frog and it said, 'Kiss me and I will turn into a genie and grant you three wishes.'"

"No shit?" says the barman.

"Anyway, so I looked around to make sure there was no one watching and gave the frog a kiss. The frog turned into a beautiful, voluptuous, naked woman. She said, 'You now have three wishes.' So I looked down at my puny 120-pound body and said, 'I want a body like Arnold Schwarzenegger.'"

"No shit!!?" says the barman.

"Yeah. Anyway, she nodded, snapped her fingers, and POOF! There I was, so huge that I ripped my clothes and was standing there butt naked. Then she asks, "What will be your second wish?"

"No shit!!?" says the barman. "What happened next?"

"So I looked at her beautiful body and said, 'I want to shag the arse off you right here by this stream.' So we made love right there by that stream for hours! Afterwards, as we lay there next to each other, she whispered into my ear, 'You do have one more wish. What will it be?' I looked at her and said, 'How about a little head?'"

★   ★   ★   ★   ★

FUNERALS

★ At the end of a funeral service the pall bearers were carrying the deceased out, when they accidentally bumped into a wall, jarring the casket. Suddenly they heard a faint but unmistakable moan. They quickly opened the casket and found that the woman inside was still alive.

  The woman lived on for ten more years before she finally died. Her funeral was held at the same place, and, at the end of the service, the pall bearers were once again carrying out her casket. As they were walking past her husband, he cried out, "Lads, watch out for that wall!"

> 66 I was thrown out of my mother-in-law's funeral the other day. When the music started playing I was the only one dancing. 99

★ A man was lying ill in hospital and was visited by his son. Suddenly, the father began to gasp for breath and grabbed the pen and pad by the bed. With his last ounce of strength he wrote a note, then dropped the pen and died. The son was so overcome with grief that he didn't remember slipping the note into his pocket. At the funeral, he reached into the pocket of his coat and felt the note. He read it, thinking it might be something that could give him some comfort in his time of grief. It read: "Take your foot off my oxygen pipe."

★ An elderly man lay dying in his bed when he suddenly imagined that he smelled the aroma of his favourite childhood meal, boiled beef and cabbage, wafting up the stairs. He gathered all his remaining strength and somehow heaved himself from the bed. Leaning unsteadily against the wall, he slowly made his way out of the bedroom, and with even greater effort forced himself down the stairs, gripping the railing with both hands.

With laboured breath, he leaned against the kitchen door. Were it not for the fact that he was in terrible pain, for a few moments he thought he was already in Heaven. For there, sure enough, upon the stove, was something he had all but forgotten, his favourite childhood meal, boiled beef and cabbage.

Was it Heaven? Or was it one final act of heroic love from his devoted wife, seeing to it that he left this world a happy man? Mustering one great final effort, he stumbled toward the stove, falling on his knees. His lips parted in anticipation of the mouth-watering meal, seemingly bringing him back to life. His raised his withered hand towards the food, when it was suddenly smacked with a spatula by his wife.

"You can piss off," she said, "this is for the funeral."

Larry La Prise, the man who wrote *The Hokey Cokey*, died peacefully on 11 April 1996, aged eighty-three. For his family, however, the funeral was traumatic. It began when they were getting him into the coffin. They put his left leg in – and things just started to go downhill from there.

✳ A young woman was married and had twelve children before her husband died. However, she was soon married again and had seven more children. Sadly, her second husband died. She remarried and this time had five more children. Alas, worn out by constant childbearing, she died.

At her funeral the preacher prayed to God, thanking him for this loving woman who fulfilled his commandment to "Go forth and multiply".

In his final eulogy, he noted, "Thank you Lord, they're finally together."

One of the mourners thought about this and whispered to the stranger standing next to him by the graveside: "That was beautiful. But which husband was he referring to: the first, second or third husband?"

"None of them. He was talking about her legs."

★ I hate it at weddings when some old dear prods me and says, "You're next."

They soon stopped when I started saying it to them at funerals.

★   ★   ★   ★   ★

GAMBLING

❖ A Jewish guy is working in his store when he hears a booming voice from above: "Levi, sell your business." He ignores the voice but it goes on for days. "Levi, sell your business for $3 million." After weeks of this, Levi relents and sells his store. The voice says, "Levi, take the $3 milion and go to Las Vegas."

"Why?" Levi asks.

The voice just repeats, "Levi, take the $3 million to Las Vegas."

So he obeys the voice from above and takes his $3 million to Las Vegas and goes to a casino. The voice says, "Levi, go to the blackjack table and put it all down on one hand."

Levi hesitates, but knows that he must. He sits down at the blackjack table and is dealt an eighteen with his first two cards. The dealer has a six showing.

"Levi, take a card," the voice booms.

"What? The dealer has—"

"Take a card!" the voice booms again.

So he tells the dealer to hit him. Levi gets an ace. Nineteen. He breathes a huge sigh of relief.

The voice booms, "Levi, take another card."

"What?"

"TAKE ANOTHER CARD!"

So Levi asks for another card. It's another ace – he has twenty!

"Levi, take another card," the voice commands.

"I have twenty!" Levi shouts.

"TAKE ANOTHER CARD!!" booms the voice.

"Okay, hit me," Levi tells the dealer. He gets another ace. Twenty-one.

The voice from above booms: "UN-FUCKING-BELIEVABLE!"

❖ A man walks into a bar and sees a dog playing poker. Unable to believe his eyes, he says to the dog's owner, "Is that your dog playing poker?"

"Yep, it certainly is," the owner replies.

"That's amazing!" says the man.

"Nah, not really. Every time the fucker has a good hand he wags his tail."

❖ A man is strolling down the street when he comes across an old lamp. He picks it up, gives it good rub and out pops a genie. The genie offers to grant him one wish, to which he replies, "I've always wanted to be lucky." The genie grants his wish.

So the man strolls on, wondering if the wish has worked, when he sees a £10 in the gutter. "Fuck me," he says to himself. "Not a bad start!"

Just then he notices a betting shop across the road. He strolls over, looks through the racing newspapers and sees a horse called Lucky Lad at 100/1 in the third race at Chester. He puts £10 on the horse for a straight win. Unbelievably, his horse romps home in first place. Feeling that he's definitely on a bit of a roll, he heads straight for the local casino, goes to the nearest roulette table and puts the entire £1,010 on "lucky" seven. Round and round the wheel spins – and the ball lands on seven.

He's now more than £35,000 up! What better way to celebrate than to head to the local brothel? He knocks and enters. All of a sudden he is showered with streamers and handed a glass of champagne. The madam of the establishment puts her arm around him and says, "Welcome sir! We have much pleasure to inform you that you are our lucky thousandth customer and you have won the right to take any room and any girl who works here, on the house, absolutely free of charge!"

Our hero says that he's always fancied bedding an Indian girl. So he is ushered into one of the rooms. A couple of minutes later, the most gorgeous Indian girl he has ever seen walks into the room – a real Bollywood stunner. For the next hour or so they put the Karma Sutra through its paces. The guy pauses and says to the girl, "You are the most beautiful woman I've ever seen in my life. I can't believe how lucky I am. But there is one thing I don't really don't get about Indian women – that stupid red spot that you all have on your forehead."

The Indian girl looks him in the eye and replies, "Sir, I am here to please you and fulfil your every desire. If my caste mark offends you, then you have my permission to scratch if off."

So he starts scratching at the girl's caste mark with his fingernail. Suddenly he stops and begins laughing hysterically.

"What's wrong sir?" the Indian girl asks, really worried.

He replies, "You're not going to believe this sweetheart, but I've just won a car!"

*　　*　　*　　*　　*

GARY GLITTER

* What's two foot tall, silver and stands at the end of a little girl's bed?
Gary Glitter's boots.

* What is the difference between Gary Glitter and a plastic bag?
You would let your children play with a plastic bag.

✳ McDonald's are launching a Gary Glitter burger. It is made of sixty-year-old meat inside ten-year-old buns.

✳ Gary Glitter announced from his cell today that after he has served his time he and his family will be jetting off to Florida, USA to start afresh. Apparently he's going to Tampa with the kids.

Gary Glitter and his girlfriend are in a video hire shop, looking for something to hire for the evening. Gary's girlfriend asks him what he wants to watch.

Gary says: "How about we get *Aladdin*?"

His girlfriend replies: "Can't we just get a video? You're in enough trouble already."

✳ Gary Glitter was on a ship with 100 boy scouts and 100 girl guides, when it hit an iceberg and started to sink. The captain announced "We're sinking! Everyone abandon ship!"

Gary Glitter asked, "What about the children?"

The captain replied, "Fuck the children!"

Gary Glitter looked around and said, "Do we have time?"

✳ Gary Glitter has bought 100 cases of Glenfiddich scotch whisky. Apparently the shop assistant told him it was a cheeky little twelve-year-old that goes down well.

* Gary Glitter is sitting in his living room, surfing the Internet on his laptop. All of a sudden, the door of the apartment whips open and his girlfriend storms through. She screams, "You bastard!" and heads into the bedroom sobbing. Stunned, the Leader switches off the computer and walks toward the bedroom, wondering to himself, "Now what have I done?"

  Inside the bedroom he finds the girl furiously packing a suitcase. He asks her what's up. She responds with a sob, "My friends say that you're a paedophile!"

  "Wow!" says Gary. "That's a big word for an eight-year-old."

* I was in the pub last night and Gary Glitter came on the jukebox. I knew we shouldn't have put on St Winifred's School Choir.

*   *   *   *   *

GEORGE BEST

* George Best is lying seriously ill in hospital and the doctor says to him: "George, I have some good news and some bad news. Which do you want first?'

  "Bad, please," says George.

  "Well," says the doctor, "the bad news is you only have about one hour left to live."

  "Oh my God!" says George, "that is really bad news. What's the good news, doc?"

  The doctor replies: "It's happy hour."

* What's the similarity between Jill Dando and George Best?

  They both finished their careers at Fulham.

❖ When Calum Best was born, George Best went straight down the pub with his mates to wet the baby's head.

Later he rang his wife and said, "How's the baby doing?"

She said, "Not bad. He just got a B in history."

❖ What's yellow and goes beep . . . beep . . . beep?
George Best.

❖ What was the similarity between George Best and Gary Glitter?
They both enjoy the occasional tot.

* * * * *

GERBILS

* How can you tell if you are in a gay amusement park?
They hand out gerbils at the tunnel of love.

* What did the brown gerbil say to the white gerbil?
"You're new around here, aren't you."

* * * * *

GERMAN JOKES

★ How many thalidomides does it take to change a light bulb?
   None, they are unable to reach. They will have to either get someone else to do it for them or sit in the dark.

★ A man walks into a bar and orders a drink. He has several more drinks; he gets pretty hammered because he has a drinking problem. Eventually he goes home, hits his wife and cries himself to sleep.

★ A horse walks into a bar. It has a long face.

★ A couple on their honeymoon want to have a bash at anal sex, but the woman declines on the basis that they have not known each other long enough for this kind of sexual deviance.

★ Have you seen Stevie Wonder's new video?
   Well, it is really quite good.

★ My father used to say, "Whatever doesn't kill you, makes you stronger." However his opinion was not based on any firm medical evidence.

★ Did you hear about the Amish mechanic?
   He did not own a car.

★ A bus hit my brother and he had both of his legs amputated. He now wears prosthetic limbs.

★ Why did the little girl fall off the swing?
   Because she had no arms.

★ "I say, I say, my dog has no nose."

"Oh no! How does it smell?"

"Well, it doesn't, but it has two ears and a fully functioning pair of eyes and that compensates for it."

★ One day, little Johnny was outside when it started to rain. But the rain was different from normal rain, this rain was green. Johnny laughed as it fell on him. He opened his mouth and caught it on his tongue. "I will call it 'goo'!" he said. Johnny collected a bottle of the green rain and took it to his school to show everyone. In class, Johnny's teacher saw the jar and asked him what it is. Johnny said "It's 'goo'! I named it!" The teacher laughed and all his friends were jealous.

Later Johnny took his jar of goo to his science teacher. "Look at my jar of goo, Mr Schmidt!" Mr Schmidt said,

"Johnny, this is not 'goo', this is 'nuclear waste'. The nearby reactor had a leak, causing nuclear acid rain." Mr Schmidt continued, "Johnny, you didn't happen to drink any, did you?" Johnny admitted that he had. "Johnny, I'm afraid you're going to get cancer and die."

How many kangaroos does it take to change a light bulb?

None – a kangaroo has neither the intelligence nor dexterity to do any kind of electrical repair work. At best it could try to indicate that the bulb needed changing by hopping around, but it would not actually be able to do anything about it.

★ What's worse than finding a worm in your apple?

The Holocaust.

★ A necrophiliac walks into a bar. All the while he harbours a pathological compulsion to have sex with dead people.

* "Doctor, I've broken my leg."
  Doctor: "I'm afraid it is a very bad break. You will never walk
    properly again."

* There's a German, a Jew and an Arab sitting in a pub.
  What a prime example of an inter-racial harmony.

* My wife is so fat she has to wear clothes in large sizes.

* What do you call it when someone wipes out an entire race
  of people?
  Genocide.

* Stevie Wonder walks into a store. He is unaware of his
  predicament, so to derive humour from the situation would
  be cruel and exploitative.

* Knock-knock.
  Knock-knock.
  It appears that there is no one home, I'll come back later.

* A man walks into a bar. As a result he needs stitches on his forehead because he hit it quite hard.

* How many Irish people does it take to screw in a light
  bulb?
  It shouldn't take more than one person to complete this
  task, regardless of nationality.

* Little Johnny comes back from school crying, and says,
  "Mommy, all the kids in the school say I have a big head."
  His mother replies, "Yes, Johnny. This is because you
  suffer from encephalitis and the other children are merely
  observing your symptoms."

★ How do you stop a clown from smiling?
  Hit him with an axe.

★ How are a strawberry and a rabbit alike?
  They are both red, except for the rabbit.

★ A white man, a Mexican and a black man find a genie lamp and rub it. The Mexican wishes for all Mexicans to go back to Mexico. The black wishes for all blacks to be brought back to Africa. The white man, who misses his friends, wishes for an annual holiday for his black and Mexican friends, so that they may visit America again if they so wish.

★ What do you get if you cross an elephant with a poodle?
  An unfortunate interbreeding between two different species which will result in undesirable characteristics.

★ "Doctor, doctor. I feel like a pair of curtains!"
  "Unfortunately this the least of your problems. You also have an inoperable brain tumour."

★ What do you call five Pakistanis in some quicksand?
  If you are unfamiliar with their names, just say, "Excuse me."

★ How do you get 100 Jews into a Volkswagen?
  You would have to manufacture a very large Volkswagen. This will solve your problem.

★ Why did the black guy get lynched?
Because he was the victim of a terrible race-hate crime.

★ What is the difference between Michael Jackson and a plastic bag?
Michael Jackson was the "King of Pop". A plastic bag is a type of flexible packaging made of thin, plastic film, and is used for containing and transporting goods such as foods, produce, powders, ice, chemicals and waste.

★ My mother-in-law is so fat that it may have an adverse effect on her health, leading to reduced life expectancy.

★ ★ ★ ★ ★

GERMANS

★ A German couple have a baby and name him Klaus. As time goes by Klaus grows up and yet he never utters a word. After years of trying to find out what is wrong with him, his parents just accept that he is mute. When Klaus reaches his fourteenth birthday his parents throw a party for him and he is given a slice of his favourite cake. Suddenly, Klaus turns to his mother and says: "Mother, zis cake is dry."

His mum can't believe her ears. Overcome with emotion she hugs him and cries, "Klaus, you can speak! Why have you never spoken before?"

"Well," replies Klaus, "until now, everything has been satisfactory."

★ "Knock knock."
"Who's there?"
"Hitler."
"Hitler who?"
"For denying the holocaust you are now sentenced to ten years in an Austrian prison."

★ A teenager was playing on his Playstation when his grandad came in the bedroom and sat down next to him. "What are you doing?" asked the grandad. "You're eighteen years old and you're wasting your life! When I was your age I went to Paris, I went to the Moulin Rouge, drank all night, had my way with the dancers, pissed on the bar and left without paying! I knew how to have a good time!"

A few weeks later the grandfather comes to visit again. He finds the lad still in his room, but with a broken arm in plaster, two black eyes and missing all his front teeth.

"What happened to you?" asked the grandfather.

"Well, grandad," replied the boy, "I did what you did! I went to Paris, went to the Moulin Rouge, drank all night, had my way with the dancers, and pissed all over the bar . . . and the barman beat seven shades of shit out of me!"

"Oh dear!" replied the grandad. "Who did you go to Paris with?"

"Just a couple mates, why? Who did you go with?"

His grandad replied: "The Third Panzer Division."

★ I don't hate Germans, I just miss my grandparents.

★ What is the difference between the Dresden bombing and Germany's best comedian?
Only the first one can make you laugh.

★ We had a German plumber round the other day to fix our radiators. He accidentally connected the gas supply to the water supply. I suppose old habits die hard!

Ten Reasons Why it's Really Great to Be German

1 Oktoberfest.
2 Oktoberfest.
3 BMW.
4 VW.
5 Audi.
6 Mercedes.
7 You can drive at speeds that would have you locked up in any other country in the world.
8 You do not have to learn German as a foreign language.
9 You think Sauerkraut is delicious.
10 Contrary to common belief, laughing is not forbidden by law.

★ What's the difference between Lady Diana and the East Germans?
    The East Germans survived the wall.

★ I bought a sun lounger from eBay last week. It arrived with a German towel already on it.

★　★　★　★　★

GINGER PEOPLE

★ What's the difference between a ginger pussy and a bowling ball?
  You could eat a bowling ball if you really had to.

★ A man's wife is in labour. After the birth, the doctor takes the man on one side and says: "You have a son. Unfortunately we have some good news and some bad news."
  The man says "Okay, tell it me straight."
  The doctor continues: "Well, your baby is brain damaged. He is unable to feed himself, will never be able to walk or see and will require constant care throughout his life. I'm afraid this sort of thing isn't covered by insurance, so it's going to cost you a fortune and you may have to remortgage your home to pay for it."
  The man is visibly shocked. He recovers his composure and says: "Well, that's awful. But please, tell me the good news."
  The doctor looks at him and says: "Sorry, that was the good news. The bad news is that your baby is ginger."

★ What do ginger people miss most about parties?
  The invitation.

★ What's the difference between a ginger and a brick?
  The brick gets laid.

★ What's the best thing about being black?
  You won't have ginger kids.

Why do ginger people sunburn easily?
  It's nature's way of telling them they should be locked indoors.

★ Why did God invent colour blindness?
  So someone will fancy the ginger kids.

★ What do you call a good-looking woman with a ginger man?
  A hostage.

★ I've just seen the new Harry Potter film, but it's pretty unrealistic. I mean, a ginger kid with two friends?

★   ★   ★   ★   ★

GOD

❖ On the sixth day, God created the duck-billed platypus. And God saw that it was good and said, "Let's see the evolutionists try and figure out this motherfucker."

❖ Why did God make homosexuality a sin?
  Because his boyfriend thought that would make sex hotter.

❖ What if God is a woman? Not only am I going to hell, I'll never know why.

❖ God says to one of his angels: "I'm absolutely knackered. I just created a 24-hour period of alternating light and darkness on Earth."
  The angel says, "What are you going to do now?"
  God replies, "Fuck it, I think I'll call it a day."

❖   One day God calls down to Noah and says, "Noah, love, I want you to make me a new ark."

Noah replies, "*Au naturellement*, anything you want, oh Mighty One, you're the boss!"

God continues, "But I want this to be a very special ark, Noah. I want an ark with not just a couple of decks, I want twenty decks, one on top of the other."

"Twenty decks?" says Noah. "Okay, Lord, whatever you say, you're the boss. Should I fill it up with all the animals just like last time?"

"Yes, that's right. Well, not exactly. This time I want you to fill it up with fish," says God.

"Fish?" says Noah.

"Yes, fish. And not just any old fish, Noah. I want carp."

"Carp, oh Mighty One?" queries Noah.

"Yes, Noah. Just carp."

Noah looks to the skies, "Okay, God, let me get this right, you want a new ark?"

"Correct."

"With twenty decks, one on top of the other?"

"Correct."

"And you want it full of carp?"

"You've got it."

"Please," says the perplexed Noah, "may I ask why, oh Lord?"

"Well," says God, "I just always fancied a multi-storey carp ark."

❖   The Yorkshire Ripper died and went to meet his maker. When he arrived, St Peter opened the pearly gates and let him in, whereupon God hit him thirteen times with a hammer and then kicked him directly in the bollocks.

The Ripper, doubled up in pain, gasped, "Why did you do that?"

God replied, "You killed thirteen women. That was a blow for each of your victims."

The Ripper said, "Yes, yes, I understand that, but why kick me in the balls?"

"For blaming me."

❖　Moses and God are walking around Heaven when God complains of being bored. Moses suggests a holiday.

"That's a good idea," says God, "but where?"

"What about Jupiter?" suggest Moses. "Lovely scenery."

"Mmmm, but the gravity gives me a backache," says God.

"Okay, what about Saturn then? Impressive rings!"

"Yes, but a bit too cold and dull. I fancy a bit of excitement."

"Well, if it's excitement you want, what about Earth? It's the happening place to be."

"Earth?" God says in disgust. "No way. Last time I was there, I got some bitch pregnant and I haven't heard the end of it for the last 2,000 years."

A boy says to his mother, "Mum, is God a man or a woman?"

His mother thinks carefully for a while and says, "Well, son, God is neither man nor woman."

The son is confused, so he asks, "Is God black or white?"

The mother replies, "God is both black and white, dear."

The son, still curious, says after a while, "Is God gay or straight, mum?"

The mother, getting a little anxious, answers, "Son, God is both gay and straight."

The son thinks about it, then his face lights up. "Mum, is God Michael Jackson?"

★　★　★　★　★

GOLF

✳ Three golfers, Tom, Dick and Harry, are looking for someone to make up a foursome. Tom mentions that his friend Bob is a pretty good golfer so they decide to invite him along the following weekend.

"Thanks, guys, I'd love to play," says Bob, "but I might be about ten minutes late, so wait for me."

The weekend rolls around. Tom, Dick and Harry arrive at the first tee promptly at 9 a.m. and find Bob waiting for them. He plays right-handed and beats them all. Quite pleased with their new golf partner, they ask him if he'd like to play again the following weekend.

"Sounds good to me," says Bob. "But wait for me because I might be ten minutes late."

The following weekend all four golfers show up on time, but this time Bob plays left-handed and still beats them all easily. As they are getting ready to leave, Bob says: "See you next weekend, but I might be about ten minutes late, so wait for me."

This goes on for several weeks and Bob always turns up on time and plays out of his skin – right-handed, left-handed, it doesn't seem to bother him. Every week, he leaves his golfing friends with the same message.

After a couple of months, the other three are fairly irritated by this routine, so Dick says, "Hang on a minute, Bob. Every week you give us the same old crap. You say you might be about ten minutes late, but you never are. And what's with this left-handed, right-handed shit?"

"Well," says Bob, "I'm very superstitious. When I get up in the morning, I look at my wife. If she's sleeping on her left side, I play left-handed. If she's sleeping on her right side, I play right-handed."

"So what do you do if she's sleeping on her back?" Dick asks.

"Then I'm about ten minutes late," says Bob.

❋ Two men had just finished the first nine holes in their round of golf, and it was obvious to one of them that his friend was having a bad day. "You're just not your old self today. What's the matter?"

His friend looking glum, said, "I think my wife's dead."

"My God! That's terrible," said his friend. "But what do you mean, you think she's dead. Aren't you sure?"

"Well, I just don't know," he responds. "The sex is still the same, but the dishes are piling up."

❋ What's the difference between a G-spot and a golf ball?

A man will make the effort to search for a golf ball.

❋ Two women were playing golf. One teed off and watched in horror as her ball headed directly toward a foursome of men playing the next hole. The ball hit one of the men and he immediately fell to the ground and rolled around in agony clasping his groin. The woman rushed down to the man, and began to apologize. "Please allow me to help. I'm a physical therapist and I know I could relieve your pain if you'd allow me."

"No, no, I'll be okay in a few minutes," the man protested, even though he was still obviously in agony, lying in the foetal position, still clasping his hands at his groin. She persisted, however, and he finally allowed her to help.

She gently took his hands away and laid them to the side, loosened his pants and put her hands inside. She administered tender and artful massage for several minutes and asked, "How does that feel?"

"Pretty good," he replied, "but I still think my thumb's broken."

* A man takes a week off and decides to spend every day improving his golf. First thing Monday morning he sets off on his first round and soon catches up with the player in front. He notices that she's a very attractive woman. He suggests that they play the rest of the round together. She agrees and she turns out also to be a very talented golfer and she wins their little competition on the eighteenth hole. He congratulates her on her game and offers to give her a lift home. All in all, he has had a really enjoyable morning.

On the way to her place, she thanks him for the morning's game and says she hasn't enjoyed herself so much for ages. "In fact," she says, "I'd like you to pull over so I can show you how much I appreciated everything." He pulls over, they kiss and she gives him the best oral sex he's ever had.

The following day he sees her at the first tee and suggests they play together again. This time he's very competitive – his sense of pride is slightly dented by the fact that she beat him the previous day. Once gain they have a magnificent day, enjoying each other's company and playing a good competitive round of golf. Yet again she pips him at the last, yet again he drives her home and again she shows her appreciation with a blow job. This goes on all week, with the lady beating him narrowly every day.

In the car on the way home from their Friday afternoon round, he tells her that he has had such a fantastic week that he has a surprise planned: dinner for two at a fancy candle-lit restaurant, followed by a night of passion in the penthouse apartment of an expensive hotel. To his surprise, she bursts into tears. He can't work out what the fuss is about but eventually she sobs: "I can't go with you. You see, I'm a transsexual."

At this he swerves violently off the road, pulls the car to a halt and curses madly and violently.

"I'm sorry," she repeats.

"You scumbag!" he screams, red in the face. "You cheating bastard. You've been playing off the women's tees all week!!"

A young woman was taking golf lessons and had just started playing her first round of golf when she suffered a bee sting. Her pain was so intense that she decided to return to the clubhouse for medical assistance. The golf pro saw her heading back and said, "You are back early. What's wrong?"

"I was stung by a bee," she said.

"Where," he asked.

"Between the first and second hole," she replied.

He nodded, and said, "Your stance is far too wide, madam."

* Frank and Emily met on holiday and Frank fell head over heels in love. After a couple of romantic weeks, during which Frank took Emily out to various night clubs, restaurants and concerts, he was convinced that he wanted to spend the rest of his life with her. On the very last night of his holiday the two of them went to dinner and had a serious talk about how the relationship would continue. "It's only fair to warn you that you're going to be a golf widow," Frank said to his new ladyfriend. "I eat, sleep and breathe golf, so if that's going to be a problem you'd better say so now!"

Emily was quiet for a moment. Then she took a deep breath and replied: "Since we're being honest with each other, there's something you also need to know. I'm a hooker."

"I see," Frank replied. He looked down at the table, as though deep in thought, then he nodded, "You know, it's probably because you're not keeping your wrists straight when you tee off."

✳ A couple were on their honeymoon, lying in bed and getting ready to consummate their marriage, when the new bride says to the husband, "I have a confession to make, I'm not a virgin."

The husband replies, "That's no big deal in this day and age."

The wife continues, "I've only been with one other guy."

"Oh yeah? Who was he?"

"Tiger Woods."

"You mean Tiger Woods the golfer?"

"Yes."

"Well," says the husband. "He's very rich, famous and handsome. I can see why you went to bed with him."

The husband and wife then make passionate love. When they are through the husband gets up and walks to the telephone.

"What are you doing?" says the wife.

The husband says, "I'm hungry. I'm going to call room service and get something sent up."

"Tiger wouldn't do that," replies his wife.

"Oh yeah? What would Tiger do?"

"He'd come back to bed and fuck me again."

The husband puts down the phone and goes back to bed to make love with his wife a second time. When they have finished, he gets up and goes over to the phone.

"What are you doing?" she says.

The husband says, "I'm still hungry so I was going to get room service to get some food."

"Tiger wouldn't do that."

"Oh yeah? What would Tiger do?"

"He'd come back to bed and fuck me again." The husband puts down the phone and goes back to bed and makes love to his wife one more time.

When they finish, he's absolutely knackered. He drags himself out of bed, staggers over to the phone and starts to dial.

The wife asks, "Are you calling room service?"

"No," replies her husband. "I'm calling Tiger Woods to find out what the par is for this hole."

✳ A man arrives home from a round of golf, looking shattered. His wife says, "You look terrible, what happened?"

He replies, "Well, everything was going great until we got to the third tee. Then Bob got up to hit his tee shot and he collapsed with a heart attack."

"Oh God, that's awful, but why do you look so tired?" the wife asks.

"Well, for the rest of the round, it was like, play the shot, drag Bob, play the shot, drag Bob . . ."

The Olympic sprinter Usain Bolt decided to take up golf, so he went down to the local course. "Hi," said Usain. "I'd like to join your golf club."

The receptionist called the club captain, who came to meet Bolt at reception.

"Hi," said Usain, "I'd like to join your golf club."

"I'm terribly sorry," said the club captain, "but we don't let black people join our club. However, if you turn right out of the main gates there is a public golf course about fifteen minutes up the road. You'll have absolutely not problem getting a game there."

"I don't think you understand," said Usain. "I am Usain Bolt."

"Oh, I see, I'm terribly sorry," said the club captain. "In that case, the public course is five minutes up the road."

✳ A father, son and grandfather go out to play a round of golf. Just as the son is about to tee off, a really fine-looking woman approaches them, carrying a bag of golf clubs. "Excuse me," she says. "My partner hasn't shown up. Would you mind if I joined you". Naturally, the guys all agree. Soon afterwards the guys begin to realize that perhaps it wasn't such a great idea after all because they really have to work hard to mind their language in her presence. The lady gets wind of this and turns to the three of them and says, "Listen, boys, I don't care what the three of you do or say out here. Go ahead, swear, smoke, spit or whatever, just don't try to coach me on my game." She then proceeds to tee off.

All eyes are on her arse as she bends over to place the ball on the tee. She then knocks the hell out of the ball, right up the middle of the fairway. She continues to amaze the three men, shooting par or better on every hole.

When they get to the eighteenth green she has a six-foot putt for par. She turns around and says, "I want to thank you gentlemen for not trying to coach me. But I'll be honest with you, I've never, ever shot par on this hole before and I want your opinions on this putt. If you can help me sink this putt I'll give each of you a blow job."

The son steps forward, eyes up the putt for a couple of minutes and finally says, "Madam, aim that putt six inches to the right of the hole. The ball will break left twelve inches from the hole and will go into the cup."

Then the father steps up to the green. "Don't listen to the kid. Aim twelve inches to the right and the ball will break left two feet from the hole and fall into the cup."

At this, the grandfather looks at both of them in disgust. He walks over to her ball on the green, picks it up, and says, "That's a gimme, sweetheart."

★   ★   ★   ★   ★

GORILLAS

★ A dwarf walks into a pub, throws a £5 note on the bar and says to the barman, "Give me a double shot of your best whisky! And who's the toughest son of a bitch in this bar tonight?"

The barman pours the dwarf a double shot of Jack Daniels and says, "Well, in my opinion, sir, I'd say the large chap at the end of the bar is the toughest son of a bitch in the premises this evening."

The dwarf knocks back his Jack Daniels in one, walks to the end of the bar and smacks the big fellow in the teeth, knocking him out cold, then walks out of the bar.

"Well," thinks the barman, "that's something you don't see every day."

The following evening the same dwarf walks into the bar, throws down a £5 note and says to the barman, "Give me a double shot of your best whisky! And who's the toughest son of bitch in this bar tonight?"

So the barman pours him his double whisky and says, "Well, sir, I'd say that big old biker sitting by that table over there is the toughest son of a bitch in this bar tonight."

The dwarf knocks back his shot, walks over to the biker, punches him square in the jaw, knocking him out, and walks out of the bar.

Well, by this time the barman is getting a mite cheesed off about having this little fellow hitting his customers. So, the next day he goes down to the local zoo and rents out a very large gorilla, then hides him in the men's toilets. Sure enough, the following evening the dwarf returns. He walks in the pub, throws down his fiver and says, "Give me a double of your best whisky! And who's the toughest son of a bitch in this bar tonight."

The barman pours him his shot and says, "You know, sir, there really isn't anybody in here tonight quite up to your standard of toughness, but I gather that there is a gentleman in the men's toilets who is, as it were, the baddest son of a bitch in the premises this evening."

The dwarf knocks back his drink and heads for the men's toilets. From the bar everyone hears the toilet door slam and the beginnings of a right royal ruckus. Suddenly it goes quiet, the dwarf walks back into the bar, brushing himself down. He says to the barman: "Oi, barman. Tell the black guy in the men's when he wakes up, his fur coat's in the wheelie bin out the back."

★ In the jungle there lived a gorilla and a rhino. They had been best mates for several years and they did everything together. One spring day the gorilla was feeling a bit randy. It had been months since he had been able to pull, and he was starting to get a bit desperate for a shag. As he was walking down to the waterhole he saw his mate the rhino bending over, having a drink. This was too much for the gorilla who saw the rhino's arse right there in front of him swaying gently from side to side as he drank. The gorilla couldn't contain himself any more and ran straight at the rhino and buggered him senseless for a good half-hour. All the time the rhino was screaming, "Get off me, I'm going to kill you, you bastard!" but he couldn't do anything because the gorilla was holding on too tight.

Eventually the gorilla finished and climbed off. "Right, I'm going to kill you!" the rhino screamed and started running after the gorilla.

The gorilla was yelling, "We've been best mates for years and we shouldn't let a trivial thing like this come between us!" The rhino, however, was having none of it and he was slowly catching up. The gorilla ran into a camp, where an explorer was sitting in a chair reading the newspaper. He ran off to the north but he couldn't get past the cliffs, so he ran back to the camp. He ran east but he couldn't get past the river, so he ran back to the camp. He ran west but he couldn't get through the undergrowth, so he ran back to the camp. Therefore he broke the explorer's neck, grabbed his clothes and newspaper, threw the explorer over the trees, sat down and started to read.

Soon afterwards the rhino charged into the camp. He ran off to the north, but couldn't find the gorilla so he ran back into the camp. He ran off to the east, but couldn't find the gorilla so he ran back into the camp. He ran off to the west, but couldn't find the gorilla so he ran back into the camp.

"Excuse me," he said, "but have you seen a gorilla?"

The gorilla, still hiding behind the newspaper, asked, "What, the one that buggered a rhino down by the watering hole?"

"Fuck me!" says the rhino. "Don't tell me it's in the papers already."

✶   ✶   ✶   ✶   ✶

GOTHS

❖ What's black and knocks on the window?
   A goth in a microwave.

❖ What do you call a goth lying in the road?
   A speed bump.

❖ What do you get if you cross a goth with a toilet?
   The Cisterns of Mercy.

❖ Two goths are walking down the road. One says "I just bought the new Love Like Blood CD."
   The other replies, "Fuck me, a talking goth!"

❖ How do you get a goth out of a tree?
   Cut the rope.

✶   ✶   ✶   ✶   ✶

GRANDPARENTS

* They say laughter is the best medicine. I'm not sure about that. My grandad is suffering from Alzheimer's and we have been laughing at him for years but he hasn't got any better.

* Little Johnny went to see his grandad. "Grandad, could you please do a frog impression?"
  Grandad, a little confused, replied, "Excuse me?"
  Johnny said again, "Grandad, can you make the sound of a frog?"
  Grandad said, "Of course I can, but why?"
  Little Johnny said, "Good, because mummy said that, just as soon as you croak, we can all fuck off to Disneyland!"

> " You have to stay in shape when you get older. My grandmother started walking five miles a day when she was sixty-five. She is ninety today and we haven't a fucking clue where she is. "

* My grandfather knew the exact hour of the exact day of the exact year he was going to die. The judge told him.

* We cleared out my grandmother's house this morning. We sorted out the good stuff and put it on eBay, took the rest down to charity shop, then went to the estate agents to put her house on the market. I'd love to see her face when she gets back from bingo.

* My grandmother spends all of her time out in the garden. That's where we buried her.

* My grandfather came out of the closet yesterday. He's not gay, he has Alzheimer's and thought it was the car.

✳ I drove past my grandmother's house and saw a dozen pints of milk on her doorstep. "Christ," I thought, "she must be thirsty today!"

✳ My grandmother has had Alzheimer's for several years. I guess I should just be grateful for the £5 I get for my birthday every week.

✳ My grandfather finally came out of his coma today. He's dead.

✳ I'm sure that wherever my grandfather is, he's looking down on me. He's not dead, he's just incredibly condescending.

✳ My grandmother refuses to grow old gracefully. Only last week she won first prize in a wet shawl contest.

✳ My grandmother died on her ninetieth birthday. It was a terrible shame. We were only half-way through giving her the bumps at the time.

✳ I call my grandad Spiderman. He hasn't got any special powers or anything, he's just really shit at getting out of the bath.

✳ A grandmother complained to her grandson, "I find that the young men of today just aren't as polite and charming as they were when I was young."

He replied: "That's because they aren't trying to fuck you now, Gran."

✳ It's been my job to give my grandmother her pill every day for the last ten years. She hates taking it, so I grind it up and slip it in her afternoon tea. Frankly the routine is a bind, but I'd never forgive myself if she got pregnant.

My grandmother passed away yesterday. She was in her nineties and she had a good innings and she went peacefully. She just sat down in a chair, relaxed, closed her eyes and drifted off to sleep. She didn't wake up again. It was a lovely way to go. Mind you, she caused fucking uproar in the dentists.

✳ I got a Valentine's Day card from my grandmother. It was very sweet of her, but unnecessary – we stopped having sex three years ago.

* * * * *

GRAVEYARDS

✳ Two women are walking through a graveyard on their way back from a night out when they find themselves desperate for a pee. As there is no one around they drop their pants and take a leak behind a couple of gravestones. As they don't have any tissue paper between them, one of the women wipes herself dry with her knickers while the second uses a wreath. The next day the two women's respective husbands are in the pub comparing notes.

"I'm keeping an eye on my missus from now on," says the first husband. "She went out last night and came back without any knickers on!"

The second replies, "You should worry! My wife came home with a card wedged half-way up her arse saying, 'We'll always miss you, from all the lads at the station.'"

★ Worse for wear after a heavy night on the piss, I awoke in a cemetery, where I saw a bloke hiding behind a gravestone. I said "Morning."

He replied, "No, just having a shit."

★   ★   ★   ★   ★

GREEKS

❖ A man goes into a bar and notices a beautiful woman sitting at the other end. He catches her eye and, much to his surprise, she winks back at him. It doesn't take long before he is sitting on the stool next to her. They talk for about an hour over a couple of drinks, when the woman says to him, "You're pretty cute. I'll tell you what. I live just around the corner. What do you think about coming up to my place?"

"That sounds great!" the man replies, barely able to believe his luck.

"Before we go up there, though," the woman says, "I have to ask you one question: do you like doing it Greek style?"

"Well, I'm not exactly sure what that is," the man answers, "but I'm willing to learn, let's go!"

So the two of them walk over to her apartment. As soon as they get through the door, the woman rips off all her clothes. He can't believe his eyes: she has an amazing body.

"Now you're sure you want it Greek style?" she asks.

"Let's do it, babe!" the man replies.

"All right, then," says the woman. "Take off all your clothes, and get up on the bed on your hands and knees."

He rips off his clothes and climbs on to the bed on his hands and knees. The woman goes around and gets on to the bed right in front of the man. She kneels down in front of his head. She asks him again, "Are you sure that you want to do it Greek style?"

"Yes! Yes!" pleads the man.

So she grabs the man with her arms right under his armpits, getting him in a lock hold. He can't move at all, his face is pressing right into her tits.

Again she says, "Are you sure that you want to do it Greek style?"

The man's muffled voice can barely be heard from between her breasts. "Yes!" he mumbles, "Greek style!"

The woman's grip on him tightens like a vice, and she yells out, "Georgiou!"

❖ What is the definition of a nice Greek boy?

One who takes his girl out twice before shagging her brother.

★ ★ ★ ★ ★

GYNAECOLOGISTS

✳ An unemployed man sees a notice for a gynaecologist's assistant in the Aberdeen job centre. So he goes to the counter and asks for more details. They tell him that the job description involves preparation of the female patient for exam, including removal of her underwear, washing and shaving of her nether regions and applying oil to the shaved parts. He is also informed that the job carries a salary of £50,000 and that he should go to Plymouth.

He asks, "Why, is that where the job is located?"

"No," comes the reply. "That is where the end of the queue is."

✳ What does a gynaecologist do when he feels sentimental?

He looks up an old girlfriend.

* What do the gynaecologist and the pizza delivery man have in common?

    They both get to smell the goods but neither one of them can eat it.

* A gorgeous, voluptuous woman went to see a gynaecologist. The doctor took one look at this woman and his professionalism immediately went out of the window. He told her to undress. After she had disrobed, the doctor began to stroke her thigh. Doing so, he asked her, "Do you know what I'm doing?"

    "Yes," she replied, "you're checking for any abrasions or dermatological abnormalities."

    "That is right," said the doctor. He then began to fondle her breasts. "Do you know what I'm doing now?" he asked.

    "Yes," the woman said, "you're checking for any lumps or breast cancer."

    "Correct," replied the shady doctor.

    Finally, he mounted his patient and started having sexual intercourse with her. He asked, "Do you know what I'm doing now?"

    "Yes," she said. "You're catching herpes, which is precisely why I came here in the first place."

* Did you hear about the gynaecologist who decorated his house through the letter box?

* Why do they call it a cervical smear?

    Because if you called it a cunt scrape, nobody would turn up for one.

* What's the difference between a genealogist and a gynaecologist?

    A genealogist looks up your family tree, whereas a gynaecologist looks up your family bush.

* A woman walks into a gynaecologist's office for an examination. She gets up on the stirrups and the doctor peers between her legs. He says: "You have a really enormous pussy. You have a really enormous pussy."

  The woman replies: "You didn't have to say it twice."

  The doctor says: "I didn't."

* A woman in her seventies goes to a gynaecologist to see if there is any remote possibility that she can have a baby. The gynaecologist tells her to lift up her skirt and pull down her panties. After a close inspection, he says, "Madam, you are seventy-five years old. Your vagina smells kipperus, which is a condition to describe the breeding ground for kippers."

  "Pardon?" says the old lady.

  "Okay, I'll make it simple for you," says the gynaecologist. "You have a kipperus vagina and if you have a baby it will be a miracle."

  The old lady thanks him and goes home to her husband.

  "What did the doctor say?" asks her husband.

  "Not good news," the old lady replies. "I have a kipper as a vagina and if I have a baby it will be a mackerel."

* ## What do a near-sighted gynaecologist and a puppy have in common?
  A wet nose.

* A six-year-old boy says to his best friend, "Yesterday after school, my mum caught me playing gynaecologists and nurses with the girl next door."

  "No shit! – I bet YOU were in trouble," replies the friend.

  "Not really, it was Wednesday so we were playing golf."

* Definition of a gynaecologist: a spreader of old wives' tails.

* * * * *

GYPSIES

* What happens if you stick your hand up a gypsy's skirt?
  You get your palm read every twenty-eight days.

* How many gypsies does it take to pave a driveway?
  It depends on how thin you slice them.

* Why are cigarettes like gypsies?
  They stink, they come in packs of twenty and they are banned from bars.

* A boy came home from school and asked his father, "Dad, am I a Jew or am I a gypsy?"
  "Why do you want to know, son?"
  "Because a kid at school is selling a bike for thirty quid. Should I offer him fifteen or just steal it?"

* Why do seagulls have wings?
  To beat the gypsies to the tip.

* What's the difference between a gypsy and a traveller?
  Political correctness.

> **I once got into a row with a gypsy and I was bricking it after he threatened to come back with his brother, his uncle and his cousin to find me and beat me up. Imagine my relief when they all turned out to be the same person.**

* What do gypsies do when the lights go out in their caravans?
  They light the candles under their kids noses.

* What does a gypsy get for his birthday?
  Your bicycle.

★   L'Oreal has launched a new shampoo for gypsies.
    It's called "Go and Wash".

★   A woman goes to the doctor's. "Doctor, I've got this problem. I'll have to take my clothes off to show you." The doctor tells her to go behind the screen and disrobe. She does so, and the doctor goes round to see her when she is ready.
    "Well, what is it?" he asks.
    "It's a bit embarrassing," she replies. "These two green circles have appeared on the inside of my thighs."
    The doctor examines her and finally admits he has no idea what the cause is. Then he suddenly asks, "Have you been having an affair with a gypsy lately?"
    The woman blushes and says, "Well, actually I have."
    "I thought as much," says the doctor. "Tell your boyfriend his earrings aren't made of real gold."

★   ★   ★   ★   ★

HAIR LOSS

❖   A woman is at the undertaker's arranging her late husband's funeral.
    The undertaker asks her: "Do you have any special requests?"
    "Well," says the widow, "he lost all of his hair when he was young and he never went anywhere without his toupee, but every time I try put it on his head it slides off."
    "No problem, I'll sort that out for you. Come back in an hour," says the undertaker. An hour or so later she returned and the toupee was perfectly placed on the dead man's head.
    "Oh, thank you so much," she says, "you must let me give you something for your trouble and I won't take no for an answer."
    The undertaker says, "All right, just give me a couple of quid for the nails."

❖ During his regular visit to the hairdresser's, a man asked his barber if he had any tips on how to treat his increasing baldness. After a brief pause, the barber leaned over and confided that the best thing he'd come across was female juices. "But you're balder than I am," replied the customer.

"You have a point," admitted the barber, "but you have to admit I've got one hell of a moustache."

❖ Why did the bald man cut holes in his pockets?

So he could run his fingers through his hair.

❖ A bald guy with a wooden leg was invited to a fancy dress party. He was very self-conscious about his baldness and his disability and didn't quite know what costume to wear to hide his head and his leg. He decided to send an email to a fancy-dress hire company to explain his predicament.

A few days later he received a parcel with a note: "Dear Sir, please find enclosed a pirate outfit. The spotted handkerchief will cover your bald head – and with your wooden leg, you will be perfect as a pirate."

The man was annoyed about their lack of tact and felt they had completely missed the point by emphasizing his wooden leg. He returned the costume with a very terse letter complaining about their appallingly inappropriate advice.

A week passed and he received another parcel and a note, which read: "Dear Sir, we are very sorry. Please find enclosed a Monk's habit. The long robe will cover your wooden leg and with your bald head you will really look the part."

Now the man was really annoyed and upset because they have added insult to injury by making a feature of his baldness. This time he wrote the company a very rude letter of complaint. The next day he received a small parcel and a note, which read –

"Dear Sir, please find enclosed a tin of treacle. Pour the tin of treacle over your bald head, stick your wooden leg up your arse and go as a toffee apple, you cunt."

HAROLD SHIPMAN

* Hollywood are making a film about Dr Harold Shipman starring Robert De Niro. It's going to be called *The Old Dear Hunter.*

* What's the difference between Harold Shipman and the government?
   Shipman actually did something about the NHS waiting lists.

* What did Harold Shipman and Gary Glitter have in common?
   They both enjoyed euthanasia.

The prison boxing team were saddened by the news that Harold Shipman took his own life. They said it was a great shame because he had a lethal jab.

* Harold Shipman's last meal was a curry. He said it was okay but he could have murdered a nan.

* Knock, knock?
   Who's there?
   Doctor.
   Doctor who?
   No, Doctor Shipman. Is your gran in?

★   ★   ★   ★   ★

HEAVEN

★ One day God says to St Peter, "We have a problem, Pete. Heaven is full to bursting. However, we have a number of celebrity candidates waiting at the gates and we are suffering from falling popularity. So I'm going to chuck out Mother Teresa and let in one of the high-profile dudes at the gate. You'll have to go and decide who is most suitable."

St Peter goes down to the pearly gates and finds Freddie Mercury, Gianni Versace and Princess Di waiting for him.

He says: "I'm afraid I can only let one of you in, so each of you must come up with a plausible reason for admission into Heaven."

Freddie says, "I've been gifted with one of the most amazing voices to ever grace the earth. I'll spend my time in Heaven singing praises to God with the choirs of angels. Heaven will never have sounded better."

Gianni says, "I was earth's greatest fashion designer. I will clothe the cherubs and angels in all the latest fashions – long silky gowns, satin cloaks and nightwear spun from the very clouds we stand on. Heaven will never have looked better."

Diana looks around nervously and seems lost for words. Suddenly, she strips off her skirt and panties, whips out a bottle of Perrier, shakes it up and douches with it.

St Peter says, "Ok, Diana, you may enter. Have a nice day."

Freddie and Gianni are furious. "What the hell's going on here? We could make Heaven look and sound better than ever before and she performs a pornographic act, but she gets in and we don't?"

St Peter just shrugs his shoulders and says, "Sorry lads, but a royal flush beats a pair of queens any day."

★ A Pakistani dies and goes up to Heaven. He knocks on the gates and St Peter opens them.

"What do you want" asks St Peter.

"I am here for Jesus," says the Pakistani.

St Peter turns around and shouts, "Jesus, your taxi's here."

★ Three friends die in a car accident, and before they are allowed into Heaven, St Peter asks each of them one question. "When you are in your coffin and family and friends are grieving for you, what would you like to hear them say about you?"

The first man says, "I would like someone to say that I was a terrific doctor and a great family man."

The second man says, "I would like someone to say that I was a marvellous husband and a great school teacher who made a huge difference."

The third man replies, "I would just like to hear someone say: 'FUCK . . . HE'S MOVING!'"

★ ★ ★ ★ ★

HEATHER MILLS

❖ My gran always gets me socks for my birthday and Christmas. She says, "You can never have too many socks." You can if you're Heather Mills.

❖ I can't stand Heather Mills. I've tried, but she keeps falling over.

❖ Heather Mills has made her will. She is going to leave 90 per cent of her body to science when she dies. The other 10 per cent will go to IKEA.

❖ It's a very sad world we live in when all people seems to want to do is make jokes about Heather Mills' leg. Personally I think it's prosthetic.

❖ Paul McCartney once bought Heather Mills a new artificial leg for Christmas, but it wasn't her main present, it was just a stocking filler.

❖ Paul McCartney was interviewed on TV about his failed second marriage. He was asked: "Do you think you will ever go down on one knee again?"

   Paul replied: "Actually, I'd prefer it if you'd call her Heather."

❖ Heather Mills was given a plane as part of her divorce settlement. On her other leg she still uses Immac.

❖ According to new reports, Madonna paid out £50 million in her divorce settlement with Guy Richie. That's more than twice the amount Paul McCartney paid out to Heather Mills. She must be kicking herself.

❖ After another outburst on TV, a psychologist described Heather Mills as "clearly unbalanced". Later Sir Paul phoned in offering advice – a couple of beer mats under her left foot normally does the trick.

❖ What's the difference between Heather Mills and your car?
   You don't laugh every time your car has a breakdown.

❖ **Heather Mills: great tits, but totally shit at Twister.**

* * * * *

HITCHHIKERS

* A hitchhiker is standing by the roadside shouting abuse and making rude gestures at passing cars. Eventually a car slows down and stops and the driver says to him, "You'll never get a lift like that mate."

   "It's okay," says the hitchhiker. "I was on my lunch break."

∗ A long-haired youth was hitchhiking from a music festival. A lorry stopped and he got a ride from a mean-looking trucker. After riding about thirty miles in silence, the youth finally said, "Well, aren't you going to ask me?"

"Ask you what?" replied the lorry driver.

"If I'm a boy or a girl," answered the youth.

"Don't matter," replied the trucker. "I'm going to fuck you anyway."

∗ A trucker picks up a hitchhiker, who climbs into the cab and notices a monkey on the dashboard. After a few miles, he says to the driver, "What's the monkey for?"

The driver says "I'll show you," and with that he smacks the monkey with the back of his hand, sending it rolling across the dash. The monkey goes down between the drivers legs, unzips his pants, pulls out his prick and proceeds to give the trucker a blow job. When he's finished, the monkey zips him up again and jumps back up on the dashboard.

"See that?" says the trucker.

"Amazing!" says the hitchhiker.

"You want to try it?"

"Okay," says the hitchhiker. "But don't hit me as hard as you hit that monkey!"

★ ★ ★ ★ ★

HOMELESSNESS

❖ Two tramps were walking down the road and they see a squashed dead cat. One of them picks it and starts eating it. "Gross!" says the other, "I can't believe you're actually doing that!"

Twenty minutes later, his friend is on his hands and knees in the gutter, retching violently. His mate quickly gets down and starts gobbling up the puke.

"I thought you didn't eat dead cat!" says the first tramp.

"Well, no, not when it's cold I don't!"

❖ A homeless guy walks into a jeweller's shop, puts his hands down his trousers and starts fingering his arsehole. The sales assistant is aghast and shouts: "Oi! Stop what you're doing and get out!"

"You want to make your fucking minds up," replies the tramp indignantly. "You've a sign on the window says come inside and pick your ring in comfort."

❖ Knock, knock jokes. Completely wasted on the homeless.

❖ What's the best thing about dating a homeless female tramp?

It doesn't matter where you drop her off.

❖ Why did the homeless guy cross the road? To get to the other cider.

❖ A homeless guy is having a shag in the cemetery. Another homeless guy comes along and says, "Oi, can I have a go?"

"No," he replies. "Fuck off and dig your own up."

❖ A pub landlord is shutting up for the night when there is a knock at the door. When he answers, a tramp asks him for a toothpick. The landlord obliges and the tramp leaves. A few minutes later there is a second knock. When he answers, there is a second tramp who also asks for a toothpick. He gets his toothpick and off he goes.

There is a third knock at the door and a third tramp. The landlord says, "Don't tell me, you want a toothpick."

"No, a straw," says the tramp.

The landlord gives him a straw but is curious as to why he wants it.

The tramp replies, "Some bloke just threw up outside. But all the good stuff's already gone."

❖ I went out for a walk last night and I came across a tramp. It was cheaper than paying a prostitute.

❖ Two tramps are walking down the street when one of them starts sniffing the air. He says to the other tramp, "Have you shit your pants?"

The other tramp replies, indignantly, "No!"

The first tramp says, "Are you sure?"

"Yes!"

"Pull your pants down and let me see."

So he pulls his pants down and reveals that they are full of shit.

"See, I told you you had shit yourself!" says the first tramp.

"Oh, right," says his mate. "I thought you meant today."

❖ A tramp finds a £5 note in the gutter, so he takes it to the off-licence and buys himself a bottle of white wine. After knocking back the plonk, the tramp collapses in a drunken stupor in a small alleyway.

About ten minutes later a passing homosexual happens upon the sprawled body of the tramp. The quick-thinking fudge-packer whips down the tramps trousers and gives him a good seeing to. As the turd-burglar is just about to leave, he feels a pang of conscience and tucks a £5 note into the tramp's hand.

Upon waking up the next day, the tramp discovers the fiver. Hardly believing his good luck, he rushes back to the off-licence and purchases another bottle of white wine. Yet again he downs the plonk and falls into a drunken sleep in his favourite alleyway. A little later the same player-of-the-pink-oboe passes the alleyway and spies the tramp. Unable to contain himself, the arse bandit divests the tramp of his shitty boxer shorts and gives him another seeing to. Again he leaves £5 out of guilt for his actions.

Upon waking up, the tramp discovers another fiver in his hand and so makes his way back to the off-licence. The sales assistant sees him enter the shop and automatically reaches for the usual bottle of cheap white wine. To which the tramp responds, "No thanks, I'll have a bottle of red."

"Why the change?" the assistant enquires.

The tramp says: "I like the white wine, but Christ, it doesn't half make your ring piece sore."

❖ Two tramps were sitting in McDonald's when one them caught of a whiff of something foul. He asks the other; "Did you just shit yourself?"

"Oh, yeah," says the second tramp.

"Why don't you go and clean yourself up then?"

"I'm not finished yet."

❖ How do tramps connect wirelessly? Brown tooth.

❖ Two tramps were walking along the railway track one day when one tramp said to the other, "I'm the luckiest man in the world."

"How's that?" asked the other tramp.

"Well, I was walking down these tracks last week and I found a £20 note. I went into town and bought a case of wine and was pissed for three days."

The other tramp said, "Not bad, but I think I'm the luckiest man in the world. I was walking down these very tracks about two weeks ago when I found a gorgeous naked woman tied to the tracks. I untied her and took her up there in the woods and I had sex with her for two days."

"Jesus," said the first tramp. "Did you get a blow job as well?"

"Nope," the other tramp replied ruefully. "I never found her head."

❖ A tramp is weaving his down the main street of the town, blind drunk. Somehow he manages to stagger up the steps of a cathedral, where he goes inside and crashes from pew to pew, finally making his way to a side aisle and into a confessional.

A priest had observed all of this and he enters his side of the confessional. The priest sits in silence for a couple of minutes, then says, "I thought perhaps you could use some help, my son."

"I don't know," comes the drunk's voice from behind the partition. "You got any paper on your side?"

I was walking through the town centre the other day when this homeless guy asked me if I had any loose change. I gave him a penny: I figured it was the least I could do.

❖ I was in a very affluent part of London the other day when this homeless person came up to me. He said, "Sir, I haven't tasted food in a week."

"Don't worry," I reassured him. "It still tastes the same."

* * * * *

HOMOSEXUALS

★ Which is better, being born black or gay?
  Black, because you don't have to tell your parents.

★ How do you know if your best mate is gay?
  He gets an erection when you take him up the arse.

★ What do you call a gay bar with no bar stools?
  A fruit stand.

★ How do you know if you're at a gay barbecue?
  The hotdogs taste like shit.

★ How do you get four homosexuals on a bar-stool?
Turn it upside down.

★ Colin comes home one day and says to his room-mate, "Can you do me a favour please. It feels like something's stuck up my arse. Could you check it out for me?"

His room-mate lubes up his finger and shoves it up Colin's arse, has a good feel around, and says, "I can't find anything."

"Trust me," says Colin. "There's definitely something up there. Try lubing up your whole hand and checking it out."

So his room-mate lubes his whole hand and sticks it up. He feels around and then pulls out a Rolex watch.

"I found your problem. There was a watch stuck up your arse."

Colin starts singing, "Happy birthday to you, happy birthday to you . . ."

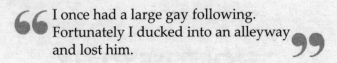

I once had a large gay following.
Fortunately I ducked into an alleyway and lost him.

★ Dr Watson is working away one day when suddenly he is hit on his head and becomes unconscious. When he wakes up, he is stripped naked and bent over a chair. Sherlock Holmes is squeezing a lemon and the juice is running all over his buttocks.

"Good grief, Holmes. What are you doing?" cries Doctor Watson.

"A lemon entry, my dear Watson, a lemon entry."

★ What do you call a gay man's scrotum?
Mud flaps.

★ Why do gay men wear ribbed condoms?
For traction in the shit.

★ How do you make a fruit cordial?
Say something nice about his shoes.

✶ What do you get when a homosexual gets Alzheimer's?

A bloke who spends all day wondering why his arse hurts.

✶   ✶   ✶   ✶   ✶

HONEYMOONS

✶ A man about to get married is confiding to his best man on his stag night. "You know, I don't think my bride is a virgin. She says she is, but I don't believe her."

"No problem," replies his friend. "There is an easy test for that. All you need is some red paint, some blue paint and a shovel. On your honeymoon, you paint one of your balls red and the other ball blue.

"How will that help?"

"When you get into bed, if she laughs and says they are the funniest bollocks she's ever seen, you simply hit the slag with the shovel."

✶ A couple returned from their honeymoon and it's obvious to their friends that all was not well. So the groom's best man took him aside and asked him what the problem is.

"Well," replied the newlywed guy, "when we had finished making love on the first night, when I got up to go to the bathroom, I put a £50 note on the pillow without thinking."

"Shit! That was bad!" said his friend. "All the same, don't sweat it. I'm sure your wife will get over it soon enough. She can't really expect that you have been saving yourself all these years!"

The groom nodded thoughtfully. "I still don't know if I can get over this though."

"What do you mean?" said his friend.

"Well, she gave me £20 change."

＊ After a whirlwind romance Frank decided to propose to his girlfriend, but before accepting his offer she thought she had to confess to her man about a childhood illness. She told Frank that she suffered a disease that left her breasts at the maturity of a twelve-year-old. Frank listened and, to her huge relief, replied it was okay – he loved her so much. Frank, however, felt this was also the right time for him to open up and admit to a secret he had kept from her. He looked her in the eyes and said: "I too have a deformity. My penis is the same size as an infant. I hope you can deal with that once we are married."

"Yes! Yes!" she cried. "I will marry you and learn to live with your infant-sized penis because I love you so much."

So Frank and his girl got married and they could barely wait for the honeymoon. Frank whisked her off to their hotel suite and they dived on the bed and started to tear at each other's clothes. She put her hands in Frank's pants, then began to scream uncontrollably and ran out of the room.

Frank ran after her. "What's wrong?" he asked her.

"You told me your penis was the size of an infant!"

"Yes, it is . . ." said Frank, "eight pounds, twelve ounces and nineteen inches long."

＊ A woman approaches her doctor for some advice. "Doctor, I'm getting married this weekend and my fiancée thinks I'm a virgin – which I am not. Is there anything you can do to help me?"

The doctor says, "Medically, no, but here's something you can try. On the wedding night, when you're getting ready for bed, take an elastic band and slide it up your upper thigh. When your husband puts it in, snap the elastic band and tell him it's the sound of your virginity going."

The woman takes his advice and after their wedding they retire to the honeymoon suite. The wife gets ready for bed in the bathroom, slips the elastic band up her leg, finishes preparing and climbs into bed with her man.

Just as he is reaching the vinegar strokes, she snaps the elastic band.

"What the hell was that?" yells her husband.

"Oh nothing, honey, that was just my virginity going."

"Well, can you ask it to come back, it's got my balls on the end of it!"

✳ A man met a woman on holiday and enjoyed a whirlwind romance. It was the best time of their lives. In a mad, impulsive moment he asked her to marry him right away.

"But we don't know each other at all, what if we don't get on?" she asked. The man replied that was a chance he was prepared to take: he had never felt that way about anyone before and was sure it would work and they could get to know each other during their marriage.

So the woman agreed and they were married. They were lazing by the poolside a couple of days later, when the husband said he fancied a dip. His new wife watched him as he climbed up to the very highest diving board and jumped off backwards. He did a triple somersault and double back-flip before entering the water with barely a ripple.

His wife was amazed and when he came back to her she clapped her hands and said: "That was amazing! I didn't know you could dive like that!"

He replied: "Yes, I used to be an Olympic high diver and I was the British champion for ten years running." They agreed that there was lots to learn about each other and that they were going to have loads of fun finding out.

Then the wife decided to go for a swim. She dived into the water, swam twenty lengths butterfly stroke, twenty lengths backstroke, twenty lengths crawl, then climbed out of the water and lay on her sun lounger, barely out of breath. Her husband was astonished. "I don't believe it! Were you an Olympic swimmer as well?"

"Nah," she replied. "I used to be a prostitute in Hull but I worked both sides of the river."

✳ After Brian proposed marriage to Jill, his father took him to one side. "Son, when I first got married to your mother, the first thing I did when we got home was to take off my trousers. I gave them to your mother and told her to try them on, which she did. They were huge on her and she said that she couldn't wear them because as they were too large. I said to her, 'Of course they are too big for you. I wear the trousers in this family and I always will.' Ever since that day, son, we have never had a single problem."

Brian took his dad's advice to heart. On his wedding night, as soon as he and Jill alone were alone, he took off his trousers and handed them to her and told her to try them on. She did as Brian had asked and said, "What is the point of this? I can't wear these, they're far too large for me."

"Exactly," Brian replied. "I wear the trousers in this family and I always will. I don't want you to ever forget that."

Then Jill took off her knickers and gave them to Brian. "Try these on," she said.

So Brian went along with it and tried them on, but they were far too small. "What's the point of this? I can't get into your knickers," said Brian.

"Exactly," Jill replied. "And if you don't change your fucking attitude, you never will."

A newly married couple are in the honeymoon suite. "Before we make love," said the bride, "I must tell you the truth. I've been hiding something from you." With that, she slipped off her wig, revealing her completely bald head.

"I don't have a problem with that, in fact I think it makes you look quite sexy," the groom replied.

"Wait, there is more," she said. She then removed wads of padding from her bra, slipped out her glass eye and removed her false leg.

With that, the groom walked towards the bedroom door.

"You're not leaving me, are you?"

"No, I'm going downstairs. Just throw it down when you are ready."

✳ A newlywed couple arrived at the hotel for the first night of their honeymoon. They cracked open a bottle of champagne and began undressing. When the bridegroom removed his socks, his new wife saw that his toes were all twisted and discoloured.

"What happened to your feet?" she asked.

"I had a childhood disease called tolio."

"Don't you mean polio?"

"No, tolio, it only affects the toes."

He then removed his trousers and revealed an awful looking pair of knees, all lumpy and deformed.

"What happened to your knees?" she asked.

"Well, I also had kneesles."

"Don't you mean measles?"

"No, kneesles, it only affects the knees."

Then he removed his underpants.

"Let me guess," said his wife. "Smallcox?"

★　★　★　★　★

HOTELS

★ A businessman found a card offering sexual services in a nearby phone box. Back in his hotel room he rang the number and a woman with a silky soft voice asked if she could be of assistance. "Yes," he said. "I'd like a doggie in bondage gear, leather, PVC, whips, the lot. And then some hardcore spanking, rounded off with a blow job. What do you think?"

The woman replied, "That sounds really good. But if you press nine first, sir, you'll get an outside line."

★ I asked the hotel receptionist for a wake-up call. She rang my room and said, "What the fuck are you doing with your life?"

★ A vicar was staying overnight in a hotel and before he went to sleep for the night, he had a look at the Gideon Bible in the bedside drawer. The following morning he was awoken by the maid with a cup of tea.

"Good morning, dear," said the vicar. "Fancy a quick shag?"

"But you're a man of the cloth," said the maid. "That can't be right!"

"It's perfectly all right, dear," replied the vicar. "I assure you, it says so in the Bible!" So the maid hopped into bed with the vicar. When it was over she got out of the bed and said: "I trust you, reverend, but I would feel better about this if you showed me the passage in the Bible where it says it's all right."

The vicar opened the bedside table drawer, took out the Gideon Bible and opened it. Someone had written on the inside cover: "Ask the maid if she fancies a fuck. She usually does."

★ A newly married couple show up at a hotel and ask for the honeymoon suite.

"Do you have reservations?" enquires the receptionist.

"Just the one," replies the groom. "She doesn't take it up the arse."

★ A man and his wife and two children book into a family room in a hotel. The man says to the hotel receptionist, "I hope the porn in my room is disabled."

The receptionist replies, "No it's just the regular porn, you sick bastard!"

★　　★　　★　　★　　★

HUNTING

✴ Bill asks his friend Derek if he fancies a spot of duck hunting. Derek says to Bill, "I'll send my dog out to see if there are any ducks out in the pond. If there aren't any ducks out there, I'm not going hunting." So he sends the dog out to the pond. The dog comes back and barks twice. Derek says, "Well I can't be bothered to go out. He only saw two ducks out there."

Bill says, "Hang on a minute, you're relying on the dog to count how many ducks there are out there? You have to be joking."

So Bill goes to look for himself and, lo and behold, there are just a couple of ducks. When he gets back he says to Derek, "I don't believe it. Where did you get that dog? There really are only two ducks out there!"

Derek says, "Well, I got him from the breeder up the road. If you want, you can get one from him, too."

So Bill goes to the dog breeder and says he wants a dog like the one his friend Derek has. The breeder obliges and Bill brings the dog home, tells it to go out and look for ducks. Minutes later the dog returns with a stick in its mouth and starts humping Bill's leg. He takes the dog back to the breeder and complains, "This dog is a fraud. I want my money back!"

The breeder asks Bill what the dog did exactly. Bill explains that when he sent the dog out to look for ducks, it came back with a stick in its mouth and started humping his leg.

The breeder says, "I see. He was just trying to tell you that there are more ducks out there than you can shake a fucking stick at."

A hunter was walking through the woods when he discovered a naked woman stretched out on the ground. He said to her, "Excuse me, madam, are you game?"

"I certainly am," she replied with a knowing wink.

So he shot her in the tits.

★ A big-game hunter walked in the bar and started bragging to everyone about his hunting skills. Not only was he a good shot, he claimed that if he was blindfolded he could recognize any dead game bird or animal pelt simply by feel. Not only that, if he could locate the bullet hole, he could even tell them what calibre the bullet was that killed the animal.

The barman challenged him to put his money where his mouth was, so the hunter agreed to prove his skills if the other customers put up the drinks, and so the bet was on. They blindfolded him carefully and took him to his first item. After feeling it for a few moments, he said "Hare." Then he felt around for the bullet hole and added, "Shot with a .308 rifle." He was dead right.

They brought him another skin, one that someone had in their car boot. He took a bit longer this time and then said, "Deer, shot with a 7-mm rifle." He was right again. For the rest of the evening he proved his skills again and again, every time against a round of drinks. Finally he staggered home, blind drunk and fell into bed. The next morning he got up with a sore head and when he looked in the bathroom mirror found that he had one hell of a shiner.

He said to his wife, "I know I was pissed last night, but not so pissed that I got in a fight I don't remember it. Where did I get this black eye?"

His wife angrily replied, "I gave it to you. You got into bed and woke me up by putting your hand inside my knickers. Then you stuck three fingers inside me and shouted, "Skunk, killed with an axe."

★ A man went out hunting with a double-barrelled shotgun. As he was climbing over a fence, he dropped the gun and it went off, shooting him directly through the genitalia. When he came round from surgery several hours later, he found that the doctor had done what appeared to be a very satisfactory job of repairing the damage. He thanked the doctor profusely and as he was getting ready to go home, the doctor gave him a business card. "This is my brother's card. I'll make an appointment for you to see him."

The farmer asks: "Is your brother a specialist?"

"No," the doctor replies, "he plays the flute. He'll show you where to put your fingers so you don't piss in your eye."

★ Two men are out in the woods hunting, when one of them collapses. He doesn't appear to be breathing and his eyes are glazed. His friend takes out his mobile phone and calls the emergency services. He gasps: "My friend is dead! What can I do?"

The operator says: "Calm down, I can help. First, let's make sure he's dead."

There is a silence, then a gunshot is heard. Back on the phone, the guy says: "Okay, now what?"

HURRICANE KATRINA

❖ How do you get thousands of poor people out of New Orleans before a flood?
  You don't.

❖ Which part of New Orleans was the first to surrender to the Hurricane Katrina flood waters?
  The French Quarter.

❖ The FBI say that they have proof that Al-Qaeda was responsible for the New Orleans floods. They are stepping up their hunt for a Suicide Plumber.

❖ Why are hurricanes normally named after women? When they come they're wild and wet, but when they go they take your house and car with them.

❖ A black guy swims into a bar . . .

★ ★ ★ ★ ★

ICE CREAM

✳ A man walks past an ice-cream shop that advertises, "Every flavour ice cream in the world."

"Bullshit," thinks the man and walks in. "Okay, give me three scoops of cunt-flavoured ice cream, please."

"No problem, sir," replies the assistant, giving the man three scoops of ice cream in a cone.

"This doesn't taste like cunt, it tastes like shit!" says the man, grimacing.

The assistant replies, "Of course it does. Try taking shorter licks."

❝ I went to make a purchase from the ice-cream van the other day and found the vendor lying dead on the floor of his van, covered in hundreds and thousands. Apparently he topped himself. ❞

* A paraplegic goes to an ice-cream van. The vendor asks him what flavour he'd like. "It doesn't matter" the customer replies: "I'm going to drop it anyway."

INCEST

* A teenager and his twin sister were approaching their end-of-term school prom night and neither of them had a date. So one day, the girl approached her brother and said, "You got a date for the prom yet?"

"No, why? Have you got someone lined up for me?"

"Not exactly. Why don't you take me?"

"Take you? You have to be joking, you're my sister!" he grimaces.

"Well, are you taking somebody else out?"

"You know I don't have a date, sis."

"Neither do I. But we both want to go to the prom, don't we? So we should go with each other."

The brother can't see anything wrong with her reasoning, so he told his sister that if neither of them has a date by Wednesday evening, he would take her to the prom. Wednesday evening rolled around and neither sibling had a date, so the brother told his sister that he'd take her to the prom on Friday.

At the dance, both of them have a great time. The brother was glad that his sister talked him into taking her. Then, while he was standing at the bar, his sister said, "Hey, bro, let's dance."

He looked around to make sure that nobody heard her, "Look, sis, I'm not going to dance with my own sister at the prom, okay?"

"Don't be so shy. Look, John is dancing with his cousin. So why can't you dance with your sister?" The brother reluctantly agreed, and they danced a slow number. The rest of the prom passed and it was time for them to go.

Both of them have had a good time. In the car, the sister looked over at her brother at the wheel and said, "I don't want to go straight home."

He gave her a curious look. "What did you have in mind?"

"Oh, I don't know. Just drive around."

He agreed, and after they had driven around a while, she looked over at him again and said, "Want to find some place to park?"

"Jesus!" said the brother, "Are you mad? You're my sister, I'm not parking up somewhere with you!"

"Who said anything about parking up? Let's just pull over somewhere and talk for a while, okay? It's been a busy year for both of us; how long has it been since we've had a chance to talk to each other?"

So she finally talked her brother into pulling the car over on a secluded back road, and after a few minutes of idle talk, she looked over at him again.

"Why don't you kiss me?"

"You've been suggesting a lot of weird things lately, you know that? I'm not going to kiss you, you're my sister!" And he reached for the ignition switch to start the car.

She reached out and took his hand. "I know I'm your sister. And you're my brother. So we love each other, right? So why shouldn't we kiss if we feel like it?" She kissed him on the cheek and he kissed her back. After a few minutes of kissing, she whispered in his ear, "Come on. Let's do it."

"Do what?" said her brother, already knowing full well what his sister had in mind. "You know what," his sister replied.

"I can't do that with you, you're my . . ."

His voice trailed off. While he was on top of her, his sister whispered "You know, you're a lot lighter than dad."

"I know," said her brother. "Mum told me."

★ My daughter has reached that age where she is asking embarrassing questions about sex. For example, only this morning she asked me: "Is that the best you can do?"

★ How do you circumcise a boy from Norwich?

Kick his sister in the face.

★ A Londoner is sitting down in a bar next to a guy from Norwich. After too many beers, the Londoner says, "Is it true that everyone from your neck of the woods dates their own cousins?"

The guy from Norwich reacts with fury. "That's a fucking malicious lie made up by you cockney bastards just to poke fun at people from Norwich!"

He went on "I've lived in Norwich all of my life and never once dated my cousin. Oh, I fucked her a few times . . . but I NEVER took her anywhere first!"

I'll never forget the day I had consensual sex for the very first time without paying for it. It was a little bit embarrassing because afterwards I threw money on the mattress out of habit. Afterwards she told me I didn't have to pay, but I said, "Just keep the money, mum, you can put it towards my half of the rent this month."

★ Did you hear about the bisexual German? He went down on his Hans and niece.

★ Why is non-alcohol lager like licking your sister's vagina?

It tastes roughly the same but you know it just isn't right.

★　★　★　★　★

INFIDELITY

❖ I came home from the pub one night and said to the wife, "You know what? I heard our milkman has slept with every woman in this street except one."

"It wouldn't surprise me," she replied. "I bet it's that stuck-up bitch from number 109."

❖ A man calls his home from work to tell his wife he's working late. A strange woman answers.

He says, "Who is this?"

"This is the maid," answers the woman.

"We don't have a maid!"

"I was just hired this morning by the lady of the house."

"Well, this is her husband. Is she there?"

"Umm . . . she's upstairs in the bedroom with someone who I just figured was her husband."

The man is fuming. He says to the maid, "Listen, would you like to make yourself a lot of money?"

"Sure, what do I have to do?"

"I want you to get my gun from my desk in the back room then go upstairs and shoot that bitch and whoever she is with."

The maid puts down the phone. The man hears footsteps, followed by two gunshots. The maid comes back to the phone.

"What do you want me to do with the bodies . . . throw them in the swimming pool?"

"What? We don't have a swimming pool! Hang on – is this 01785—?"

❖ A man came home a day early from a business trip and found his wife in the bedroom in the middle of a passionate lovemaking session with a complete stranger in their bedroom. He demanded: "What the hell's going on?"

His wife turned to the other man and said, "See, I told you he was a stupid cunt."

❖ A man woke up on his fortieth birthday feeling old and depressed. He went downstairs for breakfast, hoping his wife would cheer him up by saying, "Happy Birthday!" and perhaps have a small present for him.

As it turned out, she barely said a word and all but ignored him. He thought to himself, "Well, that's fucking marriage for you . . . but the children, they will remember."

In the event his kids came downstairs to breakfast and didn't say a word. So he left for the office, feeling low and rather despondent.

As he walked into his office, his attractive young secretary Sally said brightly, "Good Morning Boss, Happy Birthday!"

It cheered him up no end that at least someone had remembered. Later that morning his secretary knocked on his door and said, "Boss, It's such a beautiful day outside and it is your birthday, what do you say we go out to lunch, just you and me."

Things were definitely picking up! He said, "Thanks, Sally, that's the nicest thing I've heard all day. Let's go!" So they went to lunch at a quiet little restaurant with a private table where they shared a bottle of wine and a lovely meal. On the way back to the office, Sally leaned over and whispered, "You know, It's such a beautiful day, we don't need to go straight back to work, do we, boss?"

He responded, "I guess not. What do you have in mind?"

She said, "Let's drop by my apartment, it's just around the corner."

After arriving at her apartment, Sally turned to him and said,

"Boss, if you don't mind, I'm going to step into the bedroom for just a moment. I'll be right back."

"Okay," he nervously replied. She went into the bedroom and, after a couple of minutes, she came out carrying a huge birthday cake – followed by his wife, two kids, and fifteen of his friends and co-workers, all singing "Happy birthday".

He just sat there, on the sofa, sobbing, naked and erect . . .

❖ A man comes home early from work one evening to find his best friend in bed with his wife. Overcome by fury, he stabs him to death. His wife looks at him and shakes her head. "Keep that up, and pretty soon you'll have no mates left!"

❖ An angry wife met her husband at the door. There was alcohol on his breath and lipstick on his collar. "I assume," she snarled, "that there is a very good reason for you to come waltzing in here at six o'clock in the morning?"

"Yes there is," he replied. "Breakfast."

★   ★   ★   ★   ★

THE INTERNET

❖ I joined an online dating agency but my profile keeps getting rejected.

Apparently, "My dick" is not an acceptable answer to the question "What do you want most in a woman?"

❖ A man joins an online dating agency and winds up going out on several dates that are very disappointing. So he emails the agency to complain. "Have you got someone on your books who doesn't care what I look like or what job I have and has a nice big pair of tits?"

The reply comes back, "Yes, we do have one. It's you."

I met this thirteen-year-old girl in an internet chat room. She was clever, funny, flirty and sexy, so I suggested we meet up. Turns out she is an undercover detective. How cool is that for a thirteen-year-old!

* I met an incredible girl on the internet: smart, sexy and uninhibited. Of course, it turned out to be a fifty-five-year-old bloke. Frankly, the sex was disappointing.

* I was surfing the net when I came across an old flame on Friends Reunited. It had been years since we'd spoken and it really was great to catch up. We were getting on well and she suggested that we should meet up for old times' sake. I was up for it and we arranged to meet up the following week. I can't tell you how nervous and excited I was as my 'date' drew nearer. Now, to be honest, I'd let myself go a bit over the years and so thought I'd come clean. I phoned her and said "It's only fair to warn you that I'm probably not quite how you remember me. I've lost most of my hair and have been indulging a little too much in the good life."

To which she started to laugh and then said to me, "Oh, don't worry! I've put on a few pounds myself!" Naturally I told her to fuck off.

* I got an email today from a "bored housewife, thirty-ish, looking for some action!" So I sent her my washing. That will keep the bitch busy.

Ten Signs That Your Partner is Having an Online Affair

1 She sits at the computer naked.
2 After signing off, he always has a cigarette.
3 The giant rubber inflatable disk drive.
4 In the morning the computer screen is fogged up.
5 He's become amazingly good at typing with one hand.
6 Every day, Bill Gates sends $10 million worth of flowers.
7 The jam in the laser printer is a pair of knickers.
8 During sex, she screams: "A COLON BACKSLASH ENTER INSERT!!!!"
9 The fax file is filled with pictures of some guy's arse.
10 Lipstick on the mouse.

IRISHMEN

★ An Irishman tried to mug an old-aged pensioner. He said, "Give me all your money now, bitch, or you're geography."
"Don't you mean history?" she replied.
He said, "Don't try to change the subject."

★ Where does an Irish family go on holiday?
A different bar.

★ Two Irish couples decide to spice up their sex lives by swapping partners.
Paddy says later: "That was fucking great. I wonder how the girls got on."

★ An Irishman pulls alongside a lorry and shouts "Oi, driver! You're losing your load!"

The lorry driver ignores him. Five miles further along, Paddy again shouts "Oi, you're losing your load!' Yet again, the lorry diver ignores him.

Five miles further along, Paddy yells "I'm not joking! Honestly, you are losing your load!"

Finally, the lorry driver pulls up, climbs out of his cab and walks over to Paddy's window and says: "Fuck off. I'm gritting!"

★ Two Irishmen were walking along a river bank when they saw a crocodile with a man's head sticking out of its mouth. One said to the other: "Will you look at that flash fucker with the crocodile skin sleeping bag."

★ A very attractive young female speech therapist was working with a group of stammerers, with absolutely no success, despite having tried every technique in the book. Finally, out of desperation, she has an idea. "If any of you can tell me the name of the town where you were born, without stuttering, I'll have wild and passionate sex with you. So, who would like to go first?"

A number of hands shoot up. She invites an Englishman to start the ball rolling. "B—b—b—b—b—b—b—irmingham," he volunteers.

"Sorry, Michael," says the speech therapist, "No sex for you, I'm afraid. Who's next?"

A Scotsman raises his hand and blurts out, "P—p—p— p—p—p—p—aisley."

"That's not much better, Angus. How about you, Seamus?" The Irishman takes a deep breath and eventually blurts out, "London."

"Brilliant, Paddy!" says the speech therapist, and they retire to an adjacent room to keep her promise. After half an hour of hot, steamy sex, the Irishman comes up for air and says, ". . . d—d—d—d—d—d—d—d—erry."

★ An Irish family is sitting in the living rom. The wife turns to the husband and says, "I know, let's send the kids out to P-L-A-Y so we can fuck."

★ How do you get a one-armed Irishman out of a tree?
  Wave at him.

★ Did you hear about the Irish family who froze to death outside a theatre in Dublin?
  They had been queuing for three weeks to see "Closed For The Winter".

Ten Reasons Why it is Really Great to Be Irish

1 Guinness.
2 You have fifteen children because you are not allowed to use contraceptives.
3 You can get into a fight just by marching down someone's street
4 Pubs never close.
5 You can cite Papal edicts on contraception to persuade your girlfriend that you can't have sex with a condom on.
6 No one can ever remember the night before.
7 You get to shoot people in the knees who you don't agree with.
8 Stew.
9 More Guinness.
10 Eating stew and drinking Guinness in an Irish pub after a bout of sectarian violence.

★ A local radio station in Belfast held a competition. Listeners were invited to suggest words that weren't in the dictionary, but could still be used in a sentence that would make sense. The winning prize was an all-inclusive two-week holiday in Spain.

DJ: Radio Belfast here, what's your name?
Caller: Hi, my name's Colin.
DJ: Hi, Colin, what's your word?
Caller: Goan . . . spelled G-O-A-N, pronounced "go-an".
DJ: You're correct, Dave. "Goan" is not in the dictionary. Now, for that trip to Spain: what sentence can you use that word in where it would make sense?
Caller: Goan fuck yourself!
The DJ immediately cut the man off and took other calls from listeners, none of which were successful.
DJ: Radio Belfast here, what's your name?
Caller: Hi there, me name's Dave.
DJ: Hi, Dave, so what's your word?
Caller: Smee . . . spelled S-M-E-E, pronounced "smee".
DJ: That works, Dave, "Smee" is not in the dictionary. Now, for that trip to Spain: what sentence can you use that word in where it would make sense?
Caller: Smee again . . . goan fuck yourself.

★ Seamus and Paddy are walking home after a night on the ale. They have no money left to get a taxi and have missed their last bus home. They find themselves staggering past the bus depot. Paddy has a brainwave. "Seamus, get in there and steal a bus. I'll stay out here and keep lookout."

So Seamus climbs over the wall into the bus depot. Twenty minutes later, Paddy is standing there like a prick, wondering what the hell his mate is doing. Eventually Paddy climbs over the wall as well and sees Seamus running from bus to bus looking at the numbers on the front.

"What the feck are you doing?" says Paddy.

Seamus replies, "I can't find a number 32 anywhere, Paddy."

"You feckin' idiot," says Seamus. "We'll just steal a number 30 to the roundabout and walk the rest of the way."

★ Ireland's worst ever air disaster occurred early this morning when a small two-seater Cessna plane crashed into a cemetery. So far the body count is 1,267 and rising.

★ Two men are sitting next to each other at a bar. After a while one looks at the other and says, "Excuse me, but I couldn't help overhearing just now and I'm guessing from your accent that you're from Ireland."

The other guy responds proudly, "Yes, that I am at that."

The first man says, "So am I. And where about from Ireland might you be?"

The other man answers, "I'm from Dublin, I am."

The first guy responds, "Sure, and so am I. And what street did you live on in Dublin?"

The other man says, "A lovely little area it was. I lived on McCleary Street in the old central part of town."

The first man says, "Bejesus, it's a small world, so did I. And to what school would you have been going?"

The other man answers, "Well now, I went to St Mary's, of course."

The first man gets really excited and says, "And so did I. Tell me, what year did you leave school?"

The other man answers, "Well, let's see, I left school in 1964."

The first guy shouts: "The Good Lord must be smiling down upon us! I can hardly believe our good luck at winding up in the same bar tonight. Can you believe it, I graduated from St Mary's in 1964 my own self!"

At this the barmaid walks over to the bartender, shaking her head and muttering. "It's going to be a long night tonight," she says.

He replies, "Why do you say that?"

"The Murphy twins are pissed again."

★ What do you call three Irishmen in a ditch? A sleep over.

⭐ Ireland declares war on France. The French President, little Nicolas Sarkozy, is sitting in his office, sipping a Martini and tickling wife Carla's bum, when his telephone rings.

"Hello there, Mr Sarkozy," says a voice at the other end. "This is myself Paddy, down in County Clare, Ireland. I am ringing to inform you that we are officially declaring war on you!"

"Well, Paddy," little Sarkozy smirks, "this is indeed terrible news! How big is your army?"

"Right now," says Paddy "there is myself, my cousin Seamus, the next door neighbour Mick and the whole of the pub darts team. Hang on now . . . that makes eight of us!"

Sarkozy replies, "I have to inform you, Monsieur Paddy, that I have at my disposal a standing army of around 100,000 men."

"Bejesus!" says Paddy. "I'll call you back."

The following day *le petit* Sarkozy takes another call from Paddy. "Mr President sir, I'm calling you to tell you the war is still on. We have found some military equipment!"

"And what equipment would that be, Monsieur Paddy?" Sarkozy enquires.

"We have two combine harvesters, a bulldozer and a flat-bed truck."

Sarkozy replies: "I must tell you, Paddy, that I have 5,000 tanks and 3,000 armoured troop carriers. Also, I have increased my army to 150,000 since we last spoke."

"Fecking hell," says Paddy. "I'll have to get back to you."

Sure enough, Paddy rings again the next day. "Mr President, the war is still on! We have managed to get ourselves an air force. We have modified Shamus's ultra-light with a couple of shotguns in the cockpit. What's more, four lads from the pub down the road have agreed to join in.

Sarkozy stifles a laugh and replies, "I must tell you, Monsieur Paddy, that I have 100 bombers and 200 fighter planes. My military bases are surrounded by laser-guided, surface-to-air missile sites. By the way, since we last spoke, I have increased my army to 200,000!"

"Jesus, Mary and Joseph!" says Paddy, "I will have to ring you back."

Sure enough, Paddy calls again the next day. "Hello Mr President. I am sorry to inform you that we have had to call off the war."

"Really? I am sorry to hear that, Monsieur Paddy," says Sarkozy. "Why the change of heart?"

"Well," says Paddy, "we had a chat over a few pints of Guinness and decided there is no way we can feed 200,000 prisoners."

★ An Irishman walks up to the counter and says, "Can I have some Irish sausages please?" The assistant looks him up and down and says: "Are you Irish?"

The Irishman was indignant. "If I had asked you for Italian sausages, would you ask me if I was Italian?" he demanded.

"Well, no . . ."

"If I asked for German Bratwurst, would you ask me if I was German?"

"No."

Or if I asked you for a Kosher hot dog, would you ask me if I was Jewish? Or if I asked you for a taco, would you ask me if I was Mexican?"

"No."

"And if I asked you for frogs' legs, would you ask me if I was French? What about Danish bacon, would you ask me if I was Danish?"

"Well, no, I probably wouldn't," conceded the assistant.

The Irishman went on: "So why did you ask me if I'm Irish just because I asked for Irish sausages?"

"Because this is a library, sir."

★ How did the Irish acid-bath murderer lose his hand?

Pulling out the plug.

Mick and Paddy went down to the local river every Sunday morning to hire a boat and do a spot of fishing. One day they hit form and find themselves reeling in fish after fish. Mick turns to Paddy and says, "This is the perfect spot for fish. Quick, Paddy, put a mark on the side of the boat so we know where to come next week."

"Don't be such a fecking idiot," replies Paddy. "We might not get the same boat next time."

* * * * *

ITALIANS

❖ Did you hear about the half-Irish, half-Sicilian schizophrenic?

He made himself an offer he couldn't understand.

❖ Why do Italians whistle in the toilet?
So that they know which end to wipe.

❖ What would you call it when an Italian has one arm shorter than the other?
A speech impediment.

❖ What do you call an Italian man eating pussy?
Cunnilinguini.

❖ An old Italian guy went to his parish priest and asked if the priest would hear his confession.

"Of course, my son," said the priest.

"Well, father, during the Second World War, a beautiful woman knocked at my door one day and asked me to hide her from the Germans, so I hid her in my attic, and they never found her."

"You did a very wonderful thing, my son. This is nothing that you need to confess," said the priest.

"Hang on, father. It's worse. I was weak and told her that she had to pay for rent of the attic with her sexual favours," continued the old man.

"Well, it was a very difficult time and you took a big risk, my son," said the priest. "If the Germans had found you out, they would have tortured you and you would have suffered terribly. I know that God, in his wisdom and mercy, will balance the good and the evil, and judge you favourably."

"Thank you, father," said the old man. "That is a great load off my mind. Can I ask another question?"

"Of course, my son," said the priest.

The old man asked, "Do I have to tell her that the war is over?"

❖ Why is Italy shaped like a boot?

Because you couldn't get that much shit into a shoe.

❖ A black guy and a gorilla walk into a bar in Rome. The guy says to the barman, "I'd like a beer and a gin and tonic for my girlfriend here."

The barman says, "Sorry, pal, we don't serve gorillas in here."

So the guy takes the gorilla home, shaves off all her hair, gives her a nice wig, lipstick, red dress, etc. He takes her back to the bar and says, "I'd like a beer and a gin and tonic for my girlfriend here." The bartender gives them the drinks and they go off and sit down at a table.

The barman turns to a customer at the bar and says, "You know what drives me mad? Every time a good-looking Italian chick comes in here, she's with some black guy."

❖ How is the Sicilian version of Christmas different?
They have one Mary, one Jesus and twelve wise guys.

❖ Why don't Sicilians like Jehovah witnesses?
Nothing personal, they just don't like witnesses.

Ten Reasons Why it's Great to Be Italian

1 You have an in-depth knowledge of little-known pasta shapes.
2 You are not embarrassed to wear your jumper draped around your shoulders like a shawl.
3 No need to worry about tax returns.
4 Glorious military history prior to AD 400.
5 You wear sunglasses indoors.
6 A new government every other month.
7 Flexible working hours.
8 You live near the Pope.
9 You can spend hours braiding your girlfriend's armpit hair.
10 Your country is run by Sicilian murderers.

★   ★   ★   ★   ★

THE JAPANESE

* A Jewish American tourist is in a London bar watching a television documentary about the Japanese attack on Pearl Harbour. The narrator says: "On 7 December 1941, the Imperial Japanese Navy launched an unprovoked air attack on Pearl Harbour in Hawaii." The Jew shakes his head and stares into his beer.

   The narrator continues: "A third of the US Fleet was destroyed in the single worst attack of the Second World War." The Jew shakes his head again.

   "Twenty-five thousand American men and women died that day, some of them burned beyond recognition." By now, the Jew, much the worse for drink, is fighting mad and wants to vent his anger. He turns round and sees a little oriental-looking guy on a bar stool at the end of the bar. He runs over and punches the oriental-looking bloke in the face, knocking him off his stool. The guy picks himself off the floor and says, "What the hell was that for, you fucking idiot?"

   "That was for Pearl Harbour!"

   "You stupid bastard, that was the Japanese, I'm Taiwanese!"

   The Jew replies, "Japanese, Chinese, Taiwanese, same difference. You're all slanty-eyed yellow bastards!!" Feeling really proud of himself, he sits back on his stool and starts drinking his beer.

   The next moment, the Taiwanese bloke goes flying across the bar and plants a flying kung-fu-style kick on the side of the American Jew's head, sending him crashing into the wall.

   The Jew says, "What the fuck was that for, you slanty-eyed twat?"

   "That was for the Titanic!"

   "What the fuck are you on about? That was an iceberg!!"

   "Goldberg, Weinberg, Spielberg, Iceberg, same difference, you're all thieving Jew cunts!"

* What do the Japanese use for blindfolds?
   Dental floss.

✳ Why do Japanese people have slanted eyes?
   Because they're still squinting from the blast.

✳ Yamada Kaaru has been revealed as the only known survivor of both the Hiroshima and Nagasaki atomic bomb attacks. He has survived to the ripe old age of ninety-three and, although details of his medical history have been kept private, he is described as slightly deaf in one ear. The hearing in the other three is said to be very good.

✳ Stevie Wonder is playing his first gig in Tokyo and the place is rammed to the rafters. In a bid to break the ice with his new audience, he asks if anyone would like him to play a request. A little old Japanese man jumps out of his seat in the first row and shouts at the top of his voice, "Play a jazz chord! Play a jazz chord!"

   Amazed that this guy knows about the jazz influences in his long career, Stevie goes into a freeform jazz riff for about ten minutes. When he finishes the crowd goes wild, but the little old man jumps up again and shouts, "No, no, play a jazz chord, play a jazz chord."

   Stevie, being the professional that he is, dives straight into another jazz improvisation and really tears the place apart.

   The crowd really appreciates this amazingly complex technical improvisation, but the little old man jumps up again, "No, no. Play a jazz chord, play a jazz chord."

   Well and truly miffed that this little Japanese man doesn't seem to appreciate his technical expertise, Stevie calls to him from the stage, "Okay. You get up here and do it."

   The little old man climbs up on to the stage, takes hold of the mike and starts to sing . . . "A jazz chord to say I ruv you . . ."

✳ An American businessman is in Japan for a meeting. One night he gets drunk and solicits a Japanese prostitute. All the time he's having sex, the hooker keeps moaning, "Nagachi ana! Nagachi ana!" The businessman assumes that she is complimenting his technique and keeps banging away.

   The next day he is playing a round of golf with a few

Japanese business associates. One of the Japs tees off and lands a hole in one. The American, trying to impress his colleagues with his knowledge of Japanese, claps and shouts, "Nagachi ana!"

The Japanese businessman turns to him and says, "What the fuck do you mean, wrong hole?"

★　　★　　★　　★　　★

JEHOVAH'S WITNESSES

★ A man arrives at the gates of Heaven.

St Peter asks, "Religion?"

The man says, "Church of England."

St Peter looks down his list, and says, "Okay, go straight ahead to room twenty-four, but be very quiet when you go past room eight."

Another man arrives at the gates of Heaven. "Religion?"

"Catholic."

"Okay, go to room eighteen, but be very quiet as you pass room eight."

A third man arrives at the gates. "Religion?"

"Jewish."

"Okay. Go to room eleven, but be very quiet when you go past room eight."

"I can understand there being different rooms for different religions, but why must I be quiet when I pass room eight?"

St Peter tells him, "The Jehovah's Witnesses are in room eight. They think they're the only ones here."

What do you get when you cross a Tourette's sufferer with a Jehovah's Witness?

Someone who knocks on your door on a Sunday morning and tells you to fuck off.

Ten Ways to
Get Rid of a Jehovah's Witness

1 When they ask, "Can I talk to you about God?" reply, "Certainly, what would you like to know?"

2 Invite them in to see your fine collection of dinosaur fossils.

3 Answer the door with an automatic weapon and say, "Allah be Praised!"

4 Ask them for their address. When they ask why you want it, claim that you want to appear on their doorstop uninvited so that you can peddle your own beliefs.

5 Look smug and tell them that your God can beat up their God.

6 Tell them you already have your own religion. When they ask what it is, reply, "I'm not sure if it's legal in this country."

7 Make a chalk outline of a human body on your drive next to a copy of the *Watchtower*.

8 Answer every one of their questions with "What do you mean by that?" (Warning: this might take a while).

9 Ask them to explain the story of Elisha and the forty-two children.

10 Answer the door with a bloody knife and say, "I'm sorry, could you come back in half an hour? We're not done with the virgin yet."

★ Two Jehovah's Witnesses knock on the door of an elderly lady. She opens the door and they explain who they are and she lets them both inside.

She invites them to take a seat on her sofa and asks if they would like a cup of tea.

"Two teas without would be nice, please," they reply.

The old lady asks them if they would like a custard cream.

"Oh, yes please, that would be nice," they reply.

A few minutes later the old lady returns and places the tea and biscuits on the table, sits down and says: "So. What is it that you nice boys want to talk to me about?"

The Jehovah's look at each other for a while. Then one shrugs his shoulders and says to the old lady: "Buggered if we know, actually. This is the furthest we have ever got."

★   ★   ★   ★   ★

JESUS

❖ Jesus and St Peter go for a game of golf. St Peter steps up to the tee on a 120-yard par three and hits one long and straight. The ball bounces twice and rolls on to the green, leaving him a four-foot putt. Jesus is up next. He slices his shot. It flies over the fence, out of bounds and into traffic on an adjacent street. The ball bounces off a truck, on to the roof of a nearby conservatory and rolls into the rain gutter. The ball falls down the drain spout and rolls on to a lily pad in a garden pond. A frog jumps up and snatches the ball in his mouth. A kestrel swoops down and grabs the frog. As the kestrel flies over the green, the frog croaks and drops the ball. The ball rolls gently into the hole.

St Peter looks at Jesus, exasperated. "Are you going play golf?" he asks "Or are you just going to fuck around?"

❖ The three wise men arrive to visit the infant lying in the manger, bearing gifts of gold, incense and myrrh. One of the wise men, who is very tall, accidentally bumps his head on the low doorway as he leaves the stable. "Jesus Christ!" he exclaims.

Joseph says, "Write that down, Mary. It's better than Dave."

❖ It is the second coming of Christ. Before the world ends, he wants to take in some fishing, so he and his friend Moses head up to the lake to fish. They are about to rent a canoe when Moses says: "Jesus, can't you still walk on water? Why not just walk out there?" So Jesus takes his reel and tackle and steps on to the lake . . . and falls knee deep in water.

Moses says, "Well, maybe you need a head start or something, why not try it off the end of the dock."

So Jesus takes his reel and tackle, steps off the end of the dock and falls in the water up to his waist. Moses says, "Jeez, that's embarrassing. Tell you what, why not rent the boat, go out to the middle of the lake and try from there."

So they rent the boat and go to the middle of the lake. Jesus is about to step off and try again, when Moses says, "Hang on a minute. Just to be safe, why not get yourself into the state of mind you were in the first time you did it."

So Jesus sits down meditates for a few minutes. Finally he's all psyched up, and steps out of the canoe . . . and sinks to the bottom of the lake. Moses dives in and pulls Jesus up into the boat. He is really humiliated by this and just can't see what's going wrong. Moses just sits there staring down at the bottom of the boat. Suddenly, Moses says, "I got it! I know what's wrong! Did you have those holes in your feet last time?"

❖ **I know Jesus was a carpenter, but he never actually sang on any of their records.**

❖ Jesus came upon a small crowd who had surrounded a young woman they believed to be an adulteress. They were preparing to stone her to death.

To calm the situation, Jesus said: "Whoever is without sin among you, let them cast the first stone."

Suddenly an old woman at the back of the crowd picked up a huge rock and lobbed it at the young woman, scoring a direct hit on her head. The unfortunate young lady collapsed dead on the spot. Jesus looked at the old lady and said: "Mother, sometimes you are a real fucking embarrassment."

❖ Jesus and St Paul are sitting in Heaven discussing global warming, pollution and mankind's generally filthy ways. Jesus decides to pop down to see the situation for himself and asks Paul to join him. They go to the seaside and when they arrive, Jesus sees a huge metal pipe leading out to sea and asks what its purpose is. Paul explains that it is used to take human effluent out to sea, where the muck kills marine life. Jesus decides to take action and strides across the waves. Walking alongside, Paul is soon knee deep in shit, while Jesus scoots along imperiously on top of the water. Ever hopeful of some help, Paul slogs on while Jesus continues to walking on water. Soon the water is up to Paul's chin.

"Master," he calls, "I will follow you anywhere, but I'm up to my neck in shitty water and I think I'm going to drown."

At this Jesus stops walking and looks at Paul. "Well," he says, "why don't you just walk on the pipe like me, dickhead?"

Jesus was making his usual rounds in Heaven when he noticed a little white-haired old man sitting in a corner looking very disconsolate. He was saddened to see the old man looking so miserable so he stopped to talk to him.

"Old man," said Jesus gently, "this is Heaven. The sun is shining, you have all you could want here and you're supposed to be blissfully happy! What's wrong?"

"Well," said the old man, "you see, I was a carpenter on earth, and lost my only, dearly beloved son at an early age. And here in Heaven I was hoping more than anything to find him."

Tears sprang from Jesus' eyes. "FATHER!" he cried.

The old man jumped to his feet, bursting into tears, and sobbed, "PINOCCHIO!"

❖ An Irishman, an Australian and an Englishman are in a bar, and they notice Jesus sitting at a table in the corner, quietly drinking on his own. They each send him a drink over and he sips each one slowly.

When he's finished, Jesus walks over to the Irishman and shakes his hand and thanks him for the Guinness. "Bejesus, my arthritis has gone!" exclaims the Irishman.

Jesus then thanks the Aussie for the Fosters. "Christ, mate, my bad back's cured!"

Jesus approaches the Englishman, who runs away shouting, "Fuck off – I'm on disability benefit!"

★　　★　　★　　★　　★

JEWS

✳ Two Jewish businessmen meet in the street. "Abraham, I'm sorry to hear about that fire at your warehouse."

"Ssh!" hisses the other, looking over his shoulder. "It's not till next week."

They meet in the street again six months later. "Well, Abraham, how's your new warehouse business going?"

"Oi vey, it's not going so good, we had a flood last week."

"So," whispers his friend, "how do you start a flood?"

> An elderly Jewish lady is leaving her job in the clothing sweatshop and is on her way home. Suddenly a flasher blocks her path and opens up his raincoat. She takes a look and says, "This you call a lining?"

✳ What is the definition of a Jewish dilemma?
Free ham.

* A young Jewish boy goes to a new school in a small American mid-west town. The teacher asks the class, "Who was the greatest man that ever lived?"

  A girl raises her hand and says, "I think George Washington was the greatest man that ever lived because he is the father of our country."

  The teacher replies, "Well, that's a very good answer, but that's not quite the answer I am looking for."

  Another young student raises his hand and says, "I think Abraham Lincoln was the greatest man that lived because he freed the slaves and helped end the civil war."

  "Well, that's another good answer, but that is not quite the one I was looking for."

  Then the new Jewish boy raises his hand and says, "I think Jesus Christ was the greatest man that ever lived."

  The teacher's jaw drops in astonishment. "Yes!" she says, "That's the answer I was looking for." She then brings him up to the front of the classroom and gives him a lollipop.

  Later, during break time, another Jewish boy approaches him as he is licking his lollipop. "I can't believe you said 'Jesus Christ'?"

  The boy replies, "I know it's Moses and you know it's Moses, but business is business."

* ## Why do Jewish fathers have their sons circumcised?

  ## Because Jewish women can't resist anything with 10 per cent off.

* What is the difference between a Jewish mother and a rottweiler?

  The rottweiler will eventually let go.

* ## How do you say "fuck you" to a Jew?
  ## "Trust me!"

✳ What's a Jew's definition of embarrassment?

Running into a wall with a hard-on and breaking your nose.

✳ A Frenchman, a German and a Jew are lost in the desert and have been wandering for days.

The Frenchman says, "I'm tired and thirsty. I must have some wine."

The German says, "I'm tired and I'm thirsty. I must have a beer."

The Jew says, "I'm tired and I'm thirsty. I must have diabetes."

✳ Why do Jews have double-glazing?

So their kids can't hear the ice-cream van.

✳ An old Jewish guy has been hoping for years to win the lottery. One week, he goes to the synagogue and he prays: "Oh lord of Heaven and earth, imagine how much good I could do with the money if I won the lottery! Imagine how much charity I could give! Please Lord, help me win the lottery and I will use the money selflessly!"

The next week, he returns to the synagogue again and says, "Oh, lord of Heaven and earth, you must not have heard me last week! Imagine how many lives I could make easier with the money from the lottery! Please Lord, help me win the lottery!"

The following week, he goes to synagogue and prays again in a similar vein. Suddenly, he hears a voice from the heavens: "Help me, help me!"

The old Jew replies, "Lord of Heaven and earth, what can I do to help you?"

"Buy a ticket, motherfucker."

* How do you know if a family of Jews are living next door?
  There's wet toilet paper on their clothes line.

A Jewish guy is run over by a car. The paramedic arrives and says, "Are you comfortable?"
He replies, "I make a good living."

* Once upon a time long ago the mighty Emperor of Japan advertised for a new chief samurai. After a year, only three applied for the job: a Japanese, a Chinese and a Jewish samurai. "Demonstrate your skills!" commanded the Emperor.

  The Japanese samurai stepped forward, opened a tiny box and released a fly. He drew his ceremonial sword and, swish, the fly fell to the floor, neatly bisected in two matching halves.

  "Fantastic!" enthused the Emperor. "Samurai number two, show me your skills."

  So the Chinese samurai bowed, stepped forward and opened a tiny box, releasing a fly. He drew his ceremonial sword and, swish, swish, the fly fell to the floor neatly quartered.

  "That is indeed a formidable skill," nodded the Emperor. "How are you going to top that, samurai number three?" The Jewish samurai stepped forward, opened a tiny box, releasing one fly, drew his ceremonial sword and, swish, flourished it so mightily that it produced a gust of wind. The fly, however, was still buzzing around the room.

  "I am disappointed," said the Emperor. "What kind of skill is that? The fly isn't even dead."

  "Dead, schmead," replied the Jewish samurai. "Dead is easy. Now circumcision, that takes skill . . ."

* What's the difference between a Jew and a canoe?
  A canoe tips.

* What is the difference between karate and judo?

  Karate is a martial art, while judo is what bagels are made from.

* Two old Jewish ladies were shopping one afternoon when one says to the other, "Wish me good luck. My son finally met a girl and maybe they will get married. But the only thing I know about her is that my son says that she has Herpes. What is herpes?"

  Her friend replies, "I don't know, but I have a medical dictionary at home and I will look it up for you."

  The next day the ladies again meet. She says to her friend, "It's okay. You don't have to worry. Apparently It's a disease of the gentiles."

★   ★   ★   ★   ★

KINKY SEX

❖ A Scottish mate of mine is into heavy S&M. He likes nothing more than being beaten up by a vicious woman whilst naked and vulnerable. He told me he visits brothels for this several times a week.

  "Christ, that must cost you a fortune," I said.

  "Not a penny," he replied, "I just book a normal service, shag the arse off her, then tell her I haven't got any money."

❖ What do you call kinky sex with chocolate?

  S&M&M.

❖ What's the difference between kinky and perverse?

Kinky is using a feather, perverse is using the whole chicken.

❖ A man was arrested yesterday after being caught with his dick in the bank vault. He said he was only having safe sex.

❖ What's the best thing about kinky sex?

Wiping the blood off the hammer.

❖ Why do blow-up dolls make great lovers?

Because they always look shocked at the size of your cock.

❖ Vertigo fetishists. The bigger the fall, the harder they come.

❖ I was in the middle of an asthma attack the other day when I got an obscene phone call. Half way through the call, the guy at the other end paused and said, "Er . . . just remind me. Did I call you, or did you call me?"

❖ A man is sitting in a pub one evening on his own when he catches the eye of a beautiful woman at the far end of the bar. Eventually he musters the courage to go over and speak to her. "Hi, what brings a gorgeous lady like you here?" he asks

"I've broken up with my boyfriend, so I'm just sitting here drowning my sorrows. He said I was too dirty in the bedroom."

"Believe it or not, I'm here for the same reason. My girlfriend has just thrown me out, said I was too filthy as well!"

They sit drinking together for the rest of the evening. As she is about to leave, she asks if he'd like to come back to hers; he accepts. When they get back to her place, she motions to the sofa and says, "I'll be right back, I'm just going to slip into something more comfortable." She goes into the bathroom and gets out her strap-on dildo, anal beads, whip, gimp mask and a leather dominatrix outfit.

When she returns she sees the man heading towards the door. "Where are you going to?" she asks.

"Well," says the man, "I've fucked your dog and had a shit in your handbag – thanks, I'm off."

❖ My wife's back on the bottle. Apparently fisting just isn't the same.

❖ My friend was placed on the sex-offenders' list for simulating sex with a bicycle. He was bike curious.

❖ Why does Dr Pepper come in bottles? Because his wife is dead.

❖ Three women, one engaged, one married and one a mistress, were having a coffee and chatting about the state of their rather stale relationships. They decide to surprise their men that night, by wearing bondage-style leather bodices, stilettos and masks. A week later they meet again to compare notes.

The engaged girlfriend says, "The other night when my boyfriend came back home he found me with the leather bodice, six-inch stilettos and mask. He took one look at me and said: 'You are fantastic, I love you' – then we made passionate love all night long."

The mistress says, "Me too: the other night, I met my lover in the office and I was wearing the leather bodice, huge stilettos, mask over my eyes and a raincoat. When I opened the raincoat, he didn't say much . . . but we had wild sex all night."

The married woman says, "I sent the kids to stay at my mother's. I got myself ready: leather bodice, six-inch stilettos, mask, the works. My husband came back from work, opened the door and said: 'Okay, Batman, what's for dinner?'"

The other day the wife and me tried a new tantric sex position called "The Plumber". You stay in all day and nobody comes.

❖ My wife suggested we should play some sex games to spice up our sex lives.
   Unfortunately, "Guess who I shagged last night?" didn't go down very well.

★   ★   ★   ★   ★

LAWYERS

✳ A lawyer woke up in the middle of the night to find the devil standing at the foot of his bed. "What do you want?" asked the lawyer.
   "I have a proposition for you. You can win every case you ever take for the rest of your life. Your clients will adore you, your colleagues will stand in awe of you and you will make embarrassing sums of money. All I want in exchange is your soul, your wife's soul, your children's souls, the souls of your parents, grandparents, and parents-in-law, and the souls of all of your friends, and I want to have anal sex with your twelve-year-old daughter."
   "Okay," said the lawyer after a moment's thought. "So, what's the catch?"

✳ A lawyer walked into a doctor's surgery with a frog on his head. "That's a nasty looking growth," said the doctor.
   "I'll say," replied the frog. 'It started out as a small pimple on my arse."

✳ What is the difference between a dead lawyer and a squished badger in the road? Crows will eat the badger.

✳ A lawyer married a woman who had previously divorced ten husbands. On their wedding night, she told her new husband, "Please be gentle with me, I'm still a virgin."

"What?" said the astonished groom. "How can you possibly be a virgin? You told me you've already been married ten times?"

"It's true," she explains, "but I've been very unlucky in love. My first husband Ken was a sales rep. All he ever did was tell me how great it was going to be.

"My second husband Martin worked for a software company. He was never really sure how it was supposed to work, but he said he'd look into it and get back to me. My third husband Desmond was a field technician. He said everything checked out diagnostically but he just couldn't get the system up.

"My fourth husband Thomas was in customer services: even though he knew he had the order, he didn't know when he would be able to deliver. My fifth husband Fred was an engineer: he understood the basic process but wanted three years to research, implement and design a new state-of-the-art method.

"My sixth husband Bernard was in finance and administration: he thought he knew how, but he wasn't sure whether it was his job or not. My seventh husband Richard was in marketing: he had a decent product, but he was never sure how to position it. My eighth husband Roy was a psychologist: all he ever did was talk about it. Husband number nine was a gynaecologist: all he did was look at it. My tenth husband Tim was a stamp collector. God! I miss him! Anyway, now that I've married you I'm really excited!"

"Great, I'm pleased to hear it," said the new husband, "but why?"

"You're a lawyer. This time I know I'm going to get fucked."

✳ A big city lawyer went pheasant hunting in the Scottish lowlands. He shot and dropped a bird, but it fell into a farmer's field on the other side of a fence. As the lawyer was climbing over the fence to retrieve the game bird, an old farmer drove up on his tractor and asked him what he was doing.

The lawyer responded, "I shot a pheasant and it fell in your field. Now I'm going to get it back."

"No you're not," the old farmer replied. "This is my property and you are not coming over here."

The lawyer smiled. "I have to tell you that I am one of the best trial attorneys in the country and if you don't let me retrieve that bird, I will sue you and take everything you own."

The old farmer smiled back. "You don't how we settle disputes around these parts. We settle small disagreements like this with the 'Three Kick Rule'."

The lawyer asked, "What is the 'Three Kick Rule'?"

The farmer replied, "Well, because the dispute occurs on my land, I get to go first. I kick you three times, and then you kick me three times, and so on until one of us gives up."

The lawyer considered the proposed contest carefully and decided that he could easily take the old man. He agreed to abide by the local custom. The old farmer slowly climbed down from the tractor and walked up to the lawyer. His first kick planted the toe of his heavy steel-toed work boot into the lawyer's balls, dropping him to his knees. His second kick was to the midriff, causing the lawyer to throw up his last meal. With the lawyer helpless on all fours, spitting blood and vomit, the farmer's third kick to his rear end sent him face-first into a fresh cow pat.

Eventually the lawyer managed to pull himself to his feet. Wiping the blood and the puke from his face with the arm of his jacket, he said, "Okay, old man, now it's my turn."

The old farmer smiled and said, "Nah, you're all right, I give up. You can have the pheasant."

* A couple are on their way to get married when they are involved in a fatal head-on car crash. They find themselves sitting outside the pearly gates, waiting for St Peter to finish the paperwork so they can enter. "Excuse me," the man says to St Peter, "but we were on our way to get married when we were killed. Is there any chance we could finish what we set out to do and get married up here?"

"Hmmm. I don't know," says St Peter. "This is the first time anyone has ever asked. Let me go find out."

The couple sit waiting and begin to have second thoughts about whether or not they really should get married in Heaven, what with the eternal aspect of it all. What if it doesn't work out? Are they stuck together forever?

After a huge amount of time, St Peter returns, looking somewhat flustered. "Yes," he informs the couple, "you can get married in Heaven."

"Terrific," the couple respond. "But we have another question. What if things don't work out? Could we also get a divorce in Heaven?"

St Peter, clearly angered, petulantly throws his clipboard on to the ground.

"We're so sorry!" exclaim the anxious couple. "Did we say something wrong?"

St Peter exclaims, "It took me three months to find a priest up here! Do you have any idea how long it's going to take for me to find a fucking lawyer?"

* A woman went to her doctor for advice. She told him that her husband had developed a taste for anal sex and she was not sure that it was such a good idea. The doctor asked her, "Do you enjoy it?"

She said that she did. He asked, "Does it hurt you?" She replied that it did. The doctor then told her, "Well, then, there's no reason that you shouldn't practice anal sex, if that's what you like, so long as you take care not to get pregnant."

The woman was mystified. "You can get pregnant from anal sex?"

The doctor replied, "Of course. Where do you think lawyers come from?"

＊ What's the difference between a lawyer and a prostitute?
   The prostitute stops fucking you after you're dead.

＊   ＊   ＊   ＊   ＊

LEPERS

＊ How can you tell if a valentine card is from a leper?
   The tongue is still in the envelope.

＊ What did the leper say to the prostitute?
   Keep the tip.

＊ How do you get a leper out of the bath?
   With a sieve.

＊ Did you hear what happened when the leper ran into a screen door?
   He strained himself.

＊ What do you call a leper in a hot tub?
   Soup.

＊ What's the definition of self-destruction?
   A leper with epilepsy.

＊ What's green and melts in your mouth?
   A leper's dick.

★ How do you fit thirty-five lepers in a Mini?
  With a blender.

★ What do you do when a female leper bats her eyes at you?
  Catch them and shout, "You're OUT!"

★ Why was the leper hockey game called off?
  There was a face-off in the corner.

★ Did you hear about the man who picked up a leper at the gay bar?
  After he pulled it out, he got himself a nice piece of ass.

★ How do you make a skeleton?
  Put a leper in a wind tunnel.

★ **Why did the prostitute leave the leper colony?**
  Business was dropping off.

★ Which was the favourite Beatles tune in leper colonies?
  "Lend me your ear and I'll sing you a song . . ."

★ What is the best part of marrying a woman with leprosy?
  She can only give you lip once.

★ What sits in the kitchen and keeps getting smaller and smaller?
  A leper combing his hair with a potato peeler.

★ What do you call a leper in a jacuzzi?
  Stew.

★ **Did you hear about the leper who failed his driving test?**
  He left his foot on the clutch.

★   A leper wins a ticket to see the men's final at Wimbledon. When he gets there, he has trouble finding a seat because pieces of him are peeling and flaking off and he's deeply embarrassed. The leper wanders around centre court, looking for a seat where his grotesque appearance won't disturb anyone else. Finally he finds an end-of-aisle seat where he might be able to watch the game. He asks the man in the adjoining seat if it would be okay to sit there. The man answers, "No problem, mate. Just sit down and watch the game."

The leper sits down and says, "As you may have noticed, I have leprosy. If it bothers you, I will move."

"It doesn't bother me. Just shut up and watch the game."

A while later, during the fifth game, the man suddenly throws up.

Undigested strawberries and cream are splattered everywhere. Seeing this, the leper gets up and says, "Thank you for letting me to sit next to you, but I can see that my appearance has caused you to be ill. I will look for another place to sit."

The man finishes spewing up, wipes his mouth and says, "Look, mate, It's not you, I promise. Just sit down, shut up and watch the game."

So the leper sits back down. But during the second set the man begins to projectile vomit: a powerful blast of puke and bile emanates from this mouth and nose until his stomach is completely emptied. At this, the leper gets up and says, "Thank you for allowing me to sit next to you, but I can see that my appearance has caused you some distress. I will find somewhere else to sit."

"Honest, it's NOT you. Just shut up and watch the game."

So the leper sits back down. But during the third set, the man begins to throw up again. This time it is dry heaving of the most painful variety. The leper feels terrible at the sight of this man's obvious suffering and once again he offers to leave. But the man insists, "Really, it's NOT you."

So the leper asks, "Well if it's not me that is making you so ill, what is it?"

"It's that bloke behind you, pal. He keeps dipping his Doritos in your back."

★ Why was the leper unable to speak?
   The cat got his tongue.

★ Why do lepers make such good neighbours?
   They're always willing to lend a hand.

★ What's a leper's favourite chocolate bar?
   Flake.

★ What's small, green and falls apart?
   A leprechaun.

★ How do you know if a leper has been using your shower?
   The bar of soap is bigger.

★ ★ ★ ★ ★

LESBIANS

❖ What is the definition of confusion?
   Twenty blind lesbians in a fish market.

❖ What do you call a lesbian with long fingernails?
   Single.

A lesbian goes to see her gynaecologist. Upon examination, the doctor says, "It's immaculate in here, the cleanest vagina I ever saw. What do you do to keep yourself so hygienic?"

"Easy," she replies. "I have a woman in twice a week."

❖ What do you call it when two lesbians in wheelchairs are in the sixty-nine position?
 Meals on Wheels.

❖ What do you call a lesbian with big hands?
 Well hung.

❖ What do you call a group of lesbians in a field of dildos?
 Squatters.

❖ Science isn't all its cracked up to be. Okay, they've put a man on the moon, but they haven't managed to get one on Martina Navratilova.

❖ How does a lesbian asthmatic breathe?
 In snatches.

❖ A lesbian goes to a nutritionist with indigestion. The nutritionist advises, "It's simple. Basically, you are what you eat."
 She replies, "Are you calling me a cunt?"

❖ How many nails are used to make a lesbian's coffin?
 None: it's all tongue and groove.

❖ **A young boy comes home from school one day and says, "Mummy, mummy! What's a lesbian?"**
 "I'm busy," replies his mother. "Ask your father when she gets home."

❖ What pickup line does a lesbian use most?
 "Your face or mine?"

❖ What do you call a load of lesbians on top of each other?
 A block of flaps.

❖ **What do you call two lesbians in a canoe?**
   Fur traders.

❖ A man walks into a bar and orders ten double vodkas then downs them in one. The barman says, "That looks like serious business. What's the problem?"

   The man replies, "My youngest son has just informed me that he's gay."

   The next day the same man goes in and orders fifteen double vodkas and sinks them in one. "What happened?" asks the barman."

   "I just found out my eldest son is also gay," he replies.

   The next day he goes in and orders twenty double vodkas.

   "Christ!" says the barman. "Does no one in your family like pussy?"

   "Yes," he replies. "The wife, apparently."

❖ How can you tell if a lesbian is really butch?
   She kick-starts her vibrator and rolls her own tampons.

❖ What's the worst thing about catching your wife in bed with another woman?
   Who's in the kitchen?

   ❝ I saw a porno film called *Anal Lesbians* the other night. It was rubbish. They spent the entire film labelling everything in the fridge. ❞

❖ What do you call a lesbian with fat fingers?
   Well hung.

❖ If homosexuals come out of the closet, do lesbians come out of the pantry?

★   ★   ★   ★   ★

LIGHT BULB JOKES

✳ How many children with Attention Deficit Disorder does it take to change a light bulb?
   Want to play on my Nintendo?

✳ How many paranoiacs does it take to change a light bulb?
   Who wants to know?

✳ How many Jehovah's Witnesses does it take to change a light bulb?
   Three – one to change the bulb and turn it on, the other two bastards to knock on your door and ask if you've seen the light.

✳ How many mice does it take to screw in a light bulb?
   Two – the difficult bit is getting them in the light bulb in the first place.

✳ How many homosexuals does it take to screw in a light bulb?
   Only one, but it takes the entire A&E department to remove it.

✳ How many feminists does it take to change a light bulb?
   Two – one to change the light bulb and the other to suck my cock.

✳ How many sex therapists does it take to change a light bulb?
   Two – one to screw it in and one to tell him he's screwing it in the wrong way.

* How many Scousers does it take to change a light bulb?
All of them – one to change the light bulb, the rest of them to have a funeral for the old light bulb and all sign a book of condolences for it.

* How many Afghans does it take to screw in a light bulb?
Irrelevant – the electricity has been off for at least a year anyway.

* How many Ethiopians does it take to change a light bulb?
Three – one to change the light and two to eat the packaging.

* How many lepers does it take to change a light bulb?
Two – one to screw it in, and the other to give him a hand.

How many Jewish mothers does it take to change a light bulb?
None – "Don't worry about me. I'll just sit here in the dark. It's not like you care. You never write. You never call . . ."

* How many swingers does it take to screw in a light bulb?
Swingers don't screw in light bulbs, they screw in hot tubs.

* How many manic-depressives does it take to change a light bulb?
What does any of it matter? Who cares anyway?

* How many dyslexics does it take to change a light bulb?
Sixty-seven – one to hold the bulb and sixty-six to read the instructions.

✳ How many blind people does it take to change a light bulb?

I've no idea, but it's a great laugh watching them try.

✳ How many cocksuckers does it take to change a light bulb?
Shut up and keep sucking. You can change it after I've come.

✳ How many cancer victims does it take to change a light bulb?
None – they're too weak to climb the ladder.

✳ How many divorcees does it take to change a light bulb?

Four – one to cry, two to provide a supportive atmosphere and one to ring the ex-husband for instructions.

✳ One.
How many psychics does it take to change a light bulb?

✳ How many Amish people does it take to change a light bulb?
What light bulb?

✳ How many Alzheimer's patients does it take to change a light bulb?
To get to the other side.

✳ How many Freudians does it take to change a light bulb?

Two – one to unscrew the light bulb and the other to fuck my stepmother, sorry, hold the stepladder.

✳ How many Americans does it take to change a light bulb?
Depends if the bulb owns any oil reserves or not.

✳ How many Frenchmen does it take to change a light bulb?
Two – one to change it and one to hold a white flag just in case.

✳ How many Essex girls does it take to screw in a light bulb?
Chavs don't screw in light bulbs, they screw in pools of their own sick.

✳ How many lawyers does it take to change a light bulb?
You won't find a lawyer who can change a light bulb. However, if you're looking for a lawyer to screw a light bulb . . .

✳ How many surrealists does it take to change a light bulb?
A fish.

How many old people does it take to screw in a light bulb?
"In my day we didn't have light bulbs. We put candles in tin cans and hung them from the ceiling with thread. And we had to walk six miles to school in a blizzard with nothing but a potato to keep us warm . . ."

⁕ A man walks down the street and on the way he meets a friend, who happens to have only one arm. "So, what are you up to?"

"I'm going to change a light bulb."

"Won't that be difficult, with just the one arm?"

"Not really. I've still got the receipt."

★   ★   ★   ★   ★

LIMERICKS

★ There was a young widow from Kent
With a cunt of enormous extent
And so deep and so wide,
The acoustics inside
Formed an echo whenever you spent.

★ There was a young fellow called Howell
Who buggered himself with a trowel.
The triangular shape
Was conducive to rape,
And easily cleaned with a towel.

★ There once was a man from Bombay
Who made a fake cunt out of clay.
He stuck in his dick
But the thing turned to brick
And chafed his foreskin away.

★ There was a young man from Harrow,
Who had a dick as big as a marrow.
He said to his tart
"Try this for a start.
My balls are outside on a barrow."

★ There was a man from Mauritius
Who said his last fuck was delicious
But the next time I cum
It'll be up your bum
Cos that scab on your clit looks suspicious.

★ There once was a young man from Sparta
Who was a magnificent farter.
On the strength of one bean
He'd fart, "God Save the Queen"
And Beethoven's Moonlight Sonata.

★ There once was a girl called Louise
Whose pubes hung down to her knees.
So the crabs in her twat
Tied her hairs in a plait
And constructed a flying trapeze.

★ There once was a rector from King's
Whose mind was on heavenly things.
But his heart was on fire
For this boy in the choir
Whose arse was like jelly on springs.

★ There was an old woman from Leeds
Who swallowed a packet of seeds.
In less than an hour
Her tits were in flower
And her cunt was covered in weeds.

★ There was a young lady from China
Who had an enormous vagina
And when she was dead
They painted it red
And used it for docking a liner.

★ There was a young gaucho called Bruno
  Who said, "There's one thing I do know.
  A woman is fine,
  A boy is divine,
  But a llama is numero uno."

★ There was a young girl called Dolores
  Whose fanny was covered in sores.
  The dogs in the street
  Used to snap at the meat
  That hung in green gobs from her drawers.

★ There was a young sailor from Brighton
  Who said, "Shit! Your hole is a tight one!"
  Said the girl, "Shut your face!
  You're in the wrong place!
  There's plenty of room in the right 'un."

★ There was a young fellow called Runyon,
  Whose penis developed a bunion.
  With every erection,
  This painful infection
  Gave off a strong odour of onion.

★ There was a young vampire called Mabel
  With periods exceedingly stable.
  By the light of the moon
  She sat down with a spoon
  And drank herself under the table.

★ There once was a lady from Crewe
Who filled her vagina with glue.
She said with a grin,
"If they pay to get in
They can pay to get out of it too."

★ There was a young stud from Missouri
Who fucked with astonishing fury,
Until taken to court
For his vigorous sport
And condemned by a poorly hung jury.

★ There was a young fellow from Perth
The dirtiest fucker on earth.
When his wife was confined
He crept up behind
And swallowed the whole afterbirth.

There once was a barmaid named Gale
On whose breasts were the prices for ale
And on her behind
For the sake of the blind
The bar snacks were printed in Braille.

★ There was an old lady of Ypres
Who got shot in the ass by some snipers,
And when she blew air
Through the holes that were there,
She astonished the Cameron Pipers.

★ There was a young girl from Detroit
Who at screwing was very adroit.
She could squeeze her vagina
To a pin-point, or finer,
Or open it out like a quoit.

★ There was a young novice called Bell
Who didn't like cunt all that well.
He would finger and fuck one,
But never could suck one,
He just couldn't get used to the smell.

★ There was a young girl from Throgmorton
Who had one long tit and a short 'un.
To make up for that,
She'd a six-foot-wide twat
And a fart like a 650 Norton.

★ There was a young girl named Priscilla
Who flavoured her cunt with vanilla.
The taste was so fine,
Men and beasts stood in line,
But she called it a day with Godzilla.

★ A lady from Texas called Jill
Used dynamite sticks for a thrill.
They found her vagina
In North Carolina
And bits of her tits in Brazil.

★ There was a young lady from Norway
Who hung by her heels from a doorway.
She said to her beau,
"Look at this, Joe,
I think I've discovered one more way!"

* There was an old man from Calcutta
  Who was having a wank in the gutter.
  A woman walked by
  Got spunk in her eye
  And thought it was Ireland's best butter.

* There was a young man from Rangoon
  Who was born a fortnight too soon.
  He hadn't the luck
  To be born of a fuck
  'Twas a wank shovelled in with a spoon.

* There was a young queer from Khartoum
  Who took a lesbian up to his room.
  They argued all night
  About who had the right
  To do what and in where and to whom.

There was a young maid from Madrid
Who would open her legs for a quid.
But a handsome Italian
With balls like a stallion
Said he'd do it for nothing, and did.

* There was a young lady from Ealing
  Who had a rather strange feeling.
  She laid on her back
  And tickled her crack
  Then pissed all over the ceiling.

* There was an old pirate named Bates
  Who was learning to rumba on skates.
  But he fell on his cutlass
  Which rendered him nutless
  And practically useless on dates.

★ There once was a girl from Sri Lanka
Whose cunt was as big as a tanker.
You could go for a swim
In the depths of her quim
And you needed a lamppost to wank her.

★ There once was a rodent called Keith
Who circumcised boys with his teeth.
It wasn't for leisure
Or sexual pleasure
But to get to the cheese underneath.

★ There was a young lady of Dover
Whose passion was such that it drove her
To cry when she came,
"Oh dear, what a shame!
Well now we just have to start over."

★ There once was a fella named Mort
Whose prick was incredibly short.
When he climbed into bed
His lady friend said
"That's not a dick, it's a wart."

★ There was a young maid named McDuff
Who had a luxuriant muff.
In his haste to get in her
One eager beginner
Lost both of his balls in the rough.

★ There was a young maid from Cape Cod
Who dreamed she was sleeping with God.
'Twas not the Almighty
Who pulled up her nightie,
'Twas Roger the lodger, the sod.

★ There was a young maiden called Flynn
Who thought fornication a sin,
But when she was tight
It seemed quite all right,
So everyone filled her with gin.

★ There was a young man from Coblenz
Whose balls were quite simply immense:
It took forty draymen
A priest and three laymen
To transport them thither and hence.

★ There was a young man from Peru
Whose lineage was noble all through.
It's surely not crud,
For not only his blood
But even his semen was blue.

★ There was a young man of Australia
Who painted his arse like a dahlia.
The drawing was fine,
The colour divine,
But the scent, alas, was a failure.

★ There was a young girl from Hoboken
Who claimed that her hymen was broken
From riding a bike
On a cobblestone spike,
But it really was broken from pokin'.

★ There was a young fella called Taylor
Who seduced a respectable sailor.
When they put him in jail
He settled the bail
By doing the same to the jailer.

★   There was a young man from Nantucket
Took a pig to a thicket to fuck it.
Said the pig, "No, I'm queer,
Get away from my rear,
Just come to the front and I'll suck it."

★   A mathematician named Hall
Had a hexahedronical ball
And the cube of its weight
Times his pecker's, plus eight
Is his phone number – give him a call.

There was a young maiden called Randall
Who caused quite a neighbourhood scandal
By walking out bare
To the main village square
And poking herself with a candle.

★   There was a young dentist called Stone
Who saw all his patients alone.
In a fit of depravity
He filled the wrong cavity,
Good Lord! How his practice has grown!

★   There was a young tyro called Fyffe
Who married the love of his life.
But imagine his pain
When he struggled in vain,
And just couldn't enter his wife.

★   A remarkable race are the Persians;
They have such peculiar diversions.
They make love the whole day
In the usual way
And save up the nights for perversions.

* There was a young virgin from Bude
Whose proclivities were often viewed
With distrust by the males
For she'd fondle their rails,
But never would let them intrude.

* There was a young woman called Dexter
Whose husband exceedingly vexed her,
For whenever they'd start
He'd let fly a great fart
With a blast that damn near unsexed her.

* There was a young lady named Sapphire
Who succumbed to her lover's desire.
She said, "It's a sin,
But now that it's in
Could you shove it a few inches higher?"

* There once was a lady from France
Who took a long train ride by chance.
The engineer fucked her
Before the conductor
While the fireman came in his pants.

* There was a young woman called Gloria
Who was had by Sir Gerald Du Maurier,
By six other men,
Sir Gerald again,
And the band of the Waldorf-Astoria.

* There was a young woman from Bicester
More willing by far than her sister.
The sister would giggle
And wriggle and jiggle,
But this one would come if you kissed her.

★ There was a sweet lady who said,
As her new beau climbed into her bed,
"I'm tired of this stunt
That they do with one's cunt,
You can slip up my bottom instead."

★ There was a young fellow called Dirk
Who dozed off one day after work.
He woke with a scream
When he had a wet dream,
And polished it off with a jerk.

★ There was a young girl called McBight
Who got drunk with her boyfriend one night.
She came to her bed
With a split maidenhead:
It was the last time she ever got tight.

★ There was a young girl called O'Clare
Whose body was covered in hair.
It was really quite fun
To probe with one's gun,
For the target might be anywhere.

★ There was a young girl from Cornell
Whose nipples were shaped like a bell.
When you touched them they shrunk,
But when she got drunk,
They quickly got bigger than hell.

★ There was a young girl from Eskdale
Who put up her sweet arse for sale.
For two threepenny bits
You could tickle her tits,
But a shilling would get you some tail.

There was a young fellow called Lancelot
Whose neighbours looked on him askance a lot.
Whenever he'd pass
A pretty young lass,
The front of his pants would advance a lot.

★ There was a young monk from Tibet,
And this is the strangest one yet –
His prick was so long,
So pointed and strong,
He could bugger six Greeks en brochette.

★ There was a young man from Racine
Who invented a knobbing machine.
Concave or convex,
It would suit either sex,
With attachments for those in between.

★ There was a young girl with angina
Who stretched catgut across her vagina.
From the love-making frock
(With the proper sized cock)
Came Toccata and Fugue in D minor.

★ There was a young man from Cape Horn
Who wished he had never been born.
He wouldn't have been,
If his father had seen
That the end of his condom was torn.

★ There once was a girl from Lahore
Who'd lie on a rug on the floor.
In a manner uncanny
She'd wiggle her fanny
And drain your balls to the core.

★   There once was a plumber from Leigh
    Who was rodding his girl by the sea.
    Said she, "Please stop plumbing,
    I think someone's coming!"
    He replied: "I know love, it's me."

★   From the depths of the crypt at St Giles
    Came a scream that resounded for miles.
    Said the vicar, "Good gracious
    Has Father Ignatius
    Forgotten the bishop has piles?"

★   There was a man from Bhoghat
    Whose arse cheeks were terribly fat.
    They had to be parted
    Whenever he farted,
    And propped wide apart when he shat.

In the Garden of Eden sat Adam
Massaging the bust of his madam.
He chuckled with mirth
For he knew that on earth
There were only two boobs, and he had 'em.

★   There once was a lady from Hitchin
    Who was scratching her twat in the kitchen.
    Her mother said, "Rose,
    You've got crabs I suppose."
    She said, "Yes, and the fuckers are itchin'."

★   There was a young man from Nantucket,
    Whose cock was so big he could suck it.
    He said with a grin,
    As he wiped off his chin,
    If my ear was a cunt I could fuck it.

★ A bather whose clothing was strewed
By breezes that left her quite nude
Saw a man come along,
And unless I'm quite wrong
You expected this line to be lewd.

★   ★   ★   ★   ★

LINGERIE

❖ A very flat-chested woman goes shopping in search of a bra in her size. She goes into an upmarket department store and approaches a sales assistant in the lingerie department, "Do you have a size 28AAAA bra?"

The assistant replies in the negative, so the woman leaves the store and finds another department store where she is rebuffed in a similar manner.

After a third unsuccessful attempt at another department store she decided to try another approach. She walks into the Anne Summers lingerie store, marching up to the sales counter, lifts up her top and demands: "Do you have anything for this?"

The assistant looks closely and replies, "Have you tried Clearasil?"

❖ Two men finish showering in the gym when one puts on a pair of lace knickers.

"Since when do you wear women's underwear?" the other asks.

"Oh, since around the time my wife found them in the glove compartment."

❖ If love is blind, why is lingerie so popular?

Top Ten Things Men Should Never Say When Shopping for Lingerie

1   Does this come in children's sizes?
2   No thanks, just sniffing.
3   I'll be in the dressing room going blind.
4   Mum will love this.
5   The size doesn't matter, she's inflatable.
6   No need to wrap it up, I'll eat it here.
7   Will you model this for me?
8   The Miracle what? This is better than world peace!!
9   £45? You are just going to end up naked anyway.
10   You're never going to squeeze your arse into that.

❖ An Englishman, Irishman and Scotsman went to play a round of golf with their respective wives tagging along as caddies. While they are walking around the course the Englishman's wife caught her foot in a rabbit hole, tripped up, and landed in a heap on the ground with her skirt over her head, revealing that she wasn't wearing any underwear. Deeply embarrassed, the Englishman stormed over and demanded a reason for her state of undress.

"Well, darling," she explained, "you give me so little housekeeping money that I have to make the odd sacrifice, usually no one notices." With that the Englishman fumbled for his wallet and said, "Here's a tenner, go to Marks and Spencer's and get some knickers."

Two holes further on, the Irishman's wife was caught by a gust of wind, lifting her skirt over her head, revealing that she wasn't wearing any knickers either. The Irishman ran over and demanded a reason for her lack of underwear.

"Well, darling," she explained "you give me so little housekeeping money that I have to make the odd sacrifice, usually no one notices." With that the Irishman put his hand into his pocket and said, "Here's a fiver, go to Primark and get some knickers."

Three holes further on, the Scotsman's wife caught her foot on an exposed root, tripped up, and landed in a heap on the ground with her skirt over her head, revealing that she too wasn't wearing any knickers. The Scotsman stormed over and angrily demanded a reason for her state of undress. "Well, darling," she explained, "you give me so little allowance that I have to make the odd sacrifice, usually no one notices."

With that the Scotsman put his hand into his pocket and said, "Here's a comb, go and tidy yourself up, woman!"

> My wife came into the bedroom wearing a sexy negligee. She said, "Tie me up and do whatever you want". So I tied her up, fucked her sister and went fishing.

❖ A wife buys a pair of crotchless knickers in an attempt to spice up a joyless sex life. She puts them on, together with a very short skirt and sits on the sofa opposite her husband while he's watching the football. At the appropriate moment she crosses and uncrosses her legs.

"Are you wearing crotchless knickers?" he asks.

"Yes," she answers, seductively.

"Thank fuck for that. I thought the stuffing was coming out of the sofa."

★   ★   ★   ★   ★

THE LOTTERY

✳ A lad from a very poor family wins £5 million on the lottery. He goes home and hands his dad £500. His dad looks at the cash and says: "Thanks son. This money will mean a lot to me. We've never had much in this family, we've always been poor. In fact, we were so poor I couldn't even afford to marry your mother."

"What!" exclaims the son. "You mean I'm a bastard?"

"Yes, son," replies his dad, "and a fucking tight-fisted one at that."

Four Jews win the lottery and scoop the £10 million jackpot. They are getting ready to divide up the cash and one says: "Right, so that's £2 million to me, £2 million to each of you, and £2 million to the Germans."

The other two are stunned. "£2 million to the Germans? What for?"

The first Jew replies, rolling up his sleeve: "To be fair lads, they did give us the numbers."

✳ Did you hear about the gypsy who won the lottery?

They paid him with travellers' cheques.

✳ A man says to his wife, "What would you say if I told you I'd won the lottery?"

She says, "I'd take half and then leave you."

"Excellent," the guy says. "I had three numbers come up and won a tenner. Here's a fiver, now fuck off!"

✳ A man walks into the local cathedral and says to the rector, "I would like to join this fucking church."

The rector is astonished. "I beg your pardon, sir . . . I must have misunderstood you. What did you say?"

"Are you deaf? I said I want to join this fucking church!"

"I'm sorry, sir, but that kind of language is not tolerated in this building."

"Okay, twat face, I want to speak to someone else."

The rector goes into the bishop's study to inform him of the situation. The bishop listens and both return to confront the man, "Sir, what seems to be the problem here?"

"There is no problem," the man says. "I just won five million fucking quid on the fucking lottery and I want to join this fucking church to get rid of some of this fucking money."

"I see," says the Bishop, "and this cunt is giving you a hard time?"

★   ★   ★   ★   ★

MAGIC

✱ A man spends several days crossing the desert without water. Even his camel has died of thirst. As he is crawling through the sands on his hands and knees, convinced he is about to die, he suddenly sees an old briefcase sticking out of the sand a few yards ahead of him. He crawls to the old briefcase and opens it and out pops a genie. This, however, is no ordinary genie. He is wearing a grey suit and sporting an Inland Revenue ID badge on his lapel. There is a calculator in his pocket and he's holding a clipboard.

"Okay," says the genie, "I'm sure you know how this works. You have three wishes."

"I'm not falling for this," says the man, "This is a mirage. I must be losing my mind."

"So what do you have to lose?" says the genie. "You're going to die anyway, right?"

The man thinks about this for a minute and decides that the genie is right. "Okay, I wish I were in a lush oasis with plentiful food and drink."

In a flash, the man finds himself in the most beautiful oasis he has ever seen and he is surrounded with jugs of wine and platters of fruit.

"What's your second wish?"

"My second wish is that I were rich beyond my wildest dreams."

In a flash the man finds himself surrounded by treasure chests filled with rare gold coins and precious gems.

"You have just one more wish. Better make it a good one!"

After thinking for a few minutes, the man says, "I wish that beautiful women will want and need me." In a flash, he is turned into a tampon.

The moral of the story: if the Revenue offers you anything, there's bound to be a string attached.

★ A gorgeous blonde walks into a bar. The man at the bar says to her, "I'm drinking magic beer. You want one?"

"No thanks," she says. "There's no such thing."

"Sure there is, I'll show you." He takes a big swig and proceeds to throw himself out of a nearby window, then he flies up and around the building and back in through the bar window.

"That's unbelievable," she gasps.

"Hey, barman, pour me another one of them magic beers." The bartender shakes his head and pours another beer and slides it down the bar. The man knocks about half of it back and proceeds to leap out of the window and circle the building again.

"Here, you try it," he says to the blonde. She takes a big gulp from the glass, jumps out of the window, and falls about thirty feet to the ground, breaking both of her legs.

The bartender says, "Superman, you're a right cunt when you're drunk."

★ A magician was working on a cruise ship. As there was a completely new audience every couple of weeks, he was able to get away with the same routine over and over again. The only problem was that the ship's captain had a parrot that saw the shows each week and began to understand and memorize how the magician did every trick. After a while the parrot started to shout out in the middle of the show, "Look, he's got a card up his sleeve", or "Look, he's hiding something under his hat" or "Why is it always the queen of clubs?" The magician wanted to kill the parrot but wasn't in a position to do anything – after all, it belonged to the ship's captain.

One evening, however, in the middle of his show there was a freak storm and the ship sank. The magician found himself floating on a piece of wood in the middle of the sea with, as fate would have it, the parrot. For a couple of days they glared at each other, but did not share a single word.

This went on for three days, then four. Finally on the fifth day, the parrot said, "Okay, I give up. Where's the fucking ship?"

* Cinderella was eighty years old, having outlived her prince by more than a decade. She spent her days sitting on her rocking chair, watching the world go by from her front porch, with only her cat Fred for companionship.

Then one evening, out of nowhere appeared her old friend, the Fairy Godmother. "Fairy Godmother, what are you doing here after all these years?" said Cinderella.

The Fairy Godmother replied, "Well, Cinderella, since you have lived a good life I have decided to grant you three more wishes. Is there anything for which your heart still yearns?"

Cinderella is overjoyed. After careful consideration she uttered her first wish: "I wish I was very rich." In an instant her rocking chair was turned into solid gold.

Cinderella said, "Oh thank you, Fairy Godmother."

The Fairy Godmother replied, "It is the least I can do. What does your heart wish for your second wish?"

Cinderella looked down at her frail body, and said: "I wish I was young and beautiful again." In an instant, her former beautiful youthful self was restored. Cinderella felt stirrings inside her that had been dormant for years and long-forgotten vigour and vitality began to course through her veins.

The Fairy Godmother spoke again; "You have one more wish, Cinderella, what does your heart desire?"

Cinderella replied: "I wish you to transform Fred my old cat into a beautiful and handsome young man."

Magically, Fred underwent a transformation. Suddenly, before her stood a young man so fair and handsome, the like of which she nor the world had ever seen.

The Fairy Godmother again spoke: "Congratulations, Cinderella. Enjoy your new life." And, in a flash of blue light, she was gone. For a few moments, Fred and Cinderella looked into each other's eyes. Cinderella sat, breathless, gazing at the most stunningly perfect young male she had ever seen. Then Fred walked over to Cinderella and held her close in his young muscular arms. He leant in close to her ear, and whispered, blowing her golden hair with his warm breath, "I bet you regret having my balls chopped off now, don't you?"

★ A woman buys a mirror and hangs it on the bathroom door. While getting undressed she says, "Mirror, mirror, on my door, make my bra size 44!" There's a blinding flash of light and her breasts grow to enormous proportions. Excitedly, she runs to tell her husband what's happened and they both return to the bathroom.

The husband crosses his fingers and says, "Mirror, mirror, on my door, make my penis touch the floor!" Suddenly, there's another blinding flash of light and his legs fall off.

★ ★ ★ ★ ★

MANCHESTER UNITED

❖ A van driver liked to amuse himself by running over Manchester United fans that he saw walking down the road in their red colours. He would swerve to hit them and listen for the satisfactory "THUD", then he would swerve back on the road. One day he saw a priest hitchhiking and thought he would do a good turn. He stopped and asked the priest, "Father, can I give you lift?"

"I'm going to say mass at a church a couple of miles down the road," said the priest.

"No problem, father – hop in!"

The priest climbed into the passenger seat and the van continued down the road. Suddenly the van driver spotted a Manchester United fan and instinctively swerved to hit him. Just in time, however, he remembered who his passenger was, so with inches to spare he swerved back to the road, narrowly missing the fan. Although he was sure he had missed him, he was puzzled to still hear the distinctive loud "THUD". Not sure where the noise came from, he looked in his mirrors.

"I'm sorry, father, I almost hit that Manchester United fan."

"That's okay, my son," replied the priest. "I got the fucker with the door."

❖ Why are Manchester United fans like rats?
   Because you're never more than three yards away from one.

❖ How do you confuse a Manchester United supporter?
   Ask him the way to Manchester.

❖ What do you call twenty Manchester United fans skydiving from an aeroplane?
   Diahorrea.

★   ★   ★   ★   ★

MARGARET THATCHER

✱ The Pope and Margaret Thatcher are sharing a balcony in front of a huge crowd. The ex-PM and His Holiness have seen it all before, so to make it a bit more interesting, Maggie says to the Pope, "Did you know that with just one little wave of my hand, I can make every Conservative in the crowd go wild?"

He doubts it, so she shows him. Sure enough, the wave is greeted with wild cheering from the Tories. Gradually, the noise subsides.

"That was impressive," says the Pope, "but did you know that, with just one little nod, I can make every person in the crowd go crazy with joy? This joy will not be a momentary display, like that of your subjects, but will go deep into their hearts and they will forever speak of this day and rejoice."

The Iron Lady seriously doubts this and says, "One nod and all people will rejoice forever? Show me."

So the Pope head-butts her.

✳ I had a wet dream about Margaret Thatcher last night.

She got hit by a bus and I pissed myself.

✳ Margaret Thatcher answers the phone. "Can I speak to the prime minister, please?" says the voice at the other end. She politely tells him she is no longer prime minister and suggests he tries another number. Half an hour later, Maggie's telephone rings again. "Can I speak to the prime minister please?"

"Look, I've told you once I'm not prime minister any longer, now piss off and leave me alone."

Ten minutes later he calls again. "Is that the prime minister?"

Maggie says, "I've told you repeatedly that I am NOT prime minister any longer, why are you doing this to me?"

"I just love hearing you say it," says the caller.

★   ★   ★   ★   ★

MARRIAGE

★ A man gets home from work and says to his wife, "Get me a beer before it starts."

So she brings him a beer and he drinks it.

"Get me another beer before it starts," he shouts.

So she brings him another beer and he downs that one as well.

"Get me another fucking beer before it starts," he shouts at her again.

"Listen here, you lazy fat bastard," she shouts at him, "you walk in here, sit down and start barking out orders."

"Fucking hell! It's started already!"

* A woman was in the kitchen, preparing to boil eggs for breakfast. Her husband walked in. She turned and said, "You've got to make love to me this very moment."

His eyes lit up and he thought, "This is my lucky day." Not wanting to lose the moment, he embraced her and then gave it his all – right there on the kitchen table.

Afterwards she said, "Thanks", and returned to the stove.

More than a little puzzled, he asked, "Hang on . . . what was that all about?"

She explained, "The egg timer's broken."

* How do you turn a fox into an elephant?
Marry it.

After twenty years of marriage, a woman looks in the bathroom mirror and sighs. "God, I look old, fat and ugly." She implores her husband; "Pay me a compliment, dear."

Her husband replies, "Well, there's nothing wrong with your eyesight."

* A husband emerged from the bathroom naked and was climbing into bed when his wife complained, "I have a headache."

"Perfect," replies her husband. "I was in the bathroom just now powdering my penis with crushed aspirin. You can take it orally or as a suppository; you choose."

* Who is the bravest man in the world?
The guy who comes home drunk, covered in lipstick and reeking of perfume, then slaps his wife on the arse and says: "You're next, fatty."

* My wife somehow got a vacuum cleaner hose stuck up her arse. I phoned the hospital to see how she was doing. They told me she was picking up nicely.

⋆ A man walks into his bedroom and sees his wife packing a suitcase. He asks, "What are you doing?"

She replies, "I'm off to London. I read that prostitutes there get paid £400 for doing what I do for you for free."

Later, on her way out, the wife walks into the bedroom and sees her husband packing his suitcase. "Where are you going?" she asks.

"I'm coming with you. I want to see how you live on £800 a year."

> " This day holds painful memories for me because it was on this day two years ago that I lost my darling wife and two children. I'll never forget that game of cards. "

⋆ I said to my wife last night: "Honey, what do you say that tonight we change positions?"

"Okay," she replied. "You stand by the ironing board and I'll lie on the sofa and watch TV."

⋆ I said to my wife the other night: "I'm going down the pub, get your coat."

"That's nice, it's about time you took me out for a drink," she said.

"Not fucking likely," I said. "I'm turning the central heating off."

⋆ After fifteen years of marriage, my wife still gets upset if I use her toothbrush. If anyone knows a better way of getting dog shit off your trainers, I'm all ears.

⋆ A woman says to her husband, "Tell me something that will make me happy and sad at the same time."

He replies, "You've got a tighter cunt than your sister."

* My wife dresses to kill. Coincidentally, she also cooks the same way.

* A married couple are in bed one morning. "I had a really good dream last night," says the wife. "I dreamt that I was at a penis auction. Long dicks were going for £100 each and thick dicks were going for £200."

   "Really?" says the husband. "What would mine have fetched?"

   "They were giving dicks like yours away for free," says the wife.

   "That's funny, actually," he replies, "because I had a dream that I was at a vagina auction. Juicy cunts were going for £500 and tight cunts were going for a grand."

   "How about mine?" asks the wife.

   "That's where they were holding the auction."

★ I met my wife at a singles bar. Strange – I thought she was at home looking after the kids.

* Wife: "Why don't you ever call out my name when we're making love?"
   Husband: "Because I don't want to wake you."

* An Englishman, Irishman and a Scotsman are comparing their love lives.

   The Englishman says, "Before we make love, my wife and I drink a glass of wine. Then, after several hours of energetic sex, my wife tells me that she feels like she's floating a foot off the bed."

   The Scot says, "Before we make love, me and the wife have a shot of whisky. Then, after hours of sex, she tells me that she feels like she floating three feet above the bed."

   The Irishman says, "Before having sex, I get completely pissed. I fuck my wife for five minutes, wipe my cock on her nightie, burp in her face and fall asleep. She hits the fucking roof!"

✴ My wife said to me, "I need more space." So I extended the kitchen.

✴ **My wife spends a lot of time on eBay. I still haven't had a single bid for her.**

✴ A man took his wife to the county show. Among the exhibits were several breeding bulls. They went up to the first pen and there was a sign that read, "This bull mated fifty times last year." The wife nudged her husband in the ribs and said, "See that? He mated fifty times last year."

They walked a little further and saw another pen, with a sign that read, "This bull mated 100 times last year." The wife hit her husband and said, "See that? That's more than twice a week. You could learn something from that bull."

They walked a bit further and came across another, with a sign saying, "This bull mated 365 times last year." The wife hit him really hard and said: "See that? That's once a day. You could really learn something from this one."

The husband replied, "Go up and ask him if it was with the same cow."

✴ I was banging the wife last night and I asked her if she wouldn't mind moaning a bit just to get me in the mood. She replied: "When the fuck is this ceiling going to get painted?"

✴ **I asked my wife what she would like for her birthday. She said she wanted one of those big-screen TVs. So I moved her chair closer to the one we already have.**

✴ My wife makes love like a chess player. Every twenty minutes, she moves.

★ A married man keeps telling his wife "Darling, you have such a beautiful bum." In fact, all of his friends and everyone in the neighbourhood agrees that she does indeed have a very beautiful bum.

As her husband's birthday is coming up, she decides to celebrate her perfect rear by taking a trip to the tattoo parlour and having the words "Beautiful bum" tattooed on her perfect rear. She walks into a tattoo parlour and tells the tattoo artist that her husband thinks she has a beautiful bum. The tattooist can't help but agree. "You do indeed have a beautiful bum" he tells her. She then explains she wants the words "Beautiful bum" tattooed on her arse. The tattooist tells her: "I'm afraid I can't fit that on your arse, it takes up too much space. But I tell you what, I will tattoo the letters BB on each cheek and you and your husband will know that it stands for 'beautiful bum'." She agrees and has the work done.

On her husband's birthday she decided to surprise him as he comes home from work. She stands at the top of the stairs wearing only a robe. When her husband opens the door, she says, "Look, honey." She then takes off the robe and bends over.

Her husband yells "WHO THE FUCK IS BOB?"

A wife took her clothes off and asks her husband: "What turns you on more, my pretty face or my sexy body?"

He looks her up and down and replies, "Your sense of humour."

★ What's the difference between a wife and a wheelie bin?
   You only have to take out a wheelie bin once a week.

★ Why do men die before their wives?
   Because they want to.

★ A husband and wife go to visit a marriage guidance counsellor. First, the counsellor asks if he can talk to the wife alone. "You say you've been married for twenty-two years, so what seems to be the problem?" asks the counsellor.

The wife replies, "He's driving me mad! I'm going to leave him if he carries on!"

"How does he drive you mad?"

"Well, for twenty-two years," she says, "whenever we go out, he's always looking at the floor and refuses to go near anyone. It's embarrassing."

The marriage counsellor is bemused: "Is that it?"

"No. He keeps picking his nose all the time. Even in public."

"Anything else?"

The wife continues, "Whenever we're in bed, he never lets me be on top! Just for once I'd like to be on top!"

"I see," says the counsellor. "I would like a word with your husband now."

So the wife leaves the room and the husband enters. The counsellor tells him, "Your wife says that you've been driving her mad. She might leave you."

The husband looks genuinely shocked, "What? For twenty-two years I've been a loving and considerate husband and I've always given her everything she wants! I don't understand!"

The counsellor explains, "She says that you've got these habits that are driving her mad. For example, you're always acting strange in public, looking at the floor and never going near anyone else."

The husband replies, "Okay, it's something I swore to my father I would do on his death bed."

"What did he say?"

"He said that I should never step on anyone's toes!"

The counsellor shakes his head. "I think you've probably taken your father's words a little too literally. I think you will find that what he actually meant was that you should not do anything that would cause anyone else to get angry."

"Oh, really?" says the husband.

The counsellor continues, "And you keep picking your nose in public."

"Well, that's another thing dad specifically told me to do! He told me to always keep my nose clean."

The counsellor bites his lip. "I think you'll find that means that you should not indulge in any criminal activity."

"Oh, right," says the husband, looking very sheepish.

"Also, she says that you never allow her to be on top during your lovemaking."

"This is the last thing my father commanded me to do on his deathbed and it's the most important thing," says the husband, gravely.

"What did he say?"

The husband replies, "With his dying breath, he said 'Don't screw up.'"

The Four Secrets of a Happy Marriage

1 It is important that you find a woman who can cook and clean.
2 It is important that you find a woman who is financially independent.
3 It is important to find a woman who is good in bed
4 It is important that these three women never meet.

★ A husband walks into the bedroom holding two aspirin and a glass of water. "What's that for?" asks his wife
"It's for your headache," replies her husband.
"I don't have a headache!"
"Gotcha! Fancy a fuck then?"

★ Who says men can't multi-task? I can shag my girlfriend and think about her sister at the same time.

★ My wife and I do it doggy style for at least half an hour every time. Or four minutes human time.

★ A woman accompanied her husband to the doctor's for his check-up. Afterwards, the doctor called the wife into his office. He said, "I need to speak to you alone. Unfortunately your husband is suffering from a very severe stress-related illness. If you don't follow this strict regimen, your husband will certainly die. Each morning, fix him a healthy breakfast. Be nice to him and make sure he is in a good mood. For lunch, make him a nutritious meal he can take to work. And for dinner, prepare an especially nice meal for him."

The doctor continued: "Whatever you do, don't burden him with household chores because this could stress him. Try not to discuss your problems with him – that will only make his stress worse. Try to relax your husband in the evening by wearing lingerie and giving him plenty of backrubs.

"Encourage him to watch some type of team sporting event on television. And most importantly, make love with your husband several times a week and satisfy his every whim. If you can do this for the next nine months to a year I think there is an excellent chance that your husband will regain his health."

On the way home, the husband asked his wife, "What did the doctor say?"

"You're going to die."

★   ★   ★   ★   ★

MASTURBATION

❖ The local vicar was having a crafty wank in the bath. While happily tugging away and humming "Jerusalem", he realizes that he is being watched from the bathroom window by his window cleaner, his jaw agape at what he's just seen. A couple of minutes later the doorbell rings and it's the window cleaner. The vicar is too embarrassed to look the man in the eye and mumbles, "How much do I owe you?"

"Fifty pounds," comes the reply.

"That's a bit steep, isn't it?" blurts the vicar.

"Yep, fifty quid or I tell the whole parish about what I saw, you disgusting old pervert."

The vicar hands over the cash and the window cleaner goes on his way. A week later the bishop pops round to the vicar's house for a cup of tea. While the vicar is making tea, the bishop is admiring his home.

"Lovely clean windows you have there, vicar, who does them for you?"

"A man from the village does them for me," replies the vicar.

"He does a splendid job. How much does he charge?"

"Fifty pounds," replies the vicar.

"Bugger me!" says the bishop. "He must have seen you coming."

❖ What first motivated man to walk upright?
The chance to free his hands for masturbation.

> 66 There's a saying, "Talk to the hand because the face ain't listening."
> Inevitably, the hand won't listen either, so I started talking to my own hand. Well, things went well and one thing led to another. Before you know it, we were in my room having great sex. 99

❖ I was masturbating to a *National Geographic* magazine the other day. I don't know who was more embarrassed, me or my dentist.

❖ What's blue and sticky?
Smurf cum.

❖ A young lad and his teenage girlfriend were on a date. He was getting hot and finally said, "Let's shag."
She said, "Sorry I never do that."
"Well, how about a blow job?"
"Oh no. I don't do that either."
"How about giving me a hand job?"
She said she didn't know how to do that. "Do you remember when you were a kid, you used to shake a pop bottle until the pressure built up and it squirted? Just do it like that." So she took hold of his dick and began shaking. Soon he was groaning and moaning. And suddenly he began to scream.
"What's the matter?" she said.
He screamed, "TAKE YOUR THUMB OFF THE END!"

❖ Why is sex like a game of bridge?
You don't need a partner if you have a good hand.

❖ In 2008, the US government commissioned a study to find out why the head of a man's penis was larger than the shaft. After three years and $2 million, they concluded that the reason the head was larger than the shaft was to give the man more pleasure during sex.
After the Americans published the study, France decided to do their own study as well. After $250,000 and one year of research, they concluded that the reason was to give the woman more pleasure during sex.
Ireland, unsatisfied with these findings, conducted their own study. After three weeks, and at a cost of around $45.50, they concluded that it was to keep a man's hand from flying off and hitting him in the forehead.

❖ A white bloke walks into a pub, totally bladdered and shouts, "All Muslims are wankers."

A man sitting in the corner replies, "I take serious offense to that statement! It is factually incorrect."

The white guy asks, "Why? Are you a Muslim?"

He replies proudly, "No. But I am a wanker."

❖ My wife insisted I stopped masturbating.

"Why?" I replied. "It's perfectly natural."

She countered, "The kids are trying to eat their dinner."

❖ I went to see the nurse this morning for my annual check-up. She told me I had to stop wanking. I asked her why. She said, "Because I'm trying to examine you."

❖ What's the difference between pink and purple?

The grip.

❖ What's the bad news about being a test tube baby?

You know for certain that your dad is a wanker.

❖ A man is walking down a country lane late one night when he has a sudden urge for sex. He sees a pumpkin patch in the field by the lane and figures that as a pumpkin is soft inside it will be the next best thing. He cuts a hole in a pumpkin and proceeds to pleasure himself. He gets so carried away that he fails to notice that a police car had stopped at the side of the road. A police woman gets out of the car and shines a torch on him.

"Excuse me, sir," she says, "but if I'm not mistaken, you appear to be screwing a pumpkin."

The man looks horrified. "A pumpkin? Fuck! Is it midnight already?"

❖ A psychology student is conducting a survey to study the masturbatory habits of males. She approaches the first man and says, "Excuse me, sir, I'm conducting a survey and would like to know, what do you hold in your left hand while you masturbate?"

To which the man replies, "A remote controller, for the DVD."

She approaches the second man, with the same question. He answers, "I've got a magazine", and she notes down his answer.

She then approaches a third man and asks him what he holds while he masturbates, to which he answers, "A bar of soap."

Bemused by this, she asks why.

"Because I'm bathing the kids."

❖ What's the ultimate sexual rejection?
When you're masturbating and your hand falls asleep.

❖ For dads there is Father's Day. For mothers there is Mother's Day. For lovers there is Valentine's Day. And for wankers there is Palm Sunday.

❖ I was very disappointed to read that a man can get paid £60 just for donating his sperm. Just think of all that money I've let slip through my fingers.

❖ My wife has lost the urge to masturbate. She's just not feeling herself lately.

★　★　★　★　★

MECHANICS

* A mechanic dies in a road accident on his thirty-fifth birthday and finds himself at the pearly gates. The angels are singing a beautiful hymn and there is a huge crowd cheering and shouting his name and everyone wants to shake his hand. Just when he thinks things can't possibly get any better, St Peter himself comes over, apologizes for not greeting him personally at the gates, shakes his hand and says, "Congratulations, son, we've been waiting for you!"

  Totally confused and a little embarrassed, the engineer says, "St Peter, I tried to lead a decent life, I was a good husband, I loved my kids . . . but congratulations for what? I don't remember doing anything really special to deserve this."

  St Peter is amazed at the man's modesty. "Congratulations for what? We're celebrating the fact that you lived to be 160 years old! God himself wants to see you!"

  The mechanic is speechless. Eventually he says, "St Peter, I lived my life hoping that when I died I would go to Heaven, but as God is my witness, I swear I am only thirty-five years old."

  "That's impossible," says St Peter. "We've added up your time sheets!"

* How can you tell when a mechanic has just had sex?
  One of his fingers is clean.

★   ★   ★   ★   ★

MEDICAL

★ What's the difference between a rectal thermometer and an oral thermometer?
   The taste.

★ Osteoporosis. It's not what it's cracked up to be.

★ A man goes to the doctor for his test results.
   "Mr Jones, do you want the good news or the bad news?" the doctor asks.
   "Give it to me straight, doc," he replies.
   "Okay then," says the doctor, "you have less than forty-eight hours to live."
   The man is shocked and says, "Well . . . what's the good news?"
   The doctor smiles, "We're naming a disease after you."

★ Mary Poppins once said, "A spoonful of sugar helps the medicine go down."
   Not if you have diabetes, the murdering bitch.

★ What sits at the bottom of the bed and takes the piss?
   A kidney dialysis machine.

★ It's better to have loved and lost than to have never loved at all. As someone with full-blown AIDS, I beg to differ.

★ What turns a nine-stone weakling into a man of steel?
   Polio.

★ They say that whatever doesn't kill you makes you stronger. Try telling that to someone with muscular dystrophy.

★   I love playing snap with my son. He's got brittle-bone disease.

★   How can you tell which is the head nurse in a hospital?
    She's the one with the dirty knees.

★   What's the definition of machismo?
    Jogging home from your vasectomy.

★   ★   ★   ★   ★

MEN V WOMEN

Fifty Reasons Why it's Better to Be a Man Than a Woman

1   A five-day holiday requires one overnight bag.
2   Phone conversations are over in thirty seconds flat.
3   You can open all your own jars.
4   When clicking through the channels you don't have to stop at the bits where someone's crying.
5   All your orgasms are real.
6   You can go to the toilet without a support group.
7   When your work is criticized, you understand that everyone doesn't secretly hate you.
8   Nobody wonders if you swallow.
9   You never have to clean a toilet.
10 You can be showered and ready to go in ten minutes.
11 You save time and money by washing up in bulk every third week.

12 Sex never means worrying about your reputation.
13 If someone forgets to invite you to something, it means that they forgot to invite you. It doesn't mean that they hate you, and he or she can still be your friend.
14 You can quietly watch a game on TV with a mate for hours without it ever occurring to you that he's mad at you.
15 You never look at the size of a baby's head and break into a sweat.
16 You can piss anywhere, man!
17 Hot wax never comes near your pubic area.
18 One mood, all the time.
19 Same work, more pay!
20 Grey hair and wrinkles add character.
21 The remote control is yours and yours alone.
22 No such thing as bunny-hopping half an inch above the toilet seat.
23 People don't look at your chest when you're talking to them.
24 You can buy condoms without the chemist imagining you are naked.
25 If you don't call your mate when you say you will, he won't tell your other friends and they won't try to work out what the problem is.
26 One day you will be a dirty old man and you're looking forward to it.
27 You never have to miss a sexual opportunity because you're not in the mood.
28 Not liking a person doesn't exclude having great sex with them.
29 Life will go on if the bed sheets don't get changed once in a while.
30 Biological clock?

31 Having a beer belly is a perfect reason for wearing a t-shirt.

32 Your friends can be trusted never to trap you with: "So, notice anything different?"

33 None of your co-workers has the power to make you cry.

34 You don't have to shave below your neck.

35 You don't have to curl up next to a hairy arse every night.

36 You can be thirty and single, and nobody even notices.

37 You can write your name in the snow with your piss.

38 Chocolate is just another food.

39 Flowers fix everything.

40 You never have to worry about other people's feelings.

41 You get to think about sex 90 per cent of your waking hours.

42 Reverse parking is easy.

43 Foreplay is optional.

44 Window shopping is what you do when you buy windows.

45 You don't have to clean your house if the meter reader is coming.

46 You never feel compelled to stop a mate from getting laid.

47 Car mechanics tell you the truth.

48 You don't give a fuck if no one notices your new haircut.

49 Robbie Williams does not exist in your universe.

50 Angelina Jolie does.

Fourteen Reasons Why it's Better to Be a Woman Than a Man

1 You can judge a person's character just by looking at their shoes.
2 Gay waiters don't make you feel uncomfortable.
3 You can talk to members of the opposite sex without having to picture them naked.
4 You don't have to reach down every so often to check that your balls are still there.
5 You don't have to fart to amuse yourself.
6 You can sleep your way to the top.
7 You get off the *Titanic* first.
8 You can cry and get off speeding fines.
9 You have never lusted over a cartoon character, or central character of a computer game.
10 You live longer and therefore get to cash in the life insurance.
11 When you dance you don't look like a frog in a blender.
12 You know that size matters.
13 You get a whole new lease of life from a new lipstick.
14 Condoms make no significant difference to your enjoyment of sex.

*   *   *   *   *

MENSTRUATION

❖ According to a recent scientific study, women will find different males attractive depending on where they are in their menstrual cycle. When a woman is ovulating she will prefer a man with rugged, masculine features. However, just before she is menstruating she will prefer a man doused in petrol and set on fire with scissors stuck in his eyes and a cricket bat shoved up his arse.

❖ How do you confuse an archaeologist?
   Give him a used tampon and ask him which period it came from.

❖ Why do tampons have string?
   So you can floss after you eat.

❖ What's the difference between sand and menstrual blood?
   You can't gargle with sand.

❖ What's red and sits in a tree?
   A sanitary owl.

❖ What did the sanitary towel say to the fart?
   You're the wind beneath my wings.

❖ What is the difference between a woman on her period and a terrorist?
   You can negotiate with a terrorist.

❖ Susan gets her first period. Feeling uncomfortable about talking to her parents, she decides to ask little Jimmy next door. She whips off her knickers and shows him where she's bleeding from.
   "Well, I'm no expert," says Jimmy after a few minutes scratching his chin, "but it looks to me like someone's ripped your bollocks off."

❖ Two sanitary pads were floating down a sewer drain and saw two approaching tampons. One pad said to the other, "Should we say hello to those two tampons?"

"Nah", responds the other. "They're stuck up cunts."

❖ Why do women have periods?
Because they deserve them.

❖ What's the difference between normal blood and period blood?

You can't eat normal blood with a fork.

❖ How did the Red Sea get its name?
Queen Cleopatra used to bathe in it periodically.

❖ Two men are sitting in a restaurant. At the table opposite a woman was sitting with her legs wide open. One man says to his friend: "Look at the dark hair on her snatch!"

His mate replies: "No way, that isn't hair, she's wearing black knickers!" So they make a £100 bet and ask a passing waiter to find out for them. The waiter finds an excuse to go over to her table, then comes back to report.

"Neither of you is right. She had her period and there are flies on her."

❖ Why don't men trust women?

Would you trust anything that bled for three days and didn't die?

❖ Why do women stop bleeding when entering the menopause?

Because they need all the blood for their varicose veins.

★   ★   ★   ★   ★

MENTAL ILLNESS

★ My grandfather used to get up at 5 a.m. every morning and deliver milk to people's doorsteps in a horse-drawn cart. He wasn't a milkman, he was clinically insane.

✳ "Hello, thank you for calling the NHS Mental Health Hotline.

If you are obsessive-compulsive, press 1 repeatedly.

If you are co-dependent, please ask someone to press 2 for you.

If you have multiple personalities, press 3, 4, 5 and 6.

If you are paranoid, we know who you are and what you want. Stay on the line so we can trace your call.

If you are delusional, press 7 and your call will be transferred to the mother ship.

If you are schizophrenic, listen carefully and a small voice will tell you which number to press.

If you are manic-depressive, it doesn't matter which number you press, because no one will answer.

If you are dyslexic, press 9696969696969.

If you have amnesia, press 8 and state your name, address, phone number, date of birth, social security number and the third and fifth letters of your mother's maiden name.

If you have post-traumatic stress disorder, carefully press 000.

If you have bi-polar disorder, please leave a message after the beep or before the beep. Or after the beep. Please wait for the beep.

If you have short-term memory loss, press 9.

If you have short-term memory loss, press 9.

If you have short-term memory loss, press 9.

If you have short-term memory loss, press 9.

If you have low self-esteem, please hang up. Our operators are too busy to talk to you."

* A man walks in to a mental hospital and says to the receptionist: "Excuse me, is there anyone in room 30?"

  The receptionist leaves the desk to check. She comes back and says, "No, sir, there's no one in there."

  "Ah, that's good," says the man. "I must have escaped."

* I like to dress up like a white arctic bear and I have sex with men and women. I think I might be bi-polar.

* A man is visiting his mother in a mental hospital when he comes across a guy moving his arms around and making beeping noises. "Excuse me", he asks him. "What are you doing?"

  "I'm driving my car!" says the guy excitedly. "Beep beep!"

  "You are not in a car, my friend, you are in a bed in a mental hospital."

  A voice comes from the bed opposite: "Mate, shut the fuck up, will you? He's paying me twenty quid a day to wash it."

My new girlfriend broke down the other day and confessed that she self-harms. I told her, "All right love, don't beat yourself up over it."

* A large group of punters enter a bar and order a huge round of drinks. When they come to pay they give the barman milk bottle tops. "What the hell is this?" says the barman.

  The head of the group comes over to explain. "It's the annual outing from the mental institute down the road. Just humour them, keep a tab and, at the end of the night, I'll settle up with you," says the guy.

  "Okay," says the barman with a big wink.

  The night rolls on and it's a roaring success. The barman hails the group leader. "That was a great night! Not one of them is sober, and no trouble at all!" he says, amazed. "That will be £473.82, please."

  "No problem. Have you got change for a dustbin lid?"

✳ I've been taking steps to combat my kleptomania. Now my window cleaner can't reach the windows.

✳ Bill and Doris were both patients in a mental hospital. One day, while they were walking past the hospital swimming pool, Bill suddenly plunged into the deep end and sank to the bottom. Doris promptly jumped in to save him. She swam to the bottom and pulled Bill out. When the head of hospital became aware of this heroic act, she immediately ordered Doris to be discharged from the hospital, as she now considered her to be mentally stable.

When she went to inform Doris of her decision, she said, "I have good news and bad news. The good news is you're being discharged. As you were able to rationally respond to a crisis by jumping in and saving the life of another patient, I have concluded that your act displays sound-mindedness. The bad news, unfortunately, is that Bill, whose life you saved, hanged himself in the bathroom with his bathrobe belt, right after you rescued him. I am so sorry, but he's dead."

"That's sad," said Doris. "But he didn't hang himself – I put him there to dry. When can I go home?"

MEXICANS

★ Why do Mexicans eat burritos at Christmas?
So they have something to unwrap.

★ What do you call a Mexican with a broken lawn mower?
Unemployed.

★ What do you call a Mexican who can swim?
A Texan.

★ What did Jesus say to the Mexicans?
   "Don't do anything until I come back."

★ What are the first words in a Mexican cookbook?
   Steal a chicken.

★ Why did the Mexican push his wife off the cliff?
   Tequila.

★　★　★　★　★

MICE

❖ Three mice are sitting at a bar drinking. The first mouse puts down his beer and turns to the others, saying, "I'm hard, me. You know how hard I am? Well, you know that poison they put down in the kitchen? I eat that stuff for breakfast, lunch and dinner!"

   The second mouse looks unimpressed and says, "That's nothing. You know those big fucking mousetraps they got all over the place? Well, I jump in and out of them for fun. That's how hard I am!"

   The third mouse knocks back his drink and heads for the door.

   "Where are you going?" asks the first mouse.

   He replies: "See you guys later. I'm off home to shag the cat."

❖ Why do mice have such small balls?
   Because very few of them know how to dance.

❖ Why haven't scientists find a cure for AIDS yet?
   They can't get the laboratory mice to butt fuck.

★　★　★　★　★

MICHAEL JACKSON

* Victoria Beckham claims she once had an affair with Michael Jackson.

  Jacko, of course, refuted the allegation. He said he was in Brooklyn at the time.

* **Michael Jackson died of a heart attack. He really should not have looked at the man in the mirror.**

* When police swarmed all over the Neverland Ranch, they found a lot of suspicious items that needed explaining. For example, the wedding photo with Lisa Marie Presley.

* Legal experts commenting on Michael Jackson's trial were baffled because his defence team didn't play the race card. It was because they didn't know which race to play.

  Farah Fawcett died and went straight to Heaven. Upon her arrival, God asked her if there was any wish she would like granted back on earth. Farah replied that she wanted all the children of the world protected. Four hours later, Michael Jackson died. Coincidence?

* Michael Jackson went to Heaven and saw Elvis, so he went over and introduced himself as the man who married his daughter, Lisa Marie. Elvis shook him enthusiastically by the hand. "I can't tell you how pleased I am to meet you, man," said Elvis. "I heard she married a nigger."

* Michael Jackson will always be with us ... he isn't bio-degradable.

✳ What was the difference between Michael Jackson and Dick Cheney?

One had pasty white skin, fake body parts and is very creepy, the other one was Michael Jackson.

✳ When Michael Jackson's heart stopped, his chimp, Bubbles was the first to try and resuscitate him. Unfortunately he had only been trained to suck and not blow.

✳ O.J. Simpson and Michael Jackson were at Johnny Cochran's funeral. Michael corners O.J. and asks, "O.J., how do you get stains off a glove?"

✳ The first two paramedics arrive at Neverland and find Jackson's body.

The first paramedic looks at the second paramedic and says, "Okay what're we going to do first?"

The Second paramedic replies, "I don't know about you, but I'm having a go on the roller-coaster!"

✳ Paramedics at the scene knew that Michael Jackson was dead when they waved a six-year-old boy under his nose and got no response.

✳ Upon hearing the news of Michael Jackson's death, mourning fans released several white doves in his honour. Actually they were blackbirds, but with a rare skin condition.

✳ What was so unusual about Michael Jackson hanging his youngest child off the balcony? Because usually he tossed them off.

✳ Only in America can someone be born a good-looking black kid, and die an ugly white woman.

WANTED: a good home for an abandoned monkey called Bubbles. Very friendly, likes being wanked off with a white glove . . .

★   ★   ★   ★   ★

MIDGETS

★   What do you call a three-foot-tall black person?
A Yardie.

★   Why should you never take the piss out of a retarded midget?
Because it's not big and it's not clever.

★   This morning on the way to work I drove into the back of a car at some traffic lights whilst not really paying attention. When the driver got out, I saw that he was a dwarf.
He said, "I'm not happy . . ."
I replied, "Okay, so which one are you then?"

★   Did you hear about the gay midget?
It took him a lot of courage, but he finally came out of the cupboard.

★   What do you get if you leave a midget in the sun too long?
A red dwarf.

★   A dwarf walked in to a bar. The barman said "Oi, short arse, where are the other six?"
The dwarf replied, "Fuck off, you cunt, I'm off."
He must have been Grumpy.

★ Two dwarfs walk into a mini-bar.

★ A female midget goes to the doctor's. "Doctor, every time it rains, my vagina gets sore."

The doctor replies: "Hmm, that's a strange one. Well, tell you what, come back and see me when it's raining and I'll take a look."

A couple of days later it's pouring down and she goes back to the doctor's. "Right," he says. "Hop on to the bed and I'll take a look at you." So she gets on the bed and the doctor examines her. He then takes his scalpel and says "Ok, I just need to do a couple of cuts here and there." Then he tells her to stand up and asks; "How's that?"

"Much better, doctor! What did you do?"

"I just took a couple of inches off the top of your wellies."

★ I was reading in the paper about this dwarf who had his pocket picked and his wallet stolen. How could anyone stoop so low?

★ What is the difference between a clever midget and a venereal disease?

One is a cunning runt and the other is a running cunt.

★ This morning I woke up happy with a huge erection. He wasn't pleased.

★ Every day at the office a man approaches a female co-worker at the water cooler, stands very close to her, draws in a large breath of air and says: "Mmm. Your hair smells nice."

After a couple of week of this, she can't stand it any longer and complains to Human Resources. Without identifying her co-worker, she tells them what he does and that she wants to file a sexual harassment suit against him. The HR supervisor is puzzled, "What's sexually threatening about a co-worker telling you your hair smells nice?"

The woman replies, "It's Mick, the midget."

★ A man phones his friend, who is a breeder of horses. "I'm sending a mate over. He wants to buy a horse – keep an eye out for him."

The horse breeder replies: "Sure, but how will I know who he is?"

"That's easy, he's a dwarf with a speech impediment."

When the little fella arrives, the breeder asks him if he's looking for a male or female horse.

"A female horth," the dwarf replies.

He shows him a prized filly.

"Nithe lookin' horth," says the dwarf. "Can I get a clother look at her eyth?"

So the breeder picks up the dwarf, who gives the horse's eyes the once over.

"Nithe eyth, can I thee her earth?"

He picks the little fella up again and shows him the horse's ears.

"Nithe earth, can I see her mouf?"

The horse breeder is getting just a little irritated, but he picks him up again and shows him the horse's mouth.

"Nithe mouf. Can I see her twat?"

Completely pissed off by this point, the breeder grabs him under his arms and rams the dwarf's head as far as he can up the horse's twat, pulls him out and drops him on the ground.

The dwarf picked himself up from the floor, sputtering and coughing.

"Thorry. Perhapth I should rephrase the quethtion. Can I thee her wun awound a widdle bit?"

> " A female midget friend of mine says she has decided to become a prostitute. This had made me very sad. I just feel like she's selling herself short. "

★ Two dwarfs decide to treat themselves to a holiday in Las Vegas. At the hotel bar, they're captivated by two glamorous prostitutes and wind up taking them to their separate rooms. The first dwarf is disappointed, however, when, having got back to his room, he finds that he can't manage an erection. His depression is enhanced by the fact that, from the next room, he hears shouts of "ONE, TWO, THREE . . . HUP!" all night long.

In the morning, the second dwarf asks the first, "So how did it go?"

The first dwarf whispers back: "To be honest, it was so fucking embarrassing. I just couldn't get a hard-on."

The second dwarf shakes his head. "You think that's embarrassing? I couldn't even climb on to the bed."

★ A woman comes home early from work to find her husband in bed with a female dwarf. "You bastard!" she yells. "You promised you were done with playing around behind my back."

"For Christ's sake woman," replies the husband, "can't you see I'm cutting down?"

★　★　★　★　★

THE MILITARY

❖ A young soldier ran up to a nun. Out of breath, he asked, "Please, may I hide under your habit? I'll explain later." The nun agreed. A moment later two military policemen appeared and asked, "Sister, have you seen a soldier?"

"He went that way," the nun replied. After the MPs left, the soldier crawled out from under her habit and said, "I can't thank you enough, sister. You see, I don't want to go to Afghanistan."

The nun said, "I understand completely."

The soldier added, "I hope I'm not being rude, but I couldn't help noticing that you have a very hairy pair of legs!"

The nun replied, "If you'd looked a little higher, you'd have seen a pair of hairy balls. I don't want to go to Afghanistan either."

❖ **Why is the Afghan air force so easy to train?**
They only have to learn how to take off.

❖ An Englishman, an Irishman, a Welshman and a Scot are captured by the Taliban. The Taliban leader says to them, "We're going to shoot you infidels, but we are fair people and we will give you one last request. He turns to the Welshman: "What is your last request?"

The Welshman replies, "I want to hear a thousand Welshmen singing 'Land of my Fathers'."

"Okay, you will have your request." He turns to the Scotsman. "What about you?"

"I want to hear a thousand Scots pipers piping 'Scotland the Brave'," replies the Scot.

"You've got it," says the Taliban leader. He turns to the Irishman. "What is your last request?"

"I want to see a thousand Irishmen doing the Riverdance," says Paddy.

"It will be yours," says the Taliban leader.

Finally he turns to the Englishman. "And your last request?"

"Please . . ." replies the Englishman, ". . . shoot me first."

❖ **Why did the army send so many women with PMS to the war in Iraq?**
They fought like animals and retained water for four days.

❖ An army major is visiting a field hospital. He walks up to the bed of a sick private and asks, "What's your problem, soldier?"

"Chronic syphilis, sir."

"What treatment are you getting?"

"Five minutes with the wire brush each day."

"What's your ambition?"

"To get back to the front, sir."

"Good man," barks the major.

He goes to the next bed. "What's your problem, soldier?"

"Chronic piles, sir."

"What treatment are you getting?"

"Five minutes with the wire brush each day."

"What's your ambition?"

"To get back to the front, sir."

"Good man," says the major.

He moves to the next bed. "What's your problem, soldier?"

"Chronic gum disease, sir."

"What treatment are you getting?"

"Five minutes with the wire brush each day."

"What's your ambition?"

"To get the wire brush before those other fuckers, sir!"

An American destroyer is sailing in the English Channel, just off the southern coast of England, when it receives a call. "This is Britain. You need to divert your course fifteen degrees."

The American radio operator replies: "No deal, motherfucker. How about you divert your course fifteen degrees or we'll bomb your ass to kingdom come!"

The reply comes: "This is a lighthouse, your call."

❖ Two Irish soldiers in Afghanistan are given a new helicopter. They take it for a spin and Mick says to Paddy: "If I turn this helicopter upside-down, do you think we'll fall out?"

Paddy replies: "Of course not, Mick. We'll always be friends."

❖   An officer is posted to a remote desert outpost to look after a unit of troops. When he arrives he sees that there is very little in the way of entertainment, so he asks one of the men, "What do you do for sex around here?"

The trooper points to a donkey tied to a post nearby. The officer is outraged and orders the donkey to be put out in the field; he warns that if any man goes near it, he will be shot.

After several weeks without women, the officer begins to feel a bit edgy. Finally he cracks and asks for the donkey to be brought back to his tent. When it arrives he figures that he's going to be the one to go first and so drops his trousers and begins to have his way with the donkey. At this point he catches sight of his troops peering in at him, aghast, through the tent flap. "You guys have a problem with this?" he demands. "Isn't this the way you all did it?"

"Not exactly, sir," one of the men replies. "We rode the donkey into town to meet girls."

❖ My grandfather had his tongue ripped out by the Japs in Burma during the Second World War. He doesn't talk about it, though.

★   ★   ★   ★   ★

MOTHERS-IN-LAW

✳ What is the ideal weight for a mother-in-law?
About three pounds, including the urn.

❋ What do you have when you have a mother-in-law buried up to her neck in sand?
  Not enough sand.

❋ What looks good on a mother-in-law?
  A doberman.

> I was in the shopping centre the other day when I saw six hoodies attacking my mother-in-law. As I stood there and watched, my wife said, "Well, aren't you going to help?"
> I replied, "Nope. Six should be enough."

❋ A bloke brings his dog into the vet and says, "Could you please cut my dog's tail off?"
  The vet examines the tail and says, "There is nothing wrong. Why would you want this done?"
  The man replies, "My mother-in-law is coming to visit. I don't want anything in the house to make her think that she is welcome."

❋ If your wife and your mother-in-law were drowning, and you had to choose, would you go to the pub or hire a DVD?

★   ★   ★   ★   ★

MORTICIANS

✳ There were three morticians swapping stories in the bar. The first one says, "What a day I had today. This guy wasn't wearing his seatbelt and his head flew into the windshield. Took me all day to make the face look natural."

Not to be outdone, the second mortician says, "You think that's bad? I had this bloke in who got hit by a train while he was riding his bike. Took me two days to put all the pieces back together!"

The third mortician just shakes his head. "You guys have it easy. I had this female parachutist whose chute didn't open. She landed on a flagpole. It took me all week just to wipe the smile off her face."

✳ A man who had recently died is delivered to the mortuary wearing an expensive, bespoke three-piece black suit. The mortician asks the deceased's wife how she would like the body dressed. He points out that the man looks quite smart in the black suit he is already wearing. The widow, however, says that she always thought her husband looked his best in blue and insists on a blue suit. Handing the mortician a blank cheque, she adds, "I don't care what it costs, please put my husband in a blue suit for the viewing."

The woman returns the next day for the wake. To her delight, she finds her husband dressed in an expertly tailored Savile Row blue suit. It fits him perfectly. She says to the mortician, "You did an excellent job and I'm very grateful. I don't care how much this cost."

To her astonishment, the mortician presents her with the blank cheque.

"There's no charge," he says.

"No, honestly, I must reimburse you for the cost of that blue suit," she says.

"Honestly, madam," the mortician says, "it cost nothing. You see, a deceased gentleman of about your husband's size was brought in shortly after you left yesterday and he was wearing an attractive blue suit. I asked his wife if she minded him going to his grave wearing a black suit instead, and she said it made no difference as long as he looked good. After that, it was just a matter of swapping heads . . ."

A mortician was working late one night. He examined the body of Mr Dobing, who was about to be cremated, and made a startling discovery. Dobing had the biggest penis he had ever seen!

"I'm sorry Mr Dobing," the mortician commented, "I can't allow you to be cremated with such an impressive schlong. It must be saved for posterity." So, he removed it, stuffed it into his briefcase, and took it home.

"I have to show you something you won't believe," he said to his wife, opening his briefcase.

"Jesus Christ!" shrieked the wife: "Dobing's dead?"

★   ★   ★   ★   ★

MUSIC

❖ What has nine arms and sucks?
  Def Leppard.

❖ What has two heads and six legs?
  Nirvana.

❖ **What's brown and rhymes with Snoop?**
  Dr Dre.

❖ Why did it take Stevie Wonder four years to write "Song In The Key Of Life"?
   He dropped his pencil on the first day.

❖ **What happens when you sing country and western music backwards?**
   You get your wife and your job back.

❖ What's brown and sits on a piano bench?
   Beethoven's First Movement.

❖ Did you know that Neil Diamond and Sid Vicious once collaborated on a song together?
   It was called: "You don't bring me flowers any more, you cunt."

❖ What's got three breasts and can't sing?
   Kylie and Danni Minogue.

❖ What is thirty feet long, has ten teeth and stinks of urine?
   The front row of a Daniel O'Donnell concert.

❖ **What's the first sign of madness?**
   Suggs walking up your driveway.

❖ I was in Oxford Street and I bumped into Paul Weller. I said to him "Oi, Weller! I've got all your records!" I'd love to see the look on his face when the cunt gets home and realizes he's been burgled.

❖ How do you know when the stage is dead level?
   The drummer is drooling out of both sides of his mouth.

❖ What is the definition of "perfect pitch"?
   When you lob Liam Gallagher into a toilet without hitting the rim.

❖ How is an orgasm like a drum solo?
  You can tell it's coming but there's no way to stop it.

❖ **Queen guitarist Brian May has finally had his doctoral thesis in astrophysics published. He can now prove categorically that fat-bottomed girls make the rocking world go round.**

❖ Bono is at a U2 concert when he asks the audience for some quiet. Then, in the silence, he starts to click his fingers. Holding the audience in total silence, he says into the microphone . . . "Every time I click my fingers, a child in Africa dies."
  A voice from near the front pierces the silence: "Stop doing it then, cunt!"

❖ The IRA captured Ian Paisley, Margaret Thatcher and Daniel O'Donnell, but they only had two bullets. Who did they shoot?
  Daniel O'Donnell twice, just to make sure.

★   ★   ★   ★   ★

MUSLIMS

✳ Two Muslim families moved to America. When they arrived, the two men at the head of each household made a bet: in a year's time, whichever family had become more American would win. A year later they met again.
  The first man said, "My son is playing baseball, I had McDonald's for breakfast and I'm on my way to pick up a case of Bud, how about you?"
  The second man replied, "Fuck off, towel head."

You Are Almost Certainly a Member of the Taliban If . . .

1 You refine heroin for a living but you have a moral objection to beer.
2 You own a £2,000 machine gun and a £5,000 rocket launcher but you can't afford shoes.
3 You have more wives than teeth.
4 You wipe your arse with your bare left hand but consider bacon "unclean".
5 You think vests come in two styles: bulletproof and suicide.
6 You think that television is dangerous but carry explosives in your clothing.
7 You didn't know that mobile phones have uses other than setting off roadside bombs.
8 You have often said, "I love what you've done with your cave."
9 You have nothing against women; in fact you think every man should own at least one.
10 You've ever had a crush on your neighbour's goat.

✳ Why are the Taliban not circumcised?
   It gives them a place to put their bubblegum during a sandstorm.

✳ Why is the British summer just like a Muslim?
   Because it's either Sunni or Shi'ite.

✳ What does the average Pakistani weigh?
   Sweets.

★   ★   ★   ★   ★

NATIVE AMERICANS

★ The Indian chief Geronimo decides it is time to give his three sons their adult names because they have reached manhood. He gathers them in to his tent together with the elders of the tribe and turns to his eldest son.

"Son, you will be called Eagle."

The third and youngest son interrupts, "Dad, dad, what will I be called?"

"All in good time, my son," replies Geronimo.

He continues; "You will be called Eagle because you are strong and wise."

The elders agree. Geronimo then turns to his second son. Meanwhile the third son interrupts again: "Dad, dad, what will I be called?"

"All in good time, my son," he replies.

Geronimo continues to tell his second eldest, "Son, you will be called Swallow."

The third son says again, "Father, father, what will I be called?"

"All in good time, my son," comes the reply. He continues, "You will be named Swallow because you are quick and cunning."

The elders agree. He then turns to the third son, who is still impatiently asking, "Dad, dad, what will I be called?"

"Son, you will be called Thrush."

"Why is that, dad?" he asks excitedly.

"Because, my son, you are an irritating cunt."

★ Tonto and the Lone Ranger are walking through the prairie. The Lone Ranger asks Tonto how much he knows about the prairie and the nature surrounding them. Tonto suddenly drops the floor, puts his ear to the ground and says, "Buffalo come."

The Lone Ranger is amazed. He says, "Are you so knowledgeable in this world that you can hear the animals miles away and understand their acoustics via their vibrations through the ground?"

Tonto shakes his head and says, "No. Ear stuck to floor!"

★ **Did you hear about the dyslexic native American?**
They buried his knee at Wounded Heart.

★ One day an Indian chief walked into a pharmacy and asked to speak to the pharmacist. The pharmacist walks out and asks the chief, "How may I help you?"

The chief replies, "Me got heap too many children, need condoms."

The pharmacist helps the chief to select from his extensive range of condoms and sends him on his way. The next day, the chief walks back into the pharmacy with a shredded, badly mangled condom. Puzzled, the pharmacist asks him what happened.

Tossing the damaged condom on to the counter in disgust, the chief replies angrily, "Last night, me put on condom to fuck squaw. Left nut go 'Ug!', right nut go 'Ug!', condom go BOOM!" Surprised at this news, the pharmacist gives the chief a packet of special prescription, super-strength condoms. Hoping this will do the trick, the pharmacist sends the chief on his way.

The next day, the chief reappears, mad as hell with yet another shredded condom in his hand. The pharmacist asks the chief what happened.

The chief replies angrily, "Last night, me put on condom to fuck squaw. Left nut go 'Ug!', right nut go 'Ug!', condom go BOOM!" The pharmacist, by now at his wits end, asks the chief to wait, then nips out of the back of the shop and goes to a bicycle shop to buy a cycle tyre repair kit. He then takes a length of the tube, seals off one end with the repair kit and hands it to the chief. This, he tells the chief triumphantly, will definitely do the trick.

The next morning, the Indian chief limps through the door very slowly, and in obvious pain. Surprised, the pharmacist runs out and asks the chief what happened.

The chief looks him in the eye and with a very hoarse voice replies, "Last night, me put on condom to fuck squaw. Left nut go 'Ug!', condom go 'Ug!', right nut go BOOM!"

⋆ A Scouser called Steve is on a trip around North America. One day he stops off at a remote bar in the Nevada desert and gets talking to the bartender, when he sees a native American wearing full tribal gear sitting on a bar stool. Says Steve to the barman, "Who is the cool looking dude in the Red Indian gear?"

"That is the memory man," replies the bartender. "He knows everything there is to know. Has a memory like an elephant."

"Really?" says Steve.

"Sure," says the barman. "Why don't you go and check him out if you don't believe me?"

So Steve heads over to the native American, thinking that he can make him look foolish by asking him a question about English football. He asks the memory man, "Who won the 1965 FA Cup Final?"

"Liverpool," comes the swift reply.

Steve can't believe his ears. He tries again. "Who did they beat?"

"Leeds," replies the memory man.

Steve tries once more. "What was the final score?"

The wise native American replies without hesitating, "Two-one."

Steve the Scouser is impressed, but is quietly confident he will catch the memory man out with his final question. "Who scored the winning goal?"

Without blinking, the memory man says, "Ian St John."

Steve is stunned. When he gets home to Liverpool he tells everyone about the Red Indian. Several years go by and he can never quite get his strange encounter in the Nevada bar out of his head and he vows to return to American and pay his respects to the Indian. Ten years later, Steve finally saves up enough money to return, and, after weeks of searching the Nevada desert, he is delighted to find the native American living in a cave. Steve steps forward, bows, and greets the brave in the traditional manner.

"How," says Steve.

The memory man squints at him and replies: "Diving header in the six-yard box."

NECROPHILIA

❖ Necrophilia. It means never having to say you're sorry.

❖ What's the definition of disappointment?
   A necrophiliac finding someone buried alive.

❖ Necrophilia. Nature's way of telling you that your love life has gone stale.

❖ I used to be really into sadism, necrophilia and bestiality, until I realized I was just flogging a dead horse.

❖ Two necrophiliacs are at work in the morgue. One of them turns to the other and says, "You know that woman they brought in last week? They pulled her out of the water after she'd been there for three weeks. I'm telling you, her clit was just like a pickle."
   "What," the other asks, "green?"
   "No," says the first, "a bit sour."

❖ Necrophilia: the uncontrollable urge to crack open a cold one.

❖ Did you hear about the hypochondriac necrophiliac?
   He was so scared of catching something he only has sex with cadavers without removing them from the body bag.

❖ What's the difference between necrophilia and rape?
   The body temperature.

Three necrophiliacs get together in a pub to chew the fat over some of the finer points of their perversion. They start talking about the best post-mortem time for penetrating the corpse. The first necrophiliac says that he likes to shag the warm dead body moments after death. The other two beg to differ; after all, if the body is still warm, there is not much point even calling it necrophilia, is there?

The second necrophiliac says he likes to wait around for three days after death before copping off with the deceased: "Rigor mortis has set in, and it's always good to get stiff with a proper stiff."

The third necrophiliac smiles and says he prefers to wait around three months. The other two are amazed and ask him why.

He replies, "That way, I can penetrate the body anywhere I want."

❖ I used to be a necrophiliac – until some rotten cunt split on me.

★   ★   ★   ★   ★

NOSE PICKING

Nose-Picking Terms

Deep Salvage Pick: similar to the type of deep-sea exploration required to find the wreck of the *Titanic*, i.e. you probe deep into your nasal passages.

Utensil Pick: when fingers and even a thumb aren't enough to get the job done to your satisfaction.

Extra Pick: after digging for nuggets for hours on end, you suddenly hit the jackpot! Excitement only equalled by winning the lottery.

Depression Pick: when the only way to fill the void is to pick so hard and fast that the agony overcomes your feeling of remorse and depression.

Pick a Lot: abnormal amounts of picking, i.e. anything in the three digit realm is generally considered excessive within a twenty-four-hour time frame.

Kiddie Pick: alone and uninhibited you twist your forefinger into your nostril with childlike joy and freedom. The best part is there's no time limit.

Camouflaged Kiddie Pick: like the Kiddie Pick but you have company, so you wrap your forefinger in a tissue, then thrust it in deep and hold back the smile.

Fake Nose Scratch: pretend you have an itch but you're really feeling around the nostril edge for stray bogeys.

Making a Meal Out of It: done furiously and for so long, you're probably entitled to dessert.

Surprise Pickings: a sneeze or laugh causes snot to fly out of your nose and you have to gracefully wipe it off your clothing.

Auto Pick: done in a car when you think no one's looking. Can also mean automatic pick, the one you do when you're not even thinking about it, at work, while talking to a co-worker during a meeting.

Pick Your Brains: done in private, this is the one where your finger goes in so far that it passes the septum.

Pick and Save: done very quickly, just when someone looks away. Hopefully you can bide your time and pocket the snot so they don't catch on to what you just did.

Pick and Flick: a weapon against others in range around you.

Pick and Stick: intended as a "Pick and Flick", but it stubbornly clings to your fingertip.

Pipe Cleaner: you remove a chunk of snot so big it improves your breathing by 90 per cent.

★   ★   ★   ★   ★

NUNS

✳ Two nuns were taking a stroll through the park at dusk when two men jumped them, ripped off their habits, and proceeded to rape them. Sister Gregory, bruised and battered, looked up at the sky and said softly, "Forgive him, Lord, for he knows not what he is doing."

Sister Theresa looked over at her and said, "Actually, mine does."

How do you get a nun pregnant?
Dress her up as an altar boy.

Two nuns go on a shopping trip to Calais, loading up with duty free. On the way back, just as they are going to drive through "Nothing to declare", a customs officer waves them in to the side. The first nun says to the second nun, who is driving, "Don't panic, just show them your cross."

"Okay," says the seconds nun. So she winds the window down, leans out and shouts, "Fuck off!"

✳ A nun went to see her mother superior. "What troubles you, sister?" asked the mother superior. "I thought this was the day you liked to spend with your family."

"It was," sighed the sister. "I went to play a round of golf with my brother. As you may recall, I was a very keen golfer before I gave my life to Christ."

"I do recall that," agreed mother superior. "So how did your day of relaxation go?"

"Not very well," said the sister. "In fact, I'm afraid I took the Lord's name in vain today!"

"Goodness," gasped the mother superior. "You must tell me all about it, sister!"

"Well," continued the sister, "my brother and I were on the seventh tee, a 500-yard par five with a tricky dogleg right with bunkers all down the left and a green hidden behind tall trees. Anyway, I hit the drive of my life. It was a beauty. But then a herd of goose flew over and the ball hit a bird in mid-flight, about 100 yards from the tee!"

"Oh no!" said mother superior. "How desperately unfortunate! However I'm still not sure that this misfortune was sufficient to make you blaspheme, sister?"

"Oh no, no, that wasn't it," said the sister. "When I went for my ball and was trying to figure out what my next shot should be, a squirrel shot out of the woods, picked up my ball and ran off down the fairway!"

"Now that would test even my patience!" agreed mother superior. "But I trust it didn't make you blaspheme, sister!"

"No, I didn't, mother superior!" continued the sister. "I was actually wondering whether this might be a sign from God, the ball being much closer to the green and all. Just then, this eagle swooped down, grabbed the squirrel and flew off, with my ball still in the squirrel's paws!"

"Ah, I see! That's when you took the Lord's name in vain," nodded mother superior.

"No, not really, that wasn't it either," sobbed the sister. "Just as the hawk started to fly out of sight, the squirrel struggled free and the hawk dropped him right on the green. The ball dropped out of the squirrel's paws and rolled to within about two feet of the hole!"

Mother superior sat up in her chair, leaned forward and fixed the sister with her hardest stare and said, "You missed the fucking putt, didn't you?"

✳ What goes black white red, black white red?
A nun on her period doing cartwheels.

✳ Two nuns are cycling down the road. One turns to the other, saying, "I've never come this way before."
Her friend replies, "Me neither, it must be the cobblestones."

* A nun and a priest were crossing the Sahara on a camel. On the third day of their journey, the camel suddenly fell dead from exhaustion. After dusting themselves off, the nun and the priest considered their predicament. After a prolonged period of silence, the priest said: "Well, sister, I have to say that the situation looks pretty grim."

"I know, father," the nun replied. "In fact, I don't think it is likely that we can survive more than a couple of days."

"I agree," said the priest. "Sister, since you and I are unlikely to make it out of here alive, would you do something for me?"

"Anything, father."

"I have never seen a woman's breasts and I was wondering if I might see yours."

"Well, under the circumstances I don't see that it would do any harm."

The nun opened her habit and the priest enjoyed the sight of her shapely breasts. "Sister, would you mind if I touched them?"

She consented and he fondled them for several minutes.

"Father, could I ask something of you?"

"Yes, sister?"

"I have never seen a man's penis. Could I see yours?"

"I think, in the circumstances, that would be okay," the priest replied, unzipping his trousers.

"Father, do you mind if I touch it?" The priest consented and after a few minutes of fondling he was sporting a huge erection.

"Sister, you know that if I insert my penis in the right place, it can give life."

"Is that true, father?"

"Yes it is, sister."

"Then why don't you stick it up that camel's arse so we can get the fuck out of here?"

* What is black and white and screams, "YES! YES! YES!"?

A nun winning at bingo.

* A nun hails a taxi and climbs in. At the end of her journey she confesses that she isn't carrying any money. The driver observes her thoughtfully through the rear-view mirror. "You know, sister," the taxi driver says, "I hope you aren't too offended, but I've always had this fantasy of getting a blow job from a nun."

The nun thinks for a moment and says, "I'm not too offended. I just have two requirements. One, that you are single, and two, that you are Catholic."

"Oh yes, sister, I am single and Catholic," the driver replies, so the nun proceeds to satisfy the cabbie orally.

After they're finished, the driver starts laughing. "What's so funny?" the nun asks.

"I fooled you, sister. The truth is, I'm really married and I'm Jewish!"

"That's okay," the nun replies. "My name is Frank and I'm on my way to a fancy dress party."

* Sister Mary Katherine entered an order called the Monastery of Silence. Upon her arrival, the priest said, "Sister, this is a silent order. You are very welcome here for as long as you like, but you may not speak until I direct you to do so."

Sister Mary Katherine lived in the monastery for seven years before the priest said to her one day, "Sister Mary Katherine, you have been here for seven years. You are allowed to say two words."

Sister Mary Katherine replied, "Hard bed."

"I'm very sorry to hear that," the priest said. "We will get you a better bed."

After another seven years, Sister Mary Katherine was called upon by the priest. "Sister, you have been here for fourteen years. You are now allowed to speak two more words."

"Cold food," replied Sister Mary Katherine. The priest assured her that the food would be warm in the future.

On the twenty-first anniversary of her arrival at the monastery, the priest again called upon Sister Mary Katherine. "You may say two more words today, sister."

"I quit," said Sister Mary Katherine.

"It's probably for the best," said the priest. "You've done fuck all but moan ever since you got here."

* A coach load of nuns are travelling along a dangerous mountain road to Lourdes when the coach brakes give out around a particularly tight corner and it crashes down into a ravine where it explodes. All of the passengers are killed instantly. The nuns arrive at the entrance to Heaven, where they meet St Peter, who is standing next to a font filled with holy water. St Peter greets the nuns and asks the first in line, "Is any aspect of you impure in some way?"

The first nun replies hesitantly, "Well, I did once see a man's penis."

St Peter tells her not to worry as the holy water will purify her vision. He then splashes holy water on to her eyes and allows her through the pearly gates.

He asks the second nun the same thing and she replies, "I did once touch a man's penis." St Peter then purifies her vision and dips her hands in the holy water to purify her touch and then allows her through the pearly gates.

St Peter is just about to interrogate the third nun when a nun at the back barges through to the front of the queue, looking very flustered.

St Peter asks, "Is there a problem, sister?"

The nun replies, "No worries, I just want to make sure I gargle before Sister Susan dips her arse in it."

* A priest and a nun are on their way back from the seminary very late one evening when their car breaks down. The nearest garage is shut and doesn't open until morning so they decide they have no option but to spend the night in a bed and breakfast. When they get there they are told that there is only one double room available.

The priest says: "Sister, I don't think the Lord would object if we spend the night sharing this one room. I'll sleep on the sofa and you have the bed."

"I think that would be fine," agrees the nun. They prepare for bed, say some prayers and settle down to sleep. Ten minutes later the nun says: "Father, I'm very cold."

"No problem, sister," says the priest, "I'll get a blanket from the cupboard."

Another ten minutes later the nun says again: "Father, I'm still very cold."

The priest replies: "Don't worry, sister, I'll get up and fetch you another blanket."

Another ten minutes pass, then the nun murmurs softly: "Father, it's still very cold. I don't think the good Lord would mind if we acted as man and wife just for one night."

"You're right," says the priest. "Get your own fucking blankets."

Mother superior called all the nuns together and said to them, "I have to inform you that we have a case of gonorrhoea in the convent."

"Praise be," said an elderly nun at the back. "I'm sick to death of chardonnay."

✳ A small town has a monastery at one end and a convent at the other. The nuns need some supplies, so one of the priests is sent to deliver them. It's a nice day, so he decides to walk the supplies over. As he gets to the edge of town, a prostitute approaches him and asks, "Excuse me, father, fancy a blow job, £25?"

The priest says, "What's a blow job?" – at which the prostitute laughs and walks away. In the middle of town another girl approaches the priest and asks the same question, with the same result. At the other end of town, a third hooker asks the priest the same question, to which he again replies, "What's a blow job?" And, again, she laughs and walks off.

Finally the priest reaches the convent, knocks on the door, and delivers the supplies. Before he leaves, he says to the mother superior, "May I ask you a question, sister?"

"Of course," she says.

"What's a blow job?"

"£25," replies mother superior, "the same as in town."

★   ★   ★   ★   ★

NYMPHOMANIA

★ I went out with this girl who was a nympho-maniac kleptomaniac. The bitch stole all my condoms.

★ "Doctor," the woman said to the psychiatrist, "everyone says I'm a nymphomaniac."
  "I understand," said the shrink. "But I'll be able to take better notes if you'll let go of my cock."

★ Did you hear about the Mexican nympho-maniac?
  She had Juan too many.

★ ★ ★ ★ ★

OBESITY

❖ A man was driving happily along in his car with his girlfriend when he was pulled over by the police. The police officer approaches him and asks, "Have you been drinking, sir?"
  "No. Why?" replies the man. "I'm sure I wasn't weaving all over the road, was I?"
  "No," replies the officer, "you were driving superbly. It was the fat bird in the passenger seat that made me suspicious."

❖ How do you fuck a fat lass?
  Roll her in flour then go for the wet spot.

❖ What do fat people do in the summer?
   Stink.

❖ How do you know when your date is too fat?
   Your car has stretch marks.

❖ # How do you tell if a girl is too fat to fuck?
   When you pull her knickers down and her arse is still in them.

❖ How do you know when your woman is too fat? When she needs an hour to take a shit, including forty-five minutes just to align her arse to the toilet bowl.

❖ How do you get a fat girl into bed?
   A piece of cake!

❖ A friend of mine was a chubby chaser – he was really into very fat women. He went to a bar one night and saw a fat bird walk in. He went over to chat to her and they ended up back at her house and he sweet talked his way into her bed. They started shagging away, and after a while he says, "Can we turn the light off, please?"
   "Why," said the fat bird, "am I that ugly?"
   "No," he replied. "It's just that I keep burning my arse on the light bulb."

❖ # How can you tell when your girlfriend is too fat?
   When she sits on your face and you can't hear the stereo.

❖ Why do meat and potato pies have holes in the top?
   So people from Wigan can carry four in one hand.

❖ Why did God invent alcohol?
    So fat women can get laid too.

❖ How do you find a fat girl's muff?
    Flip through the folds until you smell shit, then go back one.

❖ My wife keeps telling me that obesity runs in her family. It must be the only thing that does.

> ❝ My wife doesn't like the second-hand car I got her. The ungrateful bitch said she wants something that goes from 0 to 150 in 3 seconds. So I bought her a set of bathroom scales. ❞

❖ I decided to burn some calories today. So I set a fat kid on fire.

❖ **The average obese child is expected to die at the age of fifty-four. That's the pension crisis sorted then.**

❖ My wife looks as if she has been poured into her clothes. And had forgotten to say "when".

❖ My wife is a light eater. As soon as it is light, she starts eating.

❖ An overweight housewife is on her hands and knees, scrubbing the kitchen floor, when she suddenly shouts to her husband, "Help! Frank! I'm paralysed! I can't get up!"
    Her husband runs into the kitchen, takes a look, and says, "Stand up, you stupid bitch. You're kneeling on one of your tits."

❖ I was looking at my girl this morning and I said, "You know, there are three things I really don't like about you . . ."
   "Oh, really? What are they?" she asked.
   "Your chin."

❖ What do you call an obese Chinaman?
   A chunk.

❖ I broke up with my girlfriend because she lied about her weight. When I say that, she died in a bungee-jumping accident when the elastic snapped.

❖ Why are fat girls and mopeds alike?
   They're both fun to ride until your friends find out about it.

❖ My wife told me she thought it would be very romantic if, when she dies, she could be buried in her wedding dress. I said, "You'd better hope you die of some kind of wasting disease then."

❖ I asked this young boy, "Which is your favourite Telly Tubby?"
   He replied, "Probably the new Samsung 42-inch LCD, you patronizing twat."

❖ A fat bird walks into a pub and shouts, "If anyone can guess my weight, they can shag me."
   A man in the corner replies, "Ninety-three stone, you lardy-arsed bint."
   She replies, "Close enough, you lucky bastard!"

❖ My wife said to me, "I don't want you to think I have diabetes because I'm fat. I have diabetes because it runs in our family."
   I replied, "No, darling, you have diabetes because no one runs in your family."

❖ Doctors have confirmed that the actress Dawn French has the ebola flesh-eating disease. They have given her twenty-seven years to live.

❖ I think Dawn French is a great actress. It's odd, because usually I can't stand anything that Lenny Henry has been in.

★ ★ ★ ★ ★

OLD AGE

✳ I'll never forget finding my first grey pubic hair. I wouldn't have minded, only it was in a kebab.

✳ An elderly man goes to see his doctor for a check-up. The doctor runs some tests and says to the man, "Well, everything seems to be in reasonably good condition physically, but what about mentally? How is your connection with God?"

The man says, "No problem, me and God, we're good. He takes care of me, you know."

"Really? How's that?" says the doctor.

"Every night when I have to get up to go to the toilet, he turns on the light for me and then, when I leave, he turns it back off."

Upon hearing this, the doctor is slightly baffled and calls the old man's wife. "I'd like to speak to you about your husband's connection with God. He claims that every night when he needs to use the bathroom, God turns on the light for him and turns it off for him again when he leaves. Is this true?"

She replies: "The old fool, he's been pissing in the fridge again."

✳ Two old gentlemen in their eighties are sitting by the sea front at Blackpool, staring out to sea. After a couple of hours one says "You know what I fancy?"

"No, what?" says his friend.

"One of those ice creams with hundreds and thousands and a flake."

The other says: "Wait there, I'll go and get two."

Four hours later, he returns, sits down and hands the other a paper bag. He puts in his hand and pulls out a saveloy.

"What this?" he asks.

"A steak and kidney pie."

"You useless old fool. You forgot the gravy."

✳ What's got 100 balls and fucks old ladies?
Bingo.

✳ One morning an elderly man was out playing golf, when he hit his ball into the deep rough. While searching for the ball he came across a frog. The frog looked up at him and said: "Sir, if you kiss me, I'll turn into a beautiful princess." So the old man bent down, picked up the frog, put it into his pocket, and carried on looking for his ball.

A few minutes later a voice from his pocket shouted, "Oi! I don't think you heard me. I said, if you kiss me, I'll turn into a beautiful princess."

The old man replied, "No thanks. Frankly at my age I'd rather have a talking frog."

✳ An old couple are at the doctor's. The doctor says to the old man, "I need a urine sample, a faeces sample and a blood sample."

The old man says, "What?"

The doctor repeats: "I need a urine sample, a faeces sample and a blood sample."

Once again, the old man says, "What?"

So the doctor yells: "I NEED A URINE SAMPLE, A FAECES SAMPLE AND A BLOOD SAMPLE!"

The old woman turns to her husband and says, "Bert, he wants your underpants."

✳ Two old women are sitting in a cafe. One says to the other: "Did you come on the bus?"

"Yes," replies her friend. "But I made it look like an asthma attack."

✳ What does an eighty-year-old woman have between her legs that a young woman doesn't?

Her tits.

✳ How do you know when you're getting old?

Your dreams are dry and your farts are wet.

✳ I was standing at a cashpoint machine when a frail old lady came up to and asked if I wouldn't mind checking her balance. So I pushed her over.

✳ An old woman stopped me in the street and asked me to show her how to get to the hospital. So I pushed her under a bus.

✳ What's blue and screws old ladies?

Hypothermia.

✳ What stinks and smells of dog food?

A pensioner's fart.

✳ A man went to a doctor for a check-up. The doctor told him, "You're in amazing shape for a sixty-year-old."

The man replied testily, "Did I say anything about being sixty? Actually I'm seventy-five."

"That's amazing!" replied the doctor. "Do you mind me asking, by the way, how old was your father when he died?"

The patient responded, "Hmmm! Did I say he was dead?"

The doctor was surprised and asked, "How old is he and is he very active?"

The patient replied, "Well, he is ninety-five years old and he still goes skiing three times a year and surfing three times a week during the summer."

The doctor couldn't believe it. "I'm sorry . . . how old was your grandfather when he died?"

The patient snapped back, "Did I say he was dead?"

The doctor was astonished. "You mean to tell me you are seventy-five years old and both your father and your grandfather are alive? Is your grandfather very active?"

The patient said, "He goes skiing at least once a season and surfing once a week during the summer. Not only that," said the patient, "my grandfather is 112 years old, and next week he is getting married again."

The doctor said, "At 112, why in God's name would your grandfather want to get married?"

The patient glared at the doctor and said, "Did I say he wanted to?"

Two old women were eating breakfast one morning. One noticed something funny sticking out her friend's ear. "Minnie, did you know you've got a suppository in your left ear?"

Minnie answered, "I do? A suppository?" She pulled it out and stared at it for a while. "Now I think I know where my hearing aid is."

* Statistically, 91 per cent of old people believe that we show less respect to others than we did in the past. Stupid old fuckwits!

✳ Ninety-year-old Ethel was clinically depressed over the recent death of her husband, Frank. She was so despondent that she decided that she didn't want to go on: she would just kill herself and join him in death. So she took out Frank's old army pistol and made the decision to shoot herself in the heart, since it was so badly broken in the first place. Fearing that she might just miss the vital organ and become a debilitating burden on someone else, she called the NHS helpline to enquire as to just exactly where the heart would be on a woman. The voice on the other end said, "Your heart is just below your left breast." Later that night, poor Ethel was admitted to hospital with a gunshot wound to her knee.

★　　★　　★　　★　　★

ORAL SEX

★ One night, as a couple lay in bed, the husband gently taps his wife on the shoulder and starts rubbing her arm. The wife turns over and says, "I'm sorry, darling, I've got an appointment with the gynaecologist tomorrow and I want to stay fresh." The husband, feeling rejected, reluctantly turns over and tries to sleep.

A few minutes later, he rolls back over and taps his wife again. "Er . . . I don't suppose you're seeing your dentist tomorrow, are you?"

★ ## If the dove is the bird of peace, what is the bird of true love?
The swallow.

★ Why is giving a woman oral sex like playing Monopoly?
Because it may have seemed like a good idea at the start, but it always takes too long to finish.

* A man walks into a pub and says to the barman, "Line me up ten whiskies."

   So the barman lines them up and the man gulps them down one after another. "Christ," says the landlord. "What are you celebrating?"

   "My first blow job," replies the man.

   "No shit!" says the landlord. "Have another one on the house."

   "No thanks," says the man. "If ten whiskies doesn't get rid of the taste, another one won't make any difference."

★ What do lobster thermidor and oral sex have in common?
You can't get either of them at home.

* There's a sucker born every minute, but a swallower is harder to find.

* Three mates are chatting in the pub. One says: "My wife only lets me have sex once a week." The second says: "Think yourself lucky. My wife only lets me have sex once a month." The third says: "You're both lucky. If my missus didn't sleep with her mouth open I wouldn't be getting any at all."

★ What is LXIX?
Sixty-nine the Roman way.

* What's an Australian kiss?
   The same as a French kiss, but down under.

* What is the definition of "Egghead"?
   Something Mrs Dumpty gives to Humpty.

* What's the worst thing a mother can say to her child?
   I should have swallowed you when I had the chance.

★ What's the difference between love, true love and showing off?

   Spitting, swallowing and gargling.

★ What has six legs and eats pussy?

   You, me and Martina Navratilova.

★ What is the definition of a perfect male lover?

   A man with a nine-inch tongue who can breathe through his ears.

★ How can you tell that you have an exceptionally high sperm count?

   Your date has to chew before she swallows.

★ How is pubic hair like parsley?

   You push it to the side before you start eating.

★ What did Cinderella do when she got to the ball?

   She choked.

★ A man gets up one morning to find his wife in the kitchen, apparently frying one of his socks in a pan. "What the hell are you doing?" he asks.

   "I'm doing what you asked me to do last night when you came to bed, blind drunk," she replies.

   Baffled, the man replies, "No way. I don't remember asking you to cook my sock."

★ What is the worst thing about oral sex?
   The view.

★ How is a vagina like a grapefruit?

   The best ones squirt when you eat them.

★ What do you call the space between the vagina and the arsehole?

   The chin rest.

* When is an elf not an elf?
  When she's sucking your cock, she's a goblin.

* Why do men love blow jobs so much?
They love any job they can lie back and watch a woman do.

* What's the difference between your wife and your job?
  After a couple of years your job still sucks.

* A young courting couple are locked in a passionate embrace. He asks, "Can I have a blow job, please?"

  "No chance!" replies his girlfriend.

  "Why not?" he asks her.

  "Because you won't respect me afterwards."

  Three years later they get engaged. After a celebratory meal at a posh restaurant, they go back home and he asks, "Can I have a blow job now, please?"

  "No," she replies. "You won't respect me afterwards."

  Another three years later they get married. Lying in bed together on their wedding night, he asks again, "Can I have a blow job now, please, my love?"

  "No," she replies. "You won't respect me afterwards."

  Twenty-five years later, they are sitting in bed together. He puts down his book, takes off his glasses and turns to his wife of twenty-five years, and asks "Can I have a blow job please, love?"

  "No," she replies. "You won't respect me afterwards."

  He says, "Look, I've known you for over thirty years! We've been married twenty-five years! We've got three children, one grandson with another on the way. Surely by now you must know how much respect I have for you!"

  "Okay, I suppose you have a point," she sighs. "All right, I'll give you a blow job."

  Ten minutes after she is finished, the phone rings. The husband turns to his wife and says, "Well, answer it then, you old cocksucker."

★   What do you call a woman with no arms and no legs who gives good head?
    Partially disabled.

> In a recent survey into blow jobs and why men liked them so much, 5 per cent enjoyed the sensation, 10 per cent enjoyed the excitement and 85 per cent just liked the fucking silence.

★   How do we know God is a man?
    Because if God was a woman, sperm would taste like chocolate.

★   A man in a pub finishes his pint and tells his friends he's under strict instructions, on pain of divorce, to get home at a reasonable time. One of his mates offers some advice on how to deal with situations like this, to keep both parties happy. "When you get home, tip toe up to the bedroom and crawl under the duvet from the bottom of the bed and give your wife the greatest oral sex she's ever had or is ever likely to have again. There is absolutely no way she could be in a bad mood with you."
    The man thinks it over and agrees that there is something in this, so he orders up another round of drinks for himself and his mates. Three hours and several pints later, he staggers home to find his house in complete darkness. He fumbles for his key and eventually unlocks the door, staggers inside and makes his way upstairs. When he gets in the bedroom he slips under the bottom of duvet, works his way up the bed, lifts his wife's nightie and gets to work. After a good ten-minute session and some satisfied noises from the top of the bed, he decides his work is done and he staggers off to the bathroom to brush his teeth. When he opens the bathroom door he is shocked to find his wife sitting on the toilet taking a dump.
    "What the hell are you doing in here!?" he asks.
    "Shush," hisses his wife. "You'll wake your mother up."

★ Why are pubic hairs curly?
   So they don't poke you in the eye.

★ Why is cunnilingus like being in the Mafia?
   One slip of the tongue and you're in deep shit.

★ How can you tell if you were involved in some drunken oral sex the night before?
   You wake up in the morning with a face like a glazed doughnut and a beard like an unwashed paintbrush.

★ What's the difference between a penis and a bonus?
   Your wife will always blow your bonus.

★ A lot of men are in favour of the Muslim full face veil. It solves the age-old problem of where to wipe your dick after a blow job.

★   ★   ★   ★   ★

ORGAN TRANSPLANTS

★ A prostitute went to the hospital to have a heart transplant. She said to the surgeon, "Doctor, I'm worried. What if my body rejects the organ?"

The doctor replied, "Well, you are in extremely good health apart from your heart. What do you do?"

She replied, "Actually I've been a prostitute since I was eighteen years old, but what's that got to do with anything?"

"Well," said the doctor, "if you haven't rejected an organ for the last sixteen years, it's unlikely you're about to start now."

∗   A man went to a doctor to have his penis enlarged. The highly unusual and somewhat risky procedure, known as an elephantaplasm, involved grafting a baby elephant's trunk on to the end of the patient's member.

The operation, however, was apparently a success. Overjoyed, the man went out with his girlfriend to celebrate at a very fancy restaurant.

To his horror, after preliminary cocktails, the man's penis crept out of his pants, felt around the table, grabbed a bread roll and quickly disappeared under the tablecloth.

The girlfriend was startled and exclaimed, "What was that?"

Suddenly, the penis reappeared, took another bread roll and just as quickly shot back under the tablecloth. The girlfriend sat in stunned silence for a moment, then finally said, "I don't believe I saw what I think I just saw . . . can you do that again?"

The man smiled uncomfortably and replied, "I'd like to, unfortunately I don't think my arse can take another crusty roll."

∗   What's the worst part about getting a lung transplant?
The first couple of times you cough, it isn't your phlegm.

*   *   *   *   *

ORGASMS

❖   What's the difference between a Catholic wife and a Jewish wife?
A Catholic wife has real orgasms and fake jewellery.

❖ What's the height of conceit?
Having an orgasm and calling out your own name.

The Five Types of Female Orgasm

The Optimist: Oh Yes, Oh Yes, Oh Yes . . .

The Pessimist: Oh No, Oh No, Oh No . . .

The Confused: Oh Yes, Oh No, Oh Yes, Oh No . . .

The Traveller: I'm coming, I'm coming . . .

The Religious: Oh God, Oh God . . .

❖ What is the biggest drawback for an atheist?
No one to talk to during orgasm.

❖ Why do women fake orgasms?
Because they think we care.

*   *   *   *   *

PARKINSON'S DISEASE

❖ Norman is admitted to an old folks' home. He's very lonely, so he goes in search of a friend. After wandering around for a few days, he meets Madge and they strike up a friendship. Every day they meet at the swimming pool and chat, just passing the time of day. One day Norman says "Do you know what I miss the most about youth, Madge?"
"No Norm, what?" she replies.
"Sex," he says.
"Oh, you randy old goat!" she shrieks.
"No, not like that, Madge. I just wish sometimes that somebody would take my old chap out and hold it."

Madge doesn't think it can do any harm, so out it comes. This continues for a week or so, nothing erotic, just gentle holding. One day Madge turns up to find that Norman is missing. Fearing the worst, she searches the old folks' home before finally finding him at the back of the shed shagging another old woman.

"Norman!" she sobs. "What's going on? What is it that she's got that I haven't?"

Norman replies, "Parkinson's."

Whenever my uncle tries to squeeze into a tight gap left between two parked cars, he starts to shake uncontrollably. I suspect that he suffers from parking zones disease.

❖ Doctors have found a cure for swine flu. They inject you with Parkinson's and you should be able to shake it off in a week.

❖ I've always wanted to shake Muhammad Ali's hand. Unfortunately Parkinson's beat me to it.

❖ Who is James Bond's favourite bartender?
Michael J. Fox.

❖ Which is worse – Parkinson's or Alzheimer's?
Alzheimer's – it is much better to lose half a pint than to forget where you left it.

★   ★   ★   ★   ★

PARALYMPICS

❋ What's better than winning gold at the Paralympics?
Having legs.

* What is grey, full of orange stickers and has one cunt in a yellow jacket?

   The car park at the Paralympics.

* What does a Paralympian fear the most?

   Testing positive for WD-40.

* It was the 100 metres freestyle swimming final at the Paralympics. In the first lane was an Australian who didn't have any arms. In the second lane was a Brazilian without any legs. In the third lane was the current world record holder – an Englishman without any arms, legs or torso. He was just a head. They line up, the siren blows and – splash – they're all in the pool.

   The armless Australian takes an early lead but the legless Brazilian closes on him fast. The English head meanwhile sank straight to the bottom.

   In a very tight finish the Brazilian wins. As he is celebrating victory he looks down the pool and can see bubbles surfacing from the other end. He realizes that the English contestant is still at the bottom of the pool, so he reacts quickly and dives down to rescue him. He picks up the head, swims back up to the surface and places him at the side of the pool. The head is coughing and spluttering. Eventually he breathes, and curses: "Bollocks. I got cramp in my ears."

* I can't see why some people kick up such a fuss about how some sportsmen and women don't sing the national anthem. I was watching the Paralympics and some of the gold medallists couldn't even be arsed to stand up for it.

* Did you hear about the lost-property office at the Paralympics stadium?

   They collected so many lost limbs that they were able to build another 143 athletes.

*　　*　　*　　*　　*

PARTYING

★ A woman throws a themed fancy dress party, where each guest is required to show up dressed as an emotion. The first of her guests knocks at the door, dressed from head to foot in green.

"Let me guess . . . Envy!" she says, and lets him in.

Then a lady arrives dressed from head to foot in red. She says, "Anger!" and lets her in.

Then a black man walks up to the front door, completely naked except that he is holding a bowl of pudding with his penis stuck in it.

"Wait a minute," the host says to him. "This is supposed to be an emotion party!"

The guest replies, "I know, and I'm fucking dis custard."

★ I went to an 1980s-themed party the other night. It started off great but by the end we'd all caught AIDS and lost our jobs.

★ I went to a fancy dress party wearing only a pair of boxer shorts. A really fit-looking woman at the door said to me, "This is a fancy dress party, you know. What are you supposed to be?"

"A premature ejaculation," I replied.

"What do you mean?" replied the woman.

"Well, I've just come in my pants."

★ My girlfriend was invited on a hen party recently. The invitation said "Dress to kill", so she went as Myra Hindley.

★ I was at a party last night, much the worse for drink, and I walked up to this bird and said, "Duck my sick!"

She replied, "You are drunk, don't you mean suck my dick?"

I said, "No!" then threw up all over her.

* A man goes to a fancy dress party with nothing but a naked girl on his back. "So what the fuck are you supposed to be?" the host asks.

    "I'm a turtle," the man replies.

    "Sounds like a load of bollocks to me," replies his host. "How can you be a snail when all you've got is that naked girl on your back?"

    "Well," the bloke replies, "that's Michelle."

> " I've just been to my first Muslim birthday party. The musical chairs was a bit slow but, fuck, the pass the parcel was like lightning! "

★   ★   ★   ★   ★

PENISES

❖ A man was in bed with his new Thai bride. After a couple of hours of fantastic, steamy sex, she spent the next hour stroking his penis while he enjoyed a smoke.

    "That's nice," he says. "Why do you like doing that?"

    She replies, "Because I really miss mine."

❖ Bert was happily married except for one very important aspect. His dick was so large that his wife was unable to accommodate him without it causing her great pain. One night, this frustration boiled over and he headed out to find a brothel. Surely, if he was to find a woman who could fit him, it would be there.

    As he walks into the reception he sees a woman behind the counter. "I'm Helga, the Headmistress," she says. "How can I help you?"

    He walks over to her and tells her his story. Money exchanges hands, and he's directed down the hall, first room on the left. Bert has never actually been with a prostitute before so some awkward conversation occurs before intercourse. In the act, he manages to get a third of the way in before she starts screaming in pain. He quickly withdraws, apologizes profusely and goes back to the Headmistress.

She's a little taken aback, but still proposes a solution – second door, right side. The man is a more than a little frustrated by this point, so no conversation occurs and he gets right into it. A third goes in. Then half. She screams. He dismounts and storms back to the Headmistress, not even bothering to put his clothes back on, and demands a refund.

She tells him that she has one last option for him – if it doesn't work, she will gladly refund every penny. Last door on the left. He goes in, and the room is very dark. A woman lies on the bed, waiting for him. He mounts her – a third of the way, half-way, and all the way in. She offers no complaint. Gleefully he begins thrusting, when, to his horror, he notices she appears to be foaming from the mouth. In a panic, he runs back to the Headmistress.

"That girl is frothing at the mouth! I need you to call a doctor!"

The Headmistress rolls her eyes. "For fuck's sake!" she turns and shouts behind her. "The dead girl is full again!"

❖ My last girlfriend used to call my penis "Weapon of Mass Destruction". I was flattered until I found out what she meant was it was really hard to find.

❖ Did you hear about the man with five dicks?
   His pants fit like a glove.

❖ A paperboy is doing his monthly round collecting money from his customers. He knocks on a door and is greeted by a rather voluptuous lady, who is wearing a transparent lace negligee that leaves nothing to the imagination.

❖ "Hello, madam," says the boy. "I've come for the paper money. You owe £5, please."

"Young man, I'm afraid I've no money in the house," the woman replies in a sultry voice, "but if you come in I'm sure I can think of something." So the boy enters the house and the woman throws herself on the fireside rug. Opening her negligee to reveal a pair of pendulous breasts, she says, "You can have me instead."

The boy takes off his bag, and then when whips out an unfeasibly large penis that would be more in place on a stallion. The woman can't believe her eyes. He then produces a series of big rubber rings from his bag and starts to stack them on his massive cock.

"What are you doing?" asks the woman.

"Oh these – they're just to make sure I don't go all the way in when I shag you," replies the boy.

"No way!" says the lady, "I'll take all of you!"

The boy replies, "Not for five fucking quid you won't, lady!"

❖ A Canadian, an American and an Australian were on a cruise ship, enjoying a bullshitting session. The Canadian said, "In Canada we have sheep that are so big they take all day to be shorn."

The American said, "That's nothing, in Texas our cattle are so big the steaks have to be turned with a fork lift."

The Australian replied, "That's nothing, we have women with pussies this big." He then stretched his hands so wide that it would do a fisherman justice.

"Jesus. How the hell do you screw them, then?" asked the American.

"They stretch."

★   ★   ★   ★   ★

PERSONAL HYGIENE

* A man walks into a lift and finds himself alone with an attractive woman. As the lift ascends, he asks, "Excuse me, miss, can I smell your fanny?'.
  "Certainly not!" she replied.
  "Hmmm. It must be your feet then."

* Why do women pierce their bellybuttons? It is somewhere for them to hang their air freshener.

* What's the difference between a French woman and a basketball team?
  The basketball team showers after four periods.

* What's the hardest thing about a sex change operation?
  Inserting the anchovies.

* My ex-girlfriend had a tattoo of a sea shell on her inner thigh. If you put your ear to it, I swear you can smell the ocean.

★   ★   ★   ★   ★

PET SHOPS

✳ A man sees an advert in a pet shop window for a talking centipede with a price tag at £150. Thinking he's hit upon the bargain of a lifetime, he buys the centipede and takes it away in a box. When he gets home, he opens the box and politely asks the centipede if he would like to go down the pub for a pint, but the centipede doesn't answer. A few minutes later, he asks again, but still no response.

At this point he starts to get a bit annoyed, thinking perhaps that he's been conned. He shouts one more time: "Do you want to go for a pint?!"

The centipede pops his head out of the box and says, "All right, I heard you the first time, give me a chance to put my fucking shoes on!"

❖ A vicar is in a pet shop buying a parrot. "Are you sure it doesn't know any profane words?" he asks the shopkeeper.

"Oh, absolutely. It's a very religious parrot," the shopkeeper assures him. "Do you see those strings on his legs? When you pull the right one, he recites the Lord's Prayer, and when you pull on the left he recites the 23rd Psalm."

"Wonderful!" says the vicar. "But what happens if you pull both strings?"

"I fall off my perch, you stupid cunt," screeches the parrot.

❖ My new goldfish suffers from epilepsy. The funny thing is, it never fits when it's back in the bowl.

❖ An animal rights activist walks into a pet shop and puts a bomb on the counter. He says: "You've got one minute to get out of here before the place blows!"

A tortoise in the back shouts, "You bastard!"

❖ A man buys a parrot from the pet shop but he can never get it to talk, so he goes back to the pet shop to complain. The pet shop owner says, "I know exactly what the problem is. Your bird has too much hook in its beak. What you have to do is file the beak back a bit and it will be able to talk just fine. Be careful not to file too much beak off, though, because if you take too much off, the bird won't be able to eat or drink and it will die."

The parrot owner asks how much the pet shop guy charges to do this beak modification and he says £100. So the parrot owner decides he'll do it himself.

A week or so later they bump into one another in the street. The pet shop owner enquires how the parrot is and whether it is talking yet.

The parrot owner replies, "The parrot is dead."

"I told you not to file the beak back too far – did he starve?"

"No, he was dead before I got him out of the vice."

❖ A fat woman was walking past a pet shop. Suddenly a parrot screeched at her: "Oi! I'm talking to you, you fat ugly cow!" The woman pretended not to notice and continued on her way.

The next day on her way to work she passed by the pet store again, and the parrot once more said, "Oi! I'm taking to you, you fat ugly cow!"

She was really upset by now, so she went into the shop and complained to the owner. She threatened to sue them and have the bird put down. The store owner apologized profusely and promised he would make sure the parrot would not offend her again.

The next day, she deliberately passed by the store to test the parrot. "Oi! I'm talking to you," the parrot shouted after her.

"Yes?"

"You fucking know!"

❖ A woman goes into a pet shop to buy a parrot. The assistant shows her a beautiful Norwegian Blue. "What about this one, madam? A beautiful bird, and an absolute bargain at only £25."

"Why is it so cheap?" the woman asks.

"Well," replies the assistant, "it used to live in a brothel, and as a result its language is a touch ripe."

"No matter," says the woman, making her mind up. "I'm broad-minded and it'll be a laugh having a potty-mouthed parrot."

She buys the parrot and takes him home.

Once inside his new home, the parrot looks around and squawks at the woman, "Fuck me, a new brothel and a new madam."

The woman laughs awkwardly. "I'm not a madam and this is not a brothel."

A little later, her two teenage daughters arrive home.

"Fucking unbelievable," says the parrot when he sees the two daughters. "A new brothel, a new madam and now two new prostitutes."

"Mum, tell your parrot to shut up!" complain the girls, but they all see the funny side and have a laugh at their new pet.

A short while later, the woman's husband comes home.

"Fucking incredible," says the parrot. "A new brothel, a new madam, new prostitutes, but the same old clients. How's it going, Nick?"

A woman sees an advert in a pet shop window: "Clitoris-licking frog available – apply within". She goes into the shop and says to the man behind the counter, "I'm interested in the clitoris-licking frog."

The man replies: "Bonjour, madame, fermez la porte."

❖ A woman went into a pet shop to buy her husband a pet for his birthday. After looking around for a while she found that all the pets were very expensive, so she had a word with a sales assistant and explained that she wanted to buy a pet, but she didn't want to spend a fortune. "Well," said the assistant, "I have a very large bullfrog. Apparently it has been trained to give blow jobs."

"Blow jobs? Are you sure?" the woman asked incredulously.

"It hasn't been proven, but we've sold thirty of them this month," he said.

The woman thought it would be a great joke gift and, besides, what if it's true . . . no more blow jobs for her! She bought the frog. When she got home and explained the frog's special abilities to her husband, he was extremely sceptical and laughed it off. The woman went to bed happy, dreaming that maybe, just maybe, she had performed oral sex for the last time.

In the middle of the night, she was awakened by the noise of pots and pans flying everywhere, banging and crashing around the kitchen. She ran downstairs to the kitchen, only to find her husband and the frog reading cookbooks. "What are you two doing up at this hour?" she asked.

The husband replied, "If I can teach this frog to cook, you're gone."

❖ A cute little girl walks into a pet shop and asks: "Excuthe me, do you have any widdle wabbits?"

"Aaaah," the shopkeeper thinks to himself, so he gets down on his knees so that he is on her level and says: "Do you want a widdle white wabbit, or a thoft fwuffy bwack wabbit, or one like that widdle bwown one over there?"

The little girl blushes, puts her hands on her knees, leans forward and whispers, "To be fair, I weally don't fink my anaconda gives a toth."

❖ A married couple are arguing constantly. The wife suggests that perhaps they would get along better if they have a pet for company. So the husband goes to a pet shop in search of a friend. After looking around he spots a parrot sitting on a little perch. Upon closer inspection the parrot doesn't have any feet or legs. The man says out loud, "Bloody hell! I wonder what happened to this parrot?"

"I was born this way," says the parrot. "I'm a disabled parrot."

The man laughs nervously: he could have sworn it sounded like this parrot actually understood what he said and had answered him.

"In case you're wondering, I understood every word," says the parrot. "I am a highly intelligent, well-educated parrot."

"Really?" the man asks in disbelief. "Then answer me this: how do you hang on to your perch without any feet?"

"Well," the parrot says, "this is slightly embarrassing, but since you asked, I'll tell you. I wrap my little parrot dick around this here wooden bar. You can't see it because of my feathers."

"Wow," says the man, "you really can understand and answer, can't you?"

"Of course. I can hold my own in intelligent conversation on almost any subject: politics, religion, sports, physics, philosophy. Actually, I'm an expert in ornithology. I also speak fluent French. You ought to buy me. I am a great companion." The man looks at the price tag. "Two hundred pounds!" he says. "I can't afford that."

"Pssst," the parrot hisses, motioning the man closer with one wing.

"Nobody wants me because I don't have any feet. You can get me for £20. Just make an offer."

The man offers £20 and walks away with the parrot. The new pet is sensational. He's witty, he's great company and the man is delighted. One day the man comes home from work and the parrot says, "Pssst," and motions him over with one wing. The man goes up close to the cage. "There's something you ought to know," says the parrot, "it's about your wife and the milkman."

"What?" says the man.

"Well," the parrot says, "when the milkman came to the door today your wife greeted him in a sheer negligee and kissed him on the mouth."

"What happened then?" asks the man.

"Then the milkman came into the house and lifted up the negligee and began putting his hands all over her," reports the parrot.

"Then what?"

"Then he lifted up the negligee, got down on his knees and began to look at her body, starting with her neck and slowly going down and down . . ."

The parrot pauses for a long time.

"What happened? What happened?" says the frantic man.

"Buggered if I know," says the parrot. "I fell off my perch."

*   *   *   *   *

PHARMACISTS

* A man went into a pharmacist's and asked for a vial of cyanide. The assistant asked him what he wanted it for. The man answered calmly, "I want to kill my wife." The pharmacist was shocked but kept his professional composure. "I'm sorry, sir," he replied, "but you will have to understand under the circumstances that I am unable to supply you any cyanide."

The man reached into his wallet and produced a photo of his wife. The chemist studied it for a while and returned it. "I see, sir. I'm sorry, I didn't realize you had a prescription."

* A man went into a pharmacist's and said to the assistant, "Excuse me, do you have cotton wool balls?"

He replied, "What do you think I am, a fucking teddy bear?"

❋ A man went to the pharmacist's to buy some condoms. "I wonder", said the pharmacist, "if I might interest you in our very latest product, the Artificial Vagina."

The customer couldn't believe his ears, so the pharmacist took one from behind the counter and showed it to him. "It looks just like the real thing!"

"It certainly does," replied the chemist. "Why don't you give it a real test, just smell it."

"Christ! It smells just like one!"

"A final test, just feel it."

"I can't believe it, it feels just like a real one, I'll buy it!"

"Should I wrap it up?"

"Don't bother, I'll eat it here."

❋ A little boy went to the pharmacist's for some condoms. He walked up to the counter and said, "Sir, can you tell me where the ribbed condoms are?"

The pharmacist replied, "Son, do you know what condoms are used for?"

"Yes," replied the boy. "They keep you from catching venereal diseases."

"All right," said the pharmacist, "but do you know what the ribs are for?"

The little boy thought for a minute, then looked up at the pharmacist and replied, "Well, not exactly, but they certainly make the hair on my hamster's back stand on end."

★   ★   ★   ★   ★

PHILOSOPHERS

* Socrates was widely lauded in ancient Greece for his great wisdom. One day the great philosopher came upon a friend, who ran up to him excitedly and said, "Socrates, guess what I just heard about one of your students?"

"Stop right there," Socrates replied, raising his hand. "Let's think this through. Before you tell me anything, I'd like you to pass a little test. It's called the Test of Three."

"The Test of Three?"

"That is correct," Socrates continued. "Before you talk to me about my student, let's take a moment to test what you're going to say. The first test is Truth. Are you absolutely sure that what you are about to tell me is true?"

The man thought for a while, then shook his head. "No," he replied, "actually I just heard about it from someone else."

"All right," said Socrates. "So you don't really know if it's true or not. Now let's try the second test, the test of Goodness. Is what you are about to tell me about my student something good?"

"No, on the contrary—"

"So," Socrates continued, "you want to tell me something bad about him even though you're not certain it's true?"

The man shrugged, a little embarrassed.

Socrates continued, "You may still pass the test because there is a third test – the filter of Usefulness. Is what you want to tell me about my student going to be of any use to me?"

"No, not really."

"Well," concluded Socrates, "if what you want to tell me is neither true nor good nor even useful, why tell it to me at all?"

The man was ashamed and said nothing more.

This is why Socrates was a great philosopher and held in such high esteem. It also explains why he never found out that Plato was shagging his wife.

POLES

❖ Why do so many Polish names end in "ski"?
   Because they can't spell toboggan.

❖ What is long and hard, and a Polish bride gets it on her wedding night?
   A new surname.

A man went to a Warsaw ophthalmologist. The doctor showed the patient the eye chart, displaying the letters CVKPNWXSCZ.
   "Can you read that?" the doctor asked.
   "Can I read it?" the Pole replied. "I think I shagged his sister."

❖ What do you get if you cross a Pole with a Scouser?
   Someone who steals all the jobs.

★　★　★　★　★

POLICE

* What game do policemen's children play?
  Pin the rape on the darkie.

* What's the definition of "police intelligence"?
  An excuse to raid the wrong house.

* How many metropolitan police officers does it take to push a black man down the stairs?
  None, he fell.

* A man is driving along in his car when he suddenly gets pulled over by the police. The man pokes his head out of the window and says, "What seems to be the problem, officer?"
  The policeman looks him in the eye and says, "Are you aware that a woman fell out of your car about two miles back?"
  "Thank fuck for that!" says the driver. "I thought I had gone deaf."

* What's the difference between a woman and a mobile speed camera?
  Generally, as far as a woman is concerned, you can see the cunt behind the bush.

* A man is pulled over by the police for speeding. As the police officer is writing up the ticket, the man asks, "Can you arrest me for calling you something really abusive?"
  "Yes," replies the officer.
  He then asks, "Can you arrest me for thinking something?"
  "Of course not," replies the officer.
  "In that case," says the man, "I think you're a cunt."

✳ I was driving home from the pub one night when I was stopped by a policewoman. She walked over to my car, leaned in the window and said, "Have we had a drink, sir?"

I replied, "Nope . . . but I might have shagged you at a party . . ."

✳   ✳   ✳   ✳   ✳

POLITICAL CORRECTNESS

✳ I found the girl of my dreams yesterday in the vegetable section in Tesco's.

They don't like you calling it the vegetable section any more though. It's "disabled toilets" these days.

✳ Nelson: "Order the signal, Hardy."

Hardy: "Aye, aye, sir."

Nelson: "Hold on, that's not what I dictated to the Signals. What's the meaning of this?"

Hardy: "Sorry, sir?"

Nelson (reading aloud): "England expects every person to do his duty, regardless of race, gender, sexual orientation, religious persuasion or disability. What nonsense is this, man?"

Hardy: "Admiralty policy, I'm afraid, sir. We're an equal opportunities employer now. We had a terrible job getting 'England' past the censors, in case it was considered racist."

Nelson: "Gadzooks, Hardy. Hand me my pipe and tobacco."

Hardy: "Sorry, sir. All naval vessels have been designated no-smoking working environments."

Nelson: "In that case, break open the rum ration. Let us splice the main brace to steel the men before battle."

Hardy: "The rum ration has been abolished, I'm afraid, admiral. It's part of the government's policy on binge drinking."

Nelson: "Ye Gods, Hardy. I suppose we'd better get on with it then . . . full speed ahead."

Hardy: "I think you'll find there's a four-knot speed limit in this stretch of water, sir."

Nelson: "Damn it, man! We are on the eve of the greatest sea battle in history. We must advance with all dispatch. Report from the crow's nest, please."

Hardy: "That won't be possible, sir."

Nelson: "What?"

Hardy: "Health and safety have closed the crow's nest, sir. There's no safety harness. They have also pointed out that the rope ladder doesn't meet regulations. I'm afraid they won't let anyone up there until a proper scaffolding can be erected."

Nelson: "Then get the ship's carpenter without delay, Hardy."

Hardy: "He's busy knocking up a wheelchair access to the fo'c'sle, admiral."

Nelson: "Wheelchair access? On a battleship? I've never heard anything so absurd."

Hardy: "Health and safety again, sir. We have to provide a barrier-free environment for the differently abled."

Nelson: "Differently abled? I've only one arm and one eye and I refuse even to hear mention of the word. I didn't rise to the rank of admiral by playing the disability card."

Hardy: "Actually, sir, you did. The Royal Navy is under represented in the areas of visual impairment and limb deficiency."

Nelson: "Whatever next? Give me full sail. The salt spray beckons."

Hardy: "A couple of minor problems there too, I'm afraid, sir. Health and safety won't let the crew up the rigging without hard hats and they don't want anyone breathing in too much salt because it could result in high blood pressure."

Nelson: "I've never heard such infamy. Break out the cannon and tell the men to stand by to engage the enemy."

Hardy: "The men are a bit worried about shooting at anyone, admiral."

Nelson: "What? This is mutiny."

Hardy: "It's not that, sir. It's just that they're afraid of being charged with murder if they actually kill anyone. There's a couple of no-claim, no-fee lawyers on board, watching everyone like hawks."

Nelson: "Then how are we to sink the Frogs?"

Hardy: "Actually, sir, we're not."

Nelson: "We're not?"

Hardy: "No, sir. The French are our European partners now. According to the Common Fisheries Policy, we shouldn't even be in this stretch of water. We could get hit with a claim for compensation."

Nelson: "But you must hate a Frenchman as you hate the devil!"

Hardy: "I wouldn't let the ship's diversity coordinator hear you saying that, sir. You'll be up on a disciplinary."

Nelson: "You must consider every man an enemy who speaks ill of your king."

Hardy: "Not any more, sir. We must be more inclusive. Now, please put on your kevlar vest; it's the rules. It could save your life."

Nelson: "Don't tell me – health and safety. Whatever happened to rum, sodomy and the lash?"

Hardy: "As I explained, sir, rum is off the menu! And there's a ban on corporal punishment."

Nelson: "What about sodomy?"

Hardy: "I believe that is now legal, sir."

Nelson: "In that case . . . kiss me, Hardy."

★　　★　　★　　★　　★

POLITICIANS

★ What's the difference between paedophiles and politicians?
   Politicians don't keep pictures of the little people they fuck.

★ What do politicians use for birth control?
   Their personalities.

★ A man gets stuck in traffic near Parliament. He asks a police officer what the hold-up is, and is told: "The prime minister is so depressed about the UK's debt that he's stopped his car and is threatening to douse himself with petrol and set himself alight."
   "What are you going to do?" asks the man.
   "We're putting together a collection for him," says the officer.
   "How much have you got?" asks the man.
   "About forty gallons," says the officer.

★ When politicians die, why are they buried in a hole thirty-six feet deep?
   Because deep down, they are all nice people.

★ What's the difference between a dead dog in the road and a dead politician in the road?
   There are skid marks in front of the dog.

★ What's the difference between an MP and a bucket of dirt?
   The bucket.

* A little boy goes to his father and asks, "Dad, what is politics?"

  His dad replies, "Well son, let me try to explain it this way. I'm the breadwinner of the family, so let's call me capitalism. Your mother, she takes care of the money, so we'll call her the government. We're here to take care of your needs, so we'll call you the people. The nanny, we'll consider her the working class. And your baby brother, we'll call him the future. Now, think about that and see if that makes sense."

  So the little boy goes off to bed, thinking about what dad had said. Later that night, he hears his baby brother crying, so he gets up to check on him. He finds that the baby has filled his nappy, he goes to his parents' room and finds his mother sound asleep. Not wanting to wake her, he goes to the nanny's room. Finding the door locked, he peeps in the keyhole and sees his dad in bed with the nanny. He gives up and goes back to bed.

  The next morning, the little boy says to his father, "Dad, I think I understand politics now."

  The father says, "Well done, son, tell me in your own words what you think politics is all about."

  The little boy replies, "Well, while capitalism is screwing the working class, the government is sound asleep, the people are being ignored and the future is in deep shit."

* A politician dies and goes to Heaven. When he gets to the pearly gates, St Peter takes one look at him and says, "Sorry, no politicians allowed in Heaven."

  The MP pleads that he's a good bloke who's done lots of good work.

  "Oh yeah? Like what, for example?" asks St Peter.

  The MP says, "Why, just last week I gave £20 to Children In Need, £30 to Help The Aged and £50 to Comic Relief."

  St Peter thinks for a while then says, "Wait here."

  He goes inside for a while, then comes back. "Sorry mate, I've had a word with God. He says, 'Here's your £100 back, now fuck off!'"

*   *   *   *   *

THE POPE

★ The Pope falls seriously ill and all the cardinals are very worried. They get the best doctors in Vatican City but nothing helps. Eventually one of the cardinals says: "There is only one doctor left that we haven't tried, he is the best in all Italy."

So the cardinals order him to summon the doctor to examine the Pope. The doctor comes to the council of cardinals and says: "I have good news and bad news, the Holy Father has cancer of the testicles, but the good news is he can be cured, all he needs to do is take this drug and have sex with a woman."

The cardinals recoil in shock. Obviously this treatment is impossible because he is the Holy Father and therefore must remain celibate. Unfortunately, there is no other way, so one of the cardinals approaches the Pope and explains the situation. "Holy Father, you have a terrible cancer and will die unless you have sex with a woman."

The Pope ponders this for a moment, then declares, "Ok, I'll do it, but on three conditions."

"Okay," says the cardinal. "What are the conditions?"

"One, the woman must be blind, so she will never know who she made love with."

"Okay, your Holiness, what next?"

"Two, the woman must be dumb, so if she ever realizes who she made love to, she will not be able to tell."

"Certainly, your Holiness. And the third condition?"

"She has to have big tits."

★ A man is at the barber's having his hair trimmed by Italian Tony. He mentions to the barber that he's shortly going on holiday to Italy with the wife.

"My homeland!" says Tony. "Where abouts you going?"

"Rome."

"Rome? Why would anyone want to go to Rome? It's nasty and overcrowded and dirty. You're crazy to want to go to Rome. Go to my hometown, Palermo. So, how are you getting there?"

"We're taking Alitalia," is the reply. "I got a good rate."

"Alitalia?" exclaims the barber. "You fucking crazy? That's a terrible airline. Their planes are dirty, their flight attendants are ugly and they're always late. So, where are you staying in Rome?"

"We'll be at this exclusive little place near the River Tiber called the Hotel Roma."

"Don't go any further. I know that place. It's a terrible tourist trap. Everybody thinks it's gonna be something special and exclusive, but it's a shit-hole. Stay somewhere else. So, what you gonna do in Rome?"

"We're going to go to see the Vatican and maybe get to see the Pope."

"Don't make me laugh!" snorts the barber. "Sure, you'll see him. You and a million other people. He'll look the size of an ant."

Six weeks later, the man returns for another trim. Tony asks him about his trip to Rome. "It was wonderful," explains the customer, "not only were we on time in one of Alitalia's brand new planes, but it was overbooked so they bumped us up to first class. The food and wine were fantastic and the cabin crew waited on us hand and foot. And the hotel was amazing. They'd just finished a big refurbishing job and they upgraded us to a suite for free. Then we went to see the Vatican. We were really lucky, because as we were walking around, a Swiss Guard tapped me on the shoulder and explained that the Pope likes to meet some of the visitors, and if I'd be so kind as to step into his private room and wait, the Pope would personally greet me. Sure enough, five minutes later, the Pope walked through the door and shook my hand! I knelt down and he spoke a few words to me."

"I don't believe it! What'd he say?"

He says: "'Tell me, my son, who fucked up your hair?'"

Old Hans was a minister in a small German town. He had always been a good man and lived by the Bible. One day God decided to reward him, with the answer to any three questions Hans would like to ask. Old Hans didn't have to think about it long. His first question was: "Will there ever be married Catholic priests?"

God promptly replied: "Not in your lifetime."

Hans thought for a while, and then came up with the second question: "What about female priests then, will we have them one day?"

Again God had to disappoint old Hans: "Not in your lifetime, I'm afraid."

Hans was a little disappointed to hear that. He decided to drop the subject. After having thought for a while, he asked the last question: "Will there ever be another German pope?"

God answered quickly: "Not in my lifetime."

★ ★ ★ ★ ★

PORNOGRAPHY

❖ A mother is cleaning her son's room when she finds an S&M magazine under the bed. Upset, she shows the magazine to her husband.

"Well?" his wife asks. "What do you think we should do?"

"I'm really not sure," the father replies. "But it's probably not a good idea to spank him."

Twenty Lessons We Have Learned from Watching Porn

1 Women always wear high heels to bed.
2 Men are never impotent.
3 When going down on a woman, ten seconds is more than satisfactory.
4 If a woman is discovered masturbating by a strange man, she will not scream with embarrassment, but rather insist that he shags her.
5 Women smile appreciatively when men splat them in the face with spunk.
6 Women enjoy having sex with ugly middle-aged men.
7 Women moan uncontrollably when giving a blow job.
8 Women always achieve orgasm when men do.
9 A blow job will always get a woman off a speeding ticket.
10 All women are noisy fucks.

❖ My wife said, "When you're watching pornography, do you think of me?"
    I countered, "When you're eating a cake, do you think of dogshit?"

❖ Why is porn like a KFC meal?
    It feels great when you're doing it, but afterwards, you feel really dirty and your hands are all sticky.

❖ Actors are often advised never to work with children or animals. Except in the porn industry.

11 In the 1970s people were unable to shag unless there was a wild guitar solo in the background.

12 A common and enjoyable sexual practice for a man is to take his half-erect penis and slap it repeatedly on a woman's butt.

13 There are Asian women, but no Asian men.

14 If you encounter a guy and his girlfriend having sex in the bushes, the boyfriend will not knock seven shades of shit out of you if you shove your cock in his girlfriend's mouth.

15 There is always a plot.

16 When taking a woman from behind, a man can really excite a woman by giving her a gentle slap on the bottom.

17 Nurses will suck patient's cocks.

18 When your girlfriend discovers you getting head from her best friend, she will be momentarily annoyed before fucking both of you.

19 Women never have headaches.

20 When a woman is sucking a man's penis it is important for him to remind her to "suck it".

❖ I discovered today that my grandmother once starred in a porno film. I don't know what disgusts me more, the fact she made it or the fact I carried on wanking after I recognized her.

❖ Why do women watch porn?
   To see if the characters get married at the end.

❖ Gay porn. What a load of bollocks.

★   ★   ★   ★   ★

POST

❖ A man was working in the Post Office sorting area one day when he came across a letter in shaky handwriting simply addressed to "God". As there was no other forwarding address, he thought he should open it to see what it was about.

The letter read:

Dear God,

I am an eighty-six-year-old widow, living on a very meagre pension. The other day someone stole my purse. It had £50 in it, which was all the money I have until my next pension cheque. Next Sunday is Christmas Eve and I had invited two of my friends over for dinner. Without that money I have nothing to buy food with. As I have no family to turn to, you are my only hope. Can you please help me?

Yours sincerely, Ethel.

The postal worker was very moved by the letter and showed it to all of his fellow employees. Every one of them stumped up some money – by the time he made the rounds, he had collected £46, which they put into an envelope and sent to the woman. They all felt happy in the knowledge the old lady would be able to share a meal on Christmas Eve with her friends.

Christmas came and went and a few days later another letter arrived, addressed in the same shaky handwriting, again addressed to God. All the Post Office workers gathered around while the letter was opened.

It read:

Dear God,

How can I ever thank you enough for what you did for me? Because of your generosity I had a lovely Christmas Eve with my friends and I told them all about your wonderful gift.

Yours sincerely, Ethel.

P.S. There was £4 missing. I think it must have been those thieving cunts at the Post Office.

❖ Three married women were sitting around discussing their sex lives. The first said, "I call my husband the dentist because nobody can drill like he does."

The second woman said, "I call my husband the miner because of his incredible shaft."

The third fell silent until one of the other two asked. "Well, what do you call your boyfriend?"

She said, "The postman."

"Why the postman?"

"Because he always delivers late and most of the time it's in the wrong box."

❖ **The Post Office has released a new stamp depicting a clitoris. It isn't selling too well. Apparently only 2 per cent of the population know how to lick it.**

❖ A postman was on the last delivery of his career. Everyone on his route knew him and gave him presents to say goodbye. Eventually, he got to the very last house to deliver his final letter, when the front door of the house was opened by a beautiful woman wearing nothing but a scanty robe. She grabbed his hand and took him inside. For the rest of the day and all though the night they made passionate love. The next morning when the postman awoke he thought it had all been an amazing dream. He couldn't believe his eyes when he saw the beautiful, naked woman lying in the bed beside him. She got up and made him breakfast and poured him a cup of coffee. As he was finishing his breakfast he noticed a pound coin underneath the saucer.

"What's the pound coin for?" he asked.

The women replied: "That was my husband's idea. I asked him what to do for you on your last day. He said, 'Fuck him! Give him a quid.' The breakfast was my idea."

❖ What's 100 yards long and smells of piss?

The Post Office queue on Thursday mornings.

❖ My wife is from Taiwan. People often ask me if she was a mail-order bride and I find this very insulting. The Royal Mail lose around two million letters and parcels each year and to suggest that I would trust the delivery of my wife to them is extremely insensitive. I got her via DHL next-day delivery.

✶   ✶   ✶   ✶   ✶

PREMATURE EJACULATION

✳ I was invited to a function at the Premature Ejaculation Society. When I asked if there was a dress code, they said, "No, just come as you are."

✳ Premature ejaculation isn't all bad news. I made ten sex-line calls last month and my total phone bill was less than two quid.

✳ "Doctor, I suffer from premature ejaculation. Can you cure me?"

"No. But I can introduce you to a women with a short attention span."

✳ Premature ejaculation. The greatest compliment a man can pay a woman and still they moan about it.

✶   ✶   ✶   ✶   ✶

PRIESTS

★ One day Sean and Mick were sitting having a pint in a pub across from a brothel, watching the comings and goings across the street. The two lads were taken aback when a Presbyterian minister walked into the brothel. "Bejesus," said Sean, "'Tis a terrible shame to see a man of the cloth going bad!"

A few minutes later a Jewish rabbi walked into the brothel. "Begorrah," said Mick, "would you believe that? 'Tis a shame to see the Jews giving in to temptation as well!"

A few more minutes passed and a Catholic priest walked into the brothel. Sean turned to Mick and said in a low voice, "Did you see that, Mick? One of them poor girls must be on her deathbed!"

★ Why is the Bible like a penis?
You get it forced down your throat by a priest.

★ A priest fell over a cliff and was hanging on by his fingertips. He looked up and said, "Lord, can you help me?"

A voice replied: "Let go of the cliff. Your mortal body will be dashed on the rocks below, but this time tomorrow you will be sitting on the right-hand side of God."

The priest look up again and said: "Er, is there anyone else up there who can help?"

★ I'm all for women priests. At last, a member of the clergy that teenage boys will willingly have sex with.

★ What do you give the paedophile priest who has everything?
A bigger parish.

★ One day in Ireland a golfer was out on the thirteenth tee when he hooked his shot into the woods. When he went in search of his ball he came across a little man with this huge lump on the side of his head, lying right beside his golf ball. "Goodness," said the golfer, who then proceeded to revive the poor little fellow.

Eventually the little guy sat up and said, "Well, mister, you caught me fair and square. I am a leprechaun. I will grant you three wishes."

The golfer replied: "I can't take anything from you. I'm just sorry I hit you with my ball. I'm glad that I didn't hurt you too badly."

With that, the golfer played his shot and walked away. The leprechaun said to himself: "Well, what a nice man. I have to do something for him. I'll give him the three things that I would want. I'll give him unlimited money, a great golf game and a great sex life."

A year went by and the golfer was out on the same course at the thirteenth tee again. As luck would have it, he hooked his tee shot into the same woods and went off looking for his ball. When he found the ball, he saw the same little guy and asked how he was doing.

The leprechaun said, "I'm doing just great, thanks for asking. And might I ask, how's your golf game?"

The golfer said, "Well, as a matter of fact it has improved massively since we last met. I hit under par every time."

"I did that for you," said the leprechaun. "And might I ask, how's your financial situation lately?"

"Well, now that you mention it, I keep finding these £50 notes!" he replied.

The leprechaun said, "I did that for you. And might I ask how is your sex life?"

The golfer replied, "Well, maybe once or twice a week."

The leprechaun was momentarily lost for words, "Once or twice a week? Is that all?"

The golfer looked at him sheepishly and says, "Well, that's not too bad for a Catholic priest in a small parish."

A priest suffering from a dry persistent cough goes to see his doctor. After careful examination and thorough blood tests the doctor tells him, "I am sorry, father, but you have AIDS and you are going to die."

"Oh my God!" sobs the priest.

"Yes, I understand, father," says the doctor. "You must be terrified."

"Hell, no. Everybody dies. What really disappoints me is that there was a time when you could trust altar boys."

★ What does a Catholic priest have in common with a pint of Guinness?

You need to watch your arse if you get a dodgy one.

★ A new young Catholic priest has just started working at the local church when his head priest, Father Edward, tells him he is going on a seminary for a week. Father Edward asks the new priest if he wouldn't mind doing the confessions whilst he's away. Concerned that he is inexperienced, Father David gives him the latest handbook on what to do in the confession box.

The new priest has been doing the job for only a few minutes when a young woman enters the box and says, "Forgive me, father, for I have sinned. I have had feelings of a carnal nature toward the man who mows our lawn."

The priest looks to his handbook and finds the appropriate section on sexual desire and gardening. "You must do five Hail Marys, and put something in the collection box," he tells her.

Minutes later, a second woman confesses she has kissed the man who came to fix the boiler. He looks in the handbook, finds the section on sexual relations with members of the plumbing trade and hands down a penance of ten Hail Marys and an afternoon polishing the church brass.

Minutes later, yet another woman enters the confessional box and admits that she has given the local policeman a blow job. However, the priest cannot find any mention regarding felatio and wonders what to do.

He sticks his head out of the box and says, "I don't suppose anyone knows what Father Edward's going rate is for a blow job?"

A passing choirboy replies: "A Creme Egg and a Kit-Kat."

☆ An elderly priest called Father O'Donnell was walking through his parish one sunny day when he came upon a little frog sitting by a pond. "Dear me," said Father O'Donnell, picking it up, "you're the saddest frog I ever did see. I only wish you could talk to me so that you might tell me your troubles."

The frog replied, "I can tell you. I was once a choirboy in this very parish. One day I refused to accept a sprig of heather from a malicious passing gypsy and she put a terrible curse on me, turning me into a talking frog."

Father O'Donnell couldn't believe his ears. "This is amazing," he said. "Is there anything I might do to help you?"

"Now you mention it, there is," replied the little frog. "The gypsy said that if I can find somebody to take me home and care for me, the curse will be lifted and I'll be back to normal."

"Well now, let's see about that, little fellow," replied Father O'Donnell. So he picked up the frog, put it in his pocket and took it home. That night he placed it gently on the pillow beside him and drifted off into a long, dreamy sleep. When he awoke the next morning, the frog had turned back into a choirboy, just as it had said it would.

"And that, Your Worship, is the case for the defence."

☆   ☆   ☆   ☆   ☆

PRINCESS DIANA

❖ What was Princess Di's favourite cocktail?
   A wallbanger followed by a couple of chasers.

❖ Why did Princess Diana have a Mercedes?
   She wouldn't be seen dead in a Skoda.

❖ Why did Elton John sing at Princess Diana's funeral?
   Because he was the only queen that gave a fuck.

❖ What's the difference between Princess
   Diana and a beautiful bed of flowers?
   Approximately six feet.

❖ What do Princess Diana and Ferrero Rocher have in
   common?
   They both come out of France in a fancy box.

★ Why did Princess Diana cross the road?
   She wasn't wearing her seat belt.

❖ What's the difference between a BMW and a Mercedes?
   BMW doesn't get any royalties.

❖ What do Princess Diana and a landmine have in common?
   Both were laid by Arabs.

❖ What do Princess Diana and Pink Floyd
   have in common?
   Their last big hit was *The Wall*.

❖ How did they know Princess Diana had dandruff?
  They found her head and shoulders in the glove compartment.

❖ Did you know that Princess Di was on the phone when she crashed?
  She was also on the dashboard, the windscreen, the gearstick and the headrests.

❖ What would Princess Diana be doing now if she was still alive?
  Scratching at the lid of her coffin.

❖ What is the Queen getting Fergie for Christmas?
  A black Mercedes and a trip to Paris.

❖ What do you give the princess who has everything?
  A seatbelt and an airbag.

❖ What did Princess Diana do when she heard the driver had been drinking?
  She hit the roof.

❖ Why was Diana like a mobile phone?
  They both die in tunnels.

❖ What's the one word that could have saved Princess Diana's life?
  "Taxi!"

Microsoft has announced that its new operating system is to be known, prior to launch, as "Diana, Princess of Windows". A spokesman for Microsoft said that this was in tribute to the late ex-royal. It is also appropriate because the product will look flashy, be mostly superficial, consume vast amounts of resources and will crash spectacularly.

❖ St Peter meets Mother Theresa at the pearly gates and says, "You were a good woman. I'm giving you a nice halo." Later on Mother Theresa is walking around Heaven feeling quite pleased about her lovely new halo, when she sees Princess Diana wearing a much bigger halo. Mother Theresa immediately goes back to St Peter to complain. "St Peter, I spent most of my adult life helping the poor and the sickly. Princess Diana did nowhere near the amount of charitable work I did. She was a vain self-obsessed attention seeker. Why does she have a bigger halo?"

St Peter replies, "That's not a halo. That's a steering wheel."

❖ What does Prince Philip's bumper sticker say?
"I brake for paparazzi!"

★   ★   ★   ★   ★

PRISON

★ A city hedge fund manager was nervous about being in prison, especially because his cellmate looked like a proper thug.

"Don't worry," the rough-looking cellmate reassured him, "I'm in here for a white collar crime as well."

"Well, that's a relief," said the financier. "I was sent to prison for fraud and insider trading."

"Oh nothing fancy like that for me," grinned the cellmate. "I just raped a couple of priests."

★ My father went to prison for his beliefs. He believed it was okay to have a wank on the number 88 bus from Oxford Street to Clapham.

★ A prisoner escapes from his prison after serving twelve years of a life sentence. While he is on the run he comes across a house in a remote location and breaks into it. He finds a young couple in bed. He gets the guy out of bed, ties him up on a chair, ties up the woman to the bed and while he gets on top of her, he kisses her on the neck, then gets up and goes to the bathroom.

The husband tells his wife: "Listen, this man is desperate. He probably spent a lot of time in prison and has not seen a woman in years. I saw the way he kissed your neck. If he wants sex, don't fight him, don't complain, just do what he tells you. This man is dangerous, if he gets angry, he will kill us. Be strong, darling. I love you."

His wife replies, "He has spent the last twelve years in prison. He wasn't kissing my neck, he was whispering in my ear. He told me that he finds you very attractive and asked if we kept any Vaseline in the bathroom. Be strong, darling. I love you too."

✳ After my first few prison showers, I found out why they call a prison term a "stretch".

✳ Ian Brady says to the prison guard, "I'm pissed off, I haven't had a holiday in years."

The guard says, "You're bullshitting me, Brady. A few years ago we took you up to Saddleworth Moor, you had three days up there. All those wide open spaces and fresh clean air."

Brady replies, "Fair enough, but what kind of holiday was that with the kids under me feet?"

✳ Three men are in a jail cell, discussing their crimes. The first prisoner asks the second guy, "What are you in here for?"

"Armed robbery."

"What did you get?"

"Twelve years."

They ask the third man, "What are you in for?"

"Murder."

"What did you get?"

"Twenty years."

Third man then asks the first man, "And what are you in for?"

"Setting fire to some lawyers with petrol."

"What did you get?"

"About eight to the gallon."

Paris Hilton is in prison, queuing up for some breakfast. Two guards are slopping porridge into each bowl for the prisoners. "Let's have a laugh," says one. "I'm going to wank in the porridge."

"Great idea," says the second. Both have a quick wank in the porridge before delivering it to Paris. Paris looks at the bowl and up at the guards and says, "Eeuggh!! I'm not eating this!"

The guard asks: "Why not?"

Paris replies, "It's got porridge in it."

PROFANITY

❖ A seven-year-old boy and his four-year-old brother were upstairs in their bedroom.

The seven-year-old says, "I think it's about time we started swearing." The younger brother nods his head in approval. The seven-year-old says, "When we go downstairs for breakfast, I'm going to swear first, then you swear after me, okay?"

"Okay," nods the four-year-old.

Their mother walks into the kitchen and asks the seven-year-old what he wants for breakfast. "Oh shit, mum, I don't know, I suppose I'll have some sugar puffs."

His mother gives him a sharp smack across the head, knocking him out of his chair and across the kitchen floor. He gets up and runs upstairs, crying his eyes out. She looks at the four-year-old and asked with a stern voice, "And what do YOU want for breakfast, young man?"

"I don't know," he blubbers, "but it won't be fucking sugar puffs."

❖ I was at my grandmother's house and she doesn't like swearing. I said "crap" and she told me to put 20p in the swear box. Unfortunately, I only had a pound coin and she didn't have any change. I threw in the pound and said, "Bollocks, take it all, you thieving whore."

I met this girl at a pub last night, we hit it off and she invited me back to hers for a night of sex. She asked me if I was into anything kinky and I said yes. So she slipped into a spandex cat suit with nipple-tassels, got her whip out of the cupboard and stuck a lubricated vibrator up her arse. Finally, she got me to handcuff her to the bed. Then she looked up to me and said, "Okay, now fuck me!" I made my excuses and left – there's no need for that kind of language.

❖   Bill's elderly uncle died, and in the will the uncle left him his much-prized African Grey parrot. This parrot was fully grown, with a very bad attitude and a very salty vocabulary. Every other word was an expletive, to Bill's frequent embarrassment. Bill tried hard to change the potty-mouthed bird's attitude. He was polite, he was careful not to swear in front of it, he even played soothing, classical music – in fact, just about anything he could think of to try and set a good example. Nothing worked. In sheer frustration he swore at the parrot, but the parrot just came back at him with more abuse, only this time it was ten times worse. He shook the parrot, but the bird just got angrier and more foul-mouthed.

Finally, in a moment of desperation, Bill put the parrot in the freezer to teach it a lesson. For a couple of minutes he heard the bird squawking, kicking and screaming abuse. Then, suddenly, all was quiet. Bill was frightened that he might have killed his dead uncle's prized parrot and quickly opened the freezer door. The chastened parrot quickly hopped out of the freezer and back into his cage, and said: "I am truly sorry that I might have offended you with my foul language and uncivil behaviour. I most humbly beseech your forgiveness. I will now, from this day, endeavour to behave correctly and promise that such an outburst of bad behaviour will never happen again."

Bill was completely flabbergasted at the bird's display of contrition. He was just about to ask what had caused such a dramatic change when the parrot interrupted: "May I ask, what did the chicken do?"

★   ★   ★   ★   ★

PROSTITUTES

* Three prostitutes make a bet on who has the biggest vagina. They take their clothes off and start fingering themselves and each other. They can't agree, however, which lady has the largest snatch. After a few minutes, one of the prossers has an idea. She squats on a glass top table so they measure the slimy deposit she leaves behind. The second one then squats on the table and then they measure the slimy outline she leaves, which is even bigger.

  The third one squats on the table. When she stands back up, the first prostitute says, "You didn't leave an outline."

  She laughs, "Just smell the rim!"

* ### I shagged a hooker last night. Big mistake. It's going to make the scrum very awkward on Saturday.

* A prostitute goes to the doctor complaining of morning sickness. The doctor says, "Congratulations! Do you know who the father is?"

  "Put it this way," replied the prostitute, "if you ate a tin of beans would you know which one made you fart?"

* A prostitute was visiting her doctor for a regular check-up. "Any problems you should be telling me about?" the doctor asked.

  "Well, I have noticed just lately that if I get even the tiniest cut, it seems to bleed for hours," she replied. "Do you think I might be a haemophiliac?"

  The doctor answered, "Haemophilia is a genetic disorder and it is more often found in men but it is possible for a woman to be a haemophiliac. Tell me, how much do you lose when you have your period?"

  After thinking for a moment, the hooker replied, "About £300 on a bad night."

* Why did Google invent Streetview?
  So kerb crawlers can view their meat before they pay for it.

* What do you call a prostitute with no arms or legs?
  Cash and carry.

* What's the best thing about having a sister who's a prostitute?
  The family discount.

* Did you hear about the prostitute who took up bondage?
  She was a bit strapped for cash.

A man on his way home from the pub decides to take a short cut through an unlit park. A woman approaches him and offers to fuck his brains out for £5.

He thinks to himself that this is a chance too good to miss, so hands over the £5. She leads him into a bush and they get under way. A policeman passes by, hears them at it and notices the bush shaking. He shines his torch on the pair and asks the man what he's doing. The man replies calmly, "I'm just having sex with my wife, officer. Do you mind?"

The officer responds, "I'm sorry, sir, I didn't realize it was your wife."

The man replies, "That's quite all right, officer. Until you shone your torch on her face, neither did I."

✳ A man is walking through Mayfair when a stunning London prostitute catches his eye. He strikes up a conversation and eventually plucks up the courage to ask, "How much?"

The prosser replies, "It starts at £500 for a hand job."

The man gasps: "£500? For a hand job! You have got to be kidding me, no hand job is worth that kind of money!"

The tart replies, "Do you see that block of apartments on the corner?"

"Yes."

"Do you see the block of apartments next to it?"

"Yes."

"And beyond that, do you see that third block?"

"Yes."

"Well," says the prostitute, smiling coyly, "I own those. And, I own them because I give a hand job that's worth £500."

The man thinks, "What the hell? You only live once. I'll give it a try." They retire to a nearby hotel. A short time later, one very satisfied punter is sitting on the bed realizing he has just experienced the hand job of a lifetime, worth every bit of £500. He is so amazed, he says, "I suppose a blow job is £1,000?"

The hooker replies, "Actually, £1,500."

"No one is ever going to pay that for a blow job!"

She replies, "Step over here to the window, big boy. Do you see that casino just across the street? I own that casino outright. And I own it because I give a blow job that's worth every penny of £1,500."

The guy, basking in the afterglow of that terrific hand job, says, "Sign me up."

Ten minutes later, he is sitting on the bed truly amazed. He can scarcely believe it, but he feels he truly got his money's worth. He decides to dip into the retirement savings for one glorious and unforgettable experience. He asks the prosser, "How much for some pussy?"

The hooker says, "Come over here to the window, I want to show you something. Do you see how the whole West End of London is laid out before us, all those luxury flats, gambling palaces and fancy restaurants?"

"Bugger!" the man says, in awe. "You own the whole West End?"

"No," the prostitute replies, "but I would if I had a vagina."

* What do you call a Norwegian prostitute?
    A Fjord Escort.

* What do you call a prostitute in a wheel chair?
    Park and ride.

* Judging by the itching and the rash, I think I may be allergic to prostitutes.

* Four generations of the same family of prostitutes are talking in the kitchen. The daughter prostitute says, "I got £50 for a blow job today."
    The mother prostitute says, "In my day, it was £5."
    The grandmother prostitute says, "In my day, it was 50p."
    The great-grandmother prostitute says, "Well, in my day, we were just glad for the warm drink."

* What do you get if you cross a prostitute with an elephant?
    A whore who fucks you for peanuts and remembers you forever.

* I slept with one of those high-class tarts the other week. I'm not very happy though. The bitch gave me lobsters.

✳ What do you call a prostitute on amphetamines?

A speed hump.

★   ★   ★   ★   ★

PSYCHIATRISTS

✳ A hot air balloonist is lost. He sees a man in a field below, so he shouts down, "Excuse me, can you tell me where I am and where I'm heading?"

"Sure. You are at 36 degrees 2 minutes and 14 seconds north, 96 degrees 3 minutes and 19 seconds east. You're at an altitude of 762 metres above sea level and right now you're hovering, but you were on a vector of 240 degrees at 12 metres per second."

"Thanks very much," says the balloonist. "By the way, do you by any chance suffer from Asperger's Syndrome?"

"I do indeed. How did you know that?"

"Because everything you said is true, but there was much more information than I needed and you gave me the information in a way that was of no use to me at all."

"I see. Are you a psychiatrist?"

"I am, but how on earth did you know that??"

"You don't know where you are, you haven't a clue where you're going, you got where you are by blowing hot air, you put labels on people after asking a few questions and you're in exactly the same spot you were a couple of minutes ago, but now somehow it's my fucking fault!"

✳ A man goes to the psychiatrist and says, "Doctor, sometimes I think I'm a teepee, and other times I think I'm a wigwam. What's wrong with me?"

"Ah, yes," the doctor replies, "You're too tense."

* A black woman goes to see the psychiatrist about her low self-esteem. She looks tired, overweight and generally unhealthy. After tearfully explaining her predicament, the shrink says, "Ah, yes, would you mind lying on the floor under the window?" She does as he asks. "Now over next to the door. Okay, now under the bookshelves. Thank you."

He then busies himself with writing some notes. The patient waits patiently for him to say something, but, finally exasperated, interrupts him and asks if he has anything he can offer her.

"No," he replies, "you need to see your GP about your poor diet."

"So, what was all that stuff you had me do, lying on the floor?"

"Oh, I'm having a new brown leather sofa delivered next week and I was wondering where to put it."

* After fifteen years of being in therapy, my psychiatrist said something that actually brought tears to my eyes: "No hablo Ingles."

* A patient went to see a psychiatrist. The psychiatrist gave him a Rorschach-type test – he shows a patient a circle with a dot inside it. He then asks him: "What do you see?"

The patient replied: "Two people are having sex in the middle of the circular room."

The psychiatrist then shows the patient another picture of a square with a dot inside it.

"What do you see?"

"Two people are having sex in the square room."

The psychiatrist shows the patient one more picture of a triangle with a dot outside it.

"What do you see now?"

"What are you doc, some kind of fucking pervert?"

✳ A psychiatrist goes to work and finds his colleague sitting at his desk, smiling to himself and shaking his head. "What's so funny?" his fellow psychiatrist enquires.

"You know, I thought I'd been completely analysed, but yesterday I experienced the most embarrassing Freudian slip!"

"Good Lord!" says his friend. "Do tell me more."

"Well, I was queuing at the train station ticket office and couldn't help but notice that the girl behind the counter has a massive pair of tits. It was just about impossible to take my eyes off them. Anyway, when I got to the window, instead of asking for a ticket to Tooting I asked her for a ticket to TITTING. She blushed, I blushed, I got my ticket and scarpered."

The bloke laughs and says, "Oh dear! That's very amusing!"

The following day, the other psychiatrist is sitting at his desk smiling to himself when his workmate walks in and asks, "Okay, what's tickled you?"

The first psychiatrist replies, "I had one of your Freudian slips last night. I was sitting at the dining table with my wife and I meant to say, "Please pass the mustard." But what I actually said was, "FUCK OFF, YOU FAT BITCH, YOU'VE RUINED MY LIFE!"

✳ A man went to see a psychiatrist wearing only a pair of underpants made from bubble wrap. The shrink observed him for a while and said: "Well, I can clearly see your nuts."

✳ A man walks into a bar and orders a beer. He drinks the beer than stands on the bar, drops his pants and pisses all over the place. The barman freaks out. "You dirty bastard! How dare you come into my bar and piss everywhere! I'll beat the shit out of you . . ."

The man begins sobbing. "I'm sorry! It's ruining my life. I can't sleep. I do it every time I have a drink! It's worrying me to death, please don't hit me."

The barman stops threatening him and takes pity. "Look, I have a brother who is a psychiatrist. Here's his card, why don't you see him?" The customer hugs the barman, shakes his hand and leaves.

A few months later the same man walks into the bar and orders a beer. The barman recognizes him immediately and says, "Hang on, weren't you that guy who . . ."

"Yes," says the customer, "and I took your advice and went to see your brother. I have to say he's brilliant. I am completely cured."

"I'm delighted to hear it," says the barman. "This beer is on the house."

So the man drinks the beer, stands on the bar, drops his trousers and pisses on the bar.

"You twat! I thought you said you were cured!"

"I am. It doesn't bother me any more."

★   ★   ★   ★   ★

QUASIMODO

★ Quasimodo the hunchback returns home after a hard day's bell ringing to find Esmeralda standing in the kitchen holding a wok. "Fantastic," he says, "Chinese tonight, love?"

"No, love," she replies. "I'm ironing your shirt."

★ Quasimodo comes down from his bell tower after many years and skulks in the shadows of the Notre Dame's town square. He sees an attractive young woman pass by and thinks to himself, "I've been up in that bell tower for too long. I could do with a good shag."

So off he goes to the nearest whorehouse in a back street and says to the madam on the door, "I've been up in that bell tower for many years and I could do with a proper good shag."

The madam says, "Well, you've come to the right place, the black lady through the door to the right is fifteen francs."

"The thing is," says Quasimodo, "I'm afraid I'm only good for a ten-franc fuck."

"Okay, for ten francs you get the white lady through the door to the left."

Quasimodo pays his ten francs, goes through the left door and comes out again moments later, completely satisfied.

Several years later, after being up in the bell tower on his own again, Quasimodo comes down through the shadows in to the town centre. "You know what?" he thought to himself, "I could do with a proper good shag and this time I have fifteen francs." So off he goes to the same whorehouse he went to several years earlier.

On his way there he sees a young boy, hideously disfigured with a hunch on his back, dragging one of his feet behind him. Quasimodo goes to the boy and says to him, "Excuse me, young man, how old are you?"

"I'm almost five years old, sir," replies the boy, as he looks Quasimodo up and down. "If you don't mind me asking, sir," says the young boy, "is it possible you could be my father?"

"I suppose so, it was around five years ago that I last came down from my bell tower."

"How could you do this to me, father? Look at me: I'm hideously ugly, I have a useless leg, I have a hunchback and all the people point and shout names at me. How could you bring such a creature into the world?"

"Well, think yourself lucky, son. If I had another five francs you would have been black."

*   *   *   *   *

RABBIS

❖ A man is troubled by the thorny question of whether or not sex on the Sabbath was a sin. He is not sure if sex is work or play. So he goes to the priest and asks for his opinion on this theological question.

After consulting the Bible, the priest says, "My son, after an exhaustive search, I am positive that sex is work and is therefore not permitted on Sundays."

The man thinks: "Fair enough. But then, what does a priest know about sex?" So he goes to a minister, who, after all, is a married man and more experienced in this matter, for a second opinion. Having queried the minister he receives the same reply. Sex is work and therefore not for the Sabbath.

All the same, he is not entirely happy with the reply, so he seeks out the local rabbi. The rabbi ponders the question, then announces, "My son, sex is definitely work."

The man replies, "Rabbi, how can everyone be so sure it is work?"

The rabbi replies, "Sex is work, which is why my wife won't do it, which is why the maid has to."

A priest and a rabbi find themselves sitting next to each other on a train. They get chatting and the priest asks if the rabbi, in his youth, had ever tried bacon. He coyly admits that, yes, he once did. But, the rabbi then asks, before getting his vocation, did the priest ever have sex? The priest murmurs that yes, he once did.

"Ah," says the rabbi, "much fucking better than bacon, isn't it?"

★   ★   ★   ★   ★

RABBITS

* One day a rabbit managed to break free from the laboratory where he had been born and raised. He dug a little hole under the fencing of the compound, and, as he scampered away, he felt grass under his little feet for the first time. He looked up at the sky and saw dawn breaking. "My!" he thought to himself. "What can that be? It's amazing!"

He came to a hedge and, after squeezing under it, he saw a wonderful sight. There were lots of other bunny rabbits, running around free, capering in the sunlight and nibbling at the lush green grass. "Hello!" he called out to them. "I'm a rabbit from the laboratory and I've just escaped. Are you rabbits too?"

"Yes. Come and join us," they cried. The little rabbit hopped over to his new friends and started eating the grass. It tasted so good, unlike the bland, tasteless food he had been fed all his life in the lab.

"What else do you wild rabbits do?" he asked.

"Well," one of them said. "You see that field over there? It's got carrots growing in it. We dig them up and eat them." The little rabbit spent the next hour eating the most succulent carrots he had ever eaten in his life. They were amazing. A bit later, he asked them again, "What else do you do?"

"You see that allotment over there? It has cabbages growing in it. We eat cabbages as well." The cabbage tasted fantastic, even better than the carrots.

"Brilliant!" said he little rabbit. "Is there anything else you rabbits do?"

One of the other rabbits came a bit closer to him and said in a low voice. "There is one other thing you must try. You see those rabbits over there," he said, pointing to the far corner of the field. "They're girl rabbits. We shag them. Go and give it a try."

Well, our little rabbit spent the rest of the morning banging his little heart out until, completely knackered, he staggered back over to the other rabbits.

"That was incredible," he panted.

"So, are you going to live with us then?" one of his new friends asked.

"Sorry, I had a great time but I have to get back to the laboratory".

The wild rabbits all stare at him in amazement. "Why? We thought you liked it here."

"I did – loved every minute of it," the little rabbit replied. "But I'm dying for a fag."

✳ **I gave an elderly rabbit a Viagra tablet but it died. I guess the moral of the story is, old rabbits die hard.**

✳ A little rabbit is running merrily through the forest when he stumbles upon a giraffe rolling a joint. The rabbit looks at the giraffe and says, "Giraffe, my friend, why do you do this? Come. Run with me through the forest! You'll feel so much better!"

The giraffe looks at him, looks at the joint, tosses it away and goes off running with the rabbit. Then they come across an elephant snorting cocaine. The rabbit again says, "Elephant, my friend, why do you do this? Think about your health. Come. Run with us through the lovely forest, you'll see, you'll feel so good!"

The elephant looks at them, looks at his liner of coke, then tosses it and starts running with the rabbit and giraffe. The three animals then come across a lion about to shoot up. "Lion, my friend, why do you do this? Think about your health! Come. Run with us through the beautiful forest and you'll feel so good!"

The lion looks at him, puts down his needle and mauls the rabbit to death. The giraffe and elephant look on in horror and ask: "Lion, why did you do this? He was only trying to help you."

The lion replies: "That little twat . . . he makes me run around the forest like a fucking idiot every time he takes a tab of ecstasy."

* A man comes home from work one day to find his dog with the neighbour's pet rabbit in his mouth. He panics, so he takes the dead chewed-up rabbit into the house and gives it a bath, blow dries its fur and puts it back into the cage in his neighbour's garden, hoping they will think it died of natural causes.

    A few days later, the neighbour is outside and asks him, "Did you hear that our rabbit died?"

    Lost for words, he manages to blurt, "Er . . . no . . . what happened?".

    The neighbour replies, "We just found him dead in his cage one day. The weird thing is that the day after we buried him we went outside and someone had dug him up, given him a bath and put him back into the cage. There must be some really sick bastards out there!"

* * * * *

RACISM

* How does every racist joke start?
    By looking over your shoulder.

* I was in New York riding the subway when a black man came up to me and said, "Do you know if the Yankees won?"
    I replied, "You haven't heard? Yes, the Yankees won . . . you're free!"

* Two Alabama cops are patrolling one afternoon when a young black teenager rides past on his bicycle. Seeing him, the first policeman takes out his gun and shoots the boy in the head. His partner says, "Why did you do that?"

    "Because there is a strict six o'clock curfew on all niggers," replies the shooter.

    His mate says, "Yes, but it's only 4.30."

    "I know," says the shooter, "but I know where he lives, and he'd never get home by six o'clock."

∗ A black guy dies and goes to Heaven. At the pearly gates he is greeted by St Peter. St Peter says, "Heaven is very full at the moment and we are restricting entry only to people who have done something amazing with their lives. Have you ever done anything amazing in your life?"

The black guy replies, "In fact I have. I fucked the daughter of the imperial dragon of the Ku Klux Klan."

"No way!" says St Peter, "That is truly amazing! When did that happen?"

"Oh, about three minutes ago."

∗ A young black boy is helping his mum to bake bread in the kitchen when he gets flour all over his face. He rubs the flour around a bit and turns to his mum and says, "Look, momma, I'm a white boy!"

His mother slaps him hard across the face and says, "Go and tell your daddy what you just did!" The boy goes to his dad and says, "Look, dad, I'm a white boy!"

His father grabs the boy, throws him over his knee and slaps his arse really hard and says, "Go tell your granddaddy what you said!"

The boy finds his grandfather and says sheepishly: "Look, grandad, I'm a white boy!"

The grandfather grabs the boy, drags him to the bathroom, puts a block of soap in his mouth and begins to scrub his tongue with it, before sending him to his room with no dinner. Later that evening his mother calls him down to the lounge, where his family are all seated, and says, "Have you learned anything?"

The boy replies, "Yeah. I was only white for five minutes and already I hate you black motherfuckers."

∗ Five racists corner a Pakistani down an alley. They hand him a dice and tell him: "Throw a one, two, three or five and we are going to kick your head in."

Seeing a possible escape route, the Pakistani cleverly throws a six.

"Well done," says the ringleader. "You get another go."

Police in Alabama found the body of black man hanging from a tree. His arms and legs had been removed, he had been set on fire and shot several times. The police said it was the worst suicide they had ever seen.

★ What do you call 100 black men buried up to their necks in soil?
Afro turf.

★ What is the difference between a black slave and snow tyres?
Snow tyres don't sing when you wrap them in chains.

★ My boss is black and this week he called me into his office and accused me of being racist. I replied: "I don't like your tone."

★ Why did Terry's launch a white chocolate orange?
So the black kids can have a dirty face at Easter.

★ A half-Jewish, half-black lad asks his mother, "Mum, am I mostly Jewish or mostly black?"
"That's a silly question," she replies. "Go and bother your father, already."
Off he goes to his father and asks: "Dad, would you say I'm mostly Jewish or mostly black?"
"You're just you, son, why are you asking dumb-ass questions like that?"
"Well, my friend's selling his bike for fifty quid and I don't know whether to Jew him down to twenty-five or just wait until dark and steal it."

★ How do you confuse a *Daily Mail* reader?
Tell him that asylum seekers kill paedophiles.

★ Why don't black people go on cruises?
They're not falling for that one again.

RATS

❖ A tourist wanders into a back-alley antique shop in London's Chinatown. Picking through the objects on display he discovers a detailed, life-sized bronze sculpture of a rat. He's very taken with the sculpture so he picks it up and asks the shop owner what it costs.

"Five pounds for the rat, sir," says the shop owner, "and five hundred pounds more for the story behind it."

"You can keep the story, old man," he replies, "but I'll take the rat."

The purchase complete, the tourist leaves the store with the bronze rat under his arm. As he crosses the road outside, two live rats emerge from a sewer drain and fall into step behind him. Nervously looking over his shoulder, he begins to walk faster, but every time he passes another sewer drain, more rats come out and follow him. By the time he's walked a couple of blocks, at least three dozen rats are at his heels. He quickens his pace and breaks into jog as multitudes of rats emerge from sewers and basements. By now hundreds of rats are at his heels, and, as he sees the Thames embankment just ahead of him, he panics and starts to run full tilt. No matter how fast he runs, the rats keep up, by now in their thousands. By the time he comes running up to the river's edge he has London's entire rat population behind him. Making a mighty leap towards the water, he grabs a lamp-post, and hurls the bronze rat into the Thames as far as he can. Pulling his legs up and clinging to the lamp post, he watches in amazement as the seething tide of rats surges into the river, where they drown. Shaken and dazed, he makes his way back to the antique shop.

"Ah, so you have come back for the rest of the story," says the shop owner.

"No," says the tourist, "I was wondering if you have a bronze banker."

Two rats in a sewer had been eating shit all day. One rat says to the other: "I'm sick of eating shit all day".

"Cheer up," says his friend. "We're out on the piss tonight!"

* * * * *

REDNECKS

* How many rednecks does it take to grease a combine?

Only two if you run them through real slow.

* What do you call a redneck at college?
The cleaner.

* How can you tell if a girl is a redneck?
She can suck a dick and chew tobacco at the same time and know what to spit and what to swallow.

* What's the most popular pick-up line in Arkansas?
Nice tooth!

* * * * *

RELATIONSHIPS

★ A lucky guy had three girlfriends on the go but wasn't sure which one to settle down with. So he decided to give each one £500 to see how they spent it. The first girlfriend went out and got a total makeover with the money. She bought herself clothes, a new hairdo, manicure and pedicure. When she came back she told him, "I spent the money so I could look gorgeous for you because I love you so much." He was very touched and quite aroused and they had lots of great sex.

The second girlfriend went out and bought him a new flat-screen TV. "I bought this gift for you with the money you gave me because I love you so much," she said. He loved his new telly!

The third girlfriend took his £500 and invested it in the stock market, doubled her investment, gave him the original £500 back and reinvested the rest. She told him, "I am investing the rest of the money for our future because I love you so much." She made enough money to buy him a new car.

After thinking long and hard about how each of the women spent the money, he decided to marry the one with the biggest tits.

★ What do you call a man who expects to have sex on the second date?
    Patient.

★ Two guys and a woman are sitting at a bar talking about their lives. The first guy says, "I'm a YUPPIE. You know, Young Urban Professional."

The second guy says, "I'm a DINK. You know, Double Income No Kids."

They then asked the woman, "What are you?"

She replies: "I'm a WIFE. You know, Wash, Iron, Fuck, Etc."

★ I used to think I was the world's greatest lover, until I found out that my girlfriend had asthma.

★ I met this girl in a bar and I said to her: "If I could see you naked, I'd die happy."

She replied: "If I saw you naked, I'd probably die laughing."

I said: "That works for me, as long as you are still a bit warm when I shove it up your arse."

★ The other day I told my girlfriend that she was like Marmite. She said, "What, you either love me or you hate me?"

"No," I replied, "you're black and you smell."

★ What's the funniest thing about one-night stands?

Leaving a note on the fridge telling them you have AIDS.

> My girlfriend dumped me just before she got run over. I told the ambulance men the wrong blood type. Now she knows what rejection feels like.

★ I recently broke up with my girlfriend and I was quite upset. My mum reassured me, "Don't worry, there's plenty more fish in the sea."

I replied, "Yes I know, but it isn't just the smell I miss."

★ Why do men hold hands with their girlfriends in public?

If they let go then the bitch might start shopping.

★ I met this girl last night and she was a right ugly cow. I said to her "What's your name?"

"Wednesday," she replied.

"That's a very unusual name," I said.

"She said, "Yes. Apparently when I was born my mum and dad looked in the cot and said, 'I think we'd better call it a day.'"

★ Why is sex like paintballing?
   Because you play hard for thirty minutes and when it's over you're all hot and sweaty and glad that you're not the one taking a shot to the face.

★ How can you tell if your girlfriend is frigid? When you open her legs a light comes on.

★ When I was fourteen, all I wanted was a girlfriend.
   When I was sixteen, I finally dated a girl, but there was no passion.
   So I decided I needed a passionate girl with a zest for life. In college, I got to date this really passionate girl, but she was too emotional. Everything was a drama and she cried all the time and threatened to kill herself.
   So I decided I needed a girl with some stability. I found a very nice, quite stable girl, but she was boring. She never got excited about anything.
   My life was so dull and predictable that I decided I needed a girl with some excitement. I found an exciting girl, but I couldn't keep up with her. She rushed from one thing to another, never settling on anything. She did crazy, impetuous things and flirted with all my mates. She made me miserable more times than she made me happy. She was great fun at first and very energetic, but directionless.
   So I decided to find a girl with some ambition. I found this smart, ambitious girl with her feet planted firmly on the ground and married her. Unfortunately she was so ambitious that she divorced me and took everything I owned.
   Now all I want is a bird with big tits.

★   ★   ★   ★   ★

RELIGION

❖ A Jew, a Roman Catholic and a Mormon were talking one day and the subject of family size came up.

The Jewish man said, "My wife just gave birth, so now I have enough children for a basketball team."

The Roman Catholic chipped in, "With the recent addition to our family I now have enough kids for a baseball team!"

The Mormon replied, "When I marry my next wife I'll have enough holes for a golf course."

❖ A bloke was walking across a bridge one day when she saw another man standing on the edge, about to jump. He ran over and said: "Stop. Don't do it."

"Why shouldn't I?" he asked.

"Well, there's so much to live for!"

"Like what?"

"Are you religious?"

He replied, "Yes."

"Me too. Are you Christian or Buddhist?"

"Christian."

"Me too. Are you Catholic or Protestant?"

"Protestant."

"Me too. Are you Episcopalian or Baptist?"

"Baptist."

"Wow. Me too. Are you Baptist Church of God or Baptist Church of the Lord?"

"Baptist Church of God."

"Me too. Are you original Baptist Church of God, or are you Reformed Baptist Church of God?"

"Reformed Baptist Church of God."

"Me too. Are you Reformed Baptist Church of God, Reformation of 1879, or Reformed Baptist Church of God, Reformation of 1915?"

He said: "Reformed Baptist Church of God, Reformation of 1915."

The man replied: "Die, heretic scum," and pushed him off.

Religions in Brief

Taoism – shit happens.

Buddhism – if shit happens, is it really shit?

Islam – if shit happens, blame the infidels.

Protestantism – shit won't happen if I work hard enough.

Judaism – why does this shit always happen to us?

Hinduism – this shit happened before.

Catholicism – if shit happens, it's because I deserve it.

Hare Krishna – shit happens, Ramah Lama Ding Dong

TV Evangelism – end more shit.

Jehovah's Witness – knock knock, shit happens.

Hedonism – there's nothing like a good shit happening.

Christian Science – shit happens in your mind.

Agnosticism – maybe shit happens, maybe it doesn't.

Rastafarianism – let's smoke this shit!

Existentialism – what is shit anyway?

Stoicism – this shit doesn't bother me.

Atheism – no shit.

❖ A man dies and he goes to Hell. Satan greets him and says: "Come with me. You get to choose your eternal punishment."

He walks by the first room and sees a man being whipped by a 300-lb transvestite and he thinks to himself, "Oh, God no!"

He walks by the second room and sees a man being burned with cigarettes by a 200-lb transsexual vegetarian. Again, he thinks, "No way in hell will I choose that."

He walks by the third room and sees a beautiful blonde giving an old man a blow job. He says to Satan, "Okay. I'll choose this one."

Satan agrees, walks up to the blonde and says: "You can go now, chuck. I've found your replacement."

Two bishops were discussing the decline in morals in the twenty-first century. "I didn't sleep with my wife before I was married," said one clergyman self-righteously. "Did you?"

"I don't know," shrugged the other. "What was her maiden name?"

* * * * *

RETIREMENT HOMES

✳ An old man in a nursing home walks up to a little old lady and says, "Guess how old I am!"

She unzips his fly, puts her hand inside his pants, then rummages around for a couple of minutes. "You're 82!"

He says, "That's amazing! How do you know?"

She replies, "You told me yesterday."

* A group of old people were talking at the breakfast table in a nursing home.

"My arms are so weak I can hardly lift this cup of coffee," said one.

"Yes, I know. My cataracts are so bad I can barely even see my cup of coffee," replied another.

"I can't turn my head because of arthritis in my neck," said a third, at which the rest nodded weakly.

"My blood pressure pills make me dizzy," another added.

"That's nothing," said another old man, "I've had two triple-bypass operations, a hip replacement and new knees. I've battled prostate cancer and have diabetes. I'm half blind, I can't hear anything quieter than a jet engine, I take twenty different medications for my blood pressure that make me dizzy, winded and subject to blackouts. I also have episodes of dementia and my circulation is so poor that I can no longer feel my hands or my feet. To be honest, I can't remember if I'm eighty-five or ninety-two."

"I guess that's the price we pay for getting old," said yet another lady, and again they all nodded in agreement.

Then there was a short moment of silence. "Well, it could be worse," said one old woman. "Thank God we all still have our driver's licences."

* One evening a family took their frail, elderly mother to a nursing home. The next morning the nurses bathed her, fed her a good breakfast and set her in a chair at a window overlooking a lovely flower garden. She appeared to be perfectly okay, but after a while she slowly started to fall over sideways in her chair. Two attentive nurses immediately rushed up to catch her and straightened her up. Again she seemed to be okay for a while, but after a couple of minutes she started to tilt to the other side. Again, the nurses rushed back and brought her upright. This went on all morning.

Later the family arrived to see how the old woman was adjusting to her new home. "So, mum, how is it here? Are they treating you well?" they asked.

"It's not bad," she replied. "Except they won't let you fart."

* Three old men were sitting in a retirement home chewing the fat.

"I hate being in my seventies," said the first. "You always feel like you want to piss and most of the time you stand there and nothing comes out."

"Ah, that's nothing," said the second. "When you're in your eighties, you don't have a proper bowel movement any more. You take laxatives, eat bran, sit on the toilet all day and nothing happens."

"No, being in your nineties is the worst age of all," said the third.

"Do you have trouble pissing as well then?" asked the first old man.

"No, not really, I have a piss every morning at 6 a.m. I piss like a racehorse, no problem at all."

"So, do you have a problem with your bowel movement?"

"No, I have a shit every morning at 6:30 precisely."

At this, the second old man said: "Let me get this straight. You piss every morning at 6 a.m. and shit every morning at 6:30 a.m. So what's so bad about being in your nineties?"

"I don't wake up until 7 a.m."

An old married couple were playing cards in the nursing home, as they had done every afternoon for several years. The old lady suddenly looks up and says, "I'm sorry darling. I know we've been married for many years, but for the life of me, I just can't bring it to mind ... would you please tell me your name again?"

There is dead silence for a couple of minutes, then her husband responds, "How soon do you need to know?"

* An old woman walks into the recreation room at the retirement home, holds her clenched fist in the air and announces, "Anyone who can guess what's in my hand can have sex with me tonight!"

    An elderly gentleman at the rear shouts out, "An elephant?"

    She thinks for a minute and says, "Close enough."

* Two old men sitting in a retirement home. "I'm full of aches and pains today, Ted. How do you feel?"

    His friend replies: "Like a newborn baby, Alf."

    "Really?" says Ted.

    "Yes," says Ted. "Hairless, toothless and I've just shat myself."

* ## They said that my grandad was "like a fish out of water" when he moved into the old people's home. In other words, he was dead.

* An elderly couple were sitting in an old folks' home watching the TV. All of a sudden the old man reaches over and punches his wife in the face.

    "What was that for?!" she exclaims angrily.

    "Forty years of crap sex!" her husband replies.

    She remains silent and they continue watching the TV. A couple of minutes later, the old lady gets up and kicks her husband in the balls.

    "Bloody hell," he moans, writhing on the floor. "What was that for?"

    She replies, "That's for knowing the difference!"

* I once got a gig as a stand-up comedian in an old people's home. They were a superb audience. When I say superb audience, none of them got my jokes but they still wet themselves.

* An old lady in a nursing home was trundling up and down the corridor on her Zimmer frame when an elderly retired policeman jumps out in front of her.

"You do realize you were speeding just then? Could I have your driving licence?" he says. She hands over her library card. He studies it carefully and hands it back with a raffle ticket. "Here's a speeding ticket," the old man tells her. "Be on your way, and drive more slowly this time."

A couple of hours later the same old woman is doing the same journey when the ex-copper once again jumps out in front of her. "That U-turn you did just then was illegal, can I see your driving licence?" Once again she hands over her library card; he checks it and sends her on her way.

Several minutes pass and she is coming down the corridor again. The old man jumps out of his room stark naked, nursing a wrinkly erection. The old lady says: "Oh no, not the breathalyser again!"

* * * * *

ROAD ACCIDENTS

★ Two paramedics arrived at the scene of a car crash. The driver of the car was still sitting in his seat, screaming his head off. One of the paramedics tried to calm him down. "Pull yourself together, man," he says. "At least you haven't gone through the windscreen like your passenger." He points at a girl lying unconscious on the side of the road.

The driver replied: "You haven't seen what's in her mouth."

★   A man awoke in hospital, swathed in bandages from head to foot.

"Hello," said the doctor standing next to his bed. "I see you've regained consciousness. Now you probably won't remember, but I'm afraid you were in a terrible pile-up on the M1. You're going to be okay, you'll walk again, but there is a bit of bad news and I'm going to break it to you as gently as I can. Your penis was lost in the wreckage and we were unable to find it."

The bloke groans but the doctor continues. "We've checked your insurance and you've actually got £9,000 compensation coming to you, and the good news is that we have the technology now to reconstruct your penis and it will work just as well as your old one, better in fact. Unfortunately, it doesn't come cheap. It will cost you £1,000 an inch."

The man brightened up a bit at this news. The doctor goes on. "It's your decision. You need to decide how many inches you want. But it's something you'd better discuss with your wife. If you had a five-inch dong previously, and you decide to go for a nine-incher now, she might be a bit put out. On the other hand of you had a nine-incher before and you decide only to invest in a five-incher now, she might be a bit disappointed. So it is very important that you consult with her to help you make the correct decision."

The doctor returns the next day, and asks: "Have you spoken with your wife?"

"I have, doctor."

"And has she helped you to make the decision?"

"Yes, she has."

"And what is the decision?" enquires the doctor.

"We're having a new kitchen."

★   A coach full of handicapped people has crashed in the Lake District.

Rescue workers say it will be days before they can pull the coach from the wreckage.

★ A family are driving behind a garbage truck when a used dildo flies out and thumps against the windscreen, causing the car to veer off the road into a ditch. Fortunately the occupants escape the accident unscathed.

Embarrassed, and to spare her young son's innocence, the mother turns around and says, "Don't worry, that was an insect."

Her son replies, "Funny. I'm amazed it could get off the ground with a cock as big as that."

★ One day the vicar asked if anyone in the congregation would like to express praise for answered prayers. A woman stood and walked to the podium.

She said, "I would like to say something. Two months ago, my husband Arnold had a terrible motorbike accident and his scrotum was completely crushed. The pain was agonizing and the doctors didn't know if they could help him."

At this point there was an audible collective groan from the men in the congregation as they visualized Arnold's mangled scrotum.

"My Arnold was unable to hold me or the children," she continued, "and every small movement caused him excruciating pain. We prayed as the doctors performed a very difficult and delicate operation and it turned out they were able to piece together the crushed remnants of Arnold's mangled scrotum and wrap surgical wire around it to hold it in place."

By this time all the men in the congregation were writhing in their seats, with tears in their eyes, as they visualized the operation performed on poor Arnold.

"But now", she announced in a shaky voice, "the good Lord had delivered Arnold back home to us and the doctors say that, with time, his scrotum should recover completely."

All the men sighed with relief. The vicar rose and tentatively asked if anyone else had something to say. A man stood up and walked slowly to the podium.

"I'm Arnold," he said. The entire congregation held its breath. "And I just wanted to say that the word my wife is looking for is sternum."

ROYALTY

❖ Camilla bought new shoes for her wedding to Prince Charles and, as the day wore on, they became increasingly tight around her feet. That night, when the festivities were finally over and they finally retired to their honeymoon suite, she flopped on the bed and said, "Charles, darling, please remove my shoes, my feet are absolutely killing me!" The Prince of Wales worked on her right shoe with vigour, but it would not budge.

"Harder!" yelled Camilla, "Harder!"

Charles yelled back, "I'm trying, my darling! But it's just so blooming tight!"

"Come on, my prince! Give it all you've got!" she cried.

Finally the shoe was released, Charles let out a loud groan and Camilla exclaimed, "Oh God, that feels so good!"

In their bedroom next door, the Queen said to Prince Philip, "See? I told you with a face like that, she would still be a virgin!"

Meanwhile, Charles was working hard to remove Camilla's other shoe.

"Oh, bloody hell, darling! This one's even tighter!"

Prince Philip said to the Queen: "That's my boy. Once a navy man, always a navy man!"

❖ The royal family is out for a drive in the Rolls Royce when they are flagged down by a highwayman. Prince Philip tells the Queen, "Quick, hide all the jewels in your snatch." The highwayman pokes his head in the window and seeing no valuables, tells everyone to get out of the car and drives away.

Standing beside the road, the Queen turns to Philip and says, "That was quick thinking. At least we saved one's jewellery."

"What a pity Camilla hadn't been here," says Philip. "We could have saved the Roller."

❖ The Queen was being shown around her new hospital by the matron. In the first room in the ward she sees a man furiously masturbating in bed. "Good grief!" says the Queen. "Why is one masturbating in bed?"

"Well," the matron explains, "that man has a rare disease which causes him to make too much semen. If he doesn't relieve himself five times a day, his testicles will explode."

"Oh, I see. That poor man," says the Queen.

Moving on to the second room, they look in to see a patient being given a blow job by a nurse. Clearly shocked, the Queen gathers herself and says: "This is terrible, what's one's explanation for this?"

"He has exactly the same condition as the man in the other ward," replies the matron. "Fortunately, however, he has private medical insurance."

❖ **What did Princess Diana and the Queen Mother have in common?**

They both died pushing 102.

❖ Camilla Parker-Bowles goes to see the doctor. "Doctor, whenever I swallow Charles' semen, I get heartburn and indigestion."

"I see," said the doctor. "Have you tried Andrew's?"

❖ **What was the difference between the Queen Mother and the London Underground?**

The Underground got an extension for the Jubilee.

❖ I read in the newspaper that since the death of Princess Diana, on average Camilla receives two human turds in the post every day. What I want to know is who is sending the other one?

❖ Prince Charles was visiting Stoke-on-Trent and all the civic dignitaries were lined up at Stoke station ready for the royal train to arrive. As the train came to a standstill the door to the royal carriage opened and out stepped the prince, who appeared to be wearing a piece of red carpet on his head. Upon closer inspection it turned out to be a genuine fox-fur hat. The lord mayor of Stoke-on-Trent stepped forward and whispered in the prince's ear, "Sir, it is one of the hottest days of the year. I know your views about hunting and all that, but it's hardly politically correct, is it? I mean, wearing a fox-fur hat on a hot day?"

"Oh, this old thing," Charles indicated his hat, "this was daddy's idea."

"Daddy's idea?" said the lord mayor incredulously. "You mean the Duke of Edinburgh told you to wear it?"

"Oh yes," replied Charles, "you see, he asked me where I was off to today, and when I told him I was going to Stoke-on-Trent, he said 'Stoke-on-Trent? Wear the fox hat!'"

❖ Why won't the Post Office issue stamps with a picture of Camilla on them?

Because people won't know which side to spit on.

❖ The Queen and Prince Philip were dining out in one of London's finest restaurants. The waiter comes over and asks what Philip would like to order.

"I'll have two rare steaks."

The waiter says, "Does sir mean two bloody steaks?"

Philip replies, "Yes, quite right, two bloody steaks."

To which the Queen adds, "And make sure there are plenty of fucking chips."

❖ What takes at least three strokes before it gets stiff?

Princess Margaret.

❖ Prince Charles was driving around Sandringham when he heard a soft "thud". He got out his Range Rover to discover that he had accidentally run over his mother's favourite Corgi, crushing it to a bloody pulp. Charles sat down on the grass and put his head in his hands – one's mother was going to go ballistic!

Suddenly he noticed a lamp half-buried in the ground. He dug it up, polished it and immediately a genie appeared.

"You have freed me from thousands of years of imprisonment," said the genie. "Due to the credit crunch, constant downsizing, low wages in third-world countries and fierce global competition, I can only grant you one wish. So . . . what'll it be?"

"What a terrific stroke of luck," said Charles. "The thing is, one pretty much already has all the material things in life, but let me show you this dog." They walk over to the splattered remains of the dog. "Do you think you could bring this dog back to life for me?" the Prince asked.

The genie examined the crushed remains and shook his head. "This dog is too far gone for even me to bring it back to life. Is there something else I can do for you?"

Charles thought for a minute, reached into his pocket and pulled out two photos. "I was married to this beautiful woman called Diana who everyone loved and adored," said Prince Charles, showing the genie the first photo. "But she died and now I'm married to this horse-faced old harridan called Camilla whom absolutely no one likes," and he showed the genie the second photo. "You see, Camilla isn't beautiful or popular at all, so do you think you can make Camilla as beautiful and well liked as Diana?"

The genie studied the two photographs and after a few minutes said, "Let's have another look at the Corgi."

★   ★   ★   ★   ★

SALESMEN

∗ A young Yorkshire lad moved to London and went to Harrods looking for a job. The manager asked, "Do you have any sales experience?"

The young man answered, "Yes, I was a salesman back home."

The manager liked him so he gave him the job. His first day on the job was challenging and busy, but he got through it. After the store was closed, the manager came down and asked "Okay, so how many sales did you make today?"

"One."

The manager groaned. "Only one? You're supposed to average twenty or thirty sales a day. How much was the sale for?"

"£125,699.64," the young lad replied.

The manager choked: "£125,699.64? What the hell did you sell him?"

"Well, first I sold him a small fish hook, then a medium fish hook, and then, I sold him a new fishing rod. Then I asked him where he was going fishing and he said down at the coast, so I told him he would need a boat, so we went down to the boat department and I sold him that twin-engine motorboat. Then he said he didn't think his family saloon would pull it, so I took him down to car sales and I sold him the 4 x 4 Suzuki."

The manager, incredulous, said: "You mean to tell me . . . a guy came in here to buy a fish hook and you sold him a boat and 4x4?"

"Not exactly," the young lad replied. "He came in here to buy a box of tampons for his wife, and I said, 'Well, seeing as how your weekend's fucked, you might as well go fishing!'"

A salesman knocks at the door of a house and is greeted by a twelve-year-old boy with a cigar in one hand and a half-empty bottle of whisky in the other.

The salesman asks the boy, "Excuse me, son, but is your mum or dad in?"

The boy replies, "Does it fucking look like it?"

* A little old lady answered a knock on the door one day and was confronted by a young man in a suit, carrying a vacuum cleaner. "Good morning, madam," said the young man. "If I could take a couple of minutes of your time, I would like to demonstrate the very latest in high-powered vacuum cleaners."

"Go away," said the old lady. "I don't want a new vacuum cleaner, and anyway I'm a pensioner and I'm broke."

As she was about to close the door, the young man wedged his foot in the door and pushed it wide open.

"Please hear me out," he said. "Don't send me away until you have at least seen my demonstration." And with that, he strode past her and emptied a bag of dogshit on to her hallway carpet. "If this vacuum cleaner does not remove all traces of this dogshit from your carpet, madam, I will personally eat whatever is left."

The old lady stepped back and said: "Well I hope you've got a bloody good appetite, because they cut off my electricity this morning."

★   ★   ★   ★   ★

SCHIZOPHRENIA

★ I'm completely exhausted. I shagged this beautiful girl last night but it turned out she was a schizophrenic. I wasn't allowed to stop until I brought both of them to orgasm.

★ Did you hear about the schizophrenic who threatened to kill himself?
   The police treated it as a hostage situation.

★ I had a threesome the other night. I say threesome: actually, I fucked a schizophrenic.

★ Why are schizophrenics afraid to shave?
   They don't trust that cunt with the razor.

★ Why is it that when you talk to God, it's called prayer, but when God talks to you, it's called schizophrenia?

★ What's the best thing about schizophrenia?
   It turns a wank into an orgy.

★ My doctor has diagnosed me as a paranoid schizophrenic. We think he's out to get us.

★ If I had a choice of mental illnesses, I would choose to be a schizophrenic kleptomaniac. After all, you can always take something for it.

★ I got a ticket to see the Special Olympics. I am really looking forward to the schizo-phrenic boxing.

★ ★ ★ ★ ★

SCHOOL

★ What sits in the Columbine High School Library and goes "Shhh"?

The high school quarterback's lung.

★ A nursery school teacher says to her class, "Who can use the word 'definitely' in a sentence?"

A little girl says, "The sky is definitely blue."

The teacher replies, "Sorry, Susan, but the sky can also be grey, or red."

A little boy says: "Trees are definitely green."

"Sorry," interrupts the teacher, "but in the autumn, the trees are brown."

Little Johnny from the back of the class stands up and asks: "Does a fart have lumps?"

The teacher looks horrified and says, "Johnny! Of course not!!!"

"Okay, then I definitely shit my pants."

★ Little Jimmy is sitting in class and the teacher says, "Today, children, we are going to learn multi-syllable words. Does anybody have an example of a multi-syllable word?"

Jimmy puts his hand up. "Me, Miss, Me! Me! Me!"

"Okay, Jimmy," says the teacher. "What is your multi-syllable word?"

Jimmy says, "Mas-tur-bate, miss"

The teacher smiles and says nervously, "Gosh, Jimmy, that's a mouthful."

"No, miss. You're thinking of fel-a-tio."

★ The infants' class had a homework assignment to find out about something exciting and tell it to the class the next day. When the time came for the children to give their reports, the teacher called them up one at a time. She was reluctant to call upon Jimmy, who had a reputation for being a little crude, but eventually his turn came. Little Jimmy walked up to the front of the class and, with a piece of chalk, made a small white dot on the blackboard. He then walked back to his desk and sat down. The teacher couldn't figure out what Jimmy had in mind for his report, so she asked him to explain.

"It's a period," reported Jimmy.

"Well, I can see that," said his teacher. "But what is so exciting about a period."

"Buggered if I know," shrugged Jimmy. "But this morning my sister said she missed one. Then dad had a heart attack, mum fainted and grandad shat himself."

> " We were so poor when I was a kid that my parents used to get my school clothes from the army surplus store. Have you any idea how badly bullied you get going to school dressed as a Japanese sniper? "

★ Sally: "Miss, miss, Freddy Smith has got a dick like a peanut."
Teacher: "Do you mean it's small?"
Sally: "No, it's salty."

✳ Johnny returns to school one day after an unexplained absence. His teacher asks why he was away.

"Sorry, miss," he replies. "Dad got burned."

"Oh dear," says the teacher, "I do hope it wasn't serious?"

"Well, miss, they don't fuck about at the crematorium."

∗ Jenny came home from school and gave her daddy her school report. He opened it with pride and read out aloud, "90 per cent in maths. Well done, Jenny, that is fantastic. You are going to go to university and become a maths professor!"

He read on, "94 per cent in geography. Jenny, this is fantastic. You could be a famous explorer just like David Livingstone or Ranulph Fiennes."

He continued reading her report, welling with pride, "98 per cent in French. Jenny, you are a genius. You know, you could get a fantastic job as an interpreter. Maybe even become British ambassador to the United Nations!"

Jenny's report went on in much the same fashion, with exceptionally high percentages in all subjects, until he got to her result for reading.

"30 per cent? YOU ONLY GOT 30 PER CENT? Jenny, I am ashamed of you. You are a useless, useless child. I spend all this money on your education and you repay me with 30 per cent? You are a complete disgrace!"

He then smacked her across the head with the report and locked her in a dark, cold cupboard without any dinner. Jenny started sobbing in the dark. "I'm so sorry, dad," she whimpered, "it's hard reading Braille with a hook."

∗ An infant school teacher was teaching her English class. She repeated to her students,

"Mary had a little lamb,
Whose fleece was white as snow.
And everywhere that Mary went,
The lamb was sure to go."

The teacher explained that this was an example of poetry, but that it could be changed to prose by changing the last line from, "The lamb was sure to go" to "The lamb went with her." A few days later, the teacher asked for an example of poetry or prose.

Little Jimmy raised his hand and recited,

"Mary had a little pig,
An ordinary little runt.

He stuck his nose in Mary's clothes,
And smelled her little . . ."

He stopped short and asked the teacher if she wanted poetry or prose. "Prose!" the teacher said, panicking.

So Jimmy continued, ". . . arsehole."

★ A seven-year-old at school says to her teacher: "Miss, can my mummy get pregnant?"

"How old is your mother, dear?" asks the teacher.

"Forty," she replies.

"Yes, dear, your mother could get pregnant."

The little girl then asks, "Can my big sister get pregnant?"

"Well, dear, how old is your sister?"

The little girl answers, "Nineteen."

"Oh yes, dear, your sister certainly could get pregnant."

The little girl then asks, "Can I get pregnant?"

"How old are you, dear?"

The little girl answers, "I'm seven years old."

"No, dear, you can't get pregnant . . ."

The little boy sitting behind the little girl slaps her round the back of the head and says, "See, I told you we had nothing to worry about."

★ It was the first day at school and the teacher was asking the children what their fathers did for a living. She asked a little girl, "What does your daddy do?"

She replied, "My daddy is a doctor and he helps people when they're poorly."

The teacher asked a little boy, "What does your daddy do?"

He replied, "My daddy is a mechanic. He fixes cars when they are broken."

Then the teacher asked another little boy, "What does your daddy do?"

The boy replied, "My daddy's dead."

"Well, I'm sorry to hear that," the teacher said, "but what did your daddy do before he died?"

The boy said, "He turned blue and shat on the floor."

Jimmy was sitting in class doing maths when his teacher picked him to answer a question. "Jimmy, if there were five birds sitting on a fence and you shot one with your gun, how many would be left?"

"None," replied Jimmy, "Because the rest would fly away."

"Actually, the answer is four," said the teacher, "but I like the way you are thinking."

Jimmy replies, "I have a question for you now. If there were three women eating ice cream cones in a shop – one was licking her cone, the second was biting the cone, and the third was sucking the cone – which one is married?"

"Er . . ." said the teacher hesitantly, ". . . the one sucking the cone?"

"No," said Jimmy, "the one with the wedding ring on her finger. But I like the way you are thinking."

* Little Jimmy is sitting in class one day, when the teacher says: "I'm going to give you a letter of the alphabet and you have to give me a word that starts with that letter and use it in a sentence. Let's start with A."

Little Jimmy raises his hand and shouts, "Me, miss! Me, miss! Me, miss!"

The teacher, having fallen for one of little Jimmy's crude answers a few jokes back, calls on another student instead.

Next, the teacher asks for the letters B, C and D. Each time, little Jimmy raises his hand, and each time, the teacher ignores him and calls on other students. This continues until she reaches the letter U.

By this time, little Jimmy is jumping out of his seat. The teacher thinks to herself, "What harm can it do? There isn't a bad word I can think of that starts with that letter." So she calls on little Jimmy.

"U-R-I-N-A-T-E, urinate."

The teacher says, "Okay, now use it in a sentence."

Little Jimmy responds, "Urinate, but if you had bigger tits you would be a ten."

★ A teacher gave her class of eleven-year-olds an assignment. They have to ask their parents to tell them a story with a moral at the end of it. The following day the children return to school and begin to tell their stories.

Tommy said, "My dad is a farmer and we have a lot of hens. One day dad was taking our eggs to market in a basket on the front seat of the car when we hit a big bump in the road and all the eggs got broke and made a mess."

"That's a nice story, Tommy," said the teacher. "But what is the moral of the story?"

"Don't put all your eggs in one basket," said Tommy.

"Very good," said the teacher.

Next up was little Sarah. "Our family are also farmers but we raise chickens for the meat market. One day we had a dozen eggs, but when they hatched we only got ten live chicks and the moral to this story is, 'don't count your chickens before they're hatched.'"

"That was a fine story, Sarah," said the teacher.

"David, do you have a story to share?"

"Yes. My daddy told me this story about my Auntie Muriel. Muriel was a flight engineer on a plane in Afghanistan and her plane got hit. She had to bail out over enemy territory and all she had was a bottle of gin, a machine gun and a machete. She drank the bottle of gin on the way down then she landed right in the middle of a load of Taliban soldiers. She shot fifty of them with her machine gun until she ran out of bullets. Then she killed another thirty with the machete until the blade broke, then she killed the last ten with her bare hands."

"Good heavens," said the teacher. "Does this terrible story your dad told you have a moral?"

"Yes, miss," said David. "Stay the fuck away from Auntie Muriel when she's had a drink."

✳ A young black lad asked his father, "Dad, I have the biggest dick in year three. Is it because I'm black?"

His dad replied, "No, son. It's because you're seventeen."

* * * * *

SCOTS

❖ Why do Scotsmen have blue penises?
Because they are tight-fisted wankers.

❖ An English doctor was being shown around a Glasgow hospital. He is taken into a ward full of patients who show no obvious signs of injury. He is puzzled and stops by the bed of the first patient he sees. "Excuse me," says the doctor, "What are you here for?"

The patient replies: "Fair fa' yer honest, sonsie face, Great chieftain o' the puddin' race!"

The English doctor, who hasn't understood a single word, puts it down to the local dialect and hopes for more luck with the next patient.

"Excuse, can you tell me what you are here for?"

The patient replies: "Some hae meat and canna eat, And some wad eat that want it."

This continues with the next patient: "Wee sleekit cow'rin tim'rous beastie, O what a panic's in thy breastie!"

"Well," the English doctor mutters to his Scottish colleague, "I see you saved the psychiatric ward for the last."

"Oh no," the Scottish doctor corrects him, "this is the serious Burns unit."

❖ What's the difference between a Scottish funeral and a Scottish wedding?
  — One less drunk.

❖ What's green and gets a Glaswegian drunk?
  A Giro.

❖ A Scotsman is drinking in a London bar when he gets a call on his mobile phone. Grinning from ear to ear, he announces that his wife has just given birth to a baby boy weighing twenty-five pounds, and orders a round of drinks for everybody in the bar.

Congratulations are showered on him from all around, although nobody can quite believe the baby's size. When challenged about this, the Scot just shrugs, "That's about average where I come from. My boy's a typical Scottish baby boy."

Two weeks later the Scot returns to the bar. The barman says "Aren't you the father of that massive Scottish baby? Everybody's been making bets about how big he'd be in two weeks. So, how much does he weigh now?"

The proud father answers, "Seventeen pounds."

The barman is puzzled and concerned. "What happened? You said he weighed twenty-five pounds the day he was born."

The Scot takes a slow swig from his whisky, wipes his mouth on his shirt sleeve, then replies, "We had him circumcised."

★ ★ ★ ★ ★

SCOUSERS

* A Scouser walked into the local job centre, goes straight up to the counter and said, "I'm looking for a job."

  The man behind the counter replied, "Your timing is amazing. We've just got a listing from a very wealthy man who wants a chauffeur/bodyguard for his nymphomaniac twin daughters. You'll have to drive around in a big black Mercedes, uniform provided. Because of the long hours of this job, meals will also be provided and you will also be required to escort the young ladies on their overseas holidays. The salary is £150,000 a year."

  The Scouser said, "You're bullshitting me!"

  The man behind the counter replied, "Well, you fucking started it."

* ## Why do Geordies rarely marry Scousers?
  ## They are afraid their kids will be too lazy to steal.

* What's the difference between a cow and a tragedy?
  A Scouser wouldn't know how to milk a cow.

* Eminem's gig in Liverpool is to go ahead despite concerns over a sickening attitude to women, appallingly obscene language, an irresponsible attitude to sex and violence and, of course, the booze. Eminem said that, despite these shocking traits, he would wait and "judge the Liverpudlians for himself".

* What's long, hard and fucks Scousers?
  High school.

* John Lennon Airport in Liverpool was shut for eight hours due to a "suspicious car" found within the perimeter. Apparently it had tax and insurance and the radio was still in it.

* Did you hear about the ambidextrous Scouser?
  He can sign on with both hands.

* Why does the River Mersey run through Liverpool?
  Because if it walked, it would get mugged.

* Apparently 85 per cent of Liverpudlian males say they enjoy sex in the shower.
  The other 15 per cent haven't been to prison yet.

* Two Liverpudlians die and go to meet their maker. When they get to the pearly gates, St Peter says, "No way, we don't let Scousers in here." The Scousers plead, telling him how they've been good Christians all their lives and deserve a second chance. So Peter tells them to wait while he has a word with God. God thinks it over for a while and then says, "Well, we don't really want any Scousers in here, but the rules say that we've got to admit them if they've been good Christians, so you'd better let them in."
  Peter goes off, then comes running back five minutes later: "God, God, they've gone, they've gone!"
  "What? The Scousers have gone?"
  "No, the gates!"

* **I saw a bumper sticker on a car that said, "I miss Liverpool". So I smashed the window and stole the sat-nav.**

* A Scouser is sitting in a pub having a few drinks when in walks a gay customer. The gay man eyes him up and after a few beers finally plucks up the courage to approach the Scouser.
  "Do you fancy a blow job?" he whispers.
  The Scouser picks up a bar stool and batters the guy to a pulp, kicking him out of the door. The barman comes over and says; "Christ! That was a bit brutal! What did he say to you?"
  "Dunno," replies the Scouser, "something about a job."

* Rafa Benitez flies to Baghdad to watch a young Iraqi play football and is impressed and arranges for him to come over to England. Two weeks later, Liverpool are two-nil down to Chelsea with only twenty minutes left. The manager gives the young Iraqi striker the nod and on he goes. The lad is a sensation – he scores a hat-trick in twenty minutes and wins the game for the reds! The fans are delighted, the players and coaches are delighted and the media love the new star. When the player comes off the pitch he phones his mum to tell her about his first day in English football.

   "Hello, mum, guess what?" he says. "I played for twenty minutes today, we were two-nil down but I scored three and we won. Everybody loves me, the fans, the media, they all love me. It's wonderful!"

   "Terrific!" says his mum. "Let me tell you about my day. Your father got shot and robbed in the street, your sister and I were ambushed, gang raped and beaten and your brother was beheaded by masked men, all while you were having such a wonderful time."

   The young lad is very upset, "What can I say, mum, but I'm so sorry."

   "Sorry?!!" says his mum, "Is that the best you can do? It's your fault we moved to Liverpool in the first place!"

* ## What are the four most difficult years for a Scouser?
   ### Year eleven.

* A Scouser is driving through Liverpool with his dog in the passenger seat. A police panda car follows him for about half a mile and then puts its siren and stop sign on, indicating to him to pull over. As the officer approaches the car, he sees that the Scouser is slapping the dog violently about the head. He instructs the driver to wind down his window. "Why are you hitting the dog?"

   The Scouser replies, "The little bastard just ate my tax disc."

✳ Sean Connery is being interviewed by Jonathan Ross. He brags that, despite being in his seventies, he can still have sex three times a night. Cilla Black, who is also a guest on the show, is all ears. After the show, in the green room our Cilla says, "Sean, if I'm not being too forward, I'd luv to 'ave sex with yer. Lets go back to my place, we could 'ave a lorra lorra fun."

So they go back to Cilla's house and make themselves comfortable. After a couple of drinks they go off to bed and have an hour of mad passionate sex together. Afterwards, Sean says, "If you think that was good, just let me get my head down for half an hour and we can go again if you like. But while I'm shleeping, hold my balls in your left hand and ma willie in your right hand."

Cilla looks a bit perplexed, but says, "Okay, luv."

Sean sleeps for half an hour, then wakes up and they have even better sex than before. Then Sean says, "Shilla, that was wonderful. But if you let me shleep for an hour, we can have the besht shex yet. You'll have to—"

"Yes, I know, luv," interrupts our Cilla. "Yer want me to 'old on to yer balls again. No problem hun."

Cilla complies with the routine. The sex this time is the best she's ever had. When it's all over, Sean lights a cigarette and they have a gin and tonic. Cilla asks, "Sean luv, tell me something. This holding yer balls in one hand and yer willie in de other malarkey. Does it really turn yer on that much?"

Sean replies, "No, not at all, Shilla, but the last time I shlept with a Scouser, the bitch stole ma wallet."

✳ After a poor season the Ferrari Formula One team have decided to employ Liverpudlian teenagers as their pit crew because of their renowned skill at removing car wheels quickly. At their first practice session, not only did they change all four wheels in less than six seconds, within twelve seconds they had also re-sprayed, re-badged and sold the car to the McLaren team for six cases of Stella, a bag of smack and a photo of Lewis Hamilton's bird getting shagged up the arse.

✳ What's the difference between Batman and a Scouser?

Batman can go out at night without robin.

* * * * *

SECTARIANS

✳ An Irish girl had not been home to visit her parents for five years. Upon her return, her father berated her. "Where have you been all this time? Why did you not write to us, not even a line? Why didn't you call? Can you not understand what you put your poor mother through?"

The girl, sobbing, replied, "Sorry dad. I was too ashamed. I became a prostitute."

"What!!?" yelled her father. "Get out of here, you shameless slut! You're a disgrace to this fecking family."

"Okay, dad," the girl sobbed, "as you wish. I just came back to give mum this fur coat and this diamond necklace. And for my kid brother, this gold Rolex and for you, daddy, the keys to the Mercedes limited-edition convertible parked outside, plus a membership to the country club. There's also an invitation for you all to spend Christmas on board my new yacht in the Riviera—"

"Bejesus!" interrupts her father. "Come here and give your old man a hug! You scared us half to death, lass! We thought for a minute you said you'd become a Protestant!"

✳ What is two miles long and has an IQ of forty?

An Ulster Orangemen march.

The Protestant leader Reverend Ian Paisley is telling bedtime stories to his two granddaughters. "NOW, CHILDREN," he asks gently, "WHAT WOULD YOU LIKE TO HEAR? A FAIRY TALE, OR A HORROR STORY?!"

"Horror, horror, please, grandad," squeal the kids.

"RIGHT! ONCE UPON A TIME, THERE WERE THESE TWO CATHOLICS. AND NOW THERE'S THOUSANDS OF THE BASTARDS!"

★　★　★　★　☆

SEX AND THE ELDERLY

❖ Two old age pensioners are having oral sex. After a few minutes he chokes, "Sorry, love, the smell's too bad down there, I can't carry on."

"That'll be my arthritis," she replies.

"I never heard of anyone having arthritis in their fanny before."

"No," she says. "It's in my arms and hands. I can't wipe me arse."

❖ An old man is kneeling by the bed. His wife says, "What are you praying for?"

"Guidance," he replies.

She says, "Pray for stiffness – I'll guide it in myself."

❖ What do you call a successful masturbation by a ninety-year-old man?

Miracle whip.

❖ An elderly couple in their eighties just got married and are on their honeymoon. In the hotel bridal suite she slips into something sexy and crawls into bed and waits for her new groom. Meanwhile he is in the bathroom sprucing himself up. She waits . . . and waits . . . and waits . . . until she can't wait any longer. She gets up and goes to the bathroom and opens the door. Peering in she sees him bent over on the toilet trying to put on a condom.

"Honey," she says, "what on earth are you doing? I'm eighty-six years old and can't get pregnant any more."

He looks up at her and says, "I know, darling, but you know how the damp affects my arthritis."

❖ What's the best form of birth control after fifty?
Nudity.

❖ A ninety-year-old man went to see his doctor for a check-up.

"How are feeling in general," asked his doctor.

"I've never felt better," replied the old man. "I have an eighteen-year-old bride who is pregnant with my child. What do you think about that?"

The doctor considered this for a minute and then said, "I have an elderly patient who likes to shoot rabbits. One day when he was going out he got a little confused and he accidentally picked up his umbrella instead of his gun. When he got to the woods, he saw a rabbit raised his umbrella and went, 'bang, bang' and the rabbit fell dead. What do you think of that?"

The ninety-year-old considered this for a few seconds and said, "I'd say somebody else killed that rabbit."

The doctor replied, "My point exactly."

❖ According to recent research, more money is now spent on boob jobs and Viagra than on seeking a cure for Alzheimer's. This means that, by 2040, the elderly will all have perky tits and stiff cocks, but absolutely no idea why.

❖ An elderly man goes to the doctor and says, "I have this problem with my sex life."

The doctor asks, "Can you describe the problem?"

"Well, I wake up in the morning and shag my wife, then I have a shower and a shave and I shag her again. I have my breakfast and shag her again on the table, then I get a blow job from her before I leave for work."

"Okay . . ." the doctor replies.

"I haven't finished yet. I go for a walk in the park and shag my girlfriend in the bushes. Then at lunchtime I go to the pub and shag the young barmaid a couple of times. I go back home and shag my wife again in the afternoon. Then I have my dinner and shag her again, then we go to bed and shag a couple of times before going to sleep."

"Well, I don't see what the problem is."

"Well, doctor," says the old man, "it hurts when I have a wank."

I met a much older woman in a bar last night. She was looking a bit ropey but she wasn't bad for fifty-eight and she had a massive pair of tits. We had a few drinks and flirted, then she asked if I'd ever had a mother and daughter combo.

I said, "No."

We had a couple more drinks then she told me that tonight was my lucky night. I went back to her place, barely concealing my excitement.

Then she put the hall light on and shouted upstairs: "Mother, are you still awake?"

❖ A little boy and his grandad are playing in the garden. The little boy sees an earthworm trying to get back into its hole. He says, "Grandad, I bet I can put that worm back in that hole."

The grandfather replies, "I'll bet you £5 you can't. It's too wiggly and limp to put back in that little hole."

The little boy runs into the house and comes back out with a can of hair spray. He sprays the worm until it is straight and stiff as a board. The boy then proceeds to put the worm back into the hole. His grandad hands the little boy £5, grabs the hair spray and runs into the house.

Thirty minutes later the grandfather comes back out and hands the boy another £5. The little boy shakes his head: "Grandad, you already gave me £5?"

The grandfather replies, "I know. That's from your grandma."

* * * * *

SEX EDUCATION

A young lad went to his father and asked, "Dad, what's the difference between potentially and realistically?"

The father thinks for a moment and then replied, "Go and ask your mother if she would sleep with Sean Connery for a million pounds. Then ask your sister if she would sleep with Brad Pitt for a million pounds. Then come back and tell me what you've learned."

So the lad went to his mother and asked: "Mum would you sleep with Robert Redford for a million pounds?"

His mother replied, "Definitely, I wouldn't pass up an opportunity like that."

The boy then went to his older sister and asked: "Would you sleep with Brad Pitt for a million pounds?"

His sister replied: "Would I fuck Brad Pitt? Too fucking right I would!"

The lad thought about it for a few days and went back to his father. His father asked him "Did you find the difference between potentially and realistically?"

The lad replied, "Yes, dad. Potentially we're sitting on two million quid. Realistically, however, we're living with two slappers."

The father replied, "That's my boy."

Jimmy's dad asked him, "Do you know about the birds and the bees?"

"I don't want to know!" little Jimmy cried, bursting into tears.

Confused, the father asked his son what was wrong.

"Christ, dad . . ." Jimmy sobbed, ". . . when I was seven, I got the 'There's no Santa' speech. When I was eight, I got the 'There's no Easter bunny' speech. Then when I was nine, you gave me the 'There's no tooth fairy' speech! If you're going to tell me now that grown-ups don't really fuck, I've got nothing left to live for!"

* Jimmy and Jenny are just ten years old but they are in deeply in love. One day they decide that they want to get married, so Jimmy goes to Jenny's father to ask him for her hand. Jimmy bravely walks up to him and says, "Mr Jones, me and Jenny are in love and I would like your permission for her hand in marriage."

Mr Smith smiles, "Well, Jimmy, you are only ten. Where will you two live?"

Without hesitation, Jimmy replies, "In Jenny's room. It's bigger than mine and we can both fit in there nicely."

Mr Smith says: "Okay. How will you live? You're not old enough to get a job and you'll need to support Jenny."

In an instant, Jimmy replies, "Our allowance: Jenny makes £5 a week and I make £5 a week. That's about £40 a month, and that should do us just fine."

By this time Mr Jones is a little taken aback by Jimmy's self-assurance. After a few moments he says: "Well, Jimmy, it seems that you have got everything all figured out. I just have one more question for you. What will you do if the two of you should have little ones of your own?"

Jimmy shrugs his shoulders. "That won't happen, she only lets me shag her up the arse."

* A mother and her thirteen-year-old are sitting watching the television when there's a sex scene. The daughter shifts in her seat uncomfortably but mum thinks it's a good time to show her daughter that she's an open-minded parent, and tries to get her daughter to open up and talk about dating boys and so forth.

"So," says mum, "is there anything you want to ask me about dating?"

"Oh, you know how it is," replies the daughter uneasily, feeling very uncomfortable about where this is going.

"Really now . . ." says mum, ". . . you can ask me anything. It's really important for mums and daughters to talk about these things."

"I don't know," answers the daughter.

"Don't forget," says mum, "I was a teenager once."

"Okay," says the reluctant daughter. "For starters, how do you get spunk out of your hair?"

* A mother asked her daughter what she wanted for her birthday. The little girl replied, "I want a Barbie and a G.I. Joe."

"G.I. Joe?" the mother replies. "Doesn't Barbie come with Ken?"

"No," the daughter replied. "She comes with G.I. Joe. She fakes it with Ken."

* Jane met Tarzan for the first time. After some preliminary flirting, she asked him about his sex life. "Tarzan not know sex," he replied. Jane explained to him what sex was. Tarzan said, "Oh, I understand. Tarzan use hole in trunk of tree." A little bemused, she said, "Tarzan you have it all wrong. But I will show you how to do it properly."

She took off her clothes and stood naked before him. "Here," she said. "You must put it in here." Tarzan removed his loincloth revealing a huge erection, then directed an almighty kick right in her fanny. As Jane rolled around the floor in agony, she managed to gasp: "What did you do that for?"

"Tarzan check for bees."

✳ Little Tommy was watching television in his room one evening and decided to go downstairs to ask his mum and dad about something he'd just heard.

"Dad," said Tommy "what's love juice?"

Mum and dad are horrified. Eventually, dad finishes choking on his tea and decides to bite the bullet. "Well, son, I guess one day you will need to find out anyway, so here goes." He gulps and continues, "One day you will meet a girl who you like and you will become very excited and your willy will get very hard. You might want to touch the girl all over and when you reach the top of her leg it will feel damp. This is her love juice coming out of her vagina, it means she is ready for sexual intercourse."

Tommy just sits there with his mouth wide open in astonishment. Dad finishes the talk and asks: "So, now you can tell me what it is you've been watching that you shouldn't be."

Tommy replies, "Wimbledon."

✳ A woman brings eight-year-old Jimmy home and complains to his mother that he was caught playing doctors and nurses with her eight-year-old daughter.

"Let's not be too harsh," says Jimmy's mum. "They are bound to be curious about sex at that age."

"Curious about sex?" replies the girl's mother. "He's removed her appendix!"

★   ★   ★   ★   ★

SEXIST JOKES ABOUT MEN

What a Man Means When he Says . . .

I'm hungry – I'm hungry.

I'm tired – I'm tired.

Do you want to go to see a film? – I would like to have sex with you.

Can I take you out to dinner? – I would like to have sex with you.

Can I call you sometime? – I would like to have sex with you.

Would you like to dance? – I would like to have sex with you.

Nice dress! – Nice tits!

You look tense, let me give you a massage – I would like to have sex with you, but first I want you to take your clothes off so I can fondle you.

What's wrong? – I don't see why you're making such a big fucking deal about a bit of a fondle.

What's wrong? – What meaningless self-inflicted stupid psychological trauma are you going through now?

What's wrong? – Bollocks, guess sex tonight is out of the question.

I'm bored – Do you want to have sex or not?

I love you – I want it NOW!

I love you, too – Okay I've said it, so can we please have sex NOW!?

Yes, I like what you have done with your hair – I liked it better before.

Yes, I like what you have done with your hair – £30 and it doesn't look that much different!

Let's talk – I am trying to impress you by showing you that I am a deep person and maybe then you'd like to have sex with me.

Will you marry me? – I want to make it illegal for you to have sex with other men.

I like that dress better – For fuck's sake, just buy any dress and let's go home!

I don't think that top and that skirt go well together – I am gay.

★ What's the definition of a competitive alpha male?
  Someone who finishes first and third in the same masturbation contest.

★ Why are men like lawn mowers?
  They're hard to get started, they emit noxious odours and half the time they don't work.

★ How are men and linoleum floors alike?
  You lay them right the first time and you can walk all over them for the next twenty years.

International Rules for Men

1 Two men should never share an umbrella.
2 It is only acceptable for a man to cry (a) during a film when a heroic dog dies to save its master (b) if a woman uses her teeth when giving him a blow job.
3 Any man who takes a camera with him on a stag night may be killed and eaten by his friends.
4 If you have known your mate for more than twenty-four hours his sister is off limits unless you actually marry her.
5 Never complain about the brand of free beer in your mate's fridge. You may, however, complain if the temperature is unsuitable.
6 Never buy a birthday present for another man. If you even remember your mate's birthday, you must celebrate at a strip joint of the birthday boy's choice.
7 In the mini-bus, the strongest bladder determines pit stops, not the weakest.
8 While watching a sporting event on TV in a bar, you may ask the score of the game in progress but never ask who is playing.
9 You may fart in front of a woman only after you have brought her to climax. If you trap her head under the covers for the purpose of flatulent entertainment (commonly known as a Dutch oven), she is officially your girlfriend.
10 The only time it is permissible to drink a fruity alcoholic cocktail is when you are sunning yourself on a tropical beach, and only then if it is (a) delivered by a fit waitress and (b) free.
11 It is only ever permissible to kick another guy in the bollocks if you are in a life-threatening situation.
12 A man in the company of a hot, scantily dressed woman must remain sober enough to fight.
13 Never wear Speedos. It is also your duty to remind your friends that they should not wear Speedos.

14   Never fight naked.

15   If a man's fly is open, never draw attention to it.

16   Women who claim that they enjoy watching sport should be treated as spies until they demonstrate knowledge of the game and the ability to drink as much as the other sports watchers.

17   Never hesitate to reach for the last beer or the last slice of pizza, but never both at the same time. That would be greedy.

18   If you compliment a man on his six-pack, you had better be talking about his choice of beer.

19   Never join your girlfriend or wife in discussing a friend of yours, except if she is withholding sex pending your response.

20   Never talk to a man in a toilet unless you are both urinating. For all other situations, an imperceptible nod of acknowledgment is all the conversation you need.

21   Never allow a phone conversation with a woman to go on longer than you are able to have sex with her.

22   The morning after you and a female who was previously "just a friend" have carnal, drunken monkey sex, the fact that you are feeling guilty is no reason for you not to nail each other again before the discussion occurs about what a big mistake it was.

23   Never buy a car in the colours of brown, pink, lime green, orange or sky blue.

24   The female who answers the question "What do you want for Christmas?" with "If you loved me, you would know what I want!" gets an Xbox 360.

25   There is no excuse for men to watch ice skating or men's gymnastics, ever.

26   It is not permissible to make eye contact when watching porn with your mates.

27   There are only two circumstances under which it is allowed to have an erection with male friends in the room. One is when you are watching porn, the other is when you are "spit roasting" a woman.

★ **What three words are guaranteed to destroy a man's ego?**
   "Is it in?"

★ How can you tell if a man is sexually aroused?
   He's breathing.

★ What's the difference between men and government bonds?
   Government bonds mature.

★ **How many men does it take to change a roll of toilet paper?**
   We don't know. It's never happened.

★ What is the difference between a bachelor and a married man?
   A bachelor comes home, sees what's in the refrigerator and goes to bed. A married man comes home, sees what's in the bed and goes to the refrigerator.

★ What's the difference between a boyfriend and a catfish?
   One is a dirty scum-sucking, crap-eating, bottom feeder and the other one's a fish.

★ How many bright, sensitive, caring men in the world does it take to do the dishes?
   Both of them.

What makes men chase women they have no intention of marrying?
   The same urge that makes dogs chase cars they have no intention of driving.

★ How can you tell when a man is well hung?
 When you can just barely slip your finger in between his neck and the noose.

★ What do toilet bowls, anniversaries and clitorises have in common?
 Men miss all of them.

★ Why do men find it difficult to make eye contact?
Breasts don't have eyes.

★ How do men sort out their laundry?
 Dirty, rank, rank but wearable.

★ Why don't women blink during foreplay?
There isn't enough time.

★ What do you call the useless bit of skin at the end of a penis?
 A man.

★ What do men and public toilets have in common?
 They're both either busy or full of shit.

★ What would get your man to put down the toilet seat?
A sex-change operation.

★ ★ ★ ★ ★

SEXIST JOKES ABOUT WOMEN

❖ Women are a bit like parking spaces. Normally all the good ones are taken. So occasionally, when no one's looking, you have to stick it in a disabled one.

❖ What's the difference between a bitch and a whore?
A whore sleeps with everybody at the party, and a bitch sleeps with everybody at the party except you.

❖ What woman can wash up with her left hand, cook tea with the right, sweep with one leg, dust with the other, and give a blow job and open beer with her arse?
A Swiss army wife.

❖ What's long and hard and makes women groan?
An ironing board.

❖ What is the difference between a dog and a fox?
About five pints.

❖ If your wife keeps coming out of the kitchen to nag at you, what have you done wrong?
Made her chain too long.

❖ What's the most active muscle in a woman?
The penis.

❖ Why are women like screen doors?
Once they have been banged a few times, they loosen up.

❖ I like my women like my electrical gadgets: small, Japanese and bought on the street.

❖ What is the difference between a battery and a woman?
   A battery has a positive side.

❖ What is the difference between a wife and a prostitute?
   One is contract and the other is pay-as-you-go.

❖ I met this bird in a bar. "Hey baby, what's your sign?" I asked.
   She replied: "Do not enter."
   I said: "Are you sure it isn't 'fat bird reversing'?"

❖ My girlfriend said to me, "You're always patronizing me. I really hate it when you finish my sentences."
   So I replied, "Period."

❖ How do you know when it's time to wash the dishes?
   Look inside your pants. If you have a dick, it isn't time to wash the dishes.

❖ Why do women shave under their arms?
   So they can iron faster.

❖ How do you stop a girl from falling off her bicycle?
   Remove the saddle.

❖ What's the difference between a woman from Wigan and a walrus?
   One's fat and has a moustache and smells of fish, and the other lives in the sea.

❖ Which sexual position produces the ugliest children?
   Ask your mother.

❖ What do you call a virgin on a waterbed?
    A cherry float.

❖ **If a man talking dirty to a woman is sexual harassment, what do you call a woman talking dirty to a man?**
    £2.50 a minute.

❖ How can you tell if a woman is wearing tights?
    If she farts, her ankles swell.

❖ Why do women have vaginas?
    So men will talk to them.

❖ What two things in the air can make a women pregnant?
    Her feet.

❖ Why do ballerinas wear tights?
    So they won't stick to the floor when they do the splits.

❖ Having sex with a pregnant woman isn't all bad. It's when the baby starts giving you head.

❖ What are the two most important holes in a woman's body?
    The nostrils. They enable her to breathe while she's sucking your cock.

❖ How do you know if a woman is wearing underwear?
    Look for dandruff on her shoes.

❖ Always try to treat your women the way you treat your vacuum cleaner. When it stops sucking, change the bag.

❖ What is the difference between a Harley and a Hoover?
    The position of the dirt bag.

❖ What's the difference between a man and a hog?
   A hog doesn't have to sit in a bar and buy drinks all night long just to fuck some pig.

❖ What is the definition of a perfect woman?
   Three feet tall with a round hole for a mouth and a flat head so that you can put a pint of beer on it. (N.B. The sports model has pullback ears and her teeth fold in.)

❖ How many people does it take to write a sexist joke?
   Two – the man to dictate it and the woman to type it.

❖ How do you know if your girlfriend is on anabolic steroids?
   When she flips you over, holds you down and fucks you up the arse with her clitoris.

❖ Why do women have foreheads?
   So there's somewhere to kiss them after a blowjob.

❖ Why did cave-men drag their women by the hair?
   If they dragged them by the feet, they'd fill up with rocks.

❖ Why do women have 2 per cent more brains then a cow?
   So that when you pull their tits they won't shit on the floor.

❖ How many men does it take to open a beer bottle?
   None – it should already be open when she brings it to you

❖ Why are women like Kentucky Fried Chicken?
   After you've finished with the thigh and breasts all you have left is a greasy box to put your bone in.

❖ What is the best way to brainwash your wife?
     Stand on her enema bag.

❖ Why has there never been a woman on the moon?
     Because it doesn't need cleaning.

❖ Why did God create women?
     Because dogs can't get beer out of the fridge.

A boy says to his mother one day: "Mum, why are wedding dresses white?"

She replies, "Son, this shows your friends and relatives that your bride is pure."

The son thanks his mum for this information and goes off to check this with his father. "Dad, why are wedding dresses white?"

The father looks up from reading his newspaper with some surprise.

"Well, you know, son, all household appliances come in white."

❖ Why do women have two sets of lips?
     So they can piss and moan at the same time.

❖ What is the difference between Meg Ryan and the Panama Canal?
     The Panama Canal is a busy ditch.

❖ Why do they call it pre-menstrual tension?
     Because mad cow disease was already taken.

❖ Why do women have small feet?
     So they can stand closer to the kitchen sink.

❖ Why are women like prawns?
     Their heads are full of shit but the pink bits taste great.

❖ Women are just like cartons of orange juice. It's not the shape or size that matters, or even how sweet the juice is. It's getting those fucking flaps open.

❖ Apparently a lot of women are reading this book. The dinner won't cook itself, you know.

❖ According to sex therapists, the most effective method of arousing a man is to lick his ears. Personally I think it's bollocks.

❖ How do you turn a dishwasher into a snow plough?
    Give the cow a shovel.

❖ Scientists have identified that after two years of marriage, many women develop something called "Dyson's Syndrome". They make a continuous whining noise, but no longer suck.

❖ What do you do if your boiler explodes?
    Buy her some flowers.

❖ Why do women take longer than men to reach orgasm?
    Who cares?

❖ Why does NASA always send a woman on shuttle missions?
    They weigh twenty-five pounds less than an automatic dishwasher.

❖ They say a woman's work is never done. If you ask me they should get their shit together and try to be a little better organized.

❖ What's the difference between a pit-bull and a woman with PMS?
    Lip-gloss.

Creative Insults About Women

She has a cunt like a stab wound in a gorilla's back

She looks like she's been dunking for apples in a chip pan

She has had more hands up her than Kermit the frog

She has a face like a dog licking piss off a nettle

Her face looks like she's been set on fire and put out with a golf shoe

She's got a face that could make an onion cry

I wouldn't ride her into battle

I wouldn't do her with a rusty pole

She has more chins than a Chinese phone books

She smells like an alcoholic's carpet

Shagging her is like shagging the sleeve off a wizard's cloak

❖ Why do women have legs?
   Have you seen the trail snails leave?

❖ A woman walks into a bar. Only joking, she was in the kitchen!

She has a vagina like a ripped-out fireplace

She has killed more cocks than a fowl butcher

She has a face like a sand-blasted tomato

She sweats like a dog in a Chinese restaurant

She has seen more helmets than Hitler

She has a face like a stuntman's knee

She has a cunt like a badly packed kebab

She is so ugly that even a sniper wouldn't take her out

She has a face like a blind joiner's thumb

She has piss flaps like John Wayne's saddle bags

She had a pair of flaps on her like a gutted trout

She has a cunt like a burst couch

She has been cocked more times than Elmer Fudd's shotgun

❖ Why don't women need a wristwatch?
There's a perfectly good one on the stove.

❖ What is the difference between a woman and a washing machine?

You can bung your load into a washing machine and it won't call you a week later.

❖ How do you make a woman scream for an hour after sex?

Wipe your dick on the curtains.

❖ Why do women have arms?

Have you any idea how long it would take to lick a bathroom clean?

❖ What's the cleverest thing to have come out of a woman's mouth?

Einstein's penis.

❖ Why do women wear make-up and perfume?

Because they're ugly and they smell.

★　★　★　★　★

SEXUALLY TRANSMITTED DISEASES

* What is green and eats nuts?
  Herpes.

* What's the difference between the army and a vagina?
  Army discharge is a good thing.

* What do you get when you cross Billy Ray Cyrus and a yeast infection?
  An itchy, twitchy twat.

* Why did the Essex girl name her dog Herpes?
  Because it wouldn't heel.

* A young couple went to the doctor for their annual medical check-ups.
  Afterwards, the doctor called the young man into his office and told him that he had some good news and some bad news.
  "The good news," he explained, "is that your fiancée has a rare strain of gonorrhoea, which I have only heard of once before."
  The guy blanched. "If that's the good news, then what the hell is the bad news?"
  "Well," the doctor elaborated, "the bad news is that I heard about this particular strain only last week when I took my dog to see the vet."

Doctor: "Mrs Jones, the results of your tests are back, I'm afraid you have gonorrhoea."
Mrs Jones: "I think I caught it from a toilet seat."
Doctor: "You must have been chewing it then – it's in your gums."

※ A man went to see his doctor. The doctor told him, "I have good news and bad news."

"What's the bad news?"

"Your wife has syphilis."

"Oh my God! What could possibly be good news."

"She didn't get it from you."

※ What's the difference between love and herpes?

Love doesn't last forever.

※ A British tourist goes on a trip to China. While he is there he visits a local brothel and doesn't use a condom. A week after arriving home, he finds his penis is covered with bright green spots. Horrified, he goes to see his doctor.

The doctor tells him: "I've got bad news. You've contracted Mongolian VD. It's very rare. We know little about it. We have to amputate your penis."

The man asks for a second opinion and seeks out a Chinese doctor who is working at the local clinic, figuring he'll know more about the disease.

The Chinese doctor examines him and says, "Ah, yes, Mongolian VD."

"What can you do?" asks the man. "The other doctor wants to amputate!"

The Chinese doctor shakes his head and laughs, "Stupid British doctors always want to operate. Make more money that way. No need to operate!"

"Oh, thank God!" the man replies.

"Yes!" says the Chinese doctor. "You no worry! Wait two weeks. Dick fall off by itself!"

※ How does herpes leave the hospital?

On crotches.

* The Greek god Zeus was flying over ancient Greece when he spotted a beautiful naked woman washing herself. He flew and made passionate love to her, then stroked her face and told her, "In nine months you will have a child and you will call him Hercules!"

   The woman dressed herself smiled and replied, "In nine days you will have a rash and you will call it Herpes. Now sod off."

* "I'm afraid I have some good news and some bad news, Miss Smith."

   "Well, give me the good news first, doctor."

   "Your lab tests came back today and your crabs are all gone."

   "That's terrific. But what's the bad news?"

   "We don't know what ate them."

* Which new venereal disease only affects foot fetishists?
   Athlete's tongue.

★   ★   ★   ★   ★

SHIT

★ What is ten inches long, two inches thick and starts with a P?
   A good shit.

★ Two flies were sitting on a turd when one of them farted. "Please . . ." said the other. "I'm trying to eat here."

Turd Glossary

Ghost Shit: when you feel the shit come out, have shit on the toilet paper, but there is no shit in the toilet.

Clean Shit: when you shit it out, observe it in the toilet pan, but there is nothing on the toilet paper.

Second-Wave Shit: when you're done shitting, you've pulled your pants up to your knees and you realize that you have to shit some more.

Brain-Haemorrhage Shit: also known as "Pop a vein in your forehead" shit: the kind where you strain so much to get it out that you practically have a stroke.

Sweetcorn Shit: self-explanatory.

Log Shit: your turds are so huge that you're afraid to flush the toilet without breaking them into a few pieces with your toilet brush.

Drinker's Shit: the type of shit that you have the morning after a long night of drinking. Most noticeable trait is the skid marks left on the bottom of the toilet.

I Wish I Could Shit: where you want to shit, but all you do is sit on the toilet with cramps and fart a few times.

Spinal Tap Shit: when it hurts so much that you swear it was leaving you sideways.

Groaner: so huge it cannot exit without vocal assistance.

Wet-Cheeks Shit: also known as "The Power Dump". The type that comes out of your arse so fast that your butt cheeks get splashed with the toilet water.

Liquid Shit: when yellowish-brown liquid shoots out of your arse, splashing all over the inside of the toilet bowl.

The Madras: in a class of its own.

The Crowd Pleaser: a dump so intriguing in size and/or appearance that you have to show it to someone.

Mood Enhancer: occurs after a lengthy period of constipation, allowing you to be your old self again.

The Ritual: occurs at the same time each day and is accomplished with the aid of a newspaper.

Guinness Book of Records Shit: a dump so noteworthy it should be recorded for future generations.

The Aftershock Shit: has an odour so pungent that anyone entering the vicinity within the next four hours is overpowered.

Courtesy Flush Shit: the act of flushing the toilet the instant the nose cone of the turd log hits the water and the poop is whisked away to an undisclosed location. This reduces the amount of air time the poop has to stink up the bathroom.

The Honeymoon Is Over Shit: any shit created in the presence of another person.

Floater: characterized by its floatability, this shit has been known to resurface after many flushes.

Ranger: refuses to let go. It is usually necessary to engage in a rocking or bouncing motion, but quite often the only solution is to push it away with a small piece of toilet paper.

Phantom Shit: this appears in the toilet mysteriously and no one will admit putting it there.

Peek-a-boo Shit: now you see it, now you don't. This shit is playing games with you. Requires patience and muscle control.

The Bombshell: comes as a complete surprise at a time that is either inappropriate to shit (i.e. during love making or during root canal work) or you are nowhere near shitting facilities.

Snake Charmer: a long skinny shit which has managed to coil into a frightening position. Bears a close resemblance to the Drinker's Shit.

★ Two flies are sitting on a turd. One turns to the other and says, "I haven't seen you around in a while. Where have you been ?"

The other fly replies, "Yeah, I know. I've been on the sick."

★ Two male flies are buzzing around, cruising for female flies. One of them sees a hottie sitting on a cowpat so he buzzes down and sidles up next to her.

"Excuse me," he asks, turning on his best charm, "is this stool taken?"

★ There's no such thing as a free lunch . . . unless you're a coprophiliac.

★ A little boy says to his dad one day: "Dad, where does poo come from?"

The father is a little taken aback that his five-year-old son is already asking difficult questions and thinks for a while how to respond.

"Well, you know we just ate breakfast?"

"Yes," answers the boy.

"Well, when you put food into your mouth you chew and swallow. The food then gets smaller and smaller and goes down in your oesophagus, a long tube that goes down into your tummy. Your tummy then mixes up the food and liquid with the digestive juices produced by your tummy. The digestive juices help to break down the food so the body can process it properly. Then the food comes out of your tummy and goes into your small intestine. The walls of your small intestine are filled with little hairs or fingers that stick out, called villi. The villi take the nutrients from the food into the entire body. After it leaves the small intestine, it travels into the large intestine. The only stuff that's left over when it goes into the large intestine is waste. The waste then comes out of your bottom when you go to the loo, and that is poo."

The little boy stares at his dad in stunned silence for a few seconds, then asks: "And tigger?"

★ My son was terrified after accidentally swallowing some Lego. He was shitting bricks for days.

★ ★ ★ ★ ★

SHOPPING

❖ Two blondes walk into a department store. They go up to the perfume counter and pick up a sample bottle. One sprays it on her wrist and smells it.

"That's quite nice, don't you think?"

Her friend takes a sniff and replies, "Really nice. What's it called?

"'Viens a moi'."

"'Viens a moi'? What does that mean?"

The assistant interjects, "'Viens a moi', ladies, means 'come to me' in French."

The first blonde takes another sniff, then says to her friend: "That doesn't smell anything like come to me. Does that smell like come to you?"

❖ A man was shopping in the men's department at Harvey Nichols when he spotted a stunning female assistant behind the sales counter. He went up to her and said, "Good morning, madam."

She smiled pleasantly and replied: "And what would you like?"

The man said, "I'd like to wrap my arms around you and squeeze you tight then run my hand up and down your arse and squeeze it. Then I'd like to run my hands along your inner thighs, up underneath your dress. When I get to your sweet pussy, I'd like to rub it while simultaneously ripping your dress off with my teeth and then suck on your beautiful breasts and bite your nipples lightly. What I 'need', however, is a new tie."

❖ My wife got run over on the way to the shops today. Luckily I found a tin of baked beans in the cupboard.

❖   A woman was in Oxford Street on a shopping trip during the summer sales. She bought an expensive pair of shoes in the first shop and a beautiful dress in the second. In the third, everything had just been reduced to a fiver when her mobile phone rang. It was a female doctor on the other end: "I'm sorry but your husband has just been in a terrible accident and is in a critical condition in the intensive care unit." The woman told the doctor that she'd be there as soon as possible.

As soon as she hung up, it dawned on her that she was leaving what was shaping up to be her best day's shopping ever. It was a terrible dilemma. She decided to get in a couple of more sales before heading to the hospital.

She ended up shopping the rest of the morning, finishing her trip with a complimentary cup of coffee and a slice of cheesecake from the last shop. She was ecstatic!

Suddenly she remembered her husband. Feeling guilty, she dashed to the hospital and met the lady doctor in the corridor.

The lady doctor glared at her. "You finished your shopping trip, didn't you? I hope you're proud of yourself! While you were out enjoying yourself for the past three hours, your husband has been in the intensive care unit. Unfortunately it will probably be the last shopping trip you ever take, because for the rest of his life he will require round-the-clock care and you are now his carer!"

The woman broke down and sobbed uncontrollably.

The lady doctor then laughed and said, "I'm just pulling your leg. He's dead. What did you buy?"

❖   A woman goes into her local music store looking for an old record; behind the counter is small young boy.

She says: "Excuse me sonny, but do you have 'Jingle Bells' on a seven inch?"

He replies: "No, but I've got dangling balls on a nine inch."

"That's not a record, is it?"

"No, but it's pretty good for a ten-year-old."

❖   A very ugly woman is walking down the supermarket aisle with her two sons.

A man stops her and asks: "Excuse me, are they twins?"

The woman replies: "What a stupid question. One is three years old and the other is ten. Isn't it pretty obvious they're not twins?"

The man replies: "I thought as much. I just can't believe someone fucked you twice."

❖   An elderly woman goes into fishing tackle shop to buy a rod and reel for her grandson's birthday. She doesn't know which one to get, so she just takes one over to the counter. She says to the salesman, "Excuse me, can you tell me anything about this rod and reel?"

He replies: "Madam, I'm completely blind, but if you'll drop it on the counter I can tell you everything from the sound it makes."

She is sceptical but decides to humour him anyway and drops it on the counter.

"That's a six-foot graphite rod with a 404 reel and a 10-lb test line. It's a great choice because it is on offer, this week only, for £60."

The customer is amazed. "You can tell all that just by the sound of it dropping on the counter? I'll take it!"

As she opens her purse, her credit card drops on the floor.

"American Express, if I'm not mistaken," he says.

She bends down to pick it up and accidentally breaks wind. At first she is deeply embarrassed, but then realizes that there is no way the blind shop owner could possibly tell that it was her.

The blind shop owner rings up the sale and says, "That'll be £74.50, please."

The woman is confused by this and asks, "Didn't you say that the rod and reel were on sale for £60?"

"Yes, madam."

"How did you get £74.50?"

He replies: "The rod and reel are £60, the duck caller is £11 and the bag of fish bait is £3.50."

SIAMESE TWINS

✳ A pair of Siamese twins walk into a pub in New York and park themselves on adjacent bar stools. One of them says to the bartender, "Hi there. Don't mind us, we're joined at the hip. I'm Tom, he's Dick. We'll have two Budweisers please."

The bartender, feeling a little awkward, tries to make polite conversation while pouring the beers. "Have you been on vacation yet?"

"Actually, we're off to England next week," says Tom.

"That's nice. Been there before?" asks the barman.

"Yep, we go to England every year and rent a car and drive for miles all over the country, isn't that right, Dick?"

"We sure do," says Dick.

"Ah, England!" says the bartender. "What a wonderful country to visit. London . . . Stratford upon Avon . . . Stonehenge . . . the history, the soccer . . . the beer, the culture . . ."

"Nah, we hate all that British shit," says Tom. "Warm beer, what's that all about? And as for soccer – you can shove it up your ass. Baseball and Buds beer, that's us, right, Dick? And we can't stand the English. They're such a bunch of fucking effeminate stuck-up cunts."

"So why keep going over there?" asks the bartender.

"It's the only time Dick here gets a chance to drive."

What's worse than being a Siamese twin?

Being a Siamese twin and your brother, who is attached to your shoulder, is gay, and you're not. And he has a date coming over tonight and you only have one arse.

★   ★   ★   ★   ★

SKYDIVING

★ Did you hear about the female parachutist?
She pulled the wrong string and bled to death.

★ Why do women parachutists wear tampons?
So they don't whistle on the way down.

★ What's the difference between a bad golfer and a bad skydiver?
A bad golfer goes, WHACK! "Fuck!" A bad skydiver goes, "Fuck!" WHACK!

★ If at first you don't succeed, then skydiving probably isn't for you.

★ What's the similarity between skydiving and getting a blow job from your grandmother?
They both feel exhilarating so long as you don't look down.

★ A blind man takes up skydiving, to the general amazement of his friends. When one of them asks how this was possible, he explains: "Everyone is extremely helpful. I am placed in the door with my blind dog and told when to jump. My hand is placed on my release ring for me and out I go with the dog."
"But how do you know when you are going to land?" someone asks.
"I have a very keen sense of smell and I can smell the trees and grass when I am 300 feet from the ground," the blind man replies.
"But how do you know when to lift your legs for the final arrival on the ground?"
"No problem – the dog's leash goes slack."

★   Did you hear about the Irish skydiver who fell to his death? His flippers failed to open.

★   ★   ★   ★   ★

SMOKING

❖   My doctor told me: "If you had X-ray vision and looked at your lungs, you'd never smoke again."

"Too right I wouldn't," I replied. "I would be much too busy looking through girls' underwear."

❖   Two nuns were enjoying a furtive cigarette at the back of the convent. One said, "We'd better make sure we get rid of the cigarette butts so mother superior doesn't find them."

The second nun says, "I've found a great invention called the condom that solves this problem. You just open the packet up, take out the condom, and put the cigarette butt in, roll it up, and dispose of it all later."

The first nun is quite impressed and asked where she could get them. "You get them at the pharmacist's, sister, just go in and ask."

So the next day the sister went to the pharmacist's and walked up to the counter. "Good morning, sister," said the pharmacist. "What can I do for you today?"

"I'd like some condoms, please," said the nun. He was a little taken aback, but recovered quickly and asked, "Certainly, how many would you like? There are twelve to a pack."

"I'll take six packs, that should last about a week," she replied.

The pharmacist steadied himself and asked, "Sister, so what will it be then? Ribbed, coloured, flavoured or a French tickler perhaps? We have small, medium, large and extra large."

The sister thought for a minute and said, "I'm not sure, perhaps you could recommend a good size for a Camel?"

> " I'm trying to give up two of my worst habits, smoking and wanking. I am finding it very difficult because I'm a thirty-a-day man. Also I smoke like a chimney. "

❖ Life is like a box of cigarettes. You never know which cancer you're going to get.

❖ If smoking is so bad for you, how come it cures salmon?

❖ My wife asked me how I could carry on smoking with the knowledge that I was killing myself.
"It's easy," I replied. "I also know I'm killing you through passive smoking."

★   ★   ★   ★   ★

SPERM

✳ Two Irishmen had a bad day while visiting the sperm bank in London. Patrick missed the tube and Murphy came on the bus.

✳ Two prostitutes are in a lift. One says to the other, "Can you smell spunk!"
"Sorry," says the other. "I've just burped."

✳ Why does it take one million sperm to fertilize one egg?
They refuse to stop for directions.

* A seventy-five-year-old man went to his doctor's office to get a sperm count. The doctor gave the man a jar and said, "Take this jar home and bring me back a sample tomorrow."

  The next day, the seventy-five-year-old man reappeared at the doctor's office and gives him the jar, which is as clean and empty as on the previous day. The old man explained, "Well, first I tried with my right hand, but nothing happened. Then I tried with my left hand, but still nothing. Then I asked my wife for help. She tried with her right hand – nothing. Then with her left, still nothing. She even tried with her mouth, first with the teeth in, then with the teeth out, and still nothing. We even called up the lady next door, and she tried with both hands and her mouth too, but nothing."

  The doctor couldn't believe his ears. "You asked your neighbour?"

  The old man replied, "Yes. But no matter what we tried, we couldn't get the jar open!"

* Why is a man's urine yellow and his sperm white?

So he can tell if he's coming or going.

* What's the difference between an Essex girl and an Essex boy?

  An Essex girl has a higher sperm count.

* What did one gay sperm say to another?

  "How do we find an egg in all of this shit?"

* One sperm says to the other: "How far is it to the ovaries?"

  The other one replies: "Relax, dude. We just passed the tonsils."

★   ★   ★   ★   ★

SPORT

★ I have just bought a racehorse called "My Face". It is a crap horse but I can't wait to hear all the women in the crowd screaming, "COME ON MY FACE."

★ Three men go on a skiing trip in the Austrian Alps. The ski lodge is overbooked so they all have to share a bed. The next morning, when they wake up, one guy says: "That was weird. I had a dream that this beautiful woman was wanking me off last night!"

The guy on the other side of the bed says; "No, I'll tell you what's weird – I had the exact same dream!"

The bloke in the middle suddenly looks worried.

"What's wrong?" ask his pals.

He replies, "Last night I dreamt I was skiing . . ."

★ The snooker player Steve Davis pulls a groupie after a tournament and they end up, several drinks later, in his hotel room. Desperate to shag her idol she strips her clothes off and gets on all fours presenting her arse. Steve, being a man who likes to take his time, slowly unzips his trousers, meanwhile staring at the girl's arse from every possible angle, moving from side to side and raising and lowering his head.

"Are you going to fuck me or what?" demands the girl.

"Definitely," says our Steve, "I'm just making my mind up if I should go for the easy pink or the tight brown."

★ I was once asked to run a marathon and I replied, "No chance!" But then I was told it was for disabled and blind kids, so I thought "Fuck it – I could win that!"

★ What's brown and runny?
Usain Bolt.

★ What do you call a woman who can spread her legs from one side of a tennis court to the other?
Annette.

★ What is the toughest thing about roller-blading?
Telling your parents you're gay.

★ Who was the last twenty-stone man to ride a derby winner?
Lester Piggott's cell mate.

★ Who was the last person to box Rocky Marciano?
His undertaker.

★   ★   ★   ★   ★

STEPHEN HAWKING

❖ What does Stephen Hawking do when he needs a shit?
Log out.

❖ Stephen Hawking may be a genius, but he is not setting much of an example to kids by just sitting at his computer all day.

❖ I've been trying to phone Stephen Hawking all week but he's never in. All I ever get is an automated answer.

❖ Stephen Hawking and Christopher Reeve walk into a bar. Not really.

❖ Stephen Hawking went on a blind date. She left after fifteen minutes, complaining that she didn't like his tone.

❖ Stephen Hawking has written a new book. It's called *Around the House in Eighty Days*.

❖ After divorcing his abusive wife Stephen Hawking joined a computer dating agency. After submitting all of his details and running the report he was matched up with an iPad.

❖ What did Professor Stephen Hawking say after his computer crashed?
    Nothing.

❖ If knowledge is power, how come Stephen Hawking is such a weedy little fucker?

★   ★   ★   ★   ★

STEVIE WONDER

✳ Did you know that Stevie Wonder has a tree house?
    No, neither does he.

✳ What's black and loud?
    Stevie Wonder answering the iron.

✳ What goes – Click-Click – "Is that it?" – Click-Click – "Is that it?" – Click-Click – "Is that it?"
    Stevie Wonder with a Rubik's Cube.

* Stevie walks into a store with his blind dog. Suddenly, he jerks on the leash, pulls the dog into the air over his head and starts swinging it around his head.

  The manager rushes over and says, "Stevie! Is there something wrong?"

  "Nope," replies Stevie. "I'm just having a good look around."

* ## What is the definition of endless love? Stevie Wonder and Ray Charles playing tennis.

* What does Stevie Wonder's wife do when they've had a fight?

  She rearranges the furniture.

* What is the fastest thing on land?

  Stevie Wonder's speedboat.

* ## Stevie Wonder was in a terrible car accident the other week. His whole life flashed before his ears.

* Stevie Wonder is having a meal with Tiger Woods when he challenges Tiger to a round of golf.

  "You can't be serious," replies Tiger. "At the risk of sounding rude. you're blind. How the hell are you even going to find your ball?"

  "No problem," replies Stevie. "I play regularly with a ball with a bell inside it. And I bet you $10 million that I can whup your ass!"

  "Okay then," agrees Tiger, "but on condition that we'll do it for charity."

  "Done," says Stevie.

  "Okay," says Tiger. "When do you want to do it?"

  "Any night next week."

* What is Stevie Wonder's favourite colour?
  Corduroy.

* Stevie Wonder is being interviewed by Jonathan Ross. "So, Stevie," says Ross, "you've had a fantastic career, you're a great singer, a great musician, a wonderful performer and a fabulous composer. How do you cope with being blind?"
  Stevie replies, "It's not a problem. I just thank God I'm not black."

> 66 Roses are black,
> Violets are black,
> Everything is black.
>   Stevie Wonder, aged four. 99

* * * * *

SUICIDE

★ I work for the Samaritans. I tried to call in sick this morning but the bastards talked me out of it.

★ A young woman in London was depressed and decided to end her life by throwing herself into the Thames. She went down to the docks and was about to leap into the freezing water when a handsome young sailor saw her tottering on the edge of the pier, crying. He took pity on her and said, "Look, you have so much to live for. I'm off to America in the morning, and if you like, I can stow you away on my ship. I'll take good care of you and bring you food every day."
  Moving closer, he slipped his arm round her shoulder and added, "I'll keep you happy, and you'll keep me happy."

The girl nodded in agreement. What did she have to lose? A fresh start in America could give her life new meaning.

That night, the sailor brought her aboard and hid her in a lifeboat. From that day on, every evening he brought her some sandwiches and they made passionate love until dawn. Two weeks later, during a routine inspection, the captain discovered her.

"What are you doing here?" the captain asked.

"I have an arrangement with one of the sailors," she explained. "I get food and a trip to America, and he's screwing me."

"He certainly is," said the captain. "This is the Woolwich ferry."

★ I had a friend who was suicidal. He was really depressed, so I pushed him in front of a steam train. He was chuffed to bits.

★ ## Did you hear about the suicidal wanker? He tossed himself off a bridge.

★ I've been saving a fortune lately. Instead of spending a fortune phoning expensive sex lines, I call the Samaritans and say, "Talk dirty or I'll top myself!"

★ Bruce is driving over Sydney Harbour bridge one day, listening to some music in his car, when suddenly he spots his girlfriend Sheila standing on the side of the bridge. Bruce slams on the brakes, bolts out of the car and shouts, "Sheila! What the hell are you doing, babe?"

Sheila turns around, with tears welling up in her eyes. "Bruce, honey! You got me pregnant. I don't want to be a burden, so I'm just gonna kill myself!"

Bruce gets a lump in his throat and climbs back into his car. "Sheila, not only are you a great shag, but you're a fucking good sport about it too!"

★ I phoned the Samaritans the other day and was put through to a call centre in Pakistan. When I told them I was suicidal they asked me if I could fly a plane.

★ ★ ★ ★ ★

SUICIDE BOMBERS

❖ Suicide bombers. What makes them tick?

❖ What's the difference between Basil Brush and a suicide bomber?
   A suicide bomber only goes BOOM.

❖ Two Muslim women are walking down the road with tight-fitting rucksacks, when one says to the other, "Does my bomb look big in this?"

❖ What's the difference between a Muslim extremist and a packet of Smarties?
   Smarties don't blow up in the tube.

❖ A Muslim suicide bomber dies and goes to paradise. Once there, he finds himself surrounded by seventy-two of the ugliest women anyone has ever laid eyes upon.
   "What did you expect?" Allah says to him. "Why do you suppose they're still virgins?"

❖ A man walks into a sex shop and tells the woman behind the counter he's looking for a blow-up doll. The woman asks, "Would you like a Christian or a Muslim doll?"
   Bemused, the man replies, "What's the difference?"
   "Well," replies the woman, "the Muslim doll blows itself up."

❖ Two Palestinian mothers are sitting in the cafe, reminiscing over a pint of goat's milk. One of the mothers pulls her bag out and starts flipping through pictures. "This is my oldest son Mohammed. He's twenty-four years old now."

"Yes, I remember him as a baby," says the other mother.

"He's a martyr now, though," the mum confides.

"Oh, so sad," says the other.

"And this is my second son Ahmed. He's twenty-one."

"I remember him," says the other, "he was so bonny when he was born."

"He's a martyr too," says mum.

"Oh dear . . ." says the other.

"And this is my youngest. My beautiful Khalid. He's eighteen."

"Yes," says the friend. "I remember when he first started school."

"He's a martyr also," says the mum, with tears in her eyes.

After a pause and a deep sigh, the second mother looks at the photographs and says, "They blow up so fast, don't they?"

❖ How does a shoe bomber walk?
   Very carefully.

★   ★   ★   ★   ★

SUPERMARKETS

✳ A man walked into the vegetable section of his local supermarket and asked for half a head of lettuce. The boy working there told him that they only sold whole heads of lettuce. The man was insistent and asked to speak to the manager. The boy went to see his boss and explained: "Some prick wants to buy a half a head of lettuce."

As he finished his sentence, he realized the customer was standing right behind him, so he quickly added, "and this gentleman has kindly offered to buy the other half."

The manager approved the sale and the customer went about his business. Later the manager called the boy into his office. "I was impressed with the way you got yourself out of that situation earlier. I like people who think on their feet. Where are you from, son?"

"Essex, sir," the boy replied.

"You're a long way from home. Why did you leave Essex?" the manager asked.

The boy answered, "Well sir, as my dad always said, there's nothing but whores and footballers there."

"Really?" said the manager. "My wife is from Essex."

"No shit!" the boy replied. "Who does she play for?"

✳ A woman was shopping in the local supermarket. She selects some milk, six eggs, a carton of juice and a package of bacon. As she unloads her items at the cash register to pay, a man standing behind her in the line watches her place the four items on the belt and says to her, "You must be single."

The woman looks at the four items on the belt and smiles back at him.

"That's right. How did you know?"

He replies, "Because you're very ugly."

✳ Two lions are walking down a supermarket aisle. One turns to the other and says, "Quiet in here today, isn't it?"

❋   A prostitute goes to pay for her shopping at the supermarket checkout.

"I'm awfully sorry, miss," says the assistant, "but this £50 note is counterfeit."

"Help!" she yells. "I've been raped!"

❋   I went to the supermarket and when I got to the checkout my trolley was overflowing with items. Standing just behind me was a poor old lady with only a tin of peas and a few sausages in her basket.

I said, "Is that all you've got, love?"

Her little face lit up and said, "Yes, dear."

I replied, "Well, fuck off to another till then, I'm going to be ages."

❋ I was in Tesco yesterday, and a woman dropped dead in front of me. I felt really bad for her, she'd just bought a bag for life.

❋   A little boy gets lost in the supermarket. Eventually a shop assistant sees him wandering around, and he tells her, "I can't find my mum."

The shop assistant enquires, "What's your mum like?"

He replies, "Bacardi Breezers and big dicks."

A recent study found that 35 per cent of men have been injured while undoing a woman's bra. Actually I can vouch that this is true. I was injured last week while trying to undo a woman's bra. When I undid the bra of the woman in front of me in the checkout line, she turned and hit me in the face with a jar of coffee.

✳ A man is standing in a queue at the supermarket when he sees this busty brunette staring at him. He can't quite believe she is staring at him, then she starts waving.

"Excuse me, do I know you?" he asks.

"Yes, I think you are the father of one of my kids," she says.

The man thinks hard and says, "Fuck me, are you the bird I shagged on my stag do while your friend whipped me and your other mate stuck a brush up my arse?"

"No," she replies, "I'm your son's English teacher!"

✳ A man walked into a bar with two black eyes. The barman said, "What happened to you?"

The man replied, "I was standing behind a big woman at the supermarket checkout. I noticed that her dress was caught in her crack, so I pulled it out. She turned around and punched me square in the eye."

"Where did you get the other shiner?" the barman asked.

"Well, I figured she preferred it in the crack, so I pushed it back in."

✳ A married couple are shopping in the local supermarket when the husband picks up a crate of beer and sticks it in their trolley.

"What are you're doing?" asks the wife.

"They're on offer," he replies.

"Put them back. We can't afford it!" insists the wife, and they carry on shopping. A couple of aisles later, she picks up a £20 jar of face cream and sticks it in the trolley.

"How come I have to give up stuff and you don't?" he complains.

"She countered, "The make up is so I can look good for you."

"No," he replied, "that's what the fucking beer is for."

★ ★ ★ ★ ★

SURGERY

★ Mike went to see his doctor, complaining of headaches. The doctor examined him and said, "Mike, the good news is I can cure your headaches. The bad news is that it will require castration. You have a very rare condition which causes your testicles to press on your spine, and the pressure creates one hell of a headache. The only way to relieve the pressure is to remove the testicles."

Mike was shocked and severely depressed. He wondered if he had anything to live for. His head was swimming and he couldn't concentrate enough to think straight, but realized he had no choice but to go under the knife.

When he left the hospital he was without a headache for the first time in twenty years, but he felt like he was missing an important part of himself. As he walked down the street, he felt like a different person. He could make a new beginning and live a new life. He saw a men's clothing store and thought, "That's what I need – a new suit."

He went into the shop and told the salesman, "I'd like a new suit."

The elderly tailor eyed him briefly and said, "Let's see . . . size 44 long."

Mike laughed, "That's right, how did you know?"

"I've been in the business fifty years!"

Mike tried on the suit and it was a perfect fit. As Mike admired himself in the mirror, the salesman asked, "How about a new shirt?"

Mike thought for a moment and then said, "Why not!"

The salesman eyed him and said, "Let's see, 34 sleeve & 16½ neck."

Again, Mike was amazed. "That's right, how did you know?"

"Been in the business fifty years!"

Mike tried on the shirt, and it was a perfect fit. As Mike admired his new outfit in the mirror, the salesman asked, "How about new shoes?"

Mike was on a roll and said, "Sure."

The salesman looked at Mike's feet and said, "Let's see . . . 9½ E."

Mike was astonished, "That's right, don't tell me – you've been in the business fifty years!"

They both laughed. Mike tried on the shoes and, of course, they fitted perfectly. He walked around the shop to see how they felt. The salesman asked, "How about some new underwear?"

Mike thought for a second and said, "Sure."

The salesman stepped back, eyed Mike's waist and said, "Let's see . . . size 36."

Mike laughed, "Aha! I got you! I've worn size 34 since I was eighteen years old."

The salesman shook his head, "You can't wear a size 34. A size 34 underwear would press your testicles up against the base of your spine and give you one hell of a headache."

★ **Why don't women have colostomies?**
Because they can't get the shoes to match the bag.

★ A gorgeous young girl is about to undergo a minor operation. She is gowned up and placed on a trolley by the nurse and wheeled into the corridor. After a while, a young man wearing a white coat approaches, lifts the gown and starts examining her naked body. He walks away and talks to another man in a white coat. The second man comes over and performs the same examination.

When a third man starts examining her body so closely, she starts to become a little anxious. "All of these examinations are fine, but when are you going to start the operation?"

The man in the white coat shrugged his shoulders, "I have no idea, darling. We're just painting the corridor."

★　　★　　★　　★　　★

TAXIS

❖ A businessman went to Las Vegas for the weekend to play poker. He lost the shirt off his back and had nothing left but the second half of his round-trip ticket. He left the casino and found a cab waiting. He got in and explained his situation to the cabbie and promised to send the driver money from home, but to no avail.

"Sorry pal," the cabbie said. "If you don't have fifteen bucks, get the fuck out of my cab!"

The businessman was forced to hitch to the airport and fortunately was able to catch his flight with seconds to spare.

A couple of years later the same businessman returned to Vegas. This time his luck was in and he won a fortune. Feeling pretty good with himself, he went out to the front of the casino to get a cab ride back to the airport. At the end of a long line of cabs, he suddenly recognized the driver who had refused him a ride when he was on his uppers. He thought for a moment and got into the first cab in the line.

"How much for a ride to the airport?" he asked.

"Fifteen dollars," came the reply.

"And how much for you to give me a blow job on the way?" he added.

"Get out of my fucking cab!" snarled the driver.

The businessman got into the back of the second cab and repeated the question, with similar results. He went to every cabbie in the long line with the same question.

Eventually he reached his old friend at the back of the line and got in his cab. "How much for a ride to the airport?"

The cabbie replied, "Fifteen bucks."

The businessman replied, "Okay," and off they went.

As they drove past the cabs in the long line, the businessman gave a huge smile and a thumbs-up sign to all the other drivers . . .

❖ A middle-aged prostitute gets in a taxi and when she arrives at her destination realizes that she can't pay her fare. So she lifts her skirt and shows her fanny and says: "Can I pay you with this?"

The taxi driver replies: "You got anything smaller?"

❖ An attractive woman gets into a taxi. She says, "To the airport, please."

After a while the taxi driver, watching the woman in the mirror, says, "You're the third pregnant woman I've driven to the airport today."

The woman replies: "You're mistaken. I'm not pregnant."

The taxi driver smiles; "Well, you haven't arrived at the airport yet."

❖ A man hails a taxi. He climbs in the back and the cabbie says, "Perfect timing. You remind me of Eric."

"Excuse me?" says the passenger.

The cabbie says: "Eric Smith. Eric got everything right. For example, like me coming past just when you needed a taxi. That was exactly how it always was with Eric every single time."

"No one is perfect," replies the passenger.

"Oh, Eric was," says the cabbie. "He was a great athlete. He could have been a professional footballer. He was a scratch golfer, he could sing like an opera baritone and he could dance like Broadway star. You should have heard him play the piano."

"Bloody hell," says the passenger. "Sounds like this Eric was something special."

"No kidding," says the cabbie. "He had a memory like a computer, he knew everything there was to know about wine, what food to order and which fork to eat it with. He could fix anything. Not like me. I change a fuse and the whole street blacks out. He always knew the quickest way to go in traffic and avoid traffic jams, not like me, I always seem to get into them."

"Wow," says the passenger.

"And he knew how to treat a woman and make her feel good and never answer her back even if she was in the wrong. And he was always well groomed and he wore smart clothes and highly polished shoes."

"He sounds like an amazing bloke," says the passenger. "How did you get to know him?"

"Well, I never actually met Eric," says the cabbie.

"So, how do you know so much about him?"

The cabbie replies, "I married his ex-wife."

❖   A wife decides to take her husband to a strip club for a surprise birthday treat. They arrive at the club and the doorman says, "Phil! Good to see you mate! How are you doing?"

Phil is panic struck. His wife is puzzled and asks if he's been to this club before.

"No way," says Phil quickly. "He's on my darts team."

Inside the club, they take a seat and a waitress asks, "The usual, Phil?" and before he can answer swiftly delivers a Guinness. His wife is becoming increasingly suspicious and says, "How did she know that you drink Guinness?"

"She's in the women's darts team. Sometimes we share a darts board."

Then a stripper comes over to their table, throws her arms around Phil, and says: "Hi Phil. Want your usual table dance, big boy?"

Phil's wife grabs her purse and storms out of the club. Phil chases after her and sees her getting into a taxi. Before the taxi drives off, he jumps in beside her and tries desperately to explain how the stripper must have mistaken him for someone else, but his wife is having none of it. She's going at it hammer and tongs and screaming at him, calling him every name in the book. The taxi driver looks in his mirror and says, "Looks like you picked up a real bitch tonight, Phil!"

TEACHERS

* When I misbehaved at school, the headmaster used to give me "six of the best". Now that I'm grown up I'm sure I could take the other two inches.

* A fourteen-year-old boy comes home from school and his mother asks: "What did you do today?" The boy answers: "Oh the usual, I had a maths test, I got an A in spelling and I had sex with my English teacher."

  The mother can't quite believe what she just heard and gets him to repeat it. When he does, she says angrily, "Go and tell your father what you just told me!"

  The boy goes into see his father and says, "Dad, mum's mad."

  "Why son?"

  "I just told her what I did in school today. I had a maths test, I got an A in spelling and I had sex with my English teacher."

  The father gives his son a nudge and a wink and says, "Congratulations son, you passed a milestone. I tell you what, let's go out and celebrate. We'll have some ice cream and then I'll buy you a new bike."

  The boy replies: "Great! The ice cream sounds good, dad, but can you make it a football instead of a bike? My arse is still killing me."

* A teacher starts a new job at a primary school on Merseyside. Trying to make a good impression on her first day, she explains to her class that she's a big football fan and supports Everton. She asks her students to raise their hands if they, too, are Evertonians. Everyone in the class raises their hand except one little girl. The teacher looks at the girl with surprise and says: "Sally, why didn't you raise your hand?"

  "Because I'm not an Everton fan, miss," she replies.

"Well, if you're not an Everton fan, then who are you a fan of?"

"I'm a West Ham fan, and proud of it," Sally replies.

The teacher asks: "Sally, how come you're a Hammers fan?"

"Because my mum and dad are from Barking in London and are West Ham fans, so I'm a West Ham fan too!"

"Still," says the teacher, "that's no reason for you to be a West Ham fan as well. You don't have to be like your parents all the time, do you? What if your mum was a whore and your dad was a drug addict and car thief. Would you be like them then?"

"No, Miss. I'd be an Everton fan."

TECHNOLOGY

★ Four city executives are playing golf. On the third green, they hear a mobile ringtone. One of the bankers takes the phone from his pocket, excuses himself to take the call, before returning to the game.

"Sorry, guys," says the banker smugly, "but I am so important to my bank that I carry my phone with me at all times."

At the fourth green, another phone rings. The second banker lifts the palm of his hand to his face and starts to talk into it. When he had finished, he explains: "Sorry, guys. I am such an indispensable employee that I actually have a mobile phone surgically implanted in my hand." The others examine his hand with mild interest before resuming the game.

At the fifth green, another irritating ringtone starts. A third banker splits from the group, apparently talking to himself. On his return, seeing the faces of his bemused playing partners, he explains: "My bank would fall apart without me, so I have a phone embedded in my mouth."

The game continues. At the sixth hole, a look of discomfort suddenly crosses the fourth banker's face and he squats behind the nearest bush. A couple of minutes pass and he fails to reappear. Eventually, the other three gingerly peer behind the bush, only to find him squatting with his trousers round his ankles, apparently having a shit.

"Sorry!" the first three bankers mumble, not knowing where to look.

The fourth looks up at them and smiles. "Will you look at that," he says. "I'm getting a fax . . ."

★ What do you get if you cross a PC with a nun?

A computer that will never go down on you.

★ One day at work Jim says to one of his workmates, "My elbow is killing me. I'm off to see my doctor about getting something done about it."

His mate replies, "Listen, you don't have to waste your time waiting around in a GP's waiting room. There's a brilliant new diagnostic computer in the clinic on the high street. Just give it a urine sample and the computer will tell you what's wrong and what to do about it. It takes ten seconds and costs nothing."

So Jim takes his advice and collects a urine sample in a jar and takes it to the clinic. The computer display lights up and asks for the urine sample. He pours the sample into a funnel and waits. Ten seconds later, the computer spews a printout: "You have tennis elbow. Soak your arm in warm water and avoid heavy activity. It will improve in two weeks."

That evening, while thinking how amazing this new technology was, Jim began wondering if the computer was foolproof. He mixes some tap water, a stool sample from his dog, urine samples from his wife and daughter, scrapes some oil off the driveway and masturbates into the mixture for good measure.

Jim goes back to the chemist, pours in his new sample and awaits the results.

The computer prints out the following:

1. Your tap water is too hard. Get a water softener.
2. Your dog has ringworm. Bathe him with anti-fungal shampoo.
3. Your daughter has a cocaine habit. Get her into rehab.
4. Your wife is pregnant. Twins, but they are not yours. See a solicitor.
5. Your Ford escort needs new rings.
6. And if you don't stop wanking your elbow will never get better.

★ Bill Gates dies and finds himself standing before the pearly gates, being checked over by St Peter. "Well, Bill, I have to tell you that this is a tough call," says St Peter. "I don't know whether to send you to Heaven or Hell. On the one hand, you contributed enormously to society by putting a computer in almost every home, but you also created that annoying Windows operating system. Tell you what, I'm going to do something I've never done before. I'm going to let you decide where you want to go."

"What's the difference between the two?" Bill asks.

St Peter replies, "I'm willing to let you visit both places briefly if it will help you make your decision."

"Fine," says Bill. "Where should I go first?"

"I'll leave that up to you."

"Okay, let's try Hell first," says Bill.

So Bill goes to Hell. It is a beautiful, clean, sandy beach with clear waters and lots of bikini-clad women lounging around, taking in the sun. The weather is beautiful and the temperature pleasingly warm but not too hot. Bill is very pleased. "This is great!" he tells St Peter. "If this is Hell, I really want to see Heaven!"

"Fine," says St Peter, and off they go.

Heaven is a place high in the clouds, with angels drifting about, playing harps and singing. It is very nice, but frankly a bit dull and not as enticing as Hell. Bill considers his options for a couple of minutes then delivers his decision. "All in all, I think I'd prefer Hell," he tells St Peter.

"Fine," says St Peter, "as you wish." So Bill Gates goes to Hell.

Two weeks later, St Peter decides to check to see how he is doing in Hell. When he gets there, he finds Bill, shackled to a wall in a dark cave, screaming, with hot flames licking around his feet, while demons are torturing him with branding irons.

"Hi, Bill, how's it going?" he enquires of the late billionaire.

"This is my worst nightmare!" Bill cries. "This is nothing like the Hell I visited two weeks ago! I can't believe this is happening! What happened to that other place, with the beautiful beaches, the scantily-clad women playing in the water?"

"That was a demo," replies St Peter.

★   ★   ★   ★   ★

TESTICLES

❖ If you have a green ball in your left hand, and you have a green ball in your right hand, what do you have?

The complete and undivided attention of the Incredible Hulk.

❖ Why do women rub their eyes when they wake up?

They don't have any balls to scratch.

❖ Why did the eunuch fail to cross the road?
He didn't have the balls.

❖ Did you hear about the bloke with square testicles?
He had cubic hairs.

❖ What do you call a man with three balls?
A juggler.

❖ I read somewhere that women have one breast bigger than the other.

Or is that just bollocks?

❖ The great pharaoh Ramses II was dictating to a scribe. As the great pharaoh spoke, the scribe was busily chipping away at the stone tablet. "I am going to create . . ." the monarch said slowly, "a personal bodyguard . . . of stalwart . . . and virile . . . young men."

The chips suddenly ceased flying. "Excuse me, your majesty," said the perspiring chiseller, hesitantly, ". . . but is virile spelled with one testicle or two?"

❖ A man applies to the local council for a job. The interviewer asks him; "Have you been in the armed services?"

"Yes," he says, "I was in the Falklands."

The interviewer says: "Good. That will give you extra points toward employment. Are you disabled in any way?"

The man says, "Yes, 100 per cent. A land mine blew my testicles off."

The interviewer replies: "Excellent. You're hired. The hours are from 8 a.m. to 4 p.m. You can start tomorrow. Come in at 10 a.m."

The guy is puzzled and asks, "If the hours are from 8 a.m. to 4 a.m., why do you want me to come in at 10 a.m.?"

"This is the council," the interviewer explains. "For the first two hours we sit around scratching our balls. No point in you coming in for that."

* * * * *

TOILETS

* I saw a sign in a public toilet. It said, "Please leave these premises in the condition that you would like to have found it in". So I left a porno mag and a line of coke.

* Some graffiti spotted in the ladies' public toilet, obviously written by a male intruder, read: "I'm 12 inches long and three inches wide. Are you interested?"

Written underneath, in more feminine handwriting: "Interested? I'm amazed. But what is the size of your dick?"

* Why do French men always miss the urinal?

You try pissing with both your hands in the air!

* According to a recent survey, reading, chatting and texting are among the favourite activities of Britons on the toilet. The study suggests more than fourteen million people in the UK read newspapers, books and magazines. Eight million people talk – either on the phone or to family – and one in five send texts. Personally I'd rather have a shit.

* Disabled toilets. Ironically, the only toilets so big you can run around in them.

* What is the quickest way to clear out a men's changing room?
  Say, "Nice dick!"

* A man goes into a public lavatory for a pee and sees a man standing beside him at the urinal. He realizes the man doesn't have any arms.
  "Could you help me with my zipper, please?" the disabled man politely asks.
  Feeling uncomfortable, the man obliges. The disabled man stands there for a few seconds, and then asks. "Erm, could you do me a favour and pull my trousers down for me?"
  Once again, the man feels obliged to assist and tugs at the man's trousers. The disabled guy says, "I hate to ask, but could you please take my penis out for me?"
  The man freezes, but, feeling very sorry for the guy, he reaches in and helps free the man's willy from his Y-fronts, and then steps back in shock. The man's penis is covered with green scabs and pus.
  When the disabled man finishes peeing, he says: "Thanks for helping me. I really appreciate it."
  The good samaritan starts washing his hands and says, "No problem. If you don't mind me asking – what's wrong with your dick?"
  "Fuck knows," he replies, pulling his arms free of his jacket. "But I'm not touching it."

Urinal Etiquette

Excitable: runs in, grabs for zipper, zipper is stuck; finally gets it down, finds shorts have twisted around his leg, can't find hole, rips button off in rage, pisses in pants.

Sociable: joins a friend in a piss, whether he needs one or not.

Boss-eyed: looks at a urinal to his left, pisses in one on his right.

Nosey: peers at the next guy to see how he is fixed.

Timid: unable to piss when someone is watching. Flushes urinal as if he has already used it, sneaks back later.

Indifferent: if all the urinals are in use, pisses in sink.

Show-off: no hands, fixes tie, looks around and pisses on floor.

Worried: unsure of what he has been into lately, makes quick inspection before pissing.

Drunk: holds left thumb in right hand, pisses in pants.

---

* Two pubic hairs on a toilet seat. One says to the other, "How long you here for?"

"I don't know," the other replies. "I suppose until I get pissed off."

Absent-minded: opens vest, pulls out tie, pisses in pants.

Disgusted: attempts to piss for a while, gives up, walks out, goes a few paces, turns around and charges back. Doesn't make it.

Sneaky: farts silently while pissing, knowing the man standing at the next urinal will be blamed.

Immature: pisses directly into bottom of urinal because likes to see it bubble.

Patient: stands for a very long time while reading broadsheet newspaper with free hand.

Desperate: having waited for ages in a queue, grinds his teeth while pissing in his pants.

Efficient: waits until he has to shit and then does both jobs at once.

Tough: bangs penis against side of urinal to dry it.

Obese: has to back up and take a long blind shot at urinal, misses, pisses on shoes.

Frivolous: plays his stream of piss up and down and across urinal, tries to hit fly.

✳ What's white, jelly-like and runs down a public toilet wall?
George Michael's latest release.

✳ I went into some public toilets the other day to have a shit. When I sat down and locked the door, a voice came from the cubicle next to me. "Hello mate, how are you doing?"

I thought this was a bit odd, but I didn't want to be rude so I replied, "Not too bad, thanks."

After a short pause, I heard the voice again: "Anyway, what are you up to?"

I replied, somewhat hesitantly, "Er . . . just having a quick shit actually. How about yourself?"

Then I heard the voice say, "Sorry, mate, I'll have to phone you back. There's some twat in the cubicle next to me answering everything I say."

★　　★　　★　　★　　★

TOURETTE'S SYNDROME

★ An unemployed pianist with Tourette's is walking the streets looking for work when he spies a bar with a sign in the window: "Pianist wanted for evening performances".

"Fucking ace!" he yells, and enters the bar.

"Get the cunting manager of this wank hole please, you twat," he shouts at a rather startled barman. The barman, however, obliges and his manager comes upstairs. "Can I help you sir?" he enquires.

"Yes, fuckface, you can, you fat piece of shit. I saw your advert in the window and I'm here to audition, tosser!"

The manager is naturally repelled by the man's deeply offensive behaviour. Improbably, however, his dire need for a decent pianist forces him to agree to an audition. The first tune the pianist plays is a delightful jazz number, and when he is finished the thrilled barman cries, "Bravo! Bravo! What was that piece called?"

"That song, you fat cunt, was called 'Excuse me, prime minister, but I just came in your daughter's eye and now the slut is blind'."

"I see," says the manager. "Can you play me another?"

"Tosser," replies the pianist, before launching into a powerful ballad, which leaves the manager in tears. The manager asks him the title.

"That little number was called 'Sometimes when you take a bird up the shit box you get crap on your bell end'."

"I understand," says the manager. "Have you any songs with slightly less offensive titles?"

"Well," says the pianist, "there's my jazz number 'Do you want me to split your ring piece', or there's 'I don't care if you're an older woman, you've still got the most amazing pair of tits'."

"I see," says the manager. "I think you're a superb pianist but your songs are frankly a little 'racy'. I will hire you on the condition that you do not introduce your songs or speak to the audience."

"Fuck it," says the pianist. "It's a deal, you cunt."

On his very first night everything is going superbly. The crowd loves his repertoire and his silence is received as modesty. The only thing putting off the pianist is that in the front row there is a beautiful blonde lady in a fetching black evening dress with a long split up the side revealing the tops of her stockings and a plunging neckline, which boasts a deep, inviting cleavage. During the interval the pianist has got such a stonking hard-on that he decides to retire to the men's room and knock one out.

Just as he has shot his load he hears himself being re-introduced over the tannoy, so he dashes back to the stage and finishes his act. After the show he is at the bar relaxing, when the beautiful blonde approaches him.

"Hi," she says.

"Hello," he somehow manages to reply, struggling to suppress his natural desire to accost her with a string of expletives.

She leans over and whispers in his ear, "Do you know your penis is hanging out of your trousers and spunk is dribbling on to your shoes?"

"Know it?" says the pianist with a wink. "I fucking wrote it!"

✴ I parked in a disabled space today and was accosted by a traffic warden.

"Oi, you!" he shouted, as I walked away from my car. "What's your disability?"

"Tourette's," I replied. "Now fuck off, you cunt!"

✴ A man walks in to a library and asks for a book on Tourette's.

The librarian replies, "Fuck off, you cunt."

The man says, "Yep, that's the one."

✴ A man went to visit his sister and his nephew, Mike, who had Tourette's.

He was waiting for his sister to bring in some tea, when all of a sudden his nephew looked at him and said, "Open the door, you cunt."

Naturally he was more than a little embarrassed and pretended not to hear. The nephew said again, "Open the fucking door, you cunt."

Feeling very awkward and not knowing how to respond, again he pretended he heard nothing. The nephew started getting very agitated and said once again, "You useless cunt, open the fucking door."

At this point, to his huge relief, his sister came into the room and said, "Don't worry, dear, he's just trying to tell you a knock-knock joke."

✴ **For years I thought my dad suffered from Tourette's. Turns out he just thought I was a cunt.**

✴   ✴   ✴   ✴   ✴

TRAINS

❖ A man was sitting on a train eating a bag of fresh prawns, ripping off the heads and shells and then tossing them out of the window. An older woman, sitting opposite him, said, "Do you mind not doing that? It's rather disgusting."

"Listen love," he replied, "it's got fuck all to do with you. I've paid my fare for this journey and I'll do what I want on this train." He carried on ripping off the shells, lobbing them out of the window and eating the prawns. Finally he finished the bag and settled back for a nap.

The woman then started some knitting and all the man could hear while he was trying to sleep was the incessant clicking of her knitting needles. After a while, he said to the woman, "Can't you see I'm trying to sleep?"

"It's got nothing to do with you," replied the old woman, "I've paid my fare and I'll do what I want on this train."

At that, the man grabbed the woman's knitting and threw it out of the window. The woman immediately stood up and pulled the train alarm cord.

"You'll get fined £200 for that!" laughed the man.

To which the old woman replied, "And you'll get five years when the police smell your fingers."

A bishop is sitting on a train doing *The Times* crossword. Absentmindedly, he says aloud: "Exclusively female, blank-U-N-T"

A young curate sitting next to him suggests: "Aunt?"

"You're right," says the bishop. "I don't suppose you have a rubber?"

❖ A man goes to the ticket office at the railway station and asks: "Can I have a second glass return to Mottinghab, please?"

"Sorry," replies the ticket clerk, "I don't understand."

"Can I have a second glass return to Mottinghab, please?'

"Oh I see," says the clerk. "Have you tried sucking menthol sweets, sir?'

"Why, do they cure cerebral palsy?"

❖ A few days after Christmas, a mother was working in the kitchen, listening to her young son playing with his new electric train in the living room. She heard the train stop and her son said, "All of you sons of bitches who want to get off, get the fuck off now, 'cause this is the last stop! And all of you sons of bitches who are getting on, get your asses in the train."

The mother went nuts and told her son, "We don't use that kind of language in this house. Now I want you to go to your room and you are to stay there for two hours and think about what you've done."

Two hours later, the son came out of the bedroom and resumed playing with his train. Soon the train stopped and the mother heard her son say, "All passengers who are disembarking from the train, please remember to take all of your belongings with you. We thank you for riding with us today." She heard the little boy continue, "For those of you just boarding, we ask you to stow all of your hand luggage under your seat."

As the mother smiled, the child added, "For those of you pissed off about the two-hour delay, please refer to the fucker in the kitchen."

★　　★　　★　　★　　★

TRANSVESTITES/ TRANSGENDERED

* I've got a friend who is a fat, alcoholic, transvestite. All he does is eat, drink and be Mary.

* Nelson Mandela recently met with controversial 800-metre runner Caster Semenya. It turns out that the two have much in common. Specifically, South African roots and an ability to piss while standing up.

* When I was just a little girl,
  I asked my mother: "What will I be?
  Will I be pretty? Will I be rich?"
  Here's what she said to me:
     "You're a boy. Now get out of your sister's clothes and fuck off to school."

* I've just found out that my best mate is a transsexual and has had a boob job.
     I'll never be able to look him in the face again.

* South African 800-metre star Caster Semenya was asked to take a gender test just hours before the world championship final to prove that she was a woman. According to the IAAF, the gender verification test was an extremely complex procedure, involving extensive tests, endocrinologists, gynaecologists and psychologists, to establish whether Caster Semenya is a woman or not. Or they could just get her to park a car.

* Hollywood producers are in discussions to make a film about the life of South African runner Caster Semenya. Will Smith has agreed to play the lead role.

＊ Mike was sitting by the bar knocking back a few beers after work when a beautiful woman sat down next to him. She looked vaguely familiar, but Mike couldn't quite place her.

"Hi, Mike," she said. "I haven't seen you in a long time."

"Kev, is that you?" said Mike. "Why are you dressed up like a woman?"

"Well, Mike. It's a long story, but the bottom line is that I have always felt like a woman trapped in a man's body, so I finally decided to do something about it. And, after a number of painful operations, I am now a woman."

Mike was shocked, but couldn't help staring at his friend's pert breasts, "Bloody hell, Kev, I bet it was painful to have those implants put in."

"Yep, but that wasn't the most painful part," said Kev.

"Oh Christ," said Mike. "You mean you had your dick and testicles cut off? That must have been horrific."

"Yes, that was pretty painful, but that wasn't the worst part."

"I don't believe it, mate. What could possibly be worse than that?"

"The final operation was the worst. That was when they did a craniotomy and took out half of my brain."

＊ Officials at the World Athletics World Championships launched an investigation after female competitors complained that someone had been repeatedly leaving the toilet seat up after having a piss.

★   ★   ★   ★   ★

TV

★ What do you call a dog with two dicks?
   The *X Factor* judging panel.

★ Matthew Kelly was backstage at *Stars In Your Eyes* when he saw two contestants in the corner. One was a middle-aged man in a wheelchair, the other was a younger man. Curious to know who they were, Matthew goes over to the duo and introduces himself and asks the older gentleman about his disability.
   "My nephew Simon here and I are glaziers," says the older man. "One day when Simon was up a ladder he slipped and dropped a pane of glass on me and it cut my legs clean off."
   "That's terrible," says Matthew. "But it's tremendous that you're here to support your nephew nevertheless. So who is he going to be?"
   "Oh, I'm not supporting him," said the older man. "We're singing together".
   Matthew was baffled. He knew the back-stage make-up crew were good but he couldn't figure out who these two going to become. Then the older guy put him out of his misery. "Tonight, Matthew, we're going to be Simon and Half Uncle."

★ What do you call Woody Woodpecker if his beak fell off?
   Woody Headbanger.

★ Why does Noddy have a bell on his hat?
   Because he's a cunt.

★ Why can't Miss Piggy count to seventy?
   Because she gets a frog in her throat at sixty-nine.

★ According to a football commentator on TV recently: "There is nothing more painful than missing out in a place in the FA Cup Final." Obviously, he has never experienced a paper cut on his bell end.

★ What's red and blue with a long string?
  A smurf on her period.

★ I've been banned from appearing on *Mastermind*. It turns out that masturbating over Beyoncé Knowles is not a specialist subject.

★　　★　　★　　★　　★

UNIVERSITY

❖ I was eating an orange the other day when my clever university-educated girlfriend said, "Did you know, nothing rhymes with 'orange'?"
  So I threw the orange at her head and said, "Now your face is swollen red 'cause I just threw an orange at your big fat head. Does that rhyme with 'orange', bitch?"

I was sitting on a bus in Oxford next to this university student: "Where are you from?" I asked.
  He replied: "I come from a place where we do not end our sentences with prepositions."
  I replied, "Okay . Where are you from, cunt?"

❖ A girl goes into the doctor's for a check-up. As she removes her bra, the doctor notices a large letter C in red on her chest. "How did you get that mark on your chest?" he enquires.

"Oh, my boyfriend went to Cambridge University and he's so proud of it that he never takes off his Cambridge sweatshirt, even when we shag," she replies.

A couple of days later, another girl comes in for a check-up. As she takes off her blouse, he notices a blue O on her chest. "How did you get that mark on your chest?" asks the doctor.

"Oh, my boyfriend went to Oxford and he's so proud of it that he never takes off his sweatshirt, even when we fuck," she replies.

A couple of days later, another girl comes in for a check-up. As she takes off her blouse, he notices a green M on her chest. "I don't suppose by any chance you have a boyfriend at Manchester University?" asks the doctor.

"No," she replies. "But I have a girlfriend at Warwick. Why do you ask?"

❖ An accountant, a lawyer and a window cleaner were standing side by side using a urinal in the toilets of a pub. The accountant finished, zipped up his trousers and started washing and literally scrubbing his hands clear up to his elbows. By the time he had finished he used at least twenty paper towels. Realizing that the other two men were staring at him, he turned and commented, "I graduated from Edinburgh University and they taught us about good personal hygiene."

The lawyer finished, zipped up his trousers and wet the tips of his fingers, grabbed one paper towel and commented, "I graduated from Cambridge University and they taught us to be environmentally conscious."

The window cleaner zipped up and, as he was walking out of the door, said, "I dropped out of North Staffs Polytechnic. But they taught us not to piss on our hands."

★   ★   ★   ★   ★

VALENTINES

* Roses are straight,
  Violets are twisted,
  Bend over love,
  You're about to get fisted.

* Roses are red,
  Violets are blue,
  I've got Alzheimer's,
  This little piggy went to
     market.

* Roses are red,
  Violets are blue,
  Why give her flowers
  When Rohypnol will do?

* Roses are crap,
  Violets are wanky,
  Oh God I've just come,
  Please pass me a hanky.

* Roses are red,
  It's elementary,
  Let's ring up a friend,
  And try double-entry.

* Roses are shit,
  Violets are crap,
  Show me your clit,
  And I'll cum in your lap.

* Roses are red,
  Violets aren't magenta,
  If you have a baby,
  I'll eat the placenta.

* Roses are awful,
  Violets are the pits,
  Lift up your shirt,
  And show us your tits.

* Roses are groovy,
  Violets are funky,
  I'm thinking of you
  And spanking my
     monkey.

* Roses are crap,
  Violets are shit,
  Sit on my face,
  And wiggle a bit.

* Roses are red,
  Violets are blue,
  I'm using my hand,
  But I'm thinking of you.

* Roses are dirty,
  Violets have fleas,
  Peel back my skin,
  And lick off my cheese.

* Roses are red,
  When in reality,
  Sleeping with girls
  Don't beat bestiality

* Roses are red,
  Violets are finer,
  Chickens are fowl,
  Just like your vagina.

* Roses are red,
  Skid marks are brown,
  Give us a blow job
  And swallow it down.

* Roses are red,
  Violets are blue,
  I'm schizophrenic,
  And I am too.

* Roses make me laugh,
  Violets make me titter,
  You're a dirty bitch,
  And you love it up the
      shitter.

* Roses are red,
  But I like carnations,
  You're so crap in bed,
  That I fucked your
      Alsatians.

★   ★   ★   ★   ★

VAMPIRES

★ Mummy, mummy, what's a vampire?
  Shut up, son, and eat your soup before
  it clots.

★ A vampire bat came flapping in from the night, his face
covered in fresh blood, and parked himself on the roof of
the cave to get some sleep. Soon all the other bats could
smell the blood and wanted to know where he got it. The
bat told them to clear off and let him get some sleep, but
they persisted until he finally gave in.

"Okay, follow me," he said, and flew out of the cave with
thousands of bats behind him, down through a valley, across
a river, until they arrived in a huge forest. Finally he stopped
and all the other bats milled excitedly around him, tongues
hanging out for blood.

"See that large oak tree over there?" he asked.

"Yes, yes, YES!!" the bats all screamed in a frenzy.

"Good," said the first bat. "Because I fucking well
didn't."

★ What did one lesbian vampire say to the other lesbian vampire?

"See you next month."

★ Three vampires walk into a bar. One orders a blood on the rocks. Another orders a double blood. The third asks for a mug of hot water.

"Why didn't you order blood like everyone else?" asks the bartender.

The vampire pulls out a tampon and says, "I'm making tea."

★ Why did the vampire visit the ortho-dontist?

To improve his bite.

★ ★ ★ ★ ★

VEGETARIANS

❖ Why does vegan cheese taste like shit?

Because it hasn't been tested on mice.

❖ My vegetarian wife and I were in a restaurant recently with friends and, as usual, after she passed on the meat and asked for more potatoes, I was asked the same old question: "So, where does she get her protein?"

I replied, "She swallows."

❖ Why do vegetarians give good head?

Because they are used to eating nuts.

❖ If God didn't want us to eat animals, why did he make them out of food?

❖ Mahatma Gandhi, the revered Indian leader, walked barefoot most of the time, which produced an impressive set of bunions on his feet. He also ate very little, which made him rather frail. He also endured a strict vegetarian diet, which meant that he suffered from bad breath. In short, he was a super-calloused fragile mystic hexed by halitosis.

❖ What do vegetarian worms eat?
  Linda McCartney.

❖ Paul McCartney's children are sitting down to a family dinner. Paul comes in with a tear in his eye and says "Kids, I've got some good news and some bad news. The bad news is that, tragically, your mother Linda finally lost her fight with cancer last night and died. The good news is . . . sausages for dinner!"

❖ The Koreans have recently brought out their own vegetarian version of an instant noodle snack. It's called Not Poodle.

* * * * *

VENTRILOQUISTS

* I think my uncle was a ventriloquist, He used to put his hand up my bum and tell me not to say anything.

* A ventriloquist visiting Wales walks into a small town and sees a local sitting on his porch patting his dog. He decides to have a little fun.
  "Hello my friend! Good looking dog you have there. Mind if I speak to him?"
  The Welshman looks up and down and says, "The dog doesn't talk, tosser!"

The ventriloquist continues: "Hello dog, how's it going, old friend?"

"Not bad, thanks," replies the dog.

A look of extreme shock passes across the Welshman's face.

"Is this Welsh guy your owner?"

"Yep," says the dog.

"How does he treat you?"

"No complaints. He walks me twice a day and gives me decent food." The Welshman's face is a picture of utter disbelief. The ventriloquist asks him: "Mind if I talk to your horse?"

"Err, the horse doesn't talk either, as far as I know," replies the Welshman

"Hey horse," says the ventriloquist, "how's it going, mate?"

"Cool," says the horse.

At this point the Welshman falls off his porch.

Ventriloquist: "Is this your owner?

Horse: "Yep."

Ventriloquist: "How's he treat you?"

Horse: "Not bad, thanks for asking. He rides me regularly, brushes me down and regularly changes the straw in my stable."

"Mind if I talk to your sheep?"

The Welshman replies, "The sheep's a fucking liar."

* A ventriloquist is touring the pubs and clubs in London. One night he's doing a show in a small venue above a pub in the West End. He's going through his usual routine with his dummy on his knee, reciting some dumb blonde jokes. The show is going well and the audience seem to be enjoying themselves, until a blonde woman stands on her chair and starts heckling.

"I've had enough of you and your stupid blonde jokes. What gives you the right to disrespect blonde women like that? What does the colour of a woman's hair have to do with her intelligence or her worth as a human being? It's people like you who keep people like me from reaching our full potential as a person, because you and your kind continue to stereotype not only blondes, but women in general, and all in the name of humour!"

The ventriloquist is embarrassed and begins to apologize, when the blonde interrupts, "You stay out of this! I'm talking to that little bastard on your knee!"

*   *   *   *   *

VETS

*   A man takes his rottweiler to the vet. "My dog is cross-eyed, is there anything you can do for him?"

"Well," says the vet, "let's have a look at him."

The vet picks the dog up and has a good look at his eyes. "Well," says the vet, "I'm going to have to put him down."

"What?" says the man in disbelief. "Because he's cross-eyed?"

"No," replies the vet. "Because he's heavy."

I was having some problems with my Staffordshire bull terrier so I rang the vet for some advice. I explained he was brown, stupid, aggressive and liable to attack anyone for no good reason.

"Muzzle 'im?" suggested the vet.

"No," I replied. "I'm fairly sure he's an athiest."

*   *   *   *   *

VIAGRA

❖ An woman of advanced age visited her physician to ask his help in reviving her husband's libido. "Have you thought about getting him to try Viagra?" asks the doctor.

"Not a chance," she replied. "He won't even take an aspirin."

"Well," replied the doctor. "He doesn't need to know about it. Just drop the Viagra tablet into his coffee. He won't even taste it. Give it a try and call me in a week to let me know how things went."

It wasn't even a week later that she called the doctor, who directly enquired as to progress.

The old woman exclaimed, "Oh, it was terrible! Just terrible, doctor!"

"Really? What happened?" asked the doctor.

"Well, I did as you advised and slipped it into his coffee and the effect was almost immediate. He jumped straight up, with a twinkle in his eye, and with his pants a-bulging! With one wild lunge, he ripped my clothes to tatters and took me then and there, took me passionately on the floor! It was a nightmare, I tell you, an absolute nightmare!"

"Why so terrible?" asked the doctor, "Do you mean the sex your husband provided wasn't good?"

"It the best sex I've had in twenty-five years! Unfortunately, I'll never be able to show me face in Tesco again."

❖ Why do they give Viagra to old men in nursing homes?
So they don't roll out of bed.

❖ A man goes to the chemist's and asks for a pack of Viagra. "Do you have a prescription?" the pharmacist asks.

"No," he replied, "but here's a picture of my wife."

❖ A woman asks her husband if he'd like some breakfast. "Sausage, bacon, black pudding, eggs, beans, perhaps some fried bread? Or how about a nice bowl of muesli and a cup of fresh coffee?"

"No thanks," replies her husband. "It's the Viagra. It's taken the edge off my appetite." Three hours later she asks if he would like some lunch.

"A ploughman's, maybe, or some pea and ham soup? Or I could fix you a cheese sandwich with a glass of wine?"

Again he declines. "No thanks. It's the Viagra," he says, "It's really taken the edge off my appetite."

A few hours later she asks if he wants any dinner. "I could go the chip shop and get us some fish and chips, or would you prefer a pizza? Or what about a take-away Chinese?"

Again he declines. "Nah, I'll pass, thanks. It's the Viagra. It's really taken the edge off my appetite."

"Well, then," she replies, "would you mind getting off me for ten minutes? I'm fucking starving."

❖ A man went to his chemist and asked for a double dose of Viagra.

"I'm sorry, I'm not allowed to give you a double dose," replied the chemist.

"Why not?"

"Because it isn't safe," replied the chemist.

"But I need it really badly," said the man. "My mistress is coming into town tomorrow, "I'm seeing my new girlfriend tonight and my wife comes home on Monday. Can't you see? I've got to have a double dose."

The pharmacist relented. "Okay, I'll give it to you, on one condition – you have to come in on Monday morning so that I can check you to see if there are any side effects."

On Monday morning the man dragged himself into the chemist with his right arm in a sling. The pharmacist asked, "What happened to you?"

The man said, "None of them showed up."

❖ An elderly gentleman went to the local chemist's and asked for some Viagra. The chemist said, "That's no problem. How many do you want?"

The old man answered, "Just a few, maybe four, but cut each one in four pieces."

The chemist said, "That won't do you any good."

The old man replied, "That's all right. I don't need them for sex any more. I am eighty-three years old. I just want it to stick out far enough so I don't piss on my shoes."

❖ As of today, Viagra will also be available over the counter by its correct generic medical name. Please ask your pharmacist for "Mycoxafloppin".

* * * * *

VIBRATORS

✳ What's an Aboriginal vibrator?
Eight wasps in a sherry bottle.

✳ What does an elephant use as a vibrator?
An epileptic pig.

✳ Why did God put men on earth?
Because a vibrator can't mow the lawn.

✳ I got my wife a vibrator for her birthday. She's done nothing but moan ever since.

> Ann Summers has just launched the most realistic vibrator yet. Just before you reach a climax, it ejaculates, farts, goes limp, rolls over and then it switches itself off.

✳ Three men were drinking at a bar, a doctor, a lawyer and a Geordie. The doctor said, "For my wife's birthday, I'm going to buy her a Vivienne Westwood suit and a diamond ring. Even if she doesn't like the suit, she will still love me because she got a diamond ring."

The lawyer said, "For my wife's birthday, I'm going to buy her a pair of Jimmy Choo shoes and a gold bracelet. This way, if she doesn't like the shoes, she will still love me because she got the gold bracelet."

The Geordie said, "I'm going to buy my wife a T-shirt and a vibrator. If she doesn't like the T-shirt, she can go fuck herself!"

★   ★   ★   ★   ★

VIVE LA FRANCE

★ Why did the French invent the bidet?
  It's easier than drinking out of the toilet.

★ Where's the best place to hide your money?
  Under a Frenchman's soap.

★ Why are the streets of Paris lined with trees?
  So that the Germans can march in the shade.

* What do you call a Frenchman killed in battle?
  The slowest runner.

* Why do French tanks have rear-view mirrors?
  So they can watch the battle.

* Going to war without the French is like . . . well, the Second World War actually.

* What's the difference between toast and a Frenchman?
  You can make soldiers out of toast.

* How many French troops does it take to defend Paris?
  No one knows, it hasn't been tried yet.

* How can you recognize a French war veteran?
  Sunburned armpits.

* You really do have to hand it to the French.
  After all, they won't fight for it.

* Why is the French flag made of Velcro?
  So the blue and red sections are easily removed during a time of war.

* A man goes into an army surplus store and says: "I'd like a French army knife please."
  The assistant replies, "We have Swiss army knives sir, but I've never heard of a French army knife. How does that work?"
  The man replies, "Oh, you know, no scissors or tweezers, just six corkscrews and a white flag."

Ten Reasons Why it's Great to Be French

1 When you are talking quickly you can make yourself sound gay.
2 You don't mind if your women never wash.
3 You get to eat insect food like snails and frogs' legs.
4 If there's a war you can surrender really early.
5 You don't have to read the subtitles on those late night films on Channel 4.
6 You get to test your own nuclear weapons in other people's countries.
7 You can be ugly and still be a famous film star.
8 You allow Germans to march up and down your most famous street without damaging your sense of national pride.
9 You don't have to bother with toilets, just shit in the streets.
10 People think you're a great lover even when you're not.

★ An elderly Englishman arrived at Charles de Gaulle airport in Paris. At passport control, he took a few minutes to locate his passport in his travel bag, much to the irritation of the French immigration officer.

"Have you been to France before, monsieur?" the officer asked. The elderly gentleman admitted he had been to France previously. "Then you should know well enough to have your passport ready, monsieur."

The elderly visitor replied, "I wouldn't know about that. The last time I was here, I didn't have to show a passport."

"Impossible," snorted the official. "All visitors have to show their passports on arrival in France!"

The elderly gentleman replied, "Well, the last time I was here, I came ashore on Sword Beach on D-Day in June 1944 and I couldn't find any Frenchmen to show it to."

★ What do you call a Frenchman advancing on Baghdad?
A salesman.

★ A French war hero, a Muslim pacifist and the Loch Ness Monster are sitting in a bar. Who is the odd one out?
The Loch Ness Monster – because there is a chance that he actually exists.

★   ★   ★   ★   ★

WELSHMEN

❖ What do you call a bunch of sheep tied to a tree in Wales?
The local leisure centre.

❖ What do you call a Welshman with several girlfriends?
A shepherd.

❖ How does a Welshman find sheep in long grass?
Irresistible.

❖ What do you call a Welshman who owns sheep and goats?
Bisexual.

❖ Why does a Welshman fuck a sheep next to a cliff edge?
To make sure that the sheep pushes back.

❖ Why do Welsh farmers wear Velcro on their trousers?
Because sheep have learned to detect the sound of a zipper a mile away.

❖ Why can't Welsh people count sheep to help them get to sleep?

Because when they get to three they have to stop and have a wank.

❖ Have you heard about the festival celebrated by Welsh Muslims?

It's called Ramalamb.

❖ What do you call a Welsh farmer with a sheep under each arm?

A pimp.

❖ A Welshman goes to the local livestock auctions and says, "I'd like to bid for a female sheep, please."

The auctioneer says, "Certainly sir. Are you looking for a ewe, or a lamb?"

The Welshman replies, "A ewe, obviously! What do you think I am, some kind of a nonce?"

❖ **Wales. Where else can you get a shag, a nice warm coat and a casserole all from the same date?**

❖ A Welshman is having a driving lesson. The instructor asks, "Can you make a u-turn?"

"Sure can," he replies, "I can make its eyes water if I go in dry."

★   ★   ★   ★   ★

WORK

＊ I once had a job in one of those paperless offices. It was okay until I needed a shit.

＊ **What's the worst thing about rising unemployment? It gets more difficult to shag your girlfriend with her husband at home.**

＊ A large bank hired a new chief executive officer to rid the company of deadwood. On a tour of the firm's headquarters, the CEO noticed a young man slouching against a counter with his hands in his pockets. The room was full of employees and he wanted to let them know that he meant business.

He walked up to the young man and asked, "How much money do you make a week?"

A little surprised, the young man looked at him and replied, "I make £300 a week. What's it to you?"

The CEO then handed him £1,200 in cash and bawled, "Here's a month's pay. Now FUCK OFF and don't come back!"

Feeling pretty good about himself, the CEO looked around the room and asked, "Does anyone want to tell me what that lazy bastard did around here?"

From across the room an employee shouted, "He delivered pizza from Domino's."

A man phones work and says, "Sorry, I can't come in today – I'm sick."

His boss enquires: "How sick are you?"

"Well," the man replies, "you be the judge. I'm in bed with my sister."

✳ Unemployed and desperate for work, Steve decides to accept a job, mining deep in Alaska. After a long journey he finally arrives at the mining camp, hundreds of miles from the nearest town. The camp is very small, with only a few miners. He meets the manager, who explains what his job entails. "You work for six days of the week, every day except Saturday. Your main job is to clear out the rubble and dump it into the rock quarry down the road. The work is hard but you will get used to it."

The next morning Steve goes to work. The work is very hard, but he is a strong lad and he can get through it. By the time Thursday comes around, however, he is feeling homesick and very lonely. With the nearest women 200 miles away he wonders how the other guys cope from day to day. So, he approaches the mine manager for advice.

"The job is okay and I have no complaints about the work, but I was kind of wondering what the other miners do for women around here?"

"Say no more," said the manager. "Follow me."

He leads Steve deep into the mine and turns down an unfamiliar passage. He continues on deeper into the mine into older and older tunnels until he finally stops at the end of a really ancient looking tunnel. "There," the manager says, pointing at a barrel. "The other miners use this."

"How?" says Steve.

"Well, you see that knot hole? Try it out."

Steve is more than a little embarrassed and very sceptical about this, but he is desperate, so he gives it a shot. He sticks his dick in the knot hole and can't believe the results – it actually feels like the best blow job he's ever had in his life! Friday comes around and the work is getting him down, so he goes back to the barrel to try it again. Unbelievable! This time the blow job is even better than the first time. Steve sleeps in on Saturday, his day off, and gets up for breakfast feeling really great. There isn't much to do, so he goes for a walk. On his way he bumps into the manager, who asks him: "Where do you think you're going?"

"It's my day off . . ."

"Day off? Christ, no! It's your turn in the barrel."

* A manager calls four of his employees into the office: "I'm really sorry, but I'm going to have to let one of you go."

The black employee steps forward and says, "I'm a protected minority. Fire me and I'll sue for racial discrimination."

The female employee steps forward and says: "And I'm a woman. Fire me and I'll sue for sexual discrimination."

The oldest employee says: "Fire me, son, and I'll hit you with an age discrimination suit so fast it'll make your head spin."

They all turn to look at the helpless young, white, male employee, who thinks for a moment, then says: "I think I might be gay."

★ ★ ★ ★ ★

ZOOS

* One day, while on a safari holiday in Kenya, a man was walking through the bush when he came across an elephant standing with one leg raised in the air. The elephant was clearly in some distress, so the man approached it very cautiously. As he got closer he realized that there appeared to be something sticking out of the elephant's foot. He got down on one knee and carefully inspected the bottom of the elephant's foot, only to find a large thorn deeply embedded. As carefully as he possibly could, he tugged at the thorn until it came out. The elephant gingerly put its foot down, then turned on the man with a wild look in its eyes, staring him down.

The man was frozen in panic. For what seemed like an eternity, he stood rooted to the ground with the elephant towering over him, convinced that he was about to be trampled to death. Then, to his huge relief, the elephant turned and walked away.

Over the next couple of years there wasn't a day that went by without the man pondering upon the amazing events of that day.

Several years later, the man was visiting the zoo with his small son. As they approached the elephant enclosure, one of the elephants turned and walked over to where they were standing at the rail. As it stared at him, the man saw what he thought was a flicker of recognition. He couldn't help wondering if this was the same elephant. At that moment, the man realized that he had taken his eye off his young son and that the boy had climbed the rail and fallen into the elephant enclosure. Thinking swiftly, the man climbed over the railing and made his way into the enclosure towards the elephant, which was standing over the boy as he lay on the ground. He walked right up to the elephant and looked it in the eye. Suddenly, the elephant raised his foot and crushed the boy's head, then wrapped its trunk around one of the man's legs and swung him wildly back and forth along the railing, snapping his neck and killing him. Probably not the same elephant then.

★ A man walks into a zoo, and all it has is a single dog. It was a shitzu.